The
Garland Library
of
War and Peace

The
Garland Library
of
War and Peace

Under the General Editorship of
Blanche Wiesen Cook, *John Jay College, C.U.N.Y.*
Sandi E. Cooper, *Richmond College, C.U.N.Y.*
Charles Chatfield, *Wittenberg University*

Truth
and the War
by
Edmund Dene Morel

with a new introduction
for the Garland Edition by
Catherine Ann Cline

Garland Publishing, Inc., New York & London
1972

Library of Congress Cataloging in Publication Data

Morel, Edmund Dene, 1873-1924.
   Truth and the war.

   (The Garland library of war and peace)
   Reprint of the 1916 ed.
   1. European War, 1914-1918--Causes. I. Title.
II. Series.
D511.M58 1972   940.3'11   70-147478
ISBN 0-8240-0270-9

Introduction

I

When World War I erupted in August 1914, E. D. Morel was known to the British public chiefly as the leader of the recently concluded Congo reform campaign. The talents and dedication he displayed in the course of that effort had gained him an unusual tribute from the public in the form of a national subscription in his honor,[1] an appointment to the West African Lands Committee,[2] enthusiastic adoption as the Liberal candidate for the House of Commons from Birkenhead,[3] and a respected, if poorly remunerated, place among the journalists of the day. His opposition to Britain's involvement in the war quickly lost him this wide public esteem, plunged him into bitter controversy, and led finally to his imprisonment. The views which he preached during these years of obloquy concerning the origins of the war and the proper basis of the future peace settlement were, however, increasingly accepted on the Left, and Morel emerged in the postwar years as an important influence in the formulation of the Labour party's foreign policy.

The man who is thus so intimately associated with British humanitarianism, British "pacifism," and the

5

British Labour party was born a Frenchman. Georges Edmond Pierre Achille Morel de Ville, later to be known as E. D. Morel, was born in Paris on July 15, 1873, the son of Edmond Morel de Ville and his English wife, Emmeline de Horne. The Morel de Villes were members of the "petite noblesse"[4] who were said to have had a long connection with the recently lost provinces of Alsace and Lorraine.[5] Edmond Morel de Ville, "a man of considerable talent but little ambition,"[6] was a minor official of the Ministry of Finance. His influence on his son was brief, for when Morel was four Edmond Morel de Ville died from a spinal infection thought to have been contracted while manning the defenses of Paris during the siege of 1870.[7]

It was, therefore, Morel's English mother who was responsible for his upbringing. Emmeline was a member of a middle-class East Anglian family who had been Quakers since the late seventeenth century,[8] and she displayed a courage and uncompromising adherence to principle befitting her religious background. A dispute with the Morel de Villes over legal matters led her to leave the family domicile and, since she was "too proud" to ask assistance from her own relatives,[9] to shoulder the entire burden of supporting her son. By remaining in Paris she was able to eke out a living by teaching English and music. For reasons again of "pride" she dropped the "Morel" and the particule, apparently because she regarded them as inconsonant with her reduced station in life, and she wrote her name simply as "Deville," the first of the changes that were to transform Georges Morel de Ville into E. D. Morel.[10]

She was determined that the education that she provided for her son at such sacrifice should be English. At the age of eight he was sent to Madras House, a "gentlemen's school" operating in a large private house in Eastbourne,[11] where he remained for five years. He then entered the Bedford Modern School, an institution with a reputation for providing a good education at a modest cost.[12] These school years, happy and completely undistinguished,[13] were terminated abruptly two and one-half years later when his mother's failing health necessitated his return to Paris.

Despite his mediocre academic record, Emmeline Deville recognized that she had produced a "clever son,"[14] and she worked energetically to further his career. Utilizing her contacts, she obtained a position for him at the Paris branch of the American banking firm of Drexel, Hayes and Company, an interlude which lasted two and one-half years.[15] Meanwhile, eager to return to her own country, she corresponded tirelessly with friends and relatives in an effort to find employment for him in England.[16] She was finally rewarded with the offer of a clerkship for Morel with Elder Dempster Company, a Liverpool shipping firm. In 1891 mother and son returned to England, ending what he was later to describe as their "exile."[17]

INTRODUCTION

Can the roots of Morel's later reform efforts be discovered in these early years? The de Horne family's long attachment to Quakerism, with its humanitarian tradition reaching back to the anti-slave trade movement of the eighteenth century, seems a probable source of his reforming zeal. Throughout his adult life he retained formal membership in the Church of England;[18] yet he remained aloof from, and scornful of, institutional Christianity and prided himself on the completely secular nature of his crusades. Despite these disclaimers, he certainly approached his causes with a holy enthusiasm which would have befitted his Quaker forebears. No seventeenth-century religious zealot could have been more preoccupied with the "morality" of his causes or more firmly convinced that he had been divinely selected for his various missions.

Granting the residual influence of his Quaker heritage, the problem of defining the effect of his French experience remains. It has been suggested that the violently anti-French views of Morel's later years may have been a reaction against the poverty and difficulties of his Parisian childhood.[19] Although this view cannot be entirely disproved, the evidence is not persuasive. Neither in his published writings nor in his correspondence did he reveal any dislike of France in the early years of his career. He was an enthusiastic admirer of French native policy in Africa (with the exception of the French Congo),[20] and his warnings concerning French expansion were attacks less on

INTRODUCTION

French policy than on the complacency of British officials. Morel's fierce assaults on France, which began almost twenty years after his return to England, appear to have been directly the result of his disagreement with specific French policies and explicable solely on that basis. The fact that his bitter references to his childhood in France were made only late in his life [21] suggests indeed that his memory of those years may have been darkened by his mounting disapproval of French diplomacy.

If Morel's anti-French views cannot be traced to childhood roots, his partially alien background may well have been responsible in part for those lofty expectations concerning Britain's role in the world which underlay his reform efforts. Morel was an Englishman by choice (he became a naturalized British subject in 1896), and he displayed throughout his life that extreme faith in the superior morality of the British nation which sometimes characterizes those whose foreign heritage makes them self-conscious concerning their "Englishness." His criticisms of British foreign policy, which often earned him the accusation of dubious patriotism, were in fact based on the conviction that Britain alone could provide moral leadership in international affairs.

There were other traces of his French background. His contemporaries remarked on his appearance and his temperament as reminders of his Gallic origin. A tall, handsome man with a commanding presence on the public platforms where he was to spend so much time, Morel was described as looking like "a French gentleman of good family." [22] *The passion with which he attacked abuses was more characteristic of violent political debate in France than of the relatively well-modulated discussion of public questions in England. This passion proceeded not only from genuine compassion for the downtrodden, which is a normal feature of British humanitarian crusades, but also from a wholehearted intellectual commitment to a particular analysis of the roots of the abuses — "Kingsleyism" in the Congo crusade, "Secret Diplomacy" during World War I, "The War Guilt Lie" in the postwar years. Morel's penchant for ideology, so common on the Continent, made him an unusual, and peculiarly effective, figure on the British public scene.*

II

His conversion to "Kingsleyism" was for Morel the crucial event of the 1890s, providing the path from the narrow commercial world of Liverpool to the first of his major crusades. His adoption of this ideology occurred at the end of the decade in which he had served as "the spokesman of the Liverpool shipping interests" in the press, a description which, however unfair when it was later applied to him during the Congo campaign, accurately defines his earlier role.

Morel's turn to journalism during the 1890s was a

consequence of his straitened economic circumstances. His beginning salary at Elder Dempster was £70 a year, and though this increased as he advanced in the company, the financial demands on him were growing apace. In 1896 he married Mary Florence Richardson, the daughter of a Liverpool printer, and a year later a daughter was born, to be followed, over the next few years, by three sons.[23] Part-time journalism was initially simply a means of supplementing his income in order to meet these financial responsibilities.

If economic need led Morel to journalism, his daily involvement in the world of Liverpool commerce provided him with his material. Since the days of the slave trade Liverpool had had close commercial ties with West Africa, and the African trade remained an important element in the city's economy. His post at Elder Dempster, where his command of French made him useful in connection with the firm's contract for shipping between Antwerp and the Congo, stimulated his interest in West Africa, and furnished him with information concerning developments in the region which served as the basis for the bulk of his articles.[24] By concentrating his attention on this relatively neglected portion of the Empire, Morel soon came to be regarded as an expert on West African affairs.

Improbable though it seems, this decision of a Liverpool shipping clerk to augment his income by after-hours journalism was to have important *consequences both for the King of the Belgians and the natives of the Congo. It was the coincidence of Morel's position at Elder Dempster, which made him privy to the details of the Congo trade, and his access to the public through the press which led to the exposure, and finally to the destruction, of the abuses of the Leopoldian system.*

At the outset, however, it was the welfare not of African natives but of the Liverpool commercial interests which concerned the young Morel. In a stream of contributions to the Manchester Guardian, Pall Mall Gazette, Liverpool Daily News, *and numerous other newspapers and journals, he called attention to the threats to the established trade of Liverpool resulting from the "scramble" for Africa which had begun in the 1880s.*[25] *These articles reveal an attachment to the older pattern of "informal Empire" which involved not the annexation of territory*[26] *but the use of British "influence" to maintain an open door for British trade. By the 1890s a more vigorous exercise of this influence was necessary if the competition from other powers was to be overcome, and it was the failure of the British Foreign Office to bestir itself in defense of British commercial interests in West Africa which provoked his wrath. Invoking the principles of free trade, he successfully pressured the Foreign Office to negotiate the elimination of differential tariffs in French colonies.*[27] *Meanwhile, he denounced Britain's lapse from its free trade policy on the Niger, demanding that the Niger Company's monopolistic practices be prohibited and that its charter be revoked.*

It would be a mistake to assume that this propaganda under the guise of journalism in defense of his employer's interest was regarded cynically by Morel. He was at the outset, and he remained throughout his life, genuinely committed to free trade, and the fact that such a policy best served the Liverpool firms was but an added argument in its favor. Thus Morel felt no embarrassment in later years in recording that Sir Alfred Jones, the senior partner of Elder Dempster, "knew of my press connections and often utilised them to his advantage," or in admitting that when Jones approached the Foreign Office or the Colonial Office in behalf of the Liverpool shippers "I backed up his activities in the Press." [28]

While Morel's dedication to the interests of the Liverpool traders persisted throughout, and indeed beyond, his years of employment with Elder Dempster, by 1897 his articles revealed a broadening of interest and a concern with questions more profound than the rights of competing commercial interests. The welfare of the Africans, whose presence he had hitherto scarcely noted, began to assume a mounting importance in his discussion of African affairs. Increasingly he mused on the difficulties of imposing European civilization in the tropics, [29] *finally questioning whether the benefit to the Africans could possibly be worth the price they had paid in the loss of life resulting from European penetration.*[30]

It is probable that without the influence of Mary Kingsley this incipient humanitarian concern would have remained peripheral to Morel's chief business of promoting the commercial interests of Liverpool. Early in 1899, however, a letter from Miss Kingsley, the traveler and expert on West Africa, commenting on one of his articles began the friendship which, in the course of a few months, altered his perspective on African affairs, evoked his reforming impulse, and furnished him with the doctrine which was to provide the basis for the Congo campaign.

The thirty-seven-year-old Mary Kingsley was the precise opposite of everything one would tend to associate with a Victorian lady traveler. A self-taught anthropologist,[31] *she approached Africa in a scientific spirit, going, as she said, to study "fish and fetish."* [32] *She strove to be utterly unsentimental and detached in her observations, and the result was a view of Africans rather novel for a European at the end of the nineteenth century. She saw the African neither as the "half-devil and half-child" of the pseudo-Darwinists nor as the "benighted brother" of the Christian missionaries,*[33] *but as the possessor of an admirable culture which was being threatened by disintegrating forces from without. In a characteristic passage she wrote:*

Let him [the African] have gin if he wants it, he is no

drunkard. We are in West Africa to trade not to preach. I am absolutely for Secret Societies. Witch doctors, on the whole, do more good than harm. The cannibal tribes are the finest in West Africa. Domestic slavery should not be condemned off-hand. Polygamy is a necessary institution and its chief supporters are women.[34]

Of the three groups of Europeans in Africa at this time, missionaries, government officials and traders, she approved only of the traders. The officials she considered to be ignorant of native law and custom, and the missionaries' deliberate purpose was the extinguishing of native religions which she saw as the basis of African culture. Only the traders took the African on his own terms, and she maintained that they alone, by studying the psychology of their customers, had some rudimentary understanding of native culture.[35]

Although Mary Kingsley and Morel had approached West African affairs from vastly different standpoints, they had reached remarkably similar conclusions, and the agreement of a recognized expert did much to reinforce the young man's opinions. Both were suspicious of Foreign Office and Colonial Office officials, although originally for rather different reasons. The traders, whose interests Morel had defended, she saw as the most enlightened European element in African affairs. For the random doubts that he had recently expressed concerning the effect of European religious and political activity in Africa, she provided a scientific basis and an intellectual framework.

In a practical way they were extremely useful to one another. The ambitious young journalist benefited greatly by her constant advice and her wide contacts both in the writing and the placing of his articles. In him she found, as had Sir Alfred Jones, a tireless journalistic exponent for her views.[36]

Most important, however, was the stimulus which her passionate concern for the well-being of the Africans provided to Morel's emerging humanitarian interests. Scoffing at the "white man's burden," she riveted his attention on what was, in her view, the needless suffering imposed on Africans by the policies of imperialist powers too smug in their illusion of cultural superiority to examine the cultures of those peoples they presumed to rule. The "black man's burden" of which Mary Kingsley spoke was to provide the theme of Morel's journalism for the next decade.

Mary Kingsley and her new disciple fought a single unsuccessful battle together in defense of her principles in their opposition to the hut tax in the Sierra Leone protectorate. In the course of this controversy Morel's prose took on the emotional and righteous tone which it never thereafter lost; the tax was "tyrannical and unjust," "the most colossal error which has yet marked the blundering path of British administration in West Africa . . . based upon a gross misconception of West African customs, West African modes of thought and West African law."[37] He *denounced the action of the Chambers of Commerce in dropping their early opposition to the levy under pressure from the Colonial Office,[38] thus opening a breach between himself and his employer, Sir Alfred Jones, who had played an important role in the merchants' decision.[39]*

Deprived of organized support, the opponents of the hut tax lost all hope of success, and a disheartened Mary Kingsley departed for South Africa, where she soon met her death nursing Boer prisoners of war. Her circle of admirers, including such figures as John Holt, a Liverpool shipper who approximated Miss Kingsley's somewhat idealized portrait of the "heroes of commerce," and Alice Stopford Green, the widow of the historian John Richard Green, continued, however, to encourage Morel's humanitarian concerns, finding in him a replacement for their lost leader. Inspired by Mary Kingsley's example, equipped with her ideology, and supported by her friends, Morel was soon attacking evils in the Congo Free State which made the hut tax appear, by contrast, a mere peccadillo.

III

In July 1900, the first in a series of six unsigned articles by Morel entitled "The Congo Scandal" appeared in the Speaker.[40] *He had launched the campaign which was to consume the next ten years of his life and which was to make him, in the eyes of his followers, "the modern Wilberforce."*

In attacking the abuses in the Congo Free State, Morel was exposing one of the most shocking chapters in the imperialism of the late nineteenth century. Since 1891 a system of exploitation based on a state monopoly of the land [41] and a labor tax, which required the natives to collect the products of those lands, had resulted in continuing atrocities by African forces sent on punitive expeditions against those villages which had failed to meet the insatiable demands. The pressure for ever larger collections of rubber and ivory was a consequence of the anomalous nature of the régime embodied in Leopold II, King of the Belgians and Sovereign of the Congo Free State. Unlike other European colonies in Africa, the Congo was the possession not of Belgium but of the King. Its administration was therefore deprived of access to the national treasury, while free of parliamentary supervision and control. When the costs of administration and development for this huge territory proved to be beyond the resources of the King's private fortune, he sought to raise revenue by the methods of which Morel wrote with such blazing indignation.[42]

Although he had rushed to the defense of Elder Dempster's customer, the Congo Free State, when the first efforts were made to call attention to these conditions in the 1890s,[43] Morel's conversion to "Kingsleyism" and his own investigations soon led him to alter his position decisively. His growing respect for African culture made him skeptical of the excuse, which he had himself offered earlier, that it was African barbarism, rather than the policy of the régime, which was responsible for the frequent atrocities. Even more persuasive for Morel than the stories of mutilated natives and burned villages, however, was his examination of the statistics of the Congo trade, evidence which he was particularly well-equipped to interpret. Put simply, his research disclosed that enormous quantities of rubber and ivory were being exported by the Congo Free State, and that the Congo natives, on the evidence of the amount and nature of the imports, were being paid virtually nothing in return. The rest was for Morel a simple process of logical deduction. Since it could be assumed that the Africans performed this prodigious unpaid labor reluctantly, the state must be using force to induce them to do so. The reported atrocities were thus not the scattered and unrelated acts of individuals; they were the inevitable consequence of the policy of the régime, and they would continue until the system was changed. Although in later years he greedily collected atrocity stories for propaganda purposes, it was these figures which spoke to him and ignited his passionate determination to right the wrongs of the Congo natives.[44]

Morel's attack on the Congo Free State ended his usefulness to Elder Dempster and precipitated his entrance into the career of a full-time journalist. In an atmosphere of surface politeness and underlying strain, he resigned from the employ of Sir Alfred Jones, accepting a post as sub-editor of West Africa, *a weekly newspaper. Free from the fear of embarrassing Elder Dempster, he began at this time to sign most of his articles "E. D. Morel," adopting the name in private life as well.*

Although Morel remained a prolific journalist to the end of his life, he was able to earn a living by this means only for brief periods. His association with West Africa *ended within two years after an acrimonious argument with the owner over business matters.*[45] *In 1903 he launched his own competing newspaper, the* West African Mail, *hoping to gain strong financial backing from the Liverpool firms whose interests he continued to champion. However, it did not flourish. The public for such a specialized newspaper was small, Morel's continuing exposé of the situation in the Congo alienated his former employer, Sir Alfred Jones, who initially had been a substantial advertiser,*[46] *so the* West African Mail *produced deficits each of the twelve years in which Morel was associated with it.*

The financial success of his newspaper soon became a secondary concern to Morel who increasingly viewed himself as the leader of the Congo agitation. In 1902 he had seen the "expert journalist" as the "link" who could unite philanthropic, missionary, and commercial interests in a demand for British diplomatic action against the Congo Free

State.[47] By 1905 he had ceased to think of himself primarily as a journalist; he was, he explained to one of his supporters, "the servant of a public cause." [48]

Morel's increasingly important role in the Congo agitation was transformed into a position of formal leadership by the formation in March 1904 of the Congo Reform Association (C.R.A.), whose Honorary Secretary he became. The Association was the result of his meeting three months earlier with Roger Casement, the fiery Irishman recently returned from the Congo, where he had been serving as British consul. Casement had been sent on a tour of investigation to the upper Congo, and he had returned with evidence of the brutal working of the Leopoldian system which was later published in his devastating report. As a consular official, Casement was unable to play any public role in the new organization, confining himself to contributing the first essential funds and a good deal of advice.[49] Morel, who had long regarded as ineffective the Congo agitation organized by the Aborigines Protection Society, happily assumed the position of leadership which would enable him to conduct a crusade based on his own strategy and ideology.

The Congo Reform Association built a national movement which it maintained until 1913 when, its goals achieved, the organization disbanded. Space does not permit a full treatment of the history of the agitation, but a brief description of its major features is essential to an understanding both of this phase of

INTRODUCTION

Morel's career and of the experience and attitudes with which he approached his later campaigns.

In its sustained, well-organized, and effective agitation the Congo Reform Association under Morel's leadership provides an almost classic example of that peculiarly British phenomenon, the humanitarian movement. Though such crusades had varied widely in the objects of their sympathy — their concerns ranging from Africans transported on the slave ships of the late eighteenth century to children working in the factories of the 1830s to the victims of the Bulgarian "horrors" and Armenian massacres later in the century — the leaders of the various movements evolved similar strategies and techniques. Exposure of the evils was a necessary first stage in any campaign of this kind; evidence must be collected to demonstrate that the deplorable conditions alleged by the reformers did in fact exist. An organization must be developed to circulate petitions, arrange public meetings, distribute pamphlets, and keep steady pressure on Parliament, the Cabinet, and the appropriate governmental department or departments. As the political nation grew, humanitarian leaders discovered through experience the truth of Tocqueville's observation that in a democracy "there is a necessary connection between public associations and newspapers; newspapers make associations."[50] The role of journalists in reform movements increased in importance,[51] and attention in the press was recognized as necessary to the success of any

22

agitation. Morel, who drew inspiration from these earlier struggles, studied their history carefully and adopted their proven methods. His peculiar strength lay in the systematic way in which he applied these techniques and in the refinements which he introduced.

In examining Morel's exposé of conditions in the Congo, it is necessary to refer again to the process by which he had himself become persuaded of the evils in the Congo. As noted above, it was the statistics of the Congo trade, rather than the testimony of observers, which had converted him to the reform movement. Since every financial statement issued by the Congo Free State was designed to conceal its dubious transactions, his uncovering of these facts was a considerable feat. Tedious comparisons of official documents with other evidence such as shipping records, the sale of rubber on the Antwerp exchange, and corporate reports revealing the complex relations between the Congo Free State and the concessionaires had finally provided proof of the exploitation of the natives. While he eagerly sought corroboration for his case against the régime from more conventional sources, such as missionary witnesses,[52] he grounded his exposé on what he regarded as the most irrefutable evidence — the state's own records.

Unlike earlier critics of the Congo Free State, Morel was not content, however, to expose abuses; he was intent on using the situation in the Congo as a case study of the evils that flowed from the violation of Kingsleyan principles. Mary Kingsley had preached that African customs and laws should be respected; the Congo Free State, by declaring all "vacant" lands the property of the state, had ignored native concepts of land ownership, according to which those lands on which they hunted or fished were considered the property of the tribe. She had maintained that trade provided the best basis for a mutually beneficial relationship between Europeans and Africans; the Congo Free State, by establishing a monopoly of the products in its territory, had prevented the development of trade. The result of the effort to develop a tropical colony on principles opposed to those championed by Mary Kingsley was dreadful human suffering. As Bernard Porter has observed, "Kingsleyism" provided Morel with an explanation of the Congo evils while the abuses in the Congo provided evidence to support his theory.[53]

This approach provided certain propaganda advantages. Kingsleyan doctrine invoked the authority of "science"; the reformers were no longer the sentimental and well-meaning busybodies of the old "philanthropic" school, but rather serious students of colonial problems.[54] By shifting attention from the issue of the number of atrocities to the system which produced them, Morel deprived King Leopold's apologists of their favorite defense which consisted in pointing to the instances of the mistreatment of natives in other colonies.[55] The important point,

INTRODUCTION

Morel insisted, was not the record of abuses in the past, but the certainty that they would continue as long as the system remained.

The sustained exposé which Morel carried on for ten years was supported by the very effective organization which he constructed. The Congo Reform Association established a network of auxiliaries throughout the nation which provided a mass membership, some financial support, and pressure on local churches, newspapers, and members of Parliament.[56] Wealthy contributors, chief among whom were John Holt and William Cadbury, a Quaker chocolate manufacturer, provided a significant proportion of the funds necessary for carrying on the campaign. The churches were enlisted: "Congo Sundays" were held, and bishops of the Church of England and prominent non-conformist clergymen graced the platform at Association meetings. A "Congo committee" was established in the House of Commons. Prominent supporters were persuaded to give their services to the cause. Mark Twain wrote "King Leopold's Soliloquy" (1905) at Morel's urging,[57] and Sir Arthur Conan Doyle addressed the series of meetings which marked the climax of the agitation. The owners and editors of newspapers were enlisted in the crusade by Morel's assiduous efforts, and the reformers enjoyed the nearly unanimous support of the British press.[58]

Despite its inclusion of such disparate groups and individuals, the Congo Reform Association spoke with a single voice, and it was the voice of E. D. Morel. Neither the membership, the wealthy patrons, the churchmen, the politicians, nor the other prominent figures associated with the agitation determined the policy of the organization which was firmly under the control of its Honorary Secretary. For the most part, those participating in the crusade were glad to leave decisions to the man who had so clearly mastered the intricacies of what became an increasingly complicated question, but those few who might have wished to proceed on different lines were sternly brought into line.[59] Even the executive committee of the Association, which might have been expected to exercise some control over policy, was regarded by him as "less competent in this particular matter than myself," [60] and his refusal to accept a salary for the work which consumed all of his time was motivated by the determination to remain independent of their authority.[61]

Impressive as the Congo campaign was, the destruction of the Leopoldian system was achieved only after agonizing delay. In Leopold II, Morel faced a determined and wily opponent who met each demand for reform from the British Government with the appointment of commissions of investigation and committees of reform designed to buy time while the rubber system functioned as usual. Finally forced at the end of 1906 to agree to the annexation of the Congo Free State by Belgium, the King fought for two more years to retain personal control of the colony through the provisions of the Treaty of Transfer and the Colonial Law. Leopold's resistance to British diplomatic pressure was aided by the fact that the other European powers refused all co-operation with the British on the question.[62] *Alarmed by the darkening international scene, the Foreign Office, which did not share Morel's confident view that "internationally our position has seldom been stronger,"*[63] *was careful to stop short of threats which might push Belgium into the arms of Germany.*[64]

By August 1908, King Leopold had exhausted his delaying tactics, and the Belgian Parliament voted to annex the Congo Free State. Although the elimination of the Leopoldian system was neither provided for nor promised, the King had been forced to concede greater parliamentary authority over the new colony than had originally been envisioned, and the British Foreign Office was hopeful that this would lead to reform. Morel was far from satisfied, but he admitted that "we have won a partial victory of enormous importance."[65]

The destruction of a sovereign state was indeed a feat of which any agitator might be proud, and Morel sought in his later campaigns to repeat his success by applying the techniques of propaganda and organization that he had worked out in the course of the Congo crusade. Firmly convinced by his experience in exposing the abuses of the Congo Free State that governments could be convicted of their crimes by

27

the use of their own published records, he turned confidently during World War I to the official dispatches of Allied diplomats in an effort to make his case against them. The insistence that evils were not random or accidental, but systematic, was as characteristic of his analysis of European, as of African, questions. The organization of the Union of Democratic Control, which he directed during World War I, bore many of the features of the Congo Reform Association, not least of which was the fact that it was very firmly and thoroughly controlled by its Secretary, E. D. Morel.

IV

Not only the techniques but the substance of Morel's war and postwar campaigns was crucially affected by the experience of the Congo agitation. It is indeed accurate to say that the analysis of the origins of World War I which he put forward in Truth and the War *was worked out five years before the outbreak of the conflict as a response to the final stage of the Congo question. The events of August 1914 simply confirmed the critique of European diplomacy which he had already fully developed.*

Until 1909 Morel, who viewed developments in European diplomacy entirely in terms of their probable effect on the Congo question, had been a loyal, if occasionally bothersome, ally of the British

Foreign Office and its policy. During the early stages of the Congo campaign, some of the permanent staff had encouraged the young journalist in his exposé,[66] and Morel had spoken admiringly of "the good men amongst the permanent officials."[67] He had welcomed the conclusion of the Anglo-French entente in 1904, reasoning that the increasingly close ties with France would, by strengthening Britain's diplomatic position, advance the prospects of international action against the Leopoldian system,[68] and he had approved Britain's anticipated support of France in the first Moroccan crisis for the same reason.[69] As late as January 1909, he was careful that the Congo Reform Association should refrain from any official criticism of conditions in the French Congo which might offend Britain's entente partner.[70]

When, during 1909, Morel became convinced that, far from strengthening Britain's Congo policy, friendship with France was having the effect of restraining the British Foreign Office from forceful action, he was transformed into a bitter critic of the entente. A visit to Paris in February 1909, when he met various French politicians, persuaded him that the pressure of Franco-Belgian financial interests was causing French officials to obstruct any efforts toward international action against the Leopoldian system, and he returned home disgusted with the "mass of intrigue . . . corruption and incompetence" surrounding the Congo question in France.[71] His mounting conviction that the Congo natives were being sacrificed to Britain's growing concern for the European balance of power was confirmed when, in May 1909, Sir Edward Grey, the Foreign Secretary, ruled out forceful pressure on Brussels on the grounds that ". . . if this question [the Congo] were rashly managed it might make a European question. . . ." [72] According to Morel, Grey's implication that Britain must restrain her efforts against the Leopoldian system lest Belgium co-operate with Germany in a possible European war, "DROVE" him into his fierce attacks against the Foreign Secretary's entente policy. [73] To one of his supporters he explained:

> *For the first time we were told that the Congo could not be judged on its merits but was part and parcel of the European situation. It was therefore no longer practicable for me . . . to ignore these wider issues.* [74]

To a critic of his new tactics he argued:

> *If there is one thing the Government does dread it is a campaign against the entente cordiale, and they have been told that such a campaign will be waged from Land's end to John O'Groats if they abandon the Congo natives to their fate.* [75]

Although Morel's attack on the entente was, at this stage, simply a tactic in the Congo campaign, his criticisms were by no means limited to the effect of Anglo-French agreements on Britain's Congo policy. He questioned the fundamental wisdom of the agreements. In a typical passage he insisted that he favored the Anglo-French agreements:

> *... provided that the* entente *is what the average citizen of this Empire believes it to be viz. a friendly bond which has eliminated old and deep-rooted misunderstandings; and not an arrangement with secret clauses, a sort of military convention, which necessitates on our part a state of perennial antagonism and suspicion in our relations with another great Power.*[76]

Since the entente *contained both secret clauses and a military understanding, and close observers of the diplomatic scene, including Morel, were fairly certain that this was the case, he was here challenging the central feature of Britain's European policy.*

Morel's view that the entente *was unnecessary and dangerous was persuasive only if it could be demonstrated that Germany posed no threat to British security, and he was prepared with a ready solution to that awesome difficulty. The Congo question could provide a "golden bridge" to improved Anglo-German relations.*[77] *Although Germany had demonstrated no concern whatever with the issue,*[78] *Morel was convinced that Britain and Germany, unlike France, shared a common interest in the opening of the Congo to free trade. He argued that it was the vacillations and confusions of Britain's Congo policy and her hostile stance toward Germany in Europe which accounted for the failure to enlist German co-operation earlier.*[79]

INTRODUCTION

Denouncing British foreign policy as mistaken or harmful did not satisfy Morel's need for fundamental, total explanations. Just as he had discovered the roots of the abuses in the Congo in the system of land monopoly, he now found the cause of the tragic errors in foreign policy in the system of diplomacy. In England this system was embodied in the permanent staff of the Foreign Office, and it was on them, rather than on the Foreign Secretary, that he turned his wrath. Completely reversing the views he had held at the time, he blamed the "paralytic atmosphere" of the Foreign Office for thwarting the best instincts of an earlier Foreign Secretary, Lord Lansdowne, on the Congo question.[80] *He sought, with sarcasm, to dispel the mystique surrounding professional diplomacy.*

> The picture is presented to us of anxious Ministers, holding innumerable and mysterious strings of the greatest delicacy; of a Government department harassed, but steeped in wisdom, searching with sagacious eye the bye-ways of world politics, bending a penetrating gaze upon the mystic recesses of dark intrigue, moving only when assured of absolute success, loftily indifferent in the profundity and all-embracing sweep of its trained outlook, to these rash and clamorous voices from outside, beyond the pale of official sapiency.[81]

Yet, he continued, the Congo policy of this priesthood had been a total failure. Why? Because they had failed to listen to "Public Opinion" which "permanent officialdom detests and despises perhaps

32

because the former's information is sometimes more accurate and its instincts sounder." [82]

Thus by the end of 1909 the views which guided Morel throughout the remainder of his career had been fully formulated. French diplomacy was corrupt and, by tying herself to France, Britain had been forced not only to neglect her duty toward the Congo, but also to assume a posture of hostility toward Germany in Europe. The mistakes in British policy could be traced to the system of diplomacy, operating in secret without the wholesome restraint of "Public Opinion." The solution, though Morel did not emphasize the point at the time, was clearly the substitution of democratic, for professional, control of foreign policy. In his introduction to Truth and the War *he acknowledged the crucial effect of the Congo question on his analysis of European diplomacy. The Congo campaign, he explained:*

> ... *gave me an insight into the working of what is called 'Diplomacy,' granted, I think, to few men outside the ring, and not to all within it. ... It was given to me to see behind the veil and to realize how utterly at the mercy of a Bureaucracy working in darkness and in secrecy, were the peoples, not of Africa only, but of Europe. ...* [83]

After the end of 1909, when the Congo question began moving toward a satisfactory solution, Morel increasingly shifted his attention from African to European affairs. The Belgian government established

33

a timetable for the dismantling of the Leopoldian system over a period of three years, a process facilitated by the death of Leopold II in December 1909. An Anglo-German rapprochement, *which Morel had initially desired as a means to the settlement of the Congo issue, gradually became for him an end in itself.*[84] *When the second Moroccan crisis brought Europe close to war, his book,* Morocco in Diplomacy *(1912), appeared, blaming the crisis on the* entente, *its secret agreements, and the professional diplomacy which had produced them both. This book, little read at the time of its first publication, was such a plausible, if premature, interpretation of the diplomatic origins of World War I that it went through five editions between 1915 and 1918.*[85] *When Morel was selected as the Liberal candidate for Birkenhead in 1912, his adoption address dwelt on the importance of a reconciliation with Germany and the urgent need for the democratization of foreign policy, a matter which, as he explained to a correspondent, "to my mind dwarfs everything else."* [86]

If Morel had not succeeded in making the Congo a "golden bridge" to improved Anglo-German relations, the Congo question had served as a bridge leading him from African to European affairs, and he arrived equipped with the skills of an expert propagandist, the talents of an experienced organizer, and a simple, clear explanation of the catastrophe which was about to engulf Europe.

INTRODUCTION

V

Morel was among the most prominent and, in terms of his ultimate impact on public opinion, probably the most influential, of those who opposed Britain's involvement in World War I. The outbreak of the war supplied him, in tragic fashion, with evidence to support the case which he had recently made against British foreign policy, and also provided the opportunity to make his views the basis of an organized public protest against the "Old Diplomacy." The immediate personal consequences of his crusade were grim; they included his rejection by the Birkenhead Liberals and a term in prison. By his insistence on preaching his deeply held, though unpopular, convictions he was, however, laying the groundwork for his significant role in the formulation of the foreign policy of the postwar Labour party.

The ideas motivating Morel's wartime activities are clearly, and because the book is a collection of articles, somewhat repetitiously, presented in Truth and the War. *His central point was the shared responsibility of all the belligerent nations for the outbreak of the conflict. His object, he explained, was "... to assist in destroying the legend that Germany was the sole responsible author of this war."* [87] *He maintained that "this war is ... the outcome, not of the inherent wickedness of one particular ruler, or group, or nation, but of a system of Statecraft common to all Governments"* [88] —

secret diplomacy. The responsibility for militarism, which was closely related to this diplomacy, was likewise "collective." [89] *To substantiate his contention he quoted copiously from the diplomatic documents in the White, Yellow, and Red Books published by the Foreign Offices of the belligerent nations in support of their various versions of the responsibility for the war, as well as from the Belgian diplomatic dispatches revealed by the Germans after the occupation of that country, the speeches of political leaders, the press, and statistics of military and naval expenditures and manpower in all of the warring nations.*

Although for the most part it was necessary for Morel only to document from these sources his prewar assertions concerning the aggressiveness of past French policy and the extent to which the British Foreign Office had committed the nation, without public knowledge, to the support of its entente *partner, the specific circumstances surrounding the outbreak of the war required him to extend his earlier analysis to take account of the role of Russia. Since Russia had not been a factor in the Congo problem Morel, unlike most of the prewar critics of Grey's foreign policy, had paid little attention to Britain's direct and indirect ties to Czarist autocracy.* [90] *With the beginning of the war, however, Russia replaced France as Morel's favorite villain. The fact that Russia had been the first to mobilize was one of the strongest elements in his case against the diplomacy of the* entente.[91]

The German attack on Belgium, which had been so persuasive in moving many Englishmen to support of intervention, was at first sight difficult to reconcile with Morel's relatively sympathetic picture of German diplomacy. Although the Congo campaign had made him unsentimental about "little Belgium," he admitted the immorality of the German attack on a country whose neutrality had been jointly guaranteed by the European powers. He argued, however, that there was nothing unique in Germany's lack of principle: "German diplomacy was, throughout, dishonest, as diplomacy always is." [92] *Just three years earlier, the French had treated the Moroccan agreements as a "scrap of paper," and Britain, instead of going to war in defense of the accords, had given her support to France.* [93] *Nor was Britain intervening on this occasion in support of Belgium. Had Belgian security been Britain's sole concern it could have been achieved at the price of British neutrality.* [94] *Britain entered the war in defense of the balance of power, as a consequence of secret commitments tying her to France and thus to Russia, and it was, in Morel's view, the rankest hypocrisy to pretend otherwise.*

Though no one would now dispute Morel's view that the invasion of Belgium was far less decisive in the minds of British policy makers than most Englishmen believed, few scholars would today accept his fundamental contention that Germany bore no special responsibility for the outbreak of World War I.[95] *If he was, from the perspective of present-day scholarship, mistaken in his assessment of the situation, it was doubtless in part because a desire to find vindication for his earlier attacks on the* entente *and the system of professional diplomacy predisposed him against assigning any peculiar guilt to the other side. There are, however, other explanations. Although he presumed to deal with the entire question of war origins, he was concerned primarily with the issue of the wisdom or necessity of Britain's involvement in the conflict. He therefore gave special attention to those developments, such as the two Moroccan crises, in which Britain had played an important role, while somewhat neglecting Germany's Balkan policy, recent examination of which has led to unfavorable judgments on the intentions of German leaders.*[96] *Likewise his conscientious scrutiny of diplomatic documents made him aware of the German Chancellor's last minute maneuvers, designed to mollify the German Left and Great Britain with a display of peaceful activity, but carefully calculated to fall short of success.*[97] *Taking these proposals at face value, Morel made effective use of them in building his case that German leaders were no less desirous of peace than those of any other nation.*[98]

It should be noted in Morel's defense that his rejection of German guilt for the outbreak of the war in favor of a theory of general responsibility was a view which many historians outside of Germany found persuasive throughout the inter-war period, and that present day scholars, with much more complete materials at hand, have by no means reached full agreement on the question. If Truth and the War *is to be criticized, it is less for Morel's conclusions concerning the relative responsibility of the belligerents for the war than for his characteristically overweening confidence that he had discovered in a single simplistic concept — secret diplomacy — the explanation of this major breakdown in the European system.*

The views which Morel held concerning the responsibility for the conflict did not necessarily require that he should spend the war years in a posture of dissent. C. P. Scott, the editor of the Manchester Guardian, *who sympathized with Morel's general outlook on the European scene, counseled him against a preoccupation with the past. "You have said what you thought," wrote Scott, "about the origin of the war — that's over — now we've got to deal first with the prosecution of it . . . and then with the time and the terms for stopping it."* [99] *Morel rejected such easy compromises. If the public was not disabused of its notion that the Germans were responsible for the war, they would persist in demanding a policy of "crushing Germany" which*

> *. . . if persisted in will carry this country to perdition — morally for sure; materially (in my view) for sure too. Well, we don't want this country to be materially*

overthrown and morally damned, and we have got to try to prevent it, if necessary by forcing the truth down its throat.[100]

Morel was fortunate in finding like-minded collaborators for the activist policy which his temperament required, and together they built the most effective of the "pacifist" organizations of World War I, the Union of Democratic Control (U.D.C.). The other founders included two Liberal Members of Parliament, Charles Trevelyan and Arthur Ponsonby; Ramsay MacDonald, who had resigned his chairmanship of the Parliamentary Labour Party on an issue involving the Labor party's support of the war; and Norman Angell, a journalist whose popular book, The Great Illusion *(1910), had been a vain attempt to mobilize public opinion against the approaching conflict. Although some of its members were supporters of the war, the official program was critical of the system of prewar diplomacy which had produced the conflict. The Union was dedicated to the establishment in Britain of democratic control of foreign policy to be achieved by means of a requirement that all agreements with other powers receive the sanction of Parliament. Its objectives included a peace based on disarmament, free trade, the substitution of an "International Council" for the alliance system, and the limitation of transfers of territory to cases in which the population had given*

40

its consent in a plebiscite. From the end of 1915 onward, the group threw its energies behind the demand for a negotiated peace.

As Secretary, Morel smoothly built the movement in a manner reminiscent of the Congo campaign. Despite the fact that his associates were far more experienced in public affairs than the clergymen and humanitarians whom he had mobilized during the Congo agitation, the Union was almost as thoroughly his organization as the Congo Reform Association had been. Essentially an alliance between middle-class Liberals of pacifist tendencies and working-class socialists of the Independent Labour Party, who opposèd the "capitalist" war, the organization was kept from ideological conflict by Morel's firm concentration on points on which all could agree. Branches were established, a system was instituted by which groups could affiliate, pamphlets were published, lecturers were sent throughout the country, and U.D.C. members voiced their opinions in Parliament. Despite the initial unpopularity of its views, membership in the Union reached 10,000 at the end of 1917,[101] and groups with memberships totaling 650,000 had affiliated by the end of the war.[102]

However encouraging the response in some quarters to Morel's effort to force the "truth" on the British public, the general reaction was hostile. When his views on the war became public a few weeks after its outbreak, the Executive of the Birkenhead Liberal

*Association indicated that they could no longer
support his parliamentary candidature, "flinging" him
out, as Morel remarked bitterly, "like a thief in the
night."* [103] *The lengthy justification of his position
which he sent in reply appears as Chapter One of*
Truth and the War.

*Such treatment was mild, however, compared with
the legal persecution which he was to undergo later in
the war. In August 1917 he was sentenced to a term
of six months for an infraction of a regulation of the
Defense of the Realm Act prohibiting the export of
certain anti-war publications to neutral countries. His
offense was his request to a Miss Ethel Sidgwick to
carry a copy of his pamphlet,* Tsardom's Part in the
War *(1917), to the French pacifist, Romain Rolland.
Although Morel's insistence that he did not know
that Rolland was then residing in neutral Switzerland
appears to be contradicted by evidence in the
possession of the Foreign Office,* [104] *there is every
indication that the Government had seized on a
technicality as the basis for a political trial. Miss
Sidgwick, who had actually carried the pamphlet, was
not arrested. Furthermore, the Foreign Office, the
Home Office, the Solicitor General, and the Attorney
General had been in correspondence earlier concerning what one Foreign Office official described as "Mr.
Morel's poisonous book,"* [105] Truth and the War, *in
an effort to find means to see that he was "safely
lodged in gaol."* [106] *Unlike some reformers, Morel
did not seek or relish martyrdom, and the strain of*

prison life took a toll on his health from which it never fully recovered.

During Morel's months in prison, the cause for which he had labored throughout the war gained a sudden respectability. The adoption by a special conference of the Labour movement in December 1917 of the Memorandum on War Aims *marked British Labour's enlistment in the crusade against secret diplomacy, as well as its commitment to a peace based upon the principles set forth by the Union of Democratic Control.*[107] *A few days later the Prime Minister, Lloyd George, alarmed by the unrest on the Left, delivered a statement of war aims similar to those demanded in Labour's* Memorandum. *President Wilson, encouraged by the existence of this congenial body of opinion in Britain, then enunciated his idealistic program for peace in the Fourteen Points,*[108] *of which the first, "Open covenants . . . openly arrived at," was clearly a repudiation of secret diplomacy.*

Morel emerged from prison on January 31, 1918, "a mere bundle of disordered nerves," [109] *yet within three weeks he was again addressing public meetings.*[110] *Shattered health and nerves notwithstanding, he was determined to see that the lofty principles finally proclaimed by the Allied leaders as a consequence of the rising demand from the Left, which he had done so much to encourage, would in fact serve as the basis of the peace settlement.*

VI

The postwar years saw Morel move from his accustomed role as the leader of a non-partisan, extra-parliamentary pressure group to a seat in the House of Commons and a position of influence within the Labour party. Despite such successes as the nearly universal acceptance of his foreign policy views within the Labour movement between 1918 and 1924, his defeat of Winston Churchill in the election of 1922, and his effective intervention in the negotiations leading to the Anglo-Soviet Treaty of 1924, it was for Morel a period of mounting frustration and disappointment. Accustomed to exercising firm leadership over movements devoted to a single issue, he was inexperienced in accepting the discipline of a political party and unable to understand the compromises required of party members when they attain office. His efforts in 1924 to keep his more adaptable, and perhaps more sensible, former colleagues of the Union of Democratic Control inflexibly true to their wartime faith finally debilitated his precarious health and probably hastened his death at the relatively early age of fifty-two.

Recognizing that the Labour movement's acceptance of the program of the Union of Democratic Control at the end of 1917 made it the most reliable political base for the realization of his foreign policy goals, Morel became a member of the anti-war Independent Labour Party in April 1918.[111] *Although he henceforth regarded himself as a socialist "of the reasonable and moderate kind," he was indifferent to the domestic program of British socialism, and he regarded the left-wing socialist view that war was caused by capitalism as a hindrance to the growth of the broader movement of "all really progressive forces" which he hoped would "unite under the title of the Democratic Party."*[112] *Very clearly Lenin's earlier description of him as a "pacifist bourgeoisie" remained valid in the postwar period despite his new political affiliation.*[113]

If Morel's entrance into the Labour party marked no change in his views, he had every intention of insuring that the Labour party's conversion to a program based on the foreign policy principles which he had preached would be maintained. To a German correspondent he boasted:

> The only influence since the war broke out which is 'intellectualising' — in the international sense — this vast mass of ignorance [the Labour party] is the influence wielded by our small group. . . . We are educating it daily and have been.[114]

This influence was to be exerted by the combination of propaganda and organization which Morel had twice before used so effectively. The Union's newspaper Foreign Affairs,[115] *which he edited, served as the forum from which he preached week after week his views concerning the proper basis of postwar foreign policy, and he strove valiantly, if unsuccessfully, to maintain the organization's wartime vitality.*

Morel's chief postwar goal was the revision of the Treaty of Versailles, which he vehemently opposed from the day of its publication. No provision of that document was spared his violent attacks; reparations, the territorial arrangements, and the constitution of the League of Nations all drew his wrath. Characteristically, however, he found a single root cause of the multitudinous abominations of the Treaty: the war guilt clause. He was convinced that Europe would never be pacified until the "myth" of Germany's sole responsibility for the war had been destroyed.

> *The fable of the German 'plot,' the phantasy of Allied innocence, the postulate of German sole guilt . . . this is the destructive legend accountable for all these calamities, for the tragedy of the image of Justice defaced, the tragedy of the negation of justice erected into a system, the tragedy of Europe arming once again for war.*[116]

In short, the case for the joint responsibility of all the belligerents for the outbreak of World War I, which Morel had put forward in Truth and the War, *served as the basis for his postwar crusade.*

These views led Morel and his followers to assume some curious positions. Although the Union of

INTRODUCTION

Democratic Control had been among the earliest proponents of an international organization, Morel rejected the existing League of Nations on the grounds that it was part of the hated Treaty,[117] and further that it excluded Germany and the Soviet Union from membership. The former defender of the Congo natives was the improbable author of The Horror on the Rhine (1920), a denunciation of the French for imposing the "supreme outrage" on Germany in their employment of "tens of thousands of savage men" — French African troops — in the occupation of Germany.[118] He even found himself at odds with German pacifists whose complaints that his work was being used by reactionaries in Germany to absolve their nation of all guilt for the outbreak of World War I as well as to strengthen the forces of "counter-revolution" went unheeded.[119]

By the early 1920s the Labour party had formulated a foreign policy which, in its insistence on the revision of the Treaty of Versailles, was eminently satisfactory to Morel. It is apparent that this result was effected by a number of influences including the publication of John Maynard Keynes' powerful attack on the Treaty, The Economic Consequences of the Peace (1919); the worsening economic situation in Britain, which seemed to bear out the economist's predictions concerning the harmful consequences of reparations; as well as Morel's ceaseless propaganda which was aimed particularly at working-class audiences.

47

INTRODUCTION

If Morel was not solely responsible for bringing the Labour party to its revisionist position, he had come to embody that policy in the minds of many Labourites. It therefore seemed particularly appropriate to Morel himself that he should be selected to oppose Winston Churchill at Dundee because

> *... my life's work has largely been concerned with foreign policy, anti-militarism and internationalism... [while] the personality of Churchill ... incarnates militarism and a foreign policy making for endless wars. ...*[120]

Aided by Churchill's inability to campaign because of illness, Morel won Dundee in the election of 1922, a victory which he was to repeat against other opponents in the elections of 1923 and 1924.

The establishment of the first Labour Government in 1924, which might have been expected to bring satisfaction to Morel, resulted instead in continuing frustration. He was bitterly disappointed by his failure to attain the post of Foreign Secretary.[121] *Added to this personal disappointment was his mounting disapproval of the Labour Government's foreign policy. The embarrassed admission by Ramsay MacDonald, the Prime Minister, that the Government did not intend to summon a conference for the purpose of revising the Treaty of Versailles seemed to signal a retreat from the uncompromising opposition to the Treaty with which Morel, like the Labour party, hitherto had been identified. In an*

48

attempt to work out a solution to the reparations problems that had led to the French occupation of the Ruhr, the Labour Government made friendly overtures to France, the nation which Morel regarded as the villain on the international scene. The Government's support of the Dawes Plan, which reduced the payments but retained the total of German reparations unchanged, led Morel, in July 1924, to open criticism of his party's leadership.[122]

Morel enjoyed one rather curious triumph, however, in his successful effort to "save" the Anglo-Soviet Treaty of 1924. When it was announced on August 5, 1924, that the Labour Government's negotiations with the Russians had broken down on the issue of the payment of prewar debts, six Labour backbenchers, under Morel's leadership, approached his old friend Arthur Ponsonby, the Under-Secretary of State for Foreign Affairs, warning that they would move the adjournment of the House if the Government broke off discussions. This threat of a party revolt was probably unnecessary. Ponsonby appears to have had no objection to the unofficial negotiations which followed between this group and the Soviet representatives, and he seems to have accepted with relief the face-saving formula that they produced, which provided simply that a loan would be granted to the Soviet Union when an agreement had been reached concerning the debts.[123] This insubstantial Treaty, which was to have little effect on Anglo-Soviet relations, had considerable impact on the future of the Labour party, contributing to the fall of the Labour Government and its replacement by a Conservative regime in the subsequent election.

Morel's opposition to the Dawes Plan and his successful pressuring of the Labour Government on the matter of the Russian Treaty has led to speculation that, had he lived, he would have served as the focus of a revolt against MacDonald's leadership.[124] *Certainly no considerations of party loyalty would have restrained him. A week before his death he wrote to William Cadbury, the friend who had provided financial support since the Congo days, ". . . the Party, as such, means v.[ery] little to me. I am a v.[ery] second-rate party man." He explained that "with all its faults — especially the faults of leadership" the Labour party was the most likely vehicle for the realization of his goals. He hinted, however, at his growing disenchantment.*

> *If I find that the enthusiasm, the faith, the devotion & self-sacrifice of the rank & file are betrayed by the leaders of the Party and that the impulse for good in the movement is killed by 'Party' considerations, 'Party' tactics & personal ambitions, then I shall quietly drop out of public life.*[125]

It was the first time that Morel's reaction to an unsatisfactory course of events had been anything other than the determination to stand and fight, and it was an indication that his extraordinary spirit and energy were ebbing away.

INTRODUCTION

Morel's remarkable career ended when, on November 12, 1924, he died suddenly following a heart attack. His legacy was not entirely an unmixed blessing. Certainly the distrust of professional diplomacy and the conviction that Germany had serious grievances under the Treaty of Versailles, which he had labored to inculcate in the British public, contributed to the formulation and to the acceptance of the disastrous appeasement policy of the 1930s.[126] Morel was long in his grave when that development occurred, however, and the record of his struggle against the abuses in the Congo suggests that he would have been the last to overlook the brutalities of Nazism. Perhaps the mistakes of British policymakers in the 1930s sprang less from the fact that they acted on the views that Morel had preached fifteen years earlier than that they lacked an E. D. Morel to speak to them of morality in foreign policy.

Catherine Ann Cline
Department of History
Catholic University of America

INTRODUCTION

NOTES

[1] *The subscription of £ 4,000 was presented to Morel at a testimonial dinner on May 29, 1911.*

[2] *In June 1912.*

[3] *On November 8, 1912.*

[4] *See the letter from Morel's brother-in-law, W. L. Richardson, to the editor of* Truth, *March 29, 1946. Morel's mother wrote that her son "could if he wished have his coronet on his cards." Emmeline Deville [Morel de Ville] to Emma de Horne, August 9, 1896. Unless indicated otherwise, all letters hereafter quoted are from the Morel Collection, British Library of Political and Economic Science, London School of Economics.*

[5] Sunday News *(Sydney, Australia), January 18, 1925. Clipping in the Morel Collection.*

[6] *F. Seymour Cocks,* E. D. Morel: The Man and His Work *(London, 1920), pp. 15-16.*

[7] Ibid., *pp. 16-17; Morel to Sir Patrick Hastings (copy), July 17, 1923.*

[8] *Genealogy of the de Horne family, Morel Collection.*

[9] *Cocks, p. 9.*

[10] *Emmeline Deville [Morel de Ville] to Emma de Horne, August 9, 1896.*

[11] *The author is indebted to Mr. J. C. Aspen, Chief Education Officer of the County Borough of Eastbourne, for this information.*

[12] *L. R. Conisbee,* Bedford Modern School: An Outline History *(Bedford, 1964), p. 34.*

[13] *Cocks, pp. 20-21; Reports from the Bedford Modern School, 1887-88, Morel Collection.*

[14] *Emmeline Deville [Morel de Ville] to Emma de Horne, August 9, 1896.*

[15] *Manuscript by Mary Richardson Morel, n.d. (December 8, 1951?),*

NOTES

Morel Collection.

[16] E. D. Morel's History of the Congo Reform Movement, *eds. William Roger Louis and Jean Stengers (Oxford, 1968), p. 4. This volume contains the entire text of Morel's unfinished manuscript.*

[17] *Morel to Sir Patrick Hastings (copy), July 17, 1923.*

[18] *Morel to the Archbishop of Canterbury (copy), October 27, 1906.*

[19] E. D. Morel's History of the Congo Reform Movement, *eds. Louis and Stengers, p. ix.*

[20] *See especially Morel's* Affairs of West Africa, 2nd ed. *(London, 1968), pp. 238-284.*

[21] *The only such remarks by Morel appear in* E. D. Morel's History of the Congo Reform Movement *eds. Louis and Stengers, pp. 3-4, which he began composing in 1910, and in his letter to Sir Patrick Hastings (copy), July 17, 1923.*

[22] T. P. O'Connor in the Ceylon Observer, *December 13, 1924. Clipping in the Morel Collection.*

[23] *Genealogy of the de Horne family, Morel Collection.*

[24] *His first article, "French Colonial Policy in West Africa," appeared in the* Pall Mall Gazette, *December, 1893. Clipping in the Morel Collection.*

[25] *Clippings of these articles, averaging over 100 a year between 1893 and 1901, are to be found in the Morel Collection, section A. All are dated, but it has not been possible to identify in every instance the newspapers and journals in which they appeared. Many of the articles are unsigned; others carry various signatures, including "George Morel de Ville" and "E.D.M." It is probable that Morel wished on some occasions to conceal the fact that the articles emanated from the Elder Dempster office, and, on others, to suggest a more widespread concern about some of the issues than in fact existed.*

[26] *He did, however, favor the annexation of the Ashanti territory; article entitled "Achanti," November 1, 1894. Clipping in the Morel Collection.*

[27] E. D. Morel's History of the Congo Reform Movement, *eds. Louis and Stengers, p. 31.*

[28] Loc. cit.

[29] *"Cannibalism in Sierra Leone," December 18, 1897. Clipping in the Morel Collection.*

NOTES

[30] *"Africa 'Opened Up',"* Daily Chronicle, *November 3, 1898. Clipping in the Morel Collection.*

[31] *She was the daughter of George Kingsley and the niece of Charles Kingsley, the novelist and antagonist of Newman. Throughout his life her father pursued a somewhat dilletantish interest in primitive religions, and it was reading in his rather unusual library which first stimulated her interest in African culture. Her major works were* Travels in West Africa *(1897) and* West African Studies *(1899).*

[32] *As quoted in Stephen Gwynn,* The Life of Mary Kingsley *(London, 1932), p. 55.*

[33] *See her letter to Sir Matthew Nathan which he quotes in "Some Reminiscences of Mary Kingsley,"* African Society Journal, *VII, p. 30.*

[34] *As quoted in Cecil Howard,* Mary Kingsley *(London, 1957), p. 225.*

[35] *For a perceptive analysis of Mary Kingsley's ideas see J. E. Flint's introduction to her* West African Studies, *3rd ed. (London, 1964).*

[36] *Gwynn, p. 212.*

[37] *"The Hut Tax in West Africa,"* Pall Mall Gazette, *May 5, 1899. Clipping in the Morel Collection.*

[38] *"The Hut Tax in West Africa,"* Pall Mall Gazette, *July 24, 1899. Clipping in the Morel Collection.*

[39] *For the role of the merchants in this controversy see Christopher Fyfe,* A History of Sierra Leone *(London, 1962), pp. 567 and 599.*

[40] Speaker, *II-III (July 28 - December 1, 1900), pp. 463-464, 487-488, 571-572, 595-597, 15-17, 228-229.*

[41] *In some areas the state leased its rights to concessionaires in whose companies the Congo Free State was frequently a large stockholder.*

[42] *For an excellent analysis of the chief features of the Congo Free State and the Leopoldian system see Jean Stengers, "The Congo Free State and the Belgian Congo before 1914,"* Colonialism in Africa, *1879-1960, eds. L. H. Gann and Peter Duignan (Cambridge, 1969), I, pp. 261-292.*

[43] *"A Word for the Congo State,"* Pall Mall Gazette, *July 19, 1897. Clipping in the Morel Collection. Although Morel later admitted his "slowness in finding out the facts" (*E. D. Morel's History of the Congo Reform Movement *eds. Louis and Stengers, p. 5), he omitted all mention of his active defense of the Congo Free State. His opponents appear to have overlooked the article, perhaps because it was signed "G.*

NOTES

Morel de Ville."

⁴⁴*For Morel's description of his researches see* E. D. Morel's History of the Congo Reform Movement, *eds. Louis and Stengers, pp. 35-42. An authoritative critique of his conclusions by Jean Stengers appears in the same volume, pp. 260-262.*

⁴⁵*Morel to J. A. Hutton (copy), September 22, 1902.*

⁴⁶*Morel to William Dempster (copy), July 26, 1904.*

⁴⁷*Morel to Grattan Guinness, November 24, 1902, as quoted in Ruth Slade, "English Missionaries and the Beginning of the Anti-Congolese Campaign in England,"* Revue Belge de Philologie et d'Histoire, *XXXIII (1955), p. 49.*

⁴⁸*Morel to Alice Stopford Green (copy), January 13, 1905.*

⁴⁹*For this phase of Casement's career see Galen Broeker, "Roger Casement: Background to Treason,"* Journal of Modern History, *XXIX (September, 1957), pp. 237-245; Giovanni Costigan, "The Treason of Sir Roger Casement,"* American Historical Review, *LX (January, 1955), pp. 283-302; William Roger Louis, "Roger Casement and the Congo,"* Journal of African Studies, *V (1964), pp. 99-120.*

⁵⁰*Alexis de Tocqueville,* Democracy in America, *trans and ed. by Phillips Bradley (New York, 1959), II, p. 120.*

⁵¹*The part played by W. T. Stead in the Bulgarian agitation is a case in point. See R. T. Shannon,* Gladstone and the Bulgarian Agitation 1876 *(London, 1963), pp. 69-81.*

⁵²*On the role of the missionaries in the reform movement see Slade, "English Missionaries and the Beginning of the Anti-Congolese Campaign in England."*

⁵³*Bernard Porter,* Critics of Empire *(New York, 1968), p. 265.*

⁵⁴*In fact Sir Charles Dilke, who was closely associated with the Aborigines Protection Society, was at least as sophisticated as Morel on colonial questions, and, in his avoidance of panaceas, sometimes displayed a better sense of the obstacles in the way of reform. It is true, however, that the Society was regarded with amusement in some circles, especially in the Foreign Office.*

⁵⁵*See e. g. Demetrius Boulger,* The Congo State is NOT a Slave State *(London, 1903), p. 17.*

⁵⁶*For the organization of the C.R.A. see William Roger Louis, "Morel and the Congo Reform Association, 1904-1913,"* E. D. Morel's History of the Congo Reform Movement, *eds. Louis and Stengers, pp.*

NOTES

208-209.

[57] *Samuel Clemens to Dr. Thomas Barbour, January 8, 1906.*

[58] *Congo reform was actively supported by newspapers ranging from the Conservative* Morning Post *to the Liberal* Daily News; *the* Times *was generally sympathetic.*

[59] *Determined to avoid giving the movement a sectarian aura, Morel insisted that the Congo meetings of his missionary allies have a "non-missionary character," (Morel to James Irvine, n. d. Anti-Slavery Collection, Rhodes House, Oxford), forbidding collections for their evangelistic work, and even attempting to veto an opening prayer (Porter, p. 269). The threat to his leadership posed by the Reverend John Harris, head of the London branch of the Association, was forestalled by Morel's move to London at the end of 1908 (manuscript by Mary Richardson Morel, n. d. Morel Collection).*

[60] *Morel to William Cadbury, "Very Private," May 14, 1907.*

[61] *Holt and Cadbury supported Morel during these years by means of a subsidy to the* West African Mail *from which he drew a salary as editor.*

[62] *The United States did give some support to British protests.*

[63] *Morel,* Red Rubber, *4th ed. (London, 1919), p. 166.*

[64] *For the policy of the British Government see S. J. S. Cookey,* Britain and the Congo Question, 1885-1913 *(London, 1968), pp. 91-235.*

[65] *Morel to the Reverend John Weeks (copy), November 9, 1908.*

[66] *Morel to Herbert Ward (copy), November 10, 1903.*

[67] *Morel to C. E. Middleton (copy), August 4, 1903.*

[68] West African Mail, *November 18, 1904.*

[69] *Morel to F. W. Fox (copy), April 4, 1905.*

[70] *Morel to John Daniels (copy), January 25, 1909. A somewhat milder form of the Leopoldian system, backed by interlocking French and Belgian financial interests, had been introduced into the French Congo. See Morel's* The British Case in the French Congo *(London, 1903).*

[71] *Morel to Walter Langley (copy), February 27, 1909.*

[72] *Great Britain, House of Commons, 4 Parliamentary Debates, V (1909), 1395 (May 27, 1909).*

NOTES

[73] *Morel to T. L. Gilmour (copy), October 5, 1909.*

[74] *Morel to the Bishop of Southwark (copy), July 2, 1909.*

[75] *Morel to T. L. Gilmour (copy), October 5, 1909.*

[76] *Morel,* Great Britain and the Congo, *(London, 1909), p. 262.*

[77] *Morel to W. Dorpinghaus (copy), September 27, 1909.*

[78] *On Germany's Congo policy see Jacques Willequet,* Le Congo belge et la Weltpolitik *(Brussels, 1962).*

[79] Great Britain and the Congo, *pp. 242-255.*

[80] Ibid., *p. 156. In 1903 Morel had complained that Lansdowne did not "care a 2d rush about the whole question." Morel to Sir Charles Dilke (copy), June 22, 1903.*

[81] Great Britain and the Congo, *p. 245.*

[82] Loc. cit.

[83] *p. xxxviii.*

[84] *This observation, with additional supporting evidence, appears in Willequet, p. 254.*

[85] *It was reissued as* Ten Years of Secret Diplomacy *(London, 1915). Cocks, p. 199.*

[86] *Morel to G. P. Gooch (copy), November 6, 1911.*

[87] *p. 103.*

[88] *pp. 126-127.*

[89] *p. 96.*

[90] *For a general treatment of the prewar protest against Grey's foreign policy see John A. Murray, "Foreign Policy Debated; Sir Edward Grey and his Critics,"* Power, Public Opinion and Diplomacy, *eds. Lillian Parker Wallace and William C. Askew (Durham, 1959), pp. 140-171.*

[91] *See e. g. 133-137.*

[92] *p. 22.*

[93] *See Chapter IX.*

[94] *p. 26*

[95] *For the current state of scholarship on this question see Imanuel Geiss, "The Outbreak of the First World War and German War Aims,"*

NOTES

1914: The Coming of the First World War, *eds. Walter Laquer and George L. Mosse (New York, 1966), pp. 71-87.*

[96] *See especially Fritz Fischer,* Germany's Aims in the First World War *(New York, 1967).*

[97] *Geiss, p. 84.*

[98] *See e. g. p. 133.*

[99] *C. P. Scott to Morel, August 24, 1914.*

[100] *Morel to Arthur Ponsonby (copy), August 31, 1914.*

[101] *Marvin Swartz,* The Union of Democratic Control in British Politics during the First World War *(Oxford, 1971), p. 48. This study provides a full history of the U.D.C. from 1914 to 1918.*

[102] *Lawrence W. Martin,* Peace without Victory: Woodrow Wilson and the British Liberals *(New Haven, 1958), p. 58. The sale of* Truth and the War *was another indication of the extent to which U.D.C. ideas were receiving public attention. Fifteen thousand copies had been sold by the beginning of 1918 when a third edition of 5,000 was issued.*

[103] *Morel to A. E. Wilson (copy), August 31, 1914.*

[104] *Report of Basil Thomson, Scotland Yard, "PRECIS of particulars on record regarding GEORGE EDMUND MOREL-de-VILLE, alias E. D. MOREL," August 24, 1917, F. O. 395/140/168072, Public Record Office.*

[105] *Minute by M. N. Kearney, February 12, 1917, F. O. 395/140/33236, Public Record Office.*

[106] *Minute by M. N. Kearney, October 10, 1916, F. O. 371/2828/202 398, Public Record Office. This correspondence is examined in Swartz, pp. 120-129. Morel's earlier association with Casement, who was executed for treason during the war, doubtless contributed to the suspicion with which Morel was viewed in some quarters. His publications were sufficient in themselves, however, to arouse official ire.*

[107] *For a comparison to the two programs see Catherine Ann Cline,* Recruits to Labour *(Syracuse, 1963), pp. 20-21.*

[108] *Martin, p. 158.*

[109] *Morel to William Cadbury, February 18, 1918.*

[110] *Molly Trevelyan to Mary Morel, February 20, 1918.*

[111] *There was no provision for direct membership in the Labour*

NOTES

party at this time. The Independent Labour Party was one of the socialist groups which, together with the trade unions, made up the federation which constituted the Labour party.

[112]*Morel to William Cadbury, n.d. (April, 1918?).*

[113]*Vladimir Ilyich Lenin,* Collected Works, *XVIII, 162-7 as quoted in Arno J. Mayer,* Wilson vs. Lenin: Political Origins of the New Diplomacy 1917-1918 *(New York, 1964), p. 52.*

[114]*Morel to Count Max Montgelas as quoted in Henry R. Winkler, "The Emergence of a Labour Foreign Policy in Great Britain,"* Journal of Modern History, *XXVIII (September, 1956), p. 249.*

[115]*It was known as the* U.D.C. *until July, 1919.*

[116]*Morel, "No Peace Without Truth,"* New Leader *(September 19, 1924), p. 4.*

[117]*Morel, "Why the League Fails,"* Foreign Affairs *(October, 1923), p. 71.*

[118]*Morel,* The Horror on the Rhine, *8th ed. (London, 1921), p. 13.*

[119]*H. V. Gerlach of the Bund Neuss Vaterland to the U.D.C., August 20, 1920.*

[120]*Morel to D. Watt (copy), May 12, 1920.*

[121]*Helena M. Swanwick,* I Have Been Young *(London, 1935), pp. 373-374. Morel's ambition was highly unrealistic. Neither the French nor the permanent officials at the Foreign Office could reasonably have been asked to deal with the man who had spent twenty-five years denouncing them. Furthermore, there had been growing friction between Morel and Ramsay MacDonald, the Prime Minister, since the days of their association in the U.D.C. during the war.*

[122]*Cline,* Recruits to Labour, *pp. 85-87.*

[123]*For a fuller treatment of Morel's role in the conclusion of the Anglo-Soviet Treaty see Catherine Ann Cline, "E. D. Morel and the Crusade against the Foreign Office,"* Journal of Modern History, *XXXIX (June, 1967), pp. 134-135.*

[124]*Swanwick, pp. 374-375.*

[125]*Morel to William Cadbury, November 2, 1924.*

[126]*For the loss of prestige of the Foreign Office and its consequences see Gordon Craig, "The British Foreign Office from Grey to Austen Chamberlain,"* The Diplomats, 1919-1939, *eds. Gordon Craig and Felix Gilbert (Princeton, 1953), pp. 15-48.*

Truth and the War

FIRST EDITION, JULY, 1916 10,000

REPRINT, DECEMBER, 1916 5,000

THE AUTHOR

Truth and the War

By

E. D. MOREL

Author of "Ten Years of Secret Diplomacy" ("Morocco in
Diplomacy") (The National Labour Press) ; "Nigeria :
its Peoples and its Problems" (Smith, Elder & Co.) ;
"Red Rubber: the Story of the Rubber Slave Trade flourish-
ing on the Congo in the year of grace 1907" (T. Fisher
Unwin) ; "King Leopold's Rule in Africa" (Heinemann) ;
"Affairs of West Africa" (Heinemann) ; The British Case
in French Congo" (Heinemann), etc., etc.

LONDON :
AT THE NATIONAL LABOUR PRESS LTD
1916

TO MY SONS

THIS VOLUME IS

DEDICATED

IN THE HOPE THAT THEY MAY HELP TO FREE HUMANITY
FROM THE CURSE OF MILITARISM AND WAR.

INTRODUCTION

By Philip Snowden, M.P.

"TRUTH," it has been said, "is the first casualty of war." When hostilities break out the one object of each belligerent nation is victory. "All is fair in war," and to secure and maintain national unity in support of the war every means are taken by the respective Governments to suppress criticism which, however honest and true, may be thought by them to be calculated to create a doubt as to the wholly disinterested and blameless position of their own country. It becomes a most unpatriotic act to continue to hold and to express opinions about the foreign policy of the statesmen of one's own country, which have been held and proclaimed for years before the war by large bodies of men and women, and which were then regarded as perfectly reasonable and useful criticism.

This suppression of the truth during a war is justified as being in the interests of one's own country. The test of a person's patriotism is willingness to subscribe to the declaration "My country, right or wrong." Patriotism within the limits of morality is a noble sentiment. But, as John Bright said in one of his finest passages, "the moral law was not written for individuals only, but for nations, and for nations as great as we are." When patriotism leads men and nations to ignore facts, and to refuse to hear or acknowledge the truth, it becomes a sin, for which the penalty will certainly sooner or later have to be paid. Lord Hugh Cecil recently wrote, "Mankind has suffered the prodigious evils the war has brought upon us mainly because human beings in general, and especially Germans, have come to love their countries more than they ought to do—more than they love God and His laws."

INTRODUCTION

There have been a few people in all the belligerent countries who have refused to forswear the principles they have held and proclaimed in times of peace, and who, when their prophecies have been fulfilled, have refused to deny that they ever made them. If there has been in the past foreign policy of this country, as well as in the foreign policies of other nations, something wrong, which has contributed to the present war, then it will be fatal for the future peace of Europe not to admit that truth. If another war is to be averted, there will have to be a thorough searching out of all the causes of this war, with the object of removing them. If a perverted patriotism is to be allowed to blind the people of any country to the mistakes or sins of their own Governments, then the likelihood of a permanent peace is very remote.

Among the men who have kept the impartial and judicial mind during these awful days since August, 1914, none has rendered greater service to the future of peace and internationalism than the writer of this volume. I do not expect that his attitude can be generally approved now, nor the value of his work appreciated. But Time will do justice to both. There is a certain type of very limited mental development which has not learnt that there are more numerals than two. If a word of criticism of the policy of one's own country is put forward, such persons immediately jump to the conclusion that the critic is the friend of every other nation, and that the object of his criticism is to condemn his own country and to defend all others. Criticism of the policy of statesmen is the highest patriotism, for it is aimed at removing those mistakes which detract from the reputation of our own country abroad and the well-being of our own people at home.

That is the spirit in which this book has been written. It has been written, not in the interests of the enemy, but in the interests of Great Britain. At a time when the public mind was calm and so free from passion as to be able to take an impartial view of international policy and problems, the writer's past work for oppressed peoples, and his great knowledge of and authority on international questions, would have secured for him a wide and respectful hearing. I write these few words of introduction to beseech for the book such a reception in these troublous times. The matters with which it deals are of tremendous, of the most vital importance. Without a popular knowledge of these facts it will be impossible for the people of this country to take an intelligent part in the settlement of the war.

We do not ask for the endorsement of all that is said in this volume. Let the statements stand upon their merits. Many parts of the book have already been before the public for some time. So far as I know, the facts have never been challenged. But where there are such tremendous issues involved, it is surely in the interests of truth that there should be full and free discussion, and that every side of the question should be stated and discussed. It is only by such full and frank discussion that we can hope to obtain a settlement after this war which will be permanent, because it is based upon Truth.

PREFACE TO SECOND EDITION

CONSIDERING the way in which "Truth and the War" has been boycotted by the bulk of the Press, the impossibility of getting the volume upon the bookstalls and other obstacles, it is remarkable that 10,000 copies should have been sold in three months, and that a Second Edition should now be necessary. It proves that there is even at this moment when the "great push" is counting its victims by the hundreds of thousands, and when heroism and suffering unsurpassed mark every mile of our advance, a reading public for something more than the hackneyed literature of war. And this is of good augury for the future.

One of my chief objects in publishing this book was the desire to spread the conviction I hold that sole responsibility for the war can be imputed to our enemies only by ignoring a mass of evidence which points to a distributed responsibility. And my primary object in wishing to do that, is my belief that if our national policy in this war continues to be inspired by the doctrine of a Germany solely responsible for the tragedy, the people of this country will find themselves committed beyond withdrawal to courses whose ultimate results must, in my judgment, involve them in grave and perhaps irreparable disaster.

The danger is even greater to-day than it was when the book was being written. By its acceptance of the recommendations of the Paris Conference, the Coalition Government has revolutionised the whole character of the war. With what countenance can we pose before the world as fighting for great ideals of human progress and liberty, when we simultaneously proclaim our intention to inaugurate, immediately Peace (save the mark!) has been declared, a bitter trade war upon our most energetic commercial competitors in Europe? What hopes can we entertain of convincing the world that the war is being prolonged in order to secure a lasting peace, when at the same time we

PREFACE.

announce a *post*-war policy which must inevitably perpetuate the old rivalries and hatreds, and pour fresh poison into Europe's wounds? The unhappy truth is that the Coalition Government is hurrying a blindfolded and largely inarticulate people to a great moral catastrophe, along a road littered not only with our dead but with our ideals.

And the agencies responsible are, in the main, the same from which the nation has imbibed the version of the causes and origins of this war, challenged in my book.

The nation can still avert the worst consequences which the future holds for us if the policy of the Coalition Government reaches full maturity : but it can only do so by using its thinking powers to the uttermost, *and by insisting upon the restoration of full and free public discussion of the politics of the war.*

This book ministers to these ends, and although it would be presumptuous to suppose that it can, in itself, influence in any decisive manner the course of future events, there is sufficient evidence to show that it has contributed to promote the cleavage of public opinion which is beginning to manifest itself, and in whose extension and growth lies the only hope of winning back our liberties, and with them our capacity to judge sanely of the past, the present and the future.

. . . .

It seems advisable that something should be said here as to the criticisms which the book has elicited, and its general treatment by the Press. Let us note to begin with, that it has been boycotted by the leading organs of the unlimited-liability War Party; the Party which demands the indefinite prolongation of the war—heedless of clock or calendar, reckless as to human sacrifice, indifferent as to financial drain—for the attainment of ends which it refuses to specify otherwise than in the catch-phrase "destruction of Prussian militarism," and the noble idea of "crushing German trade." *The Times* and its attendant satellites; the *Morning Post,* the *Daily Telegraph,* the *Spectator, et hoc genus omnæ* have ignored the book. That is in no way surprising. On the other hand the book has been well, and, on the whole, favourably reviewed in the Labour Press all over the country. From the Liberal Press its reception has been mixed. The *Westminster Gazette* has kept silence. The *Daily News* published a courteous but hostile review from the pen of Mr. William Archer; the *Daily Chronicle* an abusive and singularly dishonest tirade by Professor Pollard, and the *Manchester Guardian* a generous appreciation of the author's past work, coupled with strong dissent from the conclusions arrived at in "Truth and the War." The most interesting and significant notice of all appeared in the *Nation* over the initials of the Editor, Mr. H. W. Massingham, by a long way the most influential personal force in British journalism to-day. There have been other notices, some hostile, some friendly, some merely vituperative.

. . . .

On the whole, criticism of a positive kind, in the sense of disputing the facts given in the book, has been singularly lacking. Criticism has been rather of a negative kind—that I have not placed sufficient emphasis upon Germany's sins, that I have not dealt fully enough with this or that aspect of her policy, that I have not gone far enough back into history, and so on. My reply to the last criticism is that however far you may plunge into the past you will always find critics who declare that you should have gone further. It has been well said of the peoples of Europe in this war that :

We are the victims of the Past, and are carrying the burden of a thousand years: Europe's sons are dying in millions for an ancient tale of wrong, for things done long ago and crimes that are forgotten.

But my book does not deal with the history of the last thousand years. It deals with the history of the decade preceding the war. Beyond that, historical allusions are merely illustrative. My book seeks, amongst other things, to prevent a perpetuation of these very errors which the Past has handed down to us. For the rest I have neither consciously suppressed, nor consciously minimised any acts contributed by Germany before the war to the general unrest. I have endeavoured to establish a sense of perspective between the acts of the German Government and the acts of other Governments. I have condemned German diplomacy and German jingoes of the

PREFACE.

pen and of the sword; I have condemned the invasion of Belgium. But I have also condemned the diplomacy and the jingoism of other Governments, and I have refused to admit that the invasion of Belgium—wrong as it was— is without historical parallel, and places Germany outside the pale of civilised States. And when the public has been indoctrinated for two whole years with the theory that the diplomacy of the Entente Governments was throughout impeccable, and that jingoism other than German jingoism does not count, it is natural enough that an author who submits evidence to the contrary should be thought desirous of absolving Germany from all blame. That, of course, is absurd. But the contrast which such evidence presents to the accepted doctrine produces something in the nature of a violent shock in those for whom the orthodox view has become a law of the Medes and Persians.

A painful side to this was fairly and truthfully stated by a reviewer in the *Methodist Leader* when he wrote (August 31):

Perhaps what seems most obnoxious in a book of this character is its suggestion to those who have endured the agony of sacrifice and who have been borne up by the faith that not only patriotism but righteousness demanded the sacrifice that perhaps, after all, both the safer and the saner way would have been that in which such sacrifice was not needed.

I am acutely conscious of that side. Who could fail to be? We are all one family in this ghastly business. But the truth is often bitter, and if succeeding generations are to escape the horrors which indifference and intellectual sloth have so largely contributed to bring upon mankind, the present generation must drink deep of that bitterness.

The principal criticism directed against the book in regard to my having minimised German responsibility is mainly based upon the view which absolves Russia's policy of any aggressive designs; and upon the assumption that the German Government was able wholly to dictate and control the policy of Austria-Hungary. I am unable to share either the view, or the assumption, and I give some reasons in the book for my inability to do so. They could easily be multiplied. Indeed, evidence is constantly accumulating which strengthens my scepticism. But it must be readily admitted that these are matters upon which the present generation cannot hope to be fully enlightened. I have urged a case and supported it by evidence which seems to me weighty. The evidence can be added to. Until the evidence already submitted is shown to be false, the case cannot be dismissed by general statements to the effect that the Russian Government was the embodiment of virtue, and that the German Government could afford to run the risk of an open rupture with Austria-Hungary, the one Ally upon whom it could depend. The very mistakes committed by the German Government after the crisis arose, and the obviously indifferent manner in which it was served by its ambassadors at Vienna and Petrograd, seem to me alone sufficient to cast serious doubts upon the power to control events attributed to that Government.

．．．．．．．．．．．．．

There is, however, a specific criticism in the *Manchester Guardian's* review, and it is a very important one. The criticism refers to my contention that the Russian general mobilisation was the precipitating cause of the outbreak, and is concerned with the British proposal that Austria should limit her operations against Serbia to the occupation of Belgrade and its neighbourhood. I deal with this proposal in Chapter XIV. On page 134, I say :

We know now that Austria accepted the proposal King George and the British Government were so anxious that she should accept. (No. 50, Austrian Red Book.)

The *Manchester Guardian* reviewer admits the accuracy of the statement. But he goes on to remark :

But this document (Austria's acceptance) was never forwarded from Berlin to London, and though Sir Edward Grey had unofficial news of it the document itself remained unknown till published by the Austrian Government six months later.

This is an astonishing assertion. Who is my critic's authority? The assertion absolutely contradicts No. 50 in the Austrian Red Book. This document, which conveys Austria's acceptance, *did not go through Berlin at all.* There could, therefore, have been no question of Berlin forwarding it on, or keeping it back ! It begins, "I am telegraphing as follows to Berlin," and it is a despatch addressed by the Austrian Foreign Minister *to the Austro-Hungarian representatives in London and in Petrograd!*

PREFACE.

Unless the *Manchester Guardian* reviewer is prepared to adduce proof to the contrary, the fact remains on record that Austria accepted Sir E. Grey's offer, conveyed to her through the German Ambassador at Vienna—as I point out in my book, Germany supported the offer—accepted it "with pleasure," and immediately telegraphed to her Ambassadors in London and in Petrograd to that effect.

. . . .

A passing reference to Professor Pollard's performance in the *Daily Chronicle* is necessary. I will only deal with the single point in the review which is in any sense of a definite character, and which formed the subject of public correspondence between the Professor and myself in the issues of that newspaper of August 22, 24, and September 4 last. Professor Pollard declared that I adopted the German "plea of military necessity for the violation of Belgian neutrality." I had no difficulty in showing that the direct contrary was the case. Whereupon Professor Pollard wrote as follows (*Daily Chronicle,* August 26) :

I need quote but one passage in answer to Mr. Morel's disclaimer : "Germany, to stand any chance of victory, must strike instantly at France and could only hope to strike successfully by striking through Belgium, owing to the impossibility of forcing the defences of the French frontier."

Now, if the reader will turn to page 11, he will have an electrifying example of the controversial methods of the Professor of History at the London University. He will find that that "passage," which, as quoted in inverted commas, would lead anyone to suppose that it was a complete sentence, *is only part of a sentence !* The reader will find that the Professor, in his anxiety to convict me of untruth, has suppressed the first part of my sentence altogether ! The full sentence reads as under :

And the experts were all but unanimous in concluding that in the event of a general European War waged on the basis of the existing divisions in Europe—i.e., an Austro-German combination on the one side and a Franco-Russian combination on the other— Germany, to stand any chance of victory, must strike instantly at France, and could only hope to strike successfully by striking through Belgium owing to the impossibility of forcing the defences of the French frontier.

I have italicised the part suppressed by the Professor. Comment would be superfluous. The sentence occurs in the course of a developed argument in which I condemn the diplomacy which, avowedly aware that Belgium would suffer invasion in the event of a general European war based upon the then existing alliances and ententes, stirred no finger to avert it until the die was cast.

. . . .

Mr. Archer, in the *Daily News*, describes my condemnation of secret diplomacy as an "obsession." Yet he admits that the "whole diplomatic system is the acme of stupidity." He makes the interesting statement that, "the whole situation, so far as Britain is concerned," was "Germany's open determination to have Britain at her mercy by wresting from her the command of the sea." That I do not freely recognise this is, in Mr. Archer's view, astounding. To him it appears self-evident and paramount. Everything else is subsidiary. I wonder if Mr. Archer realises the implications of that attitude? We had an admitted 60 per cent. superiority over Germany in capital ships when the war broke out, and a very much greater margin in other and older types. But our superiority in metal was much greater. A high American naval authority wrote me last year :

I am struck with wonder at the passion of fear which seemed to afflict so many in England over the German fleet. In July, 1914, the British fleet in their first-class ships carried 122 13.5 inch and 140 12 inch, the Germans 98 12 inch and 86 11 inch. In the older ships Great Britain had 152 12 inch; Germany 80 11 inch. To sum up: Great Britain 122 13.5 inch, and 292 12 inch; total, 414. Germany 98 12 inch and 166 11 inch; total, 264, representing a muzzle energy in foot tons of (Great Britain) 23,301,080, (Germany) 12,328,700. Practically, in power of battleships, Great Britain was twice Germany. How in heaven's name could some of our friends have so shrieked danger?

In the decade preceding the war we spent £350,000,000 on the Navy to Germany's £185,000,000. In the same period France spent £161,000,000 and Russia (largely in re-construction) £144,000,000, while Austria only spent £50,000,000. And there was an unwritten bond between us and France involving contingent liabilities towards Russia ! In the event of a European war Germany had to reckon with the French and Russian fleets, and, hypothetically, with ours. If expenditure on naval armament is a criterion of aggressive intent, then what can be made of Mr. Archer's assertion? It is perfectly true that in 1900

PREFACE.

Germany definitely made up her mind to have a powerful fleet, but it is also true that at the time she gave effect to that intention, her potentia¹ foes, France and Russia, were spending three times as much upon their navies as Germany was on hers. Thus, in the five years, 1897-1901, France and Russia between them spent £109,000,000 on their navies to Germany's £36,000,000. These figures are all in my book, but they apparently convey nothing at all to Mr. Archer. That which lies at the root of Mr. Archer's assertion is in reality the traditional British view-point that any Continental Power which gives proof of an intention to possess a really strong and efficient navy must henceforth be regarded and treated as an enemy. This view-point is based upon the instinct of self-preservation, and is in itself perfectly natural and legitimate. But this instinct is so strong that it blinds us to two facts. First that the prosperity, and even the existence, of Continental nations is becoming dependent in an increasing degree upon oversea trade and supplies. And, secondly, arising out of this, that British sea-power becomes an increasing menace to Continental nations. The menace is potential, only so long as Britain opens her gigantic Empire to the world's trade. It becomes positive and immediate the moment British policy shows signs of reverting to protectionism. The average Englishman refuses to take this factor into consideration. He will not realise the vast changes which the last thirty years have wrought in the economy of the Continent of Europe, and the relation which those changes bear to the question of the exercise of sea-power. This is one, and for him, perhaps, the most important, of a whole series of new world-problems of whose existence he appears even now, but dimly conscious. But the German case to-day (and with the almost certain advent of a great industrial revival in Russia after the war, the Russian case to-morrow) for a strong navy is, in itself, just as respectable as our own; so long as the philosophy and practice of international relationships remain what they are at present. I have endeavoured, superficially, I admit, to indicate in the last Chapter of this book why British statesmanship must look a changed world in the face, and must realise that Continental militarism and British sea-power are not distinct problems, but parts of one and the same problem.

PREFACE.

Mr. Archer still believes that British policy was in no way committed to France before the war. He thinks, however, that "There is much more excuse for the charge of prevarication in the statements that were made after Lord Haldane's return from Berlin." But he asks, "What would Mr. Morel have done in Mr. Asquith's place?" I will answer that question when Mr. Archer is in a position to inform me whether Mr. Asquith told the nation the truth as to the character of the Haldane negotiations—in 1912, or in 1914.

.   .   .   .

In his most interesting review in the *Nation*, Mr. Massingham accurately summarises my main contention as set forth in Chapters XXXIII. and XXXIV. :

> The capital point of his indictment of Lord Grey—writes Mr. Massingham—is, I take it, that he, with Mr. Asquith and Lord Haldane, had contracted an "unwritten bond" to come to the aid of the Russo-French combination in a land war with Germany, and incidentally had neither provided the necessary army nor told the nation that it would be wanted. That is an intelligible argument.

But, continues Mr. Massingham, this argument is not consistent with my further contention that the attitude of the British Government was the "uncertain factor" in the European situation.

> Mr. Morel cannot have it both ways. If the bond, written or unwritten, held us to an intervention, there could have been no ultimate uncertainty as to our action.

In Mr. Massingham's opinion there was no bond.

My reply is this. I am guiltless of inconsistency in describing the military and naval conversations with France as an "unwritten bond," and in characterising at the same time the diplomacy of the Liberal Cabinet as the "uncertain factor" in the European situation. In the policy itself, not in my description of it, lies the inconsistency. Diplomacy could deny, in the letter, the existence of a bond. Diplomacy did so deny it to Parliament and, therefore, to the world. When the crisis arose a notable portion of the Cabinet refused to admit its existence : hence the August resignations. But its existence received consecration on August 2; its binding force was explained and defended by Lord Grey on August 3, and its obligatory and even "sacred" nature was proclaimed by Lord Lansdowne on August 6. Its unwritten character enabled the diplomacy which had contracted it to claim for years before the country and before Europe, an unfettered liberty of action. But those years had witnessed the gradual development and extension of positive and technical measures of military and naval co-operation, and these constituted a factor of a significance and actuality so overwhelming in their implications, that to set it aside would have amounted to dishonour, and would have been denounced here and in France as a betrayal. It would, in fact, have been a betrayal of France, not by the British people, but by the most powerful section of the British Cabinet. When the crash came it was that factor which decided the issue.

I might add this question : Why did Lord Morley and Mr. John Burns resign, and why did they maintain their resignations? They have both in their turn evoked strong antagonisms. But their countrymen long ago decided that they were "honest," and dubbed them so. What is the explanation of their resignations? Here is a chapter not yet written. If it ever is, I venture to predict that it will leave a mark upon British history which will not easily be effaced. And I do not think it will be my rendering of the situation in this book, which will be discredited.

But the significant part of Mr. Massingham's review is that in which he expresses "growing apprehension," lest I should be "proved right," in an "essential point" of my criticism of the policy of the Coalition Government. He summarises, very ably and accurately, my indictment of that policy as it has been disclosed in the recommendations of the Paris Conference. He declares that "it is useless to describe this as a mere Morelian libel." He indicates not obscurely that he himself possesses the detailed Government scheme for the practical execution of these recommendations, and he concludes his review which is entitled "The war we cannot wage," with the following pregnant warning :

There is one war which we know; it was not a war for the economic enslavement of half the European world. The Liberal and Free Trade parties and the Free Trade Unionists were never asked to support such an enterprise, still less the Socialist and Labour Parties. It must be waged and ended (if it ever can be ended) by a Protectionist-Conservative combination.

. . . .

I would like to say, in conclusion, that no-one is more

PREFACE.

acutely aware of the manifold imperfections of my book than I am. A collection of articles and speeches written and delivered over a period of fifteen months must necessarily contain many imperfections, both literary and structural. But the publication in this form was deliberate, and the reason for it is given on page xiii. And, after all, it is the facts that matter. So far criticism leaves these facts unshaken. In her fine Epilogue to the new and revised "History of the English People," Mrs. John Richard Green, referring to the failure of the European Powers to carry out the final consummation of their policy in partitioning the world—the division of China into spheres of influence—writes this passage:

> Europe was thrown back on herself. Her Governments, entangled in confused disputes and indiscriminate ententes endeavoured by means of independent and secret agreements to gain their several advantages, pushing back general perils and responsibilities to some later time; and the peoples, at the mercy of a secret diplomacy, became involved in engagements, responsibilities and dangers of which they knew nothing, though they must ultimately assume the burden.

Speaking at Cincinnati this month, President Wilson is reported to have said (*Daily News,* October 28):

> Have you ever heard what started the present war? It was mutual suspicion, an interlacing of alliances, a complex web of intrigue and spying.

In these two passages is crystallized my case—as stated in "Truth and the War."

It is to the peoples—the martyred peoples—that the message my book conveys is directed. It is to them, I say: Destroy this web which otherwise will become the winding sheet of your liberties and those of your children and children's children.

E. D. MOREL.

PERSONAL FOREWORD

DURING the past twelve months I have been one of the best-abused men in the British Isles. Not even my friend and colleague, Mr. J. Ramsay Macdonald, has had to endure such malignant misrepresentation. No dishonour too profound, no motive too base, but has been attributed to me.

My offence is a double one. It is that I have participated in a movement which seeks to influence public opinion in favour of the kind of settlement calculated to produce a lasting peace, and not a typical patched-up peace, solving none of the national problems peculiar to each belligerent State, in their relations with one another, such as diplomacy has given us in the past. It is that in my personal capacity I have sought, both before and since the war, to be fair to our present enemies, and, in the interest of my country, to point out that the sole responsibility for the war cannot, in justice, be wholly imputed to them. To both counts I plead guilty without any sort of reservation. I have deliberately so acted, and I shall continue deliberately to so act.

My critics have delved into my family history, and doubtless disappointed at finding no trace of German influence, either through consanguinity or associations of any sort, kind, or description whatsoever, they have discovered, to their own satisfaction, some stigma in the circumstance that I was born of a French father and of an English mother, and that twenty years ago I dropped the second portion of a double-barrelled family name, retaining the first—a circumstance of no earthly concern to anyone but myself and my relatives. Both these facts, neither of the least public importance, had been publicly accessible for many years.[1] I might add this. It is precisely because I am, in part, of French descent,[2] and have in consequence very deep natural sympathy with the

---

[1] *Vide* "Who's Who."

[2] My father died when I was an infant, and I was educated in England.

PERSONAL FOREWORD

French people, that I have criticised for some years the tendency of the powerful influences at work in France, in Russia, and in Britain, to strengthen the bellicose and reactionary influences in French political life and proportionately to weaken the elements which, in the former country, were endeavouring to establish friendly relations with Germany. For I believed implicitly in the truth enunciated seventeen years ago by the great Russian student Bloch,[1] that owing in part to her peculiar economic position, but especially to her stagnant population, France, above all Powers, should avoid entanglement in a great war. I believed with Bloch, that for France a great war under modern conditions, involving the loss of the flower of her youth, would mean " not merely national danger, but absolute ruin." And believing this, I thought that the party in France which was seeking to reach a permanent accommodation with Germany, was the party which had the truest interests of France at heart. I thought that the party in Russia which was palpably using France for its own ends, both financially and politically, constituted a real danger to the French people. I shared in that respect the views of the greatest Russian of his age, whose fears that the Franco-Russian Alliance would be "a great injury to France"[2] appeared to me only too likely to be realised. I thought that the influences in the British diplomatic and journalistic world, which were inimical to a permanent improvement in Franco-German relations lest France should fall into Germany's " orbit," were both cruelly unjust to France, and amazingly shortsighted from the point of view of British national interests. In short, my belief that British national interests lay in a thorough understanding with Germany on the principle of live and let live, and in assisting rather than hindering a Franco-German *rapprochement,* was accentuated by the conviction, to which I was personally susceptible, that, short of such an understanding, France, under the existing system of alliances, would be the chief victim of a general European war. I ministered to those convictions to the best of my ability and opportunity, from 1911, when I was released from my Congo work, until the outbreak of war.

[1] "Modern Weapons and Modern War." (Grant Richards.)

[2] Letter to an Italian Press correspondent on the Franco-Russian Alliance. Sept. 22, 1901 ("What is Religion?" And other new Articles and Letters." By Leo Tolstoy. The Free Age Press, Christchurch.)

PERSONAL FOREWORD

In their anxiety to cast discredit upon me my detractors have not even hesitated to attack the bona-fides of
one of the most generous and at the same time one of
the most powerful movements, supported by those who
were most far-seeing and morally conscious among men
eminent in British public life, which ever inspired the
people of this country—the agitation against the mis-
government of the Congo. That in so doing my detractors
were striking at their own Government, at their own
Legislature, and at their own country, has not deterred
them. Their attempts to belittle the deep moral and
spiritual significance of that movement, and grotesquely
to distort its aims, would be puerile, were it not so pathetic
and, in the true sense of the word, unpatriotic.

When these particular insinuations were first mooted,
in a paper which, under two successive editors, played an
active and honourable part in the struggle, I dealt with
them. The personal charges I have ignored. I am content to wait. But as my writings since the war broke out
have been both misquoted and distorted, I have collected
and presented them in this volume. I believe they embody
a number of facts and inferences which sooner or later
the public of this country will realise to have been the
expression of the truth, and to have been submitted with
honesty of purpose. The articles and speeches are here
reproduced as they were written or uttered, with none but
trifling verbal alterations, and they are reproduced in their
sequence. A few new chapters have been added.

In this Personal Foreword I wish to indicate as clearly
as I am able, the mental processes which have led me to
view in a different light to that in which the majority of
my countrymen at present regard them, alike the catastrophe which has overwhelmed civilisation, and the reme-
dies which need to be applied if civilisation is to be spared
the prolongation of the war until Europe crumbles into
ruin, or a repetition of it at no distant date. I am not
prompted to do so by egotism, but by the feeling that I
owe something of the sort alike to old friends and acquaintances, some of whom condemn or misapprehend my
present actions, and to new friends and acquaintances who
honour me with their confidence.

. . . .

From the year 1899 to the outbreak of the war, my
life was almost wholly absorbed in journalistic, literary,
and other work relating to the affairs of Africa. Of that

work, records exist in my own published writings, and in the writings of others in this country and abroad. From early in 1912 until the outbreak of the war, I was partly engaged at the Colonial Office in connection with the West African Lands Commission, presided over by Sir Kenelm Digby, and of which I was appointed a member by Mr. Lewis Harcourt, then Colonial Secretary, together with Sir Walter Napier, Sir Frederick Hodgson, Sir William Taylor, Mr. Josiah Wedgwood, M.P., and others.

A considerable portion of the period referred to was devoted to the unravelling and the remedying of the greatest crime perpetrated upon the African race since the days of the oversea slave trade. I refer to the maladministration by the late Leopold II. of the "Congo Free State"; the exposure of that so-called State's misdeeds, and its final removal from the map of Africa. In the course of that task, which I did not initiate,[1] but with which I became prominently identified as Honorary Secretary of the Congo Reform Association,[2] I was brought into close contact with the methods of international diplomacy, and with the proceedings of diplomats. The full story of the liberation of the Congo—a region as large as Europe *minus* Russia—from the grip of one of the most atrocious systems of slavery the world has ever known, which reduced its population by some twelve millions in a quarter of a century, and converted vast areas into absolute desert, has yet to be written. I was engaged in writing it when the war broke out. If it is ever written, the struggle will be seen to have resolved itself into a kind of duel, not only with Leopold II., himself the astutest of all contemporary diplomatists, but with the European diplomatic machine itself. For the true conditions of the Congo were known, or became in due course known, to every Chancellory in Europe. In diplomatic circles there was neither ignorance of nor dispute about the facts. The diplomatic machine itself, however, could not be induced

---

[1] The late Sir Charles Dilke and the late Mr. R .H. Foxbourne, Secretary of the Aborigines Protection Society, were the originators.

[2] The first President was Earl Beauchamp, the second Lord Monkswell. The Association was created in 1904 and dissolved in 1913. Among those who, in the course of the Association's nine years' existence, served upon its Executive Committee were the following :—Mr. Alfred Emmott (now Lord Emmott of Oldham), the Bishops of Winchester and Liverpool, Dr. Scott Lidgett and Dr. Clifford, Sir George White, Sir Gilbert Parker, Mr. J. Ramsay Macdonald, Mr. T. L. Gilmour, etc.

for many years to move. But for the constantly growing pressure of public opinion here, in Belgium, in the United States, and to some extent in Italy, which impelled certain definite steps involving certain definite results, these in turn producing other developments, the machine would never have moved at all. It is to the credit of British diplomacy that it did move—but it did so only as a result of public pressure. And public pressure alone kept it moving, slowly, with prolonged delays and frequent vacillations.

The experience of pursuing a specific aim and steering a single course in season and out of season for eleven years on end through the tortuosities of diplomatic shuffling, of removing one obstacle only to find another in its place, of personal intercourse with diplomatists here and elsewhere, with journalists in their councils and obedient to their will, with permanent officials, Ministers, and politicians, and with the flotsam and jetsam which crowd the diplomatic corridors—this experience gave me an insight into the workings of what is called "Diplomacy," granted, I think, to few men outside the ring, and not to all within it.

The experience taught me many things. I had supposed that once the facts officially established as the result of popular demand, the "scrap of paper" upon which the great Powers had inscribed their solemn vow to safeguard the rights and liberties of the Congo peoples, would be honoured in full by some at least of the signatories. But I was not long in discovering that the acknowledged truth was not to be the determining factor in the solution of the problem, which, I observed, did not depend upon the plighted troth of Governments or upon the proven martyrdom of millions of men, women, and children, but upon the ambitions, intrigues, jealousies, fears and suspicions of rival diplomatists. I found that the destruction of human life in Africa, even on a scale so unprecedented, was used merely as a counter upon the diplomatic chess-board of Europe, that the appeal to humanity, justice, and common sense was regarded intrinsically as valueless, and that joint action to redeem Europe's honour was paralysed by considerations remote from the issue at stake.

It was given me to see behind the veil, and to realise how utterly at the mercy of a Bureaucracy working in darkness and in secrecy, were the peoples, not of Africa only, but of Europe; a Bureaucracy rooted in obsolete traditions, badly informed, out of touch with and supremely indifferent to the human pulse, cynically and openly contemptuous of moral conduct, deeming the finest of arts the art successfully to lie, living in a world walled round by narrow prejudices, and absorbed in the prosecution of rivalries for the attainment of objects bearing not the remotest relation to the well-being or fundamental needs of the masses, whose destinies that Bureaucracy held in the hollow of its hands.

Such was my apprenticeship in the sphere of international diplomacy. I am fain to confess that when in September, 1914, I read, with the rest of the world, the famous phrase of the German Chancellor about the "scrap of paper," it struck me then, and it strikes me now, less on the score of its immorality than on the score of its honesty. It is the one statement, perhaps, in the whole official collection of despatches to which the word "honest" is completely applicable; the professional diplomatist in the crisis of the hour and under the stress of poignant emotion, proclaiming the dishonesty of diplomacy, not of German diplomacy alone but of "Diplomacy" itself, which in no land, under no Government, at no period, has honoured its written word when its own arbitrary interpretation of what constitutes the "national interest" has seemed to counsel repudiation.

But this impression which I here record must not be misunderstood. German diplomacy has been as immoral, as short-sighted, as treacherous as any other. And it has added to those defects, habitual to Diplomacy itself, a brutality of manifestation peculiarly its own, combined with an almost phenomenal incapacity to understand, still less to appreciate, the psychology of the nations with whom it has had to deal. But to each people belongs the task of purging its own Augean stables. To denounce the mote in a neighbour's eye is cheap enough, but it is apt, not only to prevent your detecting the mote in your own, but to induce the belief that no mote exists. That is the malady from which every belligerent nation is now suffering, and paying for in blood and tears.

. . . .

The Congo Reform Association, having accomplished its labours with the completion of the reforms promised by the Belgian Government after the substitution of Belgian national control over the Congo for the personal despotism of King Leopold, voluntarily dissolved in 1913. Shortly after my return, in the spring of 1911, from visiting our great African protectorate of Nigeria; Britain, France, and Germany were suddenly plunged into the second crisis over Morocco,[1] and for several weeks they stood on the brink of war. It was a case of another violated international treaty, another "scrap of paper," and, like the Congo one, dedicated by the signatory Governments to "Almighty God." But the circumstances differed. The Congo International Treaty was violated by the chief party to it at the expense of all the other parties, and at the expense of the natives. But as none of the other parties concerned had material interests to serve in the Congo, as the only real victims were the natives, the other parties had collectively abstained from dealing with the offender. In the Morocco International Treaty four European Powers were directly interested. Three of them—France, England, and Spain—had pushed cynicism to the length of concluding a secret pact providing for the political and economic partition of Morocco, which made their signatures at the foot of an international treaty proclaiming the independence and integrity of Morocco a more than usually dishonest farce. They had concealed this pact, not only from the fourth interested party—Germany—but from their own Parliaments and peoples. When, therefore, Germany intervened, public opinion in France and England, ignoring the true facts and cleverly played upon by the officially inspired Press, quite honestly regarded German action as wantonly provocative and designed to force a war, or at least to break up the "Entente"—so-called.[2]

A painstaking investigation of the whole diplomatic history of Morocco revealed a record of treachery and deceit towards the British and French peoples, towards Morocco and the rest of the world, by the French and British Foreign Offices, with few parallels even in the annals of diplomacy. The individual diplomatists concerned were doubtless in their private lives the most estimable and upright of men. But, as Mr. Arthur Ponsonby somewhere puts it, the mischief is that the detestable system of intrigue and secrecy in which diplomatists live, move, and have their official being is such that it sets up wholly false ethical values, and imposes a standard of morals which

---

[1] The first had occurred in 1905-06.

[2] Public opinion in Spain was incensed against France and not against Germany, for reasons set forth in my book.

would not be tolerated for a moment among decent men in social life. It seems to be a case of the impeccable Dr. Jekyll becoming the objectionable Mr. Hyde when he has breathed for a certain time the atmosphere prevailing in the Foreign Offices of Europe. It is possible in that atmosphere for men honest in their social relations, to betray the honour of their country and the cause of international justice; to draw up secret instruments, which if made public would be repudiated by the peoples, and to sacrifice the interests of the peoples by involving them in liabilities affecting their future and the future of their children in the most vital fashion, and to deny, when questioned, that they have done so.

The investigation also conveyed the certainty, at any rate to the investigator, that after the words that had been uttered and the facts that had transpired, a European war in the near future, a war which would involve the British people, was virtually inevitable unless certain things occurred. The only possible way to save the situation, so it seemed to me, was by making the true facts known to the British public, in the hope that the publication of them might lead to a revulsion of feeling, and to a clearer comprehension of the German case; and thereby provoking a full and frank discussion in Parliament as to the real character of our official relations with France, and, therefore, contingently with Russia, to whose Government official France was bound in a military and political alliance.

To these ends I laboured entirely single-handed, and obeying no outside inspiration, and following a series of articles in British and French magazines and newspapers, I published, four months after France and Germany had reached an agreement on the matter immediately under dispute, my book, "Morocco and Diplomacy."[1] Its dedication[2] indicated the purpose of the book, and in writing it I believed that I was performing a useful and patriotic, if somewhat painful task. My objects were not misjudged at

[1] Smith, Elder & Co., 1912. Since re-issued as "Ten Years of Secret Diplomacy." (National Labour Press. 1s.)

[2] "To those who believe the establishment of friendlier relations between Britain and Germany to be essential to the prosperity and welfare of the British and German peoples, and to the maintenance of the world's peace, and to those who are persuaded that the acceptance of national liabilities towards foreign Powers by secret commitments withheld from the British people, is both a menace to the security of the State and a betrayal of the national trust, this volume is respectfully dedicated."

the time, even by those who disagreed with the deductions I drew from the marshalling of facts, which to this day remain absolutely unchallenged. The bulk of the newspaper comment was wholly favourable—with the exception, of course, of the organs which had played the most prominent part in misleading the public. It is noteworthy that none of the latter attempted to dispute the accuracy of the facts presented.

Various intimations reached me that the book had not been without value in affecting influential opinion, and it may have contributed to the attempts to reach a *modus vivendi,* which afterwards took place. But Parliament did not respond. The matter was allowed to lapse. The original errors and falsities took root, and to this day are continually repeated. There was no public opinion sufficiently organised and in earnest outside Parliament, still less within it. The crisis had brought England as well as France and Germany, to the very edge of the precipice. In France a Yellow Book was issued, and an exhaustive debate, lasting several days, took place both in the Chamber of Deputies and in the Senate. In England a timid request for papers was curtly refused, and nothing in the nature of Parliamentary discussion was ever attempted. It is a satisfaction to me, albeit a somewhat melancholy one, that since the war broke out, a considerable demand for my book has arisen, and that every diligent searcher after truth has either recognised the accuracy of my analysis of the facts, or, at least, has admitted its value. In "The Policy of the Entente : 1904-14,"[1] the Hon. Bertrand Russell, when treating of Morocco, remarks of my book that : "Any new account not designed simply to whitewash the English and French Governments can only repeat what is to be found" in it, "even when, like what follows, it is derived entirely from other sources." Mr. Charles W. Hayward endorses it unreservedly in his volume, "What is Diplomacy ?"[2] His condemnation of Anglo-French diplomacy is couched in more vigorous language than my own. He concludes that the crisis of 1911 was "infamously provoked," and that in the dispute "the honour is entirely Germany's." Mr. G. Lowes Dickinson does not believe that "any instructed and impartial student will accept what appears to be the current English view, that the attitude of Germany

[1] The National Labour Press : 1s.
[2] Grant Richards Ltd. : 2s. 6d.

in this episode was a piece of sheer aggression without excuse, and that the other Powers were acting throughout justly, honestly, and straightforwardly."[1]   Mr. George Armstrong's[2] censure is more direct.   Prefacing it by the statement that, "despite the elaborate investigations and expositions of Mr. E. D. Morel, knowledge of this extraordinary chapter in our diplomatic history is far from general," and adding that the "publications of the British, French, and Belgian Foreign Offices" have "completely confirmed the accuracy" of my statements, he scathingly denounces the action of our Foreign Office, and concludes by asking :—

"Could a more damning illustration be imagined of the possibilities of secret diplomacy as an agent for the embroilment of the nations in quarrels in which they have no interest?"

Mr. G. P. Gooch[3] permits me to quote as his considered opinion that my "critical examination of European diplomacy in Morocco deserves the most careful study; it is not only one of the few cardinal works on our recent foreign policy, but it supplies several important links in the chain of events which led up to the war."

And although there are some intellectuals, posing as historians, who continue studiously to ignore, since they cannot refute, my contribution to this international tragedy, which was to become one of the chief combustibles in the great conflagration, I am satisfied that its endorsement in the works referred to is but the prelude to a wider recognition that what I wrote was true both in substance and in fact, and that in writing it I could have had no motive other than that of serving the interests of the British people, of the French people, and of international concord.

It has since transpired that at the very time I was engaged in making the investigation which resulted in the appearance of "Morocco in Diplomacy," the Belgian diplomatic representatives in Berlin, London, and Paris were expressing to their Government,[4] precisely the same

[1] "The European Anarchy." (George Allen & Unwin : 2s. 6d.)
[2] "Our Ultimate Aim in the War." (George Allen & Unwin : 2s. 6d.)
[3] Author of "History of Our Time," "History and Historians in the Nineteenth Century," and many other historical works.
[4] First published in the *Norddeutsche Allgemeine Zeitung,* and afterwards by E. S. Mittler & Sons, Berlin. An English edition, "Belgium and the European Crisis," has been published by the same firm. That a Spanish edition has been published is apparent

views in regard to the character of Anglo-French diplomacy in this matter as I had been led to form; that they were consumed by the same fears as I was in respect to the outcome, and that they had come to the same conclusions as I had, reluctantly, and by the sheer weight of evidence arrived at. And their despatches, be it noted, were written while the events examined and summarised by me were in process of accomplishment. I think it may be safely asserted that never have the statements of an author dealing with a complicated and intricate international problem, and without reference to any sources of information not publicly accessible, received, in that author's lifetime, such startling and unexpected corroboration from contemporary diplomatic documents.

.   .   .   .

That was my second intervention in public affairs, as affected by and concerned with international diplomacy. The motive which inspired both was the same. In the case of the Congo I sought, with the help of others, to emancipate an enslaved race, by ascertaining and publishing the facts and by forcing them upon the attention of my countrymen and the world. I also caressed the hope that if the international conscience could be sufficiently aroused to bring the intriguing Governments into line on this primarily human issue, in which the honour of all the great nations (Russia excepted) was closely involved; the co-operation thus secured might lead to something like agreement between the Governments for an international treatment of problems, both administrative, economic, and political, connected with the future of African and Asiatic territories. I felt that if this could be accomplished, the interests of the native races would receive greater consideration, and that the chance of critical disputes arising between the European Govern-

from a recent article in the *Cambridge Magazine,* and editions have, doubtless, appeared in every European language. Beyond a brief reference to these documents in *The Times,* when they first came out, all reference thereto has been suppressed in our newspapers. Their very existence is unknown to the great mass of the British public, but long extracts have been published in the "Notes from the Foreign Press," issued by Mrs. Buxton. They are referred to in the Introduction to the third edition of "Ten Years of Secret Diplomacy," where I urged that Parliament should call for their production as a State-paper. Copious extracts are also made from them in Mr. G. Lowes Dickinson's "The European Anarchy." For further reference to them in this volume, see Chapters IX., XIV. and XVI.

ments would be diminished, seeing that, with one exception, all the serious European crises of the previous two decades had originated in quarrels over the disposal, or exploitation, of areas in Africa and Asia. The first of these objects was finally attained. The hope that the dangers and the disgrace resulting from the Congo experiment might lead the Powers seriously to envisage the possibility of a common policy in Asia and Africa was not, unhappily, realised.

In the case of Morocco, the demonstration I sought generally to make was the helplessness of the peoples of Europe in the face of a secretive and immoral diplomacy, which might at any moment produce a situation leading to the wholesale massacre of multitudes. In the present volume I submit a series of facts and arguments designed to shòw that sole responsibility for the war is imputable to no one country, but to the egotism, ambitions, and stupidity of the ruling classes in all countries, and to a common system of international intercourse between States, which makes it impossible for the peoples, who neither desire nor make war, to prevent that egotism and those ambitions from plunging them into fratricidal and insensate strife. Between the enslavement and exploitation of African peoples at the hands of an evil King and his bodyguard of financial vampires, and the enslavement and exploitation of European peoples for whom the issues of life and death have become, by an abuse of power, the sport of a handful of public officials, whom no tolerable system of government should invest with such authority, there is a difference, not of principle, but only of manifestation and setting. I assisted in overthrowing the worst example of the former which has occurred in the last 120 years. I hope to assist, in however small a way, in swelling the stream of public purpose which will sweep away the latter. My standpoint in both cases is identical. The Leopoldian rule in the Congo was an odious and wicked wrong perpetrated upon a section of the human race. The present war is an abominable outrage upon the whole human race.

And if I am told that in issuing a collection of studies which establish that all the rights are not on one side and all the wrongs on the other, but that responsibility for this terrible war is much more universal than popular opinion in any of the belligerent countries is yet prepared to admit, I am injuring the "national cause," my reply is this :—

PERSONAL FOREWORD

The only cause I recognise as "national" will be helped and not injured by this, or any other effort similarly inspired. That cause is the welfare of ·the mass of the British people, who support the fabric of the British Commonwealth; the millions who are suffering and dying on land and on the sea; the millions who labour and suffer in the factory, the workshop, the slum; the men and boys in the trenches; the women who wait and watch with straining hearts; the children, and the unborn. Their claim to happiness, their claim to relief, their claim to a tolerable future, is the only claim that appeals to me in the national sense. And associated with them, in common rights and in common wrongs, are those, who, in other lands, also suffer and perish—victims one and all of the meaningless phrase, the empty pomp, the poisonous boast of war; victims one and all of the barbarous Statecraft, the perverted religion, the selfish exploitation of caste, and creed, and vested interest.

CONTENTS

CONTENTS

PART II.

PART I

CHAPTER I.

The Outbreak of the War[1]

You cannot afford to disinterest yourselves from foreign affairs. You cannot afford to remain indifferent to the mechanical organisation by which that branch of your national affairs is conducted. The last 20 years have seen a steady democratisation of our great public departments. But the Foreign Office has remained outside that tendency. It continues to be managed under a close Caste-System. Wealth and aristocratic connections are still considered, the first always, the second almost always, the indispensable attributes to a diplomatic career. It is a career closed to men of brains, education, and intelligence who do not possess those attributes. . . It is my profound conviction that one of the paramount interests of the people of this country, and of the people of Germany, is that the friction which has unhappily existed for some years between them should be replaced by an honourable understanding.—*Extract from the Author's " Adoption " address to the General Council of the Birkenhead Liberal Association, November 8, 1912.*

What is the policy of Great Britain supposing the forces against Peace prevail? . . . We have not been assured that, come what may, Great Britain is no party to this dispute and will not allow herself to be dragged into it. In the light of the events which took place last year, when this country found itself within measurable distance of war with Germany in connection with the Franco-German dispute over Morocco, we are warranted in asking that such an assurance should be given to us. We are, I submit, warranted in asking that we may be authoritatively assured that if the war parties on the Continent succeed in dragging the statesmen of Europe into a desolating conflict, Great Britain stands absolutely free from any entanglement with any Continental Power.—*The Author, speaking at Birkenhead on the Balkan crisis, December 3, 1912.*

One of the greatest difficulties will be seen on consideration to be that of reconciling Colonial participation in British foreign policy, with a more considerable measure of public control over foreign policy at home. It is increasingly a matter of legitimate complaint that the foreign policy of this country is decided outside the nation's knowledge, or its will, and that the power of the House of Commons adequately to discuss or criticise foreign policy has sunk almost to microscopic proportions. A growing body of thought resents the perfunctory and occasional manner in which the country is permitted a rare glimpse into the aims and methods of our foreign policy. This body of thought is disposed to question the compatibility between democratic institutions, and the conclusion, without the cognisance of the House of Commons, of treaties and conventions with foreign

---

[1]Being a letter written to the Executive of the Birkenhead Liberal Association, published in full in the Birkenhead papers of October 14, 1914. The letter was afterwards, in response to numerous requests, reproduced in pamphlet form.

Powers, which, under certain circumstances, may involve the nation in war. This feeling has been immensely strengthened by the knowledge, which has since become accessible, that the official explanation of our attitude in the Franco-German dispute over Morocco last summer twelvemonth, will not now stand the test of reasoned debate in any public assembly. If it be reasonable that the Dominions should be consulted in foreign policy, as the natural sequel to their participation in the defence of the Empire, then, *a fortiori*, is it reasonable that the British people should be consulted and kept informed through the elected representatives of the nation.—*The Author, speaking on " Democracy and Empire," at the Liverpool Reform Club, as the guest of the New Century Society, January 14, 1913.*

Now one would think that a nation, faced with these facts which are not in dispute, would bend its whole energies upon evolving effective machinery to stop this dry-rot in the national building. And here I come to the point which I should wish, if you will allow me, to impress upon you. Under present circumstances we cannot evolve that machinery, and we never shall evolve it until we realise the absurd insufficiency of our existing institutions. We have 45 millions of people in these islands, and we are trying with one Parliament to do for them what one Parliament would be utterly incapable of accomplishing even if it had nothing else to think about than the domestic needs of these people. . . But this is only half the picture. This Parliament is the Imperial Parliament as well as the domestic Parliament. It is directly responsible, with the Government of India, for the welfare of 300 millions of people. It is directly responsible, with the Egyptian Government, for 14 millions of Egyptians and Sudanese. It is wholly responsible for 43 millions of coloured peoples in the Crown Colonies and Protectorates. Then this Parliament is also supposed to be responsible for the conduct and character of our relations with foreign Powers, and for the great defensive Services, the Navy and Army, which exist to protect not these shores alone, but the Empire. . . If you will let your mind dwell upon this situation for a moment you cannot but realise that we are attempting the impossible, and that if we go on with the attempt much longer there will come a point when the over-weighted machine must break down. There will come a point when any Government, I do not care what Party it represents, will find the task of Government impossible ; and when, if you have in power a statesman of the type of Palmerston or Disraeli, or the pale prototype or either, he will plunge you, or try to plunge you, into a great war as the only way of escape from an intolerable situation.—*The Author, speaking on " Our Social Conditions," at Birkenhead, December 12, 1913.*

October 5, 1914.

I AM in receipt of your letter of the 2nd inst., in which you intimate, in effect, that my prospective candidature is no longer acceptable to the Liberals of Birkenhead. Your letter is couched in the courteous and generous terms which the uniform kindness I have received from yourselves would have led me to expect.

. . . .

I would wish to preface my remarks on the wider issue by saying that I detest as heartily as anyone can do the odious and immoral doctrines preached by the politico-militarist school of Prussia, and inculcated by the philo-sophy of Nietzsche and Treitschke which have contributed, exactly to what degree it is difficult to say, but largely there can be no doubt, to the armed tension of Europe; that I condemn as vigorously as anyone can do the blunder-ing brutality of German diplomatic methods; that I abhor as intensely as anyone can do the violation of Belgian territory and the ruthless treatment meted out to the Belgian civil population and to certain Belgian towns by the German armies. Were every counter allegation, precedently and subsequently brought against the Belgian civil population by Germany, true, it would not lessen Ger-many's responsibility one iota. Nor is Germany's moral responsibility by one fraction lowered because the Russian troops are alleged to be perpetrating wholesale excesses in East Prussia. These monstrosities are the accompani-ment of all wars. Perpetrated in Belgium they reach to a high pinnacle of shame because Belgian neutrality was guaranteed by international treaty, above all because Bel-gium was innocent of any provocative act whatever;[1] and I

[1] The German Government has since published a number of official documents discovered in the Brussels archives, on the strength of which it seeks to establish that the Belgian Government had com-mitted itself to the *Entente* long before the war, and had com-promised Belgium's neutrality. Even if these documents did prove the German contention, they would not justify Germany's invasion of Belgium, since they were admittedly discovered months after that invasion took place. The utmost that they can be held to prove is that the Belgian Government feared a request from the German Government for a passage through Belgium of the German armies in the event of a general European war; that certain consultations took place between the Belgian and British military authorities in that connection, and that the British General Staff had taken pre-cautions to secure all the topographical and other information required in view of the contingency of the *Entente* armies operating in Belgian territory with or without the active co-operation of the Belgian army. Whether a neutral Power, potentially threatened, commits a technical breach of its neutrality by consulting with certain Powers from among the guarantors of its neutrality, is a matter for the international jurist. That Belgium, seeing herself drifting into a position of national peril by the increasing tension of the European situation, would have been well advised to make a public appeal to all the guaranteeing Powers years ago is undoubted. And if Belgian foreign policy had been effectually controlled by the Belgian democracy, one may assume that such an appeal would have been made. It is equally clear that if any of the Great Powers, who were not only aware of Belgium's peril, but were contributors towards it, had been sincerely desirous of shielding their *protégée* from the con-sequences of their own rivalries, diplomacy would have raised the whole question of Belgium *de novo,* as it was raised by Gladstone

am wholly in accord with the view that future conditions of peace should include heavy compensation to Belgium for the material damage inflicted upon her and for the wrongs which she has suffered. I favour this the more since, as I shall presently show, I believe that the British Government is also heavily in Belgium's debt; a debt which the issue of loans and hospitality to refugees do not liquidate.

These sentiments, however, cannot blind me to the facts that Germany is not peculiar in possessing a politico-militarist school whose influence is pestilential; that we heard of Machiavelli before we heard of Nietzsche; that a German Association comprising some 300 of the intellectual elite of Germany published last year a scathing onslaught upon Bernhardi,[1] who himself complains in his preface that his book is necessary because his views are not shared by the mass of his countrymen; that the sanctity of international law has been flouted by every

and Granville in 1870. But Germany has no ground of complaint on the score of any technical violation of Belgian neutrality, which may, or may not, be involved in the Anglo-Belgian military conversations preceding the war; seeing that down to the very last moment Germany's official representatives continued to assure the Belgian Government that Belgian neutrality would be respected by Germany. The documents which Germany has unearthed, then, while they do strengthen the conviction that Belgium has been, fundamentally, a victim to the "balance of power," cannot be regarded as palliating in any way whatsoever Germany's action. They emphasise, however, that the British Foreign Office was fully cognisant of what the situation of Belgium would be in the event of a general European war, and that the British military authorities were concerning themselves with the matter, as it was their manifest duty to do, from the time—1906—when the military consultations between the British and French General Staffs were authorised by a section of the British Cabinet without the knowledge of the Cabinet as a whole. These documents accentuate, therefore, the moral responsibility of the *Entente* Powers towards Belgium, and should be borne in mind by the reader when perusing Chapters I., II., XXXIII., XXXIV., and XXXV. of this volume. It is generally understood that facsimiles of these documents have been widely distributed throughout the world. The American edition bears the imprint: "*The International Monthly.*" *Inc. 1123 Broadway, New York.* These documents are quite distinct from the reports of the Belgian diplomatists in foreign capitals, referred to in Chapters IX. and XV.

[1] *Der deutsche chauvinismus.* By Professor Otfried Nippold on behalf of the *Veröffentlichungen des verbandes für internationale verständigung.* (Stuttgart: Druck von W. Kohlhammer: 1913). It is a collection of the utterances of the chief German Jingoes with appropriate comments.

Government in turn whenever it considered its vital interests affected; that the last decade alone has witnessed a perfect epidemic of Treaty breaking, and finally, that despite its bragging and sabre-rattling, its offensive diplomatic procedure and the unpleasant claim of its ruler to co-partnership with the Almighty, Germany is, in point of fact, the only great European Power which, during the last forty years, has not indulged in the pastime of war, apart from the guerilla campaign against a Hottentot tribe in South-West Africa. I conclude from this that neither the German people nor yet their Government, have a monopoly of immorality, treachery, violence, and general wickedness; that to encourage the state of mind which fosters this notion is to render a dis-service and not a service to our people, between whom and the German people, I, for my part, deem it not unpatriotic to hope for reconciliation and co-operation in happier days; is to impair the judgment and distort the vision of our people who require no such stimulus to do their duty whatever it may be; and is to excite a temper calculated to encourage a repetition of the errors and a perpetuation of the systems which have occasioned this cataclysm. Nor do I believe that militarism, Prussian or other, can be destroyed by militarism; or that particular constitutions can be imposed upon a people from outside; or that the idea that a nation of eighty millions can be dismembered and reduced to a position of permanent political inferiority is other than a delusion. I should not find it possible to support a policy which proclaimed these aims to be its own and which was unprepared, after the defeat of the enemy and after the fear of invasion had passed away, to sacrifice innumerable lives in the attempt to secure them. If these opinions conflict with true Liberalism, then it is evident that I have, somehow, missed what I conceived the spirit of Liberalism to be.

The real point of divergence between us, I gather, is concerned rather with the past than with the future. It is a matter of sincere grief to me that divergence should exist on what I regard as a matter of principle and one of immense import to the democracy of this country. On this point I must be forgiven for speaking quite plainly. I hold that no Government, certainly no Liberal Government, is entitled to undertake obligations towards foreign Powers involving the use, in certain contingencies, of the armed forces of the Crown, without consulting Parliament.

(3 A)

And I submit that when a Government, be it Liberal or Conservative, having contracted such liabilities without consulting Parliament, repeatedly states in Parliament that it has not done so, and only confesses that it has on the very eve of war, a situation arises whose implications are really fundamental, because they go to the very root of our public life and of our national institutions. It is a situation which is not affected by the necessity of vigorously prosecuting a war once entered upon—on that all are agreed. Nor is it affected by the views which may be generally held as to the causes, the origin, or the expediency of this war; nor yet by the ultimate results which may ensue from the war. It is far simpler and more direct. I content myself with saying that I am unable to accommodate myself to that situation, and on no consideration whatever could I remain silent on such an issue.

I may, perhaps, be allowed to recall to you that my opinions as to the injustice and danger to the democracy of an autocratic and secret foreign policy have never been concealed from the Birkenhead electorate. I have frequently adverted to the subject in my speeches, and I have never had reason to suppose that my statements were disapproved by my audiences, or that they were incompatible with that general exposition of Liberal principles by me to which you are good enough to make generous allusion in your letter. My public attitude on that grave and urgent problem had, moreover, preceded my adoption as prospective Liberal candidate for Birkenhead. My public contributions to the secret transactions between the British and French Foreign Departments which had characterized the Morocco imbroglio were known in Birkenhead before my adoption, and my views on the whole subject of secret diplomacy had been stated beyond possibility of misconception.

Now, despite the belief, confirmed by official utterances, that the era of secret engagements towards France had finally disappeared with the French acquisition of Morocco, rumours arose last year,[1] and again in the opening months of this year,[2] that our Foreign Office had secretly committed us to render assistance to France in the event of a European War. As France was herself committed to Russia, this, if true, implied the additional

[1] 1913.
[2] 1914.

and equally grave objection that our Foreign Policy would thereby become influenced by that of Russia, towards which Power the Foreign Policy of France had become manifestly subservient. The prospect was the more alarming in view of what had happened and was happening in Persia. Rumour did not point to the conclusion of a Treaty, but, as one of the several questions put to the Prime Minister defined it, to the giving of :

. . . . assurances which in the contingency of a great European War would involve heavy military obligations on this country. . . . an obligation arising owing to an assurance given by the Ministry in the course of diplomatic negotiations, to send a very large armed force out of this country to operate in Europe.

These questions will be found in Hansard 1913, vol. l., cols. 42-43; vol. l., cols. 1316-7; 1914, vol. lxi., col. 1499; vol. lxiii., cols. 457-8. The replies were categorical. On March 11th, 1913, the Prime Minister denied that such obligations had been contracted or such assurances given. A fortnight later the Prime Minister repeated the denial in detail. On April 28 of this year the Foreign Secretary declared that the position had not altered. On June 11 he assured the House that the Prime Minister's statement " remains as true to-day as it was a year ago." These definite affirmations, although treated scoffingly enough in a great Tory newspaper, assumed, not without presumptive evidence, to be in the closest touch with certain influential permanent officials in the Foreign Office, seemed to dispose once and for all of the truth of the rumours in question to which I had personally lent credence.[1]

On August 3 last, when the tramp of armed legions had begun to shake the plains of Europe, the Foreign Secretary revealed to the House of Commons, amid shouts of approval from the Tory benches, that he had contracted liabilities towards France as far back as 1906; that they

[1] The secret transactions with France are dealt with in Chapters XXXIII. and XXXIV. The following publications may also be referred to : "The Candid Review," May, August and November, 1915; "The Policy of the Entente," by the Hon. Bertrand Russell (National Labour Press, 1916, 1s.); "Belgium and the Scrap of Paper," by H. N. Brailsford (National Labour Press, 1915, 1d.); "What is Diplomacy?" by Charles Hayward (Grant Richards Ltd., 1916, 2s. 6d.); "The European Anarchy," by G. Lowes Dickinson (George Allen and Unwin, 2s. 6d.); "La guerre qui vient," by Francis Delaisi (Paris, 8 rue Saint Joseph, 1911, 25 centimes), etc.

had been renewed on divers occasions since, and that the final seal had been placed upon them on the previous day, August 2. These liabilities had taken the form of (a) authorizing a plan of military operations on the Continent of Europe between the British and French General Staffs, (b) authorizing an arrangement between the Admiralty and the French Naval Authorities involving a strategic disposition of the French Fleet favourably affecting our naval position in the Mediterranean, but leaving the French northern and western coastline undefended, (c) undertaking to attack the German Fleet if the German Fleet made a descent upon the French coasts or interfered with French shipping.

It came, therefore, to this. While negative assurances were given to the House of Commons, positive acts diametrically opposed to these assurances had been concerted by the War Office and the Admiralty with the authority of the Foreign Office. All the obligations of an open alliance had been incurred, but incurred by the most dangerous and subtle of methods; incurred in such a way as to leave the Cabinet free to deny the existence of any formal parchment recording them, and free to represent its policy at home and abroad as one of contractual detachment from the rival Continental groups. When, in the early days of August, the situation into which the Government as a whole had drifted, became for the first time clearly apparent to the Cabinet, two of its members found themselves unable to concur in what they regarded as a breach of faith to themselves and to the nation.[1] Their standpoint, in a very differing degree of setting and circumstance, is my own. To-morrow it will, I venture to predict, be the standpoint of the Democracy of this country. For while the policy of contracting obligations of this kind towards Continental Powers may or may not be wise, a system which allows of so terrific a responsibility being assumed by a section of the Cabinet behind the back of Parliament is not a system which Democracy can tolerate with safety to itself. And a system which permits of responsible Ministers rising in Parliament to deny that which has been planned, prepared, and executed is not a system to which I, as a believer in the principle

---

[1] The Right Hon. John Burns and Lord Morley. Mr. Charles Trevelyan, a junior member of the Government, also resigned. Other members of the Cabinet also resigned, but reconsidered their position when Belgium was invaded: *Vide* Chapter XXXIV.

of government by the people for the people, can give my allegiance. The overwhelming significance of the avowals of August 3 are to-day obscured amidst the passions aroused by the war. But they constitute a challenge to the basic principles of popular government, and Democracy cannot remain indifferent to that challenge. It must take it up. If Liberalism is not behind it when it does so Liberalism will disappear from our political life.

It is possible that public opinion would have supported a case for a military and naval understanding with France, frankly placed before Parliament, on the basis of a Ministerial survey of the international situation. But in my judgment it is quite certain that the support would have been limited to sanctioning the defence of France if wantonly attacked by Germany *on an issue affecting those two countries alone.* There would have been a refusal to sanction the extension of our liabilities to contingencies arising out of France's relations with Russia, the one Power which had nothing to lose and everything to gain from a general European War. In that way would the European situation, so far as the Western Powers were concerned, have been saved. A really Liberal Foreign Policy, untrammelled by secret obligations, would have bent all its energies, during the years which followed the Morocco crisis of 1911, in an effort to secure that the impending clash (the portents were writ large upon the horizon) between Slav and Teuton in the Balkans should not fling Western Europe into the abyss. Our Foreign Policy was not free to take that course. It has been fettered by a naval and military understanding which bound us to the side, not of France alone, but to that of Russia, whose general mobilization order of July 31 was the precipitating cause of the war. These fetters they were which effectually strangled the Foreign Secretary's strenuous efforts to preserve the peace of Europe during the crisis. He was tied to France, and through France to Russia. France is at war because of her contract with Russia. We, who deem ourselves at war because of the outrage upon Belgium, are at war for precisely the same reason as the French.

The one good thing which might have evolved from the evil thing which our entanglement itself was, would have been a frank avowal of its existence in the early days of the crisis.   One of the most pregnant passages in the White Book is that in which the Russian Foreign Minister holds this language to our Ambassador :

"He (M. Sazanoff) did not believe that Germany really wanted war, but her attitude was decided by ours. If we took our stand firmly with France and Russia there would be no war. If we failed them now, rivers of blood would flow, and we would in the end be dragged into war." (No. 17.)

The Minister added, in reply to a remark by our Ambassador, that :

"unfortunately Germany was convinced that she could count upon our neutrality."

The fact that we had sacrificed our neutrality in advance by commitments secret and unsanctioned, but involving the honour of individual Ministers, was the fatal handicap to a serious attempt to deal with the Belgian issue, both in the years which preceded and in the opening days of the crisis. This, and this alone, is the explanation of the extraordinary manner in which the Belgian issue was handled. What was the position of Belgium in the event of a European conflagration involving the Western Powers? It was a position of extreme precariousness despite the international neutrality guarantee of 1839, renewed in 1870 for one year only. It was a position which the actual division of Europe into two rival groups rendered, indeed, almost desperate. For nothing was more certain than that if the embers, which these rivalries promoted, ever burst forth into stupendous fire, treaties and conventions, along with constitutions, frontiers, and even dynasties would be swallowed up in the flames. That, were this conflagration to eventuate, it would be on the Belgian plains that the future destinies of Europe would be decided, was the view of every strategist of repute in every country. It is noteworthy, however, that the experts have always omitted from their calculations the counter-balancing effect of a timely and explicit declaration of British policy. Experts upon international military strategy are not concerned with the moralities, but with the manner in which the great killing machines which Democracy tolerates and feeds to its own undoing, will be

set in motion when potentates and diplomatists fall out
and the pressure of the war captains becomes irresistible.
And the experts were all but unanimous in concluding that
in the event of a general European War waged on the
basis of the existing divisions in Europe—i.e., an Austro-
German combination on the one side and a Franco-
Russian combination on the other—Germany, to stand any
chance of victory, must strike instantly at France, and
could only hope to strike successfully by striking through
Belgium owing to the impossibility of forcing the defences
of the French frontier. All this was notorious. Equally
notorious was the fact that Germany was perfecting her
military railways and making other strategic preparations
on the Belgian frontier to be ready for the eventuality.
The facts have been published again and again. Mr.
Churchill told us on September 21 last (at Liverpool) that
he had known them for three years, and, of course, he
spoke for his colleagues ; for those of them, at least, whose
business it is to be informed on these matters.

The position of Belgium, then, was such as imperiously
necessitated a clear and unambiguous attitude on the part
of those responsible for directing the Foreign Policy of
Great Britain. The mere existence of the old neutrality
treaty was obviously insufficient to safeguard Belgium's
position since, as Mr. Churchill has told us, the Government was aware that Germany would thrust aside that
treaty if, on the outbreak of a European War she were
faced with a Russo-French combination, a combination
which, in view of the experts, would ensure her defeat
unless she could disable France rapidly by an advance
through Belgium.

Confronted with these circumstances it was a duty owed
by the British Government to its own people, to Belgium,
and to the world, to intimate in clear language to all
whom it might concern, its firm intention of using the
whole might of the Empire against any Power whose
strategic military exigencies might tempt its rulers, in
the event of a general European War, to violate the
neutrality of Belgium. It was the one influence which,
had it been timely exercised—for example, at any moment
within the last two years when our relations with Germany were recovering from the Moroccan trouble—could
have prevented the situation on the Belgian-German frontier from developing to the danger point.   There are

precedents for such warnings conveyed in friendly terms in time of peace. If the warning had been disregarded and German preparations on the Belgian frontier had persisted, our course was clear. If it had been regarded we should have had an admirable opportunity of removing from Germany—under circumstances permitting of the practicability of the course, not at a moment when an acute crisis had reached breaking point—the latent fear that England might encourage a Russo-French aggression upon her; and thus played the disinterested rôle of Peace-maker among the nations. Even if such a declaration had been made in the opening days of the crisis it might still have had a potent effect, because Germany believed at that moment that we should remain neutral.

But such an attitude was only possible to a Foreign Policy which, apart from the Belgian issue, was unfettered by commitments to either European group; or to a Foreign Policy which had sought and received national sanction to an alliance with France, but an alliance limited to the defence of legitimate French interests, an alliance unaffected by Russian aims and actions in the Balkans, an alliance designed to save France from being sacrificed to a Slav-Teuton quarrel, and in saving France, saving Belgium, and confining the theatre of potential war to Eastern and Central Europe.

Such an attitude, unhappily, was not possible, because our neutrality had been bartered away. Hence it came about that as on the general issue, so on the Belgian issue, we maintained a doubtful attitude until the position had become hopelessly compromised, and until the opportunity of saving Belgium was lost. Although, as Mr. Churchill had said, we had been aware of Belgium's peril for three years, a glance at the White Book will show that the Belgian question was never raised at all until July 31 last. On that day we asked Germany, whom for three years we had been aware would NOT respect Belgian neutrality in the event of a war with Russia and France, whether she would respect it! We asked France the same question, although the French plan of campaign had been concerted with the British General Staff! And even on that day— the day upon which war became irrevocable through the issue of a general mobilization order for all the Russian armies—the Belgian issue was not presented as a question of vital British national policy; it might not be a "decisive" but merely an "important" factor in deter-

mining our action. (No. 119.) A day later yet—August 1
—it was intimated that the British official attitude on the
Belgian issue would depend upon "public feeling." (No.
123.)

The blood of our gallant sons is poured out to-day as
the immediate consequence of the outrage committed upon
Belgium. But the time will come when the country will
ask of those in authority this question : "What did you
do to PREVENT that outrage?" For my part I put that
question now, and I find the answer in an autocratic and
secret foreign policy to which I have been consistently
opposed, and which I intend to help in rooting out of our
national life.

I believe I am doing a greater service to those who
suffer from its effects and with whom I had hoped to be
associated later on in the accomplishment of that purpose,
by speaking now than by remaining silent, even at the
price of forfeiting your and their good-will. I cannot play
the hypocrite among you.

At any rate, that is the message which seems to come
to me from those dreadful fields of senseless carnage
where millions expiate the sins, the faults, and follies of
the few.

CHAPTER II.

Belgian Neutrality and European Military Strategy[1]

THREE years ago he gave some attention to the military aspects of the problem, and he was quite sure that Germany would violate the neutrality of Belgium. All her plans were made in cold blood to do that.—*Mr. Churchill at Liverpool, September 21, 1914.*

German preparations for invading France had been made years ago. They always intended to go through Belgium.—*Mr. Bonar Law at .Belfast, September 29, 1914.*

The German Staff had for years made no secret of this intention (going through Belgium), and French military critics had accepted it as a truism.—*Nelson's "History of the War," by Mr. John Buchan (Thomas Nelson and Sons).*

I HAVE been asked by various correspondents for further information in corroboration of the assertion contained in my letter that military experts were agreed upon the necessity for Germany—from the standpoint of military strategy—to seek a passage through Belgian territory in order to attack France in the hypothesis of a general European war, and that the German preparations in view of that eventuality were notorious. Mr. Churchill's avowal really dispenses me from pursuing the matter, for in effect it is an avowal that the German intentions and preparations were known to the British War Office, as, of course, they were; and to every War Office, for that matter, in Europe. But, as my correspondents do not appear wholly satisfied, I append these notes, which make no pretence to being exhaustive.

The military situation of Germany in the hypothesis of a general European war has been frequently and minutely discussed and depicted, as have the measures taken by her strategists to cope with it, by eminent soldiers in many lands, from General Langlois (French) to General Nogi (Japanese). The German plans, their character and nature and their inevitability (from

[1] Originally published as an Appendix to the pamphlet containing the Author's letter of resignation to the Birkenhead Liberal Association (*vide* Chapter I).

14

the military standpoint) have been very fully described and explained by British students of war and by British publicists in touch with authoritative military opinion. The best known of these writings, perhaps, are those of Colonel Repington, the military writer on the *Times,* whose reputation is international, and whose alleged close association with high military circles in this country has been the subject of Parliamentary observation; and of Mr. Hilaire Belloc. Mr. Belloc's article in the *London Magazine* of May, 1912, is almost a military classic. The columns of the *Times* have abounded in allusions to this subject. The issues of that paper for January 23 and 30 and February 20, 1911, and December 3, 1912, as also the *Fortnightly Review* for August, 1911, and the *Morning Post* (which has many Service connections) of January 12, 1911, may be consulted with advantage. The Belgian papers, the French military journals of that year and the ensuing one, and the Belgian Parliamentary debates can also be referred to; and amongst the published works of military writers, Colonel Boucher's *L'Allemagne en péril*—a significant title—published early this year in Paris and Nancy. But the material is too abundant even to summarise here.

Broadly speaking, these writings and utterances display a unanimity in estimating the situation and its implications, and in regarding a German demand for a right of way through Belgium as being axiomatic in the event of a general European war. Nor is there any occasion for surprise in the fact. An explanatory *résumé* may, however, serve the process of clarification.

Throughout the nineteenth century the danger of a violation of Belgian neutrality arose from French necessities, strategically considered, of course; these notes are merely concerned with the strategical side of the question. In point of fact, the neutralisation of Belgium arose from the aggressive tendencies of French policy of that time. In 1870 Napoleon III. and his generals are supposed to have made all arrangements for a French invasion of Belgium, which the publication that year of the famous draft-treaty drawn up in 1866 by Benedetti, the French Ambassador at Berlin, and Lord Granville's ensuing act in requiring both France and Prussia to pledge themselves anew in regard to Belgian neutrality, nipped in the bud.[1]

---

[1] *Vide inter alia:* "The Life of Lord Granville," by Lord Edmond Fitzmaurice; "Life of Gladstone," by Lord Morley; "Modern Europe," by Alison Phillips, etc.

Down to the opening years of the present twentieth
century, German strategy, in the hypothesis of another war
with France, would appear to have been based upon a
concentrated offensive through Alsace-Lorraine, whose
annexation as the result of the war of 1870 was, by the
way, insisted upon by the German military chiefs from
the point of view of strategic defence, it being through
those provinces that the French invasions of Germany in
previous times had usually been directed.

But a series of new developments were destined gradually to transform the entire military outlook as between
Germany and France and) revolutionise the strategic
plans both of the German and of the French General Staffs.
These determining influences have been at once political
and military. The Franco-Russian Alliance, the lessons
of the Russo-Japanese war, the formidable character of
the French defences on the Franco-German frontier, the
perfecting of modern gun-fire, the immense increase in
military effectives, and the need of greater space for their
deployment, are the principal factors, all inter-connected,
which caused these changes.

By general consent, military opinion had reached the
following conclusions. The French lines inside the French
frontier where it faces the German, had become virtually
impassable by an attacking army, however strong, under
modern conditions of warfare, which involves the deployment of immense forces—greater than at any period in
the world's history—and which gives to the defence,
owing to the destructive character, long range, and invisi-
bility of modern gunfire, a great superiority over the
attack. Between Verdun and Lunéville and between
Epinal and Belfort—i.e., along almost the entire length
of the French lines—there was hardly a spot not com-
manded by the fire of heavy guns. The area presents
serious natural obstacles, and these had been enormously
aggravated by an uninterrupted series of batteries, forts,
and entrenched positions. Three narrow gaps did exist :
the Belfort gap, the Lunéville-Neufchâteau gap, and the
Stenay gap, north of Verdun. But, by common admission,
they were impracticable as avenues of invasion. I need
not go into technical details : they have been set forth at
considerable length by a number of expert writers. As
Colonel Repington has pointed out (1911), the difficulties
were such as to "almost preclude the notion that the
German strategist will be content to run his head against

a French line of battle in the three narrow *trouées* left open to a German invasion."

The problem, then, which faced the German Government and the German General Staff, as portrayed by a mass of authoritative military opinion, may now be briefly examined in the light of the historical events of the past twenty years. A general European war waged on the basis of the existing divisions of Europe meant that Germany would have to face a Franco-Russian combination of very great numerical superiority. The vulnerability of the German military position in such circumstances was Bismarck's haunting obsession, and his policy was ceaselessly directed to prevent their occurrence. The brilliant course of studies which Sir Charles Dilke published in the *Fortnightly Review* in 1887, and which caused a great flutter in the diplomatic dovecotes, did much to enlighten British public opinion on the subject, and the British Government of the day fully appreciated it. In the light of actual events it is, indeed, both curious and instructive to peruse the English papers of that period, which was one of great tension. They indicate an appreciation of the anxieties bulking so largely in the minds of German statesmen, and a realisation of what the German position would become if a Franco-Russian alliance were consummated. [In recent years—*i.e.,* since the actual consummation of that alliance—all this has been entirely banished from consideration and public discussion, owing to the changed character of Anglo-German relations. But the problem itself did not change with the changed character of those relations.] Thus we find the *Standard* (February 17, 1887), whose then relations with the Foreign Office were believed to be close, declaring :—

"Russia can afford to wait. So can France. Germany cannot. Germany must see to its own safety, and Prince Bismarck cannot reasonably be expected to pass his declining days impotently watching the silent conspiracy, for the silent growth of the power of France and the power of Russia against the Fatherland."

Curiously enough, the German Chancellor used almost identical language in the Reichstag in 1914. "France could wait, but we not. A French inroad on our flank in the Lower Rhine could have been fatal to us. So we were forced to set aside the just protests of the Luxemburg and Belgian Governments."[1]

Bismarck's success in staving off the danger was not perpetuated by those who came after him.   A Franco-Russian military alliance was born.   Thenceforth the situation of Germany became one of permanent and unquestionable peril.   The consciousness of that peril became the dominant factor in the considerations of German statesmen, and under its influence "Prussian militarism" became, in the opinion of all Germans, much as many of them might detest its manifestations, the one bulwark of the nation against the dangers which encompassed it. Writing in 1911, Colonel Repington remarked : "The possibility of a war on two fronts is the nightmare of German strategists, and considering the pace at which Russia has been building up her field armies since 1905, the nightmare is not likely to be soon conjured away."   An admission of that kind from a military writer of unquestioned authority, who has never troubled to conceal his anti-German sentiments, speaks for itself.   To it may be added the conclusions of Colonel Boucher in his work, *Germany in Peril,* already alluded to.   After pointing out that Germany could not attack France except through Belgium, and could not attack Russia without having France "on her back," he concludes : "Germany is, in a word, condemned to stifle on her own soil from her surplus production, from her surplus population, and from the very hugeness of her power."   A prospect, it will be concluded, not altogether pleasing for the party concerned.

From the date of the conclusion of the Franco-Russian Alliance, German strategy could have but one intelligible object—to prepare for an immediate offensive against France in the hope of striking a rapid and overwhelming blow at the Western foe before the Russian avalanche had time to gather the full force of its momentum.   Any other policy on the part of the German military chiefs would, in the opinion of the experts—and no particular knowledge of military stategy is required to demonstrate its obviousness—have been suicidal from the military point of view

---

[1] It is interesting to recall that within a fortnight of the outbreak of war a general offensive in Lorraine and Alsace was initiated by the French on a large scale.   After seizing the passes of the Vosges, they took successively Dannemarie, Thann, Mulhouse, and Saarburg, and overran Upper Alsace almost to the Rhine.   They were then defeated with heavy loss and under circumstances which have not yet transpired.

in the hypothesis of a general European war. The German
General Staff bent its energies, therefore, upon securing
the mechanical means for that accomplishment. This necessitated raising the military machine—especially in regard to
rapidity of mobilisation and in the construction of strategic
railways—to the highest possible pitch of efficiency. But
the factors already alluded to, arising from the developments of the past decade, had added immeasurably to the
difficulties of the German General Staff and to the military
danger of the German situation in the hypothesis of a
general European war. At a period which may be said
roughly to date back seven years, or possibly a year or
two earlier, Germany, owing to these developments, found
herself, militarily speaking, compelled to realise that her
armies could not force the French lines inside the French
frontier; in other words, that a German blow at France
by way of the Franco-German frontier was impracticable.
Germany's strategic necessities (*i.e.,* an immediate offensive against France) remaining, of course, unaffected by
this realisation, her General Staff had to work out a plan
for an offensive against France from other bases. What
were the other possible bases? They were Switzerland,
Belgium, and Luxemburg. Switzerland was out of the
question for obvious reasons. There remained Belgium
and Luxemburg. An offensive against France was,
thenceforth, possible only through Luxemburg and Belgium. Failing that, German strategy, in the event of a
general European war on the existing basis of international
relationships, would have to abandon all idea of an offensive
against France, and content itself with standing on the
defensive to await the French onslaught. Germany's
alternative was thus either to give up all idea of striking
a decisive blow at France before Russia had time to concentrate her masses and set them in motion, or to obtain
a passage through neutral territory, peacefully if possible,
by force if necessary. In adopting the former attitude she
would have laid herself open to a French invasion through
Alsace-Lorraine, a difficult feat, but not, in expert opinion,
an impracticable one, such as a German forcing of the
French lines had become. She would also have laid herself open to a possible invasion through Belgian and
Luxemburg territory, and in view of French records in
the past, Germany's rulers and her General Staff held,
not unreasonably perhaps, that they would be criminal to
run that risk. Rightly or wrongly, the German Govern-

ment and the German military chiefs concluded that Germany could not forego an immediate offensive against France in the hypothesis of a general European war, without endangering the national existence of their country.

Let me here remark once again that I am engaged in describing the military situation of Germany in Europe from 1906 onwards, as known to the Military Departments of all the European Governments, our own included; and as depicted for us by authoritative military opinion in Europe, including authoritative British military opinion. I am not discussing the moralities of the matter at all. My views as to the moral side of the invasion of Belgium are given in my letter.[1] But those who suppose that British policy in regard to the passage through Belgium of German or French armies has always been the fixed quantity it is now represented as being, would do well to refresh their memories by perusing the literature of 1887, when France and Germany were on the eve of war over the Schnaebele incident, *i.e., before the conclusion of the Franco-Russian Alliance and before the other material factors touched upon in these notes had, in combination, rendered a German offensive against France over the Franco-German frontier—even then extremely hazardous—virtually impossible.* A study of the writings of that time will show that "scraps of paper" are regarded with very different eyes, according to circumstances, by those whose purpose it is to influence public opinion either in one direction or in another. I cannot find, in referring to contemporary writings, that the suggestion of a possible demand by Germany, or France, of a right of way through Belgium should be treated by Great Britain, if such a demand arose, otherwise than from the point of view of British interests, and it was argued by many at that time that British interests would be met by guarantees of a restoration of the *status quo* at the conclusion of the war. British official opinion of those days was probably interpreted in the famous letter signed by "Diplomaticus," which appeared in the *Standard* of February 4, 1887, and which received strong editorial support. Its thesis, that it would be "madness" for Great Britain to oppose a passage of German troops through Belgium, was, generally speaking, endorsed. The *Pall Mall Gazette* went even further. After pointing out that considerable importance was likely to be attached to this thesis, "owing to its

[1] *Vide* Chapter I.

being understood that the *Standard* is at present the Governmental and Salisburian organ," the *Pall Mall Gazette* went on to argue that the treaties of 1831 and 1839 did not impose upon Great Britain any "obligation" as regards Belgian neutrality. Its editorial of February 4, 1887, concludes an analytical examination of those treaties as follows :—

"There is, therefore, no English guarantee to Belgium. It is possible, perhaps, to 'construct' such a guarantee; but the case may be summed up as follows : (1) England is under no guarantee whatever except such as is common to Austria, France, Russia, and Germany; and (2) that guarantee is not specifically of the neutrality of Belgium at all; and (3) is given not to Belgium, but to the Netherlands."

The *Spectator* of February 5, 1887, remarked : "The probability is that we shall insist on her (Belgium) not becoming the theatre of war, but shall not bar—as, indeed, we cannot bar—the traversing of her soil."[1]

I resume, with apologies for this digression. When once the German strategists had become fully persuaded that an offensive against France *via* the Franco-German frontier had become impracticable, the situation was accepted, and the German General Staff turned its whole attention to working out a plan for an offensive against France *via* Belgium and Luxemburg, *i.e.,* on the line of advance Aix-la-Chapelle—Trèves. I do not suppose that the German General Staff invited the military attachés of the various Powers, or the foreign newspaper representatives, to examine on the spot the actual steps which were being taken. But, apart from that, there appears to have been no particular secrecy about the German preparations. How in the nature of things could secrecy

---

[1] Palmerston, who signed the 1839 treaty, appeared to attach but mediocre importance to it. Replying to Disraeli on June 8, 1855, about the proposed neutralisation of the Danubian principalities, he said : "There certainly are instances in Europe of such propositions, and it has been agreed by treaty that Belgium and Switzerland should be declared neutral ; but I am not disposed to attach very much importance to such engagements, for the history of the world shows that when a quarrel arises and a nation makes war, and thinks it advantageous to traverse with its army such neutral territory, the declarations of neutrality are not apt to be very religiously respected." (Quoted by Brailsford in his "Belgium and the Scrap of Paper.") The quotation may be commended to those who argue that Germany's exclusion from the comity of nations is both possible and desirable after the war.

have been secured? The matter was openly debated—in diplomatic terms, of course—in the Belgian Chamber at the end of 1912, when the Belgian Minister of War made a notable statement, and the Belgian Press teemed with articles on the whole subject both in 1911 and 1912, much difference of opinion manifesting itself. Indeed, during the course of the struggle in England to obtain humane treatment for the natives of the Congo and the observance by King Leopold and the Belgian Government of the clauses of the Berlin and Brussels Acts, it was a constant practice on the part of the apologists of Leopoldianism in England to allege that the British reform movement was to be deprecated because it would "drive Belgium into the arms of Germany."

To talk about Germany's "secret preparations" in this respect is picturesque, and helps to keep up the idea of Machiavellism about German policy which it is considered desirable to maintain. But in point of actual fact, although German diplomacy was, throughout, dishonest, as diplomacy always is, Germany's preparations on the Belgian frontier became in due course as notorious as the object of them had precedently become. The strategists and military writers knew all about them in substance, and their knowledge could only have been acquired through the usual military and secret service channels. Moreover, German military writers themselves do not appear to have been in the least concerned to disguise the facts. For example, General Van Faulkenhausen, in his *Der Grosse Krieg der Zelztzeit* (quoted in the *Times,* 1911), assumed, as a matter of course, that Belgian territory would be violated in the event of a general European war. Military writers, British and others, told us that when Germany perceived she must revolutionise her whole military plans, she forthwith began a great work of strategic railway construction, flanking the whole front Aix-la-Chapelle—Trèves, linking up these new lines with the main lines and military centres at Mainz, Cologne, Bonn, and Coblentz. They told us, as far back as 1911, that the detraining platforms at Metz had been gradually trebled, and that between Aix-la-Chapelle and Trois Vièrges a fresh base of concentration for an army was in course of preparation; that, in addition to these railways, "double lined and metalled for heavy traffic," sidings had been provided at all the stations and at suitable points between them; that between Montjoie and St. Vith landing spaces sufficient for over 120,000 men had been provided; that small stations (such as Münster, Rötgen, Montjoie, etc., etc.), with no traffic at all, had been provided with platforms, "some of which extended over half a mile." They told us of entrenched camps in proximity to the Belgian frontier, of the accumulation of trucks, stores, and so on and so forth.

A word has now to be said about French policy and strategy on the hypothesis of a general European war. It has been recently suggested in various quarters that if Germany had not attacked France, France would not have attacked Germany. But this can only be in the nature of an after-thought. Had there been even a question of France's remaining neutral if Russia became involved with Germany, no *general* war would have taken place, Belgium would not now be the theatre for the contending armies of four Powers, and Britain would not be lamenting the death of thousands of her gallant sons. That the German Government did not desire war with France, the White Book and the accessory documents in combination definitely establish. When, on August 1, there seemed a chance that the British Government might be disposed to attempt to use its good offices with a view to securing French neutrality in the event of a Russo-German conflict, the rulers of Germany instantly responded. The German Ambassador in London wired the Chancellor that he had told Sir Edward Grey he (the Ambassador) thought Germany would agree. The Chancellor wired back confirming. The Kaiser wired to King George to the same effect (*vide* documents h, i, j, in Price's *The Diplomatic History of the War*). The hope turned out to have been due to a misunderstanding between Sir Edward Grey and the German Ambassador in the course of a telephonic conversation (*vide* Sir Edward Grey's statement in the House on August 28).

The language used by the French Ambassador at Petrograd to Sir George Buchanan, the British Ambassador, on July 24 (No. 6 White Book), and by M. Cambon, the French Ambassador in London, to Sir Edward Grey on July 30 (No. 105 White Book), are explicit in the sense that the French Government had no intention of remaining neutral. So much for that.

As to French strategy. Since the Franco-Russian Alliance, French military writers have been divided in their views as to the strategy to be followed by the French

armies in the event of a general European war. Two of
the most recent French military works are those by Lieut.-
Colonel A. Grouard and by Colonel Arthur Boucher respectively.[1]   Lieut.-Colonel Grouard, while admitting that
upon the outbreak of such a war France would probably
be invaded before her preparations were complete, argues,
nevertheless, that the offensive should be taken ''as rapidly
as possible,'' and that the efforts of the French should be
directed against Southern Alsace, with Thionville as main
objective.   No attempt should be made to cross the Rhine
until the French armies held the complete mastery of the
left bank of that river.   The capture of Thionville would
be followed by an attack upon Germersheim, and with the
capture of the latter place, the interests of France would be
to secure terms of peace based upon the restoration of
Alsace-Lorraine.   Colonel Boucher (author of two previous
and well-known works, *The Offensive against Germany*
and *France Victorious in the War of To-Morrow*) also
believes in making all preparations for a rapid counter-
offensive.   ''If by the eleventh day Germany has not
crossed our frontier, it is we who will cross hers by taking
the direct offensive.''   Both authors appear to regard it
as a matter of course that France will intervene in a Russo-
German war.   Colonel Boucher is particularly emphatic.
He points out—with a veracity which some British writers
have failed to imitate—that Germany's new military law
of 1913 was ''to guard against the Slav danger.''   Germany, he says, ''does not doubt that France, remaining
immutably faithful to her treaties, would support her ally
with all her strength, choosing, however, the most favourable moment to intervene. . . .''

With the penetrating logic and philosophy peculiar to
the French mind, Colonel Boucher has given what is, perhaps, the truest picture of the conditions which prevailed
in Europe at the dawn of the year of grace 1914.   The
passage is worth reproducing in full :—

''Strange is the situation in which France finds herself !   It is regret at having lost her two fine provinces of
Alsace and Lorraine, which have remained so piously
attached to us; it is our unshakable determination to
succeed in wresting them from the domination of their
invaders and our hope to see once again the Tricolour

---

[1] *La guerre éventuelle* (Paris, Librairie Chapelot, 1913) and
L'Allemagne en péril, op. cit.

waving from their public buildings; it is, therefore, a question of sentiment which is, above all, the cause of our hostility towards Germany, and this hostility compels us to undertake in the Triple Entente, covered by France and Russia, the protection of the vital interests of our allies and friends. For if we are victorious, Europe is for ever delivered from German domination; simultaneously Slavism has hurled Germanism to earth; Russia becomes completely free to consolidate her immense Empire by increasing it. If we are victorious, England remains the mistress of the seas; her fleet has no longer anything to fear from that of Germany; her trade is sheltered from competition. In order to resist attacks which threaten her on all sides, Germany is compelled to develop her military power to the supreme point, and, in the ultimate resort, this power becomes concentrated against us. . . ."

Enough has now, I think, been said to answer the query raised by my correspondents. But in order to link up the strategic situation of Germany in the reader's mind with the international position as established by the existing divisions of Europe, and thus to clarify the whole story, it may be useful to recapitulate the leading points. *Point I.* The Franco-Russian Alliance was the product of various causes. A discussion of them would be out of place here. The alliance has been alternately represented to the British public as defensive and offensive, according to the tendencies prevailing in governing circles at the moment. It has been regarded in Germany as a permanent menace, and as tilting the so-called "balance of power" heavily against her. From the moment of its conclusion Germany's military position became, in strict fact, whatever it may have been in motive, a defensive attitude against vastly superior potential forces.[1] *Point II.* If that alliance—the exact terms of which have not been published —implied French aid to Russia in the event of a Teuton-Slav conflict over the Balkans and over the position of Austro-Hungary (as we see by the White Book that it did), then an immediate offensive by Germany against France was axiomatic, and was known so to be by every Government in Europe. *Point III.* The only feasible line, strategically speaking, of German advance against France lay, in the opinion of experts, through Belgium and

[1] *Vide* Mr. Lloyd George's speeches in 1908 and 1914—Chapters X. and XXXIII.

Luxemburg. *Point IV.* The German General Staff was known to have made all preparations for that eventuality, and a request by Germany to Belgium for a right of way was as certain in 1914 as it was probable in 1887. These, for the past decade, have been the *fixed and positive factors* of the European situation in the hypothesis of war— eliminating the factor of British policy towards that eventuality and in the causes which might bring it about. The *uncertain factor* in the European situation has been the attitude of the Liberal Cabinet, and the more closely the effects of that attitude are studied through a restored faculty of critical judgment in the minds of the British people, the more certainly will that attitude be condemned. It made extension of the war to the Western area inevitable. For, on the one hand, our diplomacy, secretly pledged to France (and, therefore, to Russia, without, be it noted, even a knowledge of the exact text of the French and Russian Alliance !), refused to declare itself, despite the repeated requests of the French and Russian Governments. And, on the other, our diplomacy thus secretly pledged, was prevented from playing cards on the table with Germany in the matter of Belgium, which was the key to the situation, as these notes prove. Not only did our diplomacy fail to raise the Belgian issue with Germany until the very last moment, and then only in a manner lacking both in definiteness and precision, although it was aware that Belgium would be involved as a matter of course if war broke out; but when our diplomacy did eventually raise that issue it declined to say that Great Britain would remain neutral even if Belgian neutrality were not violated, and even if Germany, as the result of a victorious war, refrained from availing herself of her victory in order to secure any of the French Colonial possessions (No. 123),[1]

---

[1] The inquiry was made by the German Ambassador on August 1, 1914. Sir E. Grey afterwards stated, in effect, that the German Ambassador's inquiries were made on his own personal initiative and lacked official authority. (August 27.) This incident remains one of the unexplained mysteries of the negotiations. Why was the conversation recorded and subsequently published in the White Book— where it stands out as one of the really crucial documents—if it had been merely informal? Is it usual for an Ambassador to make pregnant proposals off his own bat? Considerable care is taken in connection with several documents in the White Book to differentiate between a personal communication and an official communication ; for instance, in No. 3 it is recorded that the Austrian Ambassador "explained privately," and in No. 10 we are told that the German Ambassador "asked me privately." Why, then, does the interview

and it made no effort whatsoever to secure the neutrality of France in a Russo-German quarrel. If British diplomatic policy, nominally in the hands of Sir Edward Grey, but really in the hands of the permanent officials, was a peace policy, it failed through sheer incapacity and incompetence. If it was a war policy, its success is its condemnation.

of August 1—as published in No. 123—contain no indication to the effect that the Ambassador was merely speaking in his personal capacity? It is, moreover, apparent from the German Ambassador's telegram to his Government (dated 8.30 p.m., August 1, *vide* Price, p. 411) that he had been acting on "instructions," and the general character of his inquiries—as recorded in No. 123—cannot be said to have been in disaccord with the tone of the telegrams the Kaiser and the German Minister for Foreign Affairs were even then despatching from Berlin. It would have been a simple matter, one would have thought, if Sir E. Grey was doubtful about the German Ambassador's authority, to have ascertained by wire whether the Ambassador was speaking for himself or for his Government. It would have constituted at least an attempt to save Belgium and England's entry into the war

CHAPTER III.

Was Germany wholly responsible? [1]

It is clear that the closer the study of the negotiations which led up to the world disaster are studied, the more impossible it is to put the blame entirely upon the shoulders of any one European State; and the more the evidence is sifted, the stronger becomes the conviction that the responsibility for the failure of diplomacy to save the civilisation of Europe must be laid at the door of all the European Chancelleries without distinction.—*"The Diplomatic History of the War," by Mr. Philips Price (George Allen and Unwin: second edition).*

THERE is a disposition to regard the discussion of the immediate origin of the war as out of place. But hardly a day passes without some eminent author or historian contributing his quota to the subject, the conclusion being invariably that Germany and Germany alone was to blame. To hazard a doubt as to the accuracy of some of the facts put forward in support of this conclusion is denounced as unpatriotic. But is it unpatriotic to hope for an eventual reconciliation beween the British and German peoples? The British and German peoples hold with unquestionable sincerity that each is wholly in the right. It might or might not be desirable to withhold discussion until the combatants on either side—for the most part as innocent of the causes which flung them into the death-grapple as the unborn babe—were mercifully released from their present occupation. That must be a matter of opinion. But in actual fact, non-combatant diplomatists and publicists on both sides decline to do so, and their main object appears to be to pile fresh fuel on to the flames of hatred. Under the circumstances it cannot be wrong to ask for enlightenment on a point of very considerable importance, and which remains—for many of us at least—wrapped in doubt and obscurity.

May I indicate it? Until the other day most people who have really studied the available evidence would, I imagine, have agreed in fixing the main responsibility for

[1] *The Labour Leader,* October 8, 1914.

the immediate origin of the war upon Austria's intemperance in dealing with Servia, upon Germany's inability or unwillingness to hold Austria back, and upon Russia's sudden orders for a *general* mobilisation after the Austro-Russian "conversations," momentarily broken off, had been resumed.

But with the appearance of Sir M. de Bunsen's despatch, issued as a special White Paper (Cd. 7596), we are virtually asked to revise that view and to conclude that Austria was Germany's catspaw, and that Germany rushed into war, compelling Austria to follow, when Austria had, in effect, given way to Russia's demands. I am unaware that a single newspaper in this country has read anything but this in Sir M. de Bunsen's despatch.

The more that despatch is studied, however, the more difficult does it become for some of us to reconcile its tenour with contemporary documents. For example, in discussing the actions of the Austro-Hungarian Government, Sir M. de Bunsen remarks :—

"Russia replied to a partial Austrian mobilisation and declaration of war against Servia by a partial Russian mobilisation against Austria. Austria met this move by completing her own mobilisation, and Russia again responded with results which have passed into history." (p. 2.)

The first sentence agrees with the White Book (Cd. 7467). But if "completing her own mobilisation" means, as I assume it to mean, *general* mobilisation, then the inference here is that the Austrian general mobilisation preceded the Russian. But Sir M. de Bunsen's despatch in the White Book announcing the Austrian general mobilisation is dated August 1 (No. 127), and Russia gave orders for a *general* mobilisation in the night of July 30, and announced it in the morning of July 31 (Nos. 112-113).[1] Which is right? Obviously the date is of capital importance.[2]

Sir M. de Bunsen further states :

"Unfortunately these conversations at St. Petersburg and Vienna were cut short by the transfer of the dispute

---

[1] Mr. Stephen Graham was in a village as far away from St. Petersburg as the Mongolian frontier, and the telegram to mobilize came through at 4 a.m. on July 31. (*Vide: Times,* September 11, 1914, and Price "The Diplomatic History of the War."

[2] Mr. Philips Price has since called attention also to this grave discrepancy in the second edition of his valuable work.

to the more dangerous ground of a direct conflict between Germany and Russia. Germany intervened on July 31 by means of her double ultimatum to St. Petersburg and Paris.'' (p. 3.)

What is singular in the above passage is the omission of the Russian *general* mobilisation order, which was, admittedly, the immediate cause of the German ultimatum. Can any useful purpose be served by sliding over what Germany alleges to have been the determining factor in her action, viz., the Russian *general* mobilisation?

Again, if Austria was as anxious to come to terms as Sir M. de Bunsen states, how is it that Sir G. Buchanan, in reporting the *general* Russian mobilisation order, should have given as its compelling cause, a :

'' . . . report received from Russian Ambassador in Vienna to the effect that Austria is determined not to yield to intervention of Powers, and that she is moving troops against Russia as well as against Servia.'' (No. 113.)

In fine, Sir M. de Bunsen reports the Russian Ambassador at Vienna to be ''working hard for peace'' (p. 3) and as conducting negotiations in the most hopeful spirit of compromise, at the very moment when, according to Sir M. de Bunsen's colleague at St. Petersburg, this same Russian Ambassador is telegraphing his Government that Austria is utterly irreconcilable !   These things do not hang together.   What is the explanation?

Again, how are we to explain Sir M. de Bunsen's main implication, viz., a Germany determined to drag Austria into war, together with his casual treatment of the Russian *general* mobilisation, with the despatches from his colleagues, at Berlin and St. Petersburg, which do not harmonise in the least with his? To mention but one instance. Sir G. Buchanan seems to have been under no illusion as to the probable consequences of a *general* Russian mobilisation. He told M. Sazanoff as early as July 25 :—

'' . . . that if Russia mobilised, Germany would not be content with mere mobilisation or give time to Russia to carry out hers, but would probably declare war at once.'' (No. 17.)

And if justice in controversy is permissible in a state of war, it is but the barest justice to Germany's statesmen to recall that they never concealed what the consequences of a Russian *general* mobilisation would be from the British Ambassador, as the White Book bears witness. A Russian *general* mobilisation, therefore, meant war (whether Germany was justified in regarding it as tantamount to a declaration of war is another matter). It meant war in the opinion of the British Ambassador at St. Petersburg. But the event is barely referred to in Sir M. de Bunsen's subsequent presentation of the situation preceding the outbreak, and when he does refer to it the reference is accompanied by a confusion of dates which seems to affect his presentation in a very vital manner.[1]

I pass over the charges of secret mobilising brought against Germany by Russia and against Russia by Germany, because it is not yet possible to compare their respective accuracy. But numerous quotations might be given from the White Book, did space allow, which conflict squarely with Sir M. de Bunsen's implications, or with the implications which have been read into his despatch—

[1] There is an impartial and exhaustive analysis in *"The Diplomatic History of the War"* (*supra*) of the official and unofficial evidence as to the respective dates of mobilization by the various belligerent Governments. From this analysis—the accuracy of which has not, so far as I know, been disputed—it is possible to obtain a clear idea of the actual facts. In reading the summary which follows, the reader must bear in mind that Germany's capacity to give rapid effect to a mobilization order was greater than that of any of the other belligerents. On the other hand, the attempts which have been made to represent Germany's fears of Russia, and the panic which swept over Berlin when news of the general Russian mobilization was received on July 31, as "pro-German" concoctions, because Russian mobilizing powers were necessarily slower than Germany's, must be accepted with caution. As a matter of fact, *within five days of the outbreak of war*, two powerful Russian armies had invaded East Prussia. They defeated the Germans at Gumbinnen, invested Koenigsberg, and occupied Tilsit. Before the end of August, Petrograd was wild with joy, and £20,000 had been raised to present to the first Russian soldier who entered Berlin.

July 25—Austria mobilizes against Serbia (*i.e.*, partial mobilization).

July 28—Russia mobilizes against Austria (*i.e.*, partial mobilization).

July 30 (in the night)—Russia issues a general mobilization order (*i.e.*, against Germany and Austria).

July 31—Germany proclaims a state of martial law.

July 31 (midnight)—Germany summarily demands a demobilization of the Russian army within 12 hours, in default of which Germany will mobilize.

July 31 (at the earliest; the British White Book gives August 1) —Austria orders a general mobilization (*i.e.*, against Russia).

August 1 (afternoon)—Germany issues a general mobilization order.

whichever may be preferred. Apart from the White Book, documents exist which strengthen the doubts raised by a study of Sir M. de Bunsen's despatch. For example, the *Times'* Berlin correspondent, who can hardly be suspected of German sympathies, reported on July 27 (*Times,* July 28) :—

"Germany is certainly and no doubt sincerely working for peace."

And the *Times,* commenting thereon, declared :—

"If this be the case, as we trust and believe it to be, peace ought, with a little further exertion, to be secured."

Again, the former Berlin correspondent of the *New Statesman,* writing from London, in the issue of that periodical dated August 25, states :—

"Now that war is come I can commit an indiscretion and recount an incident over which before my lips were sealed. There was some agitation in the reactionary Press for the suppression of the Socialist peace meetings on the ground that they weakened the policy of the country. On the morning of the day on which the meetings were held an important official of the Social Democratic Party was summoned to the office of the Imperial Minister of the Interior and there informed that not only had the Government no intention of forbidding the peace meetings, but that all precautions would be taken against their disturbance, and that the Government hoped that the Socialists would continue their agitation with the utmost energy. And this they did up to the moment when martial law was declared and further action was useless."

The accuracy of that statement has since been confirmed in a letter which has reached Mr. Ramsay Macdonald from Sweden from one of the German Socialist leaders. On August 1 the *Westminster Gazette* published from its correspondent in Berlin, Mr. Crozier Long, the text of a despatch to the German Ambassador at Vienna, communicated to Mr. Long by the German Government, and reading as follows :—

"BERLIN, JULY 30, 1914.—The report of Count Pourtalès [German Ambassador at St. Petersburg] does not harmonise with the account which your Excellency has given of the attitude of the Austro-Hungarian Government. Apparently there is a misunderstanding, which I beg you to clear up. We cannot expect Austria-Hungary to negotiate with Servia, with which she is in a state of war. The refusal, however, to exchange views with St. Petersburg would be a grave mistake. We are indeed ready to fulfil our duty. As an ally we must, however, refuse to be drawn into a world conflagration through Austria-Hungary not respecting our advice. Your Excellency will express this to Count Berchtold with all emphasis, and great seriousness.—BETHMANN-HOLLWEG.''

Are we to conclude that the *Times* was misinformed; the German Socialists (but to what purpose, if so?) purposely misled, and the telegram of July 30 communicated to Mr. Crozier Long a forgery? It may well be, but I am not aware that it has been so stated—still less proved. The telegram bears out the repeated assurances given to Sir E. Goschen by the German Chancellor as to the efforts the German Government was making to hang upon Austria-Hungary's coat-tails, and although those efforts may not have been as energetic as they might and should, and although they were handicapped by the German Government's original and fatal miscalculation as to Russia's intentions if Austria pushed her quarrel with Servia to the uttermost, Sir Edward Grey certainly believed in their genuine character. Otherwise, he would hardly have telegraphed as he did to the British Ambassador at Berlin on July 29 :—

"If he [the German Chancellor] can induce Austria to satisfy Russia and to abstain from going so far as to come into collision with her, we shall all join in deep gratitude to his Excellency for having saved the peace of Europe." (No. 77.)

Finally, can Sir M. de Bunsen's despatch be reconciled with, for example, the repeated statements of Austro-Hungarian statesmen that the underlying issues of the quarrel with Servia involved the very existence of the Dual Monarchy; with such despatches as Nos. 18, 76, and 95, in the latter of which Sir M. de Bunsen himself telegraphed (July) :—

"The French Ambassador hears from Berlin that the German Ambassador at Vienna is instructed to speak severely to the Austro-Hungarian Government against acting in a manner calculated to provoke European war."

And with No. 97, in which Sir G. Buchanan reports that in the course of an interview with M. Sazonoff, the German Ambassador "completely broke down on seeing that war was inevitable." According to Sir M. de Bunsen's later interpretation of the position, that German representative should have rejoiced.

My object in writing is simply to ask whether a further consideration of accessible data may not cause a modification of the judgment occasioned by Sir M. de Bunsen's despatch. For my part, I believe strongly that it is never impossible to appeal to the British sense of fair-play, whatever the circumstances of the moment may be, and even the horrors of his appalling catastrophe will not leave such enduring bitterness behind them as a charge of calculated perfidy, if that charge is unjust and untrue. I do not say that it is. But there are many others besides myself who cannot reconcile the implications of that despatch with other contemporary documents. We are all aware of Germany's blunders and Germany's faults. But this charge suggests a perfidiousness which, in the absence of conclusively-corroborative evidence and in the face of contradictory evidence, is not credible as now presented.

CHAPTER IV.

Denials and Avowals[1]

In the debate on the Address on March 10, 1913, Lord Hugh Cecil said : The right hon. gentleman and his colleague are generally believed—I speak with the utmost diffidence in regard to allegations which may not be well founded—to have entered into an arrangement, or, to speak more accurately, to have given assurances, which in the contingency of a great European war would involve heavy military obligations on this country. We do not suspect the Prime Minister or the Foreign Secretary of pursuing anything but a pacific foreign policy, and we are far from saying that their policy is in any way an aggressive one ; but certainly we believe, if the stories current are true, the policy, if it is not to be regarded as an aggressive one, is adventurous.

The Prime Minister : Will the noble lord define a little more definitely what he means?

Lord H. Cecil : I am only anxious not to use words which will convey anything but perfectly fair criticism in a matter of this sort, and any ambiguity in what I have said is due to the fact that I do not wish to go beyond the necessities of the case.

The Prime Minister : I do not complain.

Lord H. Cecil : There is a very general belief that this country is under an obligation, not a treaty obligation, but an obligation arising owing to an assurance given by the Ministry in the course of diplomatic negotiations, to send a very large armed force out of this country to operate in Europe. This is the general belief. It would be very presumptuous of anyone who has not access to all the facts in the possession of the Government. . . .

The Prime Minister : I ought to say that it is not true.

Lord H. Cecil : I am very glad to have elicited that explanation.
(*Hansard*, 1913. Vol. L., cols. 42, 43.)

On March 24, 1913, Sir William Byles asked the Prime Minister : Whether he will say if this country is under any, and, if so, what obligation to France to send an armed force in certain contingencies to operate in Europe ; and if so, what are the limits of our agreements, whether by assurance or treaty, with the French nation.

Mr. King asked the Prime Minister : (1) Whether the foreign policy of this country is at the present time unhampered by any treaties, agreements, or obligations under which British military forces would, in certain eventualities, be called upon to be landed on the Continent and join there in military operations ; and (2) whether, in 1905, 1908, or 1911, this country spontaneously offered to France the assistance of the British army, to be landed on the Continent to support France in the event of European hostilities?

[1] *The Labour Leader*, December 3, 1914. Written in reply to an attack upon the Author by Professor Conway.

The Prime Minister : As has been repeatedly stated, this country is not under any obligation not public and known to Parliament which compels it to take part in any war. In other words, if war arises between European Powers there are no unpublished agreements which will restrict or hamper the freedom of the Government or of Parliament to decide whether or not Great Britain should participate in a war. The use that would be made of the naval and military forces if the Government and Parliament decided to take part in a war is, for obvious reasons, not a matter about which public statements can be made beforehand.

—(*Hansard,* 1913. Vol. L., cols. 1316-7.)

On April 28, 1914, Mr. King asked the Secretary of State for Foreign Affairs : Whether he is aware that demands have recently been put forward for a further military understanding between the Powers of the Triple Entente with a view to concerted action on the Continent in case of certain eventualities, and whether the policy of this country still remains one of freedom from all obligations to engage in military operations on the Continent?

Sir E. Grey : The answer to the first part of the question is in the negative, and as regards the latter part the position now remains the same as stated by the Prime Minister in answer to a question in this House on March 24, 1913.

—(*Hansard,* 1914. Vol. LXI., col. 1499.)

On June 11, 1914, Mr. King asked the Secretary of State for Foreign Affairs whether any naval agreement had been recently entered into between Russia and Great Britain ; and whether any negotiations with a view to a naval agreement have recently taken place or are now taking place between Russia and Great Britain?

Sir William Byles asked the Secretary of State for Foreign Affairs whether he can make any statement with regard to an alleged naval agreement between Great Britain and Russia ; how far such an agreement would affect our relations with Germany ; and will he lay papers?

Sir Edward Grey : The hon. member for North Somerset asked a similar question last year with regard to military forces, and the hon. member for North Salford asked a similar question also on the same day as he has again done to-day. The Prime Minister then replied that, if war arose between European Powers, there were no unpublished agreements which would restrict or hamper the freedom of the Government or of Parliament to decide whether or not Great Britain should participate in a war. The answer covers both the questions on the Paper. It remains as true to-day as it was a year ago. No negotiations have since been concluded with any Power that would make the statement less true. No such negotiations are in progress, and none are likely to be entered upon so far as I can judge. But if any agreement were to be concluded that made it necessary to withdraw or modify the Prime Minister's statement of last year which I have quoted, it ought, in my opinion, to be, and I suppose that it would be, laid before Parliament.

—(*Hansard.* Vol. LXIII., cols. 457-8.)

PROFESSOR CONWAY charges me with misrepresenting "plain facts." He finds the proof of this in a passage of my letter of resignation to the Birkenhead Liberal Association, which the *Labour Leader* reproduced. In the particular passage which he quotes I had endeavoured to summarise in "plain," *i.e.,* in non-diplomatic language, the revelations, uttered in diplomatic language, by the Foreign Secretary in the House of Commons on August 3. I gather Professor Conway's main argument to be that the Anglo-French military and naval "conversations," authorised by the Foreign Secretary and by some of his colleagues, had no substantial bearing upon the formation of British foreign policy, because, in authorising them, the Foreign Secretary had expressly reserved the ultimate freedom of the Government and of the House of Commons to endorse them or otherwise. The fact that the Foreign Secretary declined to take the final plunge until August 2, although pressed to do so by the French Ambassador, appears to Professor Conway to convey additional evidence of his contention. Indeed, your correspondent goes so far as to say :—

" . . . Down to August 2 it was entirely open to the House of Commons to decide as it liked the whole policy to be pursued in relation to the crisis."

Let us, then, examine once again, since Professor Conway will have it so (although for my part, it appears to me not wholly desirable at this moment), the "plain facts" which I have so "wantonly" misrepresented. And let us examine them in such a way that the plain man, who is neither professor nor diplomatist, may root them in his mind once and for all.

The House of Commons, and through the House of Commons, the country, was solemnly assured on four occasions, twice in 1913, and twice in 1914, that our foreign policy was entirely free from any sort or kind of secret obligation towards a Continental Power calculated to involve the blood of its manhood being squandered on the plains of Europe, if the various Governments of the Continent found it impossible at a given moment to control their tempers and their appetites. Similar assurances were given by other members of the Cabinet. At least I presume so, judging from my own personal experience. Mr. Runciman, President of the Board of Agriculture, sitting by my side and speaking on behalf of my candidature at Birkenhead on April 14, 1913, denied "in the most categorical way" (to use his own words) the existence of a "secret understanding with any foreign Power." At the conclusion of his speech, a speech mainly devoted to denouncing Conscription and "inevitable wars," which he

described as, wars "in which we are involved owing to
some understanding with other Powers," I expressed
my relief to have heard his declaration.

I pause here to ask, and to suggest that my readers
should ask themselves why were the questions which
elicited these assurances put to Ministers in the House?
Why did Mr. Runciman make that "categorical" statement at Birkenhead? It was because there were a certain
number of men inside and outside the House of Commons
who had reason to believe that there did exist an
unavowed military and naval understanding authorised
by the British and French Foreign Offices, and that that
understanding was the dominating factor in British
foreign policy. In my own case—for Mr. Runciman's
declaration was the result of precedent public statements
made by me—a study of French newspapers and magazines, together with information received from French
correspondents, coupled with a pretty complete knowledge of the undersides of the Moroccan affair of 1912,
had convinced me that the secret diplomacy of the two
Foreign Offices, which had almost precipitated the two
peoples into war in 1911, had not ceased with the French
acquisition of Morocco (in violation of "a scrap of paper"
called the Algeciras Act), but was persisting; and that
the existence of a secret military and naval understanding
was looked upon in French military circles as a fact—not
to say a "plain fact."

To resume. From March 10, 1913, the date of the
Prime Minister's first denial of a military understanding
with France, to June 28, when the heir to the Austrian
throne was murdered at Sarajevo, the position of Great
Britain in the hypothesis of a European war, so far as
the House knew it, was one of complete freedom from any
entanglement with France. And that, too, was Great
Britain's position so far as the House knew it, from June
28 until the afternoon of August 3. Between July 20,
when the crisis, according to the White Book, may be said
to have begun, and August 3, not the slightest intimation
was conveyed to the House that the position of Great
Britain in the hypothesis of a European war was other
than it had precedently been described as being—the latest
declaration to that effect dated a fortnight before the
Sarajevo crime. To argue, therefore, as Professor Conway
argues, that under these circumstances, it was "entirely
open" to the House down to August 2, to "decide

the whole policy to be pursued in relation to the crisis,"
appears to me—I don't wish to be impolite—just nonsense.

On August 3 the Foreign Secretary delivered an im-
passioned plea in favour of British intervention on behalf
of France. He revealed the "conversations." He revealed
the strategic concentration of the French Fleet in the
Mediterranean as being due to our "friendship" with
France. He drew a heartrending picture of battered and
bombarded French coasts, defenceless because of that
Mediterranean concentration. He avowed that he had on
the previous day undertaken that the British Navy would
intervene if France's potential enemy, Germany, indulged
in such battering and bombardment, and he wound up by
declaring, in effect, that in his opinion the honour of the
country was engaged.

Those are the "plain facts" and no casuistry will get
over them or under them.

Let us now examine the setting in which these plain
facts are placed. What was the psychological atmosphere
on that fateful 3rd of August? A state of war already
existed in Europe. In England the public mind was
excited and on edge. For days the war-Press, headed by
the *Times,* had been steadily flogging up bellicosity. The
Tory Party in the House was solid for British intervention; so, too, had become a section of the Liberals. In
what condition was the House of Commons to exercise
a discriminating judgment, when the statesman responsible
for the conduct of the country's foreign relations, and enjoying a greater personal influence over the House of
Commons than any of his contemporaries, made the
oratorical effort of his life under circumstances favourable
to the case he urged? But, apart from that, it was, in
any event, too late. The House of Commons was presented, in every practical sense, with accomplished facts.
It could only have rejected the appeal on behalf of France
by rejecting the Minister who made it, and the Cabinet.
What House of Commons could have done so—even had
this particular House wanted to do so, which it did not —
in the face of a national emergency so momentous?

Again, of what conceivable value were the reserves
attached to these authorised military and naval conversations? "Conversations" is a diplomatic formula. Between
diplomatists "conversations" signify discussion, negotiation—talk, in short, which may have its sequel in acts,
but which may not. " Conversations" between military

men belonging to different countries, who have to work out in a country which is foreign to one of the parties practical details relating to the movement of large bodies of troops, are *acts* involving further acts, setting in train complicated and delicate machinery in a hundred different centres. When two Governments authorise their, Military and Naval Staffs to "converse" as to eventual military and naval action against a common potential foe, they set in motion the entire mechanism of their fighting services. A relationship of a particularly intimate character is thereby set up which reacts, and is bound to react in an infinity of direct and indirect ways, upon the policy of the two Governments. Mutual obligations—in a material, if not in an official sense—are incurred. The Governments which authorise such "conversations" have taken a definite step which they can only retrace at the expense of turning friendly relations into unfriendly ones. If such "conversations" merely consisted in academic and periodical debates over hypothetical strategic movements, round a map-strewn table, one might at a stretch regard them as innocuous. But when they consist, as they do and must consist, of a careful survey of the actual field of potential operations; of the selection of points for concentration and defence; of the selection of ports for disembarkation; of the settlement of a multitude of plans, interlinked one with the other, vitally affecing the disposition of both armies—their binding character is apparent.

These particular "conversations" meant the elaboration of an entire plan of campaign, replete in every detail, affecting the disembarkation and transport over rail and road of an expeditionary force of 165,000 men—or whatever the exact number may have been—with the enormous quantities of cannon, horses, motors, waggons, stores, and all the impedimenta of a modern army. And as with the military, so with the naval "conversations." You may speak of an understanding whereby France concentrated her fleet in the Mediterranean and left her western and northern coast-line undefended, in order to leave us freer to concentrate in the North Sea, as a "conversation" of no binding force until authorised by Parliament. But it is the sort of "conversation" which decides the destinies of nations, and, when carried on in secret, leaves the nations concerned entirely helpless to control the outcome. The secret "conversations," begun in 1906 and thenceforth persisted in, constituted, morally speaking, a pledge given to France by the most powerful personalities in the British Liberal Ministry, to join with France in the event of war between France and her only potential foe, Germany. Materially speaking, they constituted an Anglo-French military and naval alliance. I can understand the argument which says that it was right to give that pledge. I can even understand the argument that it was right, having given that pledge, to deny to the House of Commons that it had been given. But I do not understand the argument which says that the moral obligation and the material fact alike meant nothing, until at the eleventh hour the House of Commons became aware of both, and endorsed them.

Whatever may have been the combination of circumstances and ideas which militated against the irrevocable plunge being taken until August 2, it cannot affect the "plain facts." No carefully-edited and summarised presentment of diplomatic conversations can affect those "plain facts" in the remotest degree. At first, the motives for refusing to make the declaration demanded by both France and Russia from the beginning were probably mixed. Towards the culmination of the crisis, they were probably due to the fierce struggle going on in the Cabinet between the pro-War party and the anti-War party, which, no doubt, our children will be greatly benefited by knowing. The irrevocable step could, obviously, not have been taken until the bulk of the Cabinet was agreed to support it, and until a stage in the course of outside events had been reached, when the House of Commons was in the psychological condition to endorse it.

CHAPTER V.

"What will ye do in the end thereof?"[1]

"THE prophets prophesy falsely and the priests bear rule by their means, and My people love to have it so, and what will ye do in the end thereof?"[1]

IN the end thereof—what will ye do in the end thereof? For some of us this question clamours with our awakened conscience in the morning, obtrudes itself into our daily tasks, and haunts us as we seek our rest.

What shall mark the close of this colossal tragedy which has plunged all Europe into mourning, and the consequences of which, even the immediate and visible consequences, our imagination can hardly grasp, so catastrophic are they for millions of us, for our civilisation, our hopes, our faiths?

This tragedy was precipitated in a panic of mutual fears. But its seeds were sown in a futile and wicked Statecraft which, in every land, has held up before the peoples the foulest of idols—material security resting upon bayonets.

Will that Statecraft be shattered with the realisation of its criminal imbecility? Will that idol be overthrown now that it has been stripped of its gaudy coverings and stands revealed to us in all its hideous nakedness? Will the peoples begin to understand that their real enemies are not their neighbours against whom they hurl shot and shell; but that their real enemies are those same groups of men who, in every land, by faults of temper, by incessant secret plots and counter-plots, by the cult of a false philosophy, and by the maintenance of an impossible system of official intercourse, hound the peoples to mutual destruction?

Or, when the prophets and the high-priests have decreed the cessation of the slaughter, shall we, in sheer exhaustion and nausea, in utter weariness of body, mind, and spirit, suffer ourselves to be led back into the old

[1] Speech at a public meeting held in the Friends' Meeting House, Manchester, December 17, 1914.

paths, to worship at the old shrines, to renew allegiance to the old traditions?

Upon the answer to those questions the salvation of humanity depends. And it rests with the peoples what the answer shall be.

Amongst the masses who listened to the tocsin of war reverberating throughout Europe in the closing days of July, there was singularly little hatred—at first. But war is the perfected mechanism of hate, and the blood-fumes are potent. Hate; hate and fear reign supreme in the council chambers of the nations to-day. Among the plains and valleys of Europe, littered with the piteous evidence of human carnage and human error, among those who actually fight the battles decreed by others, hate is swallowed up in the awfulness of experience, in a loathing of horrors unsurpassed. It is not among the brave men who sway backwards and forwards in this Titanic and inconstant struggle, from the marshes of Flanders to the plains of Poland, that hate sits enthroned. For these men, despite the wall of fire and steel which separates them, are linked together in a catholicity of suffering. They kill and maim a foe they mostly do not see, just as, in happier times, they sow and reap, and labour at the desk and in the mill; in response to what they regard as a mysterious and inexorable law. It is not from them, perishing by shot and shell, by festering wounds, by exposure and bitter cold, it is not from them, assuredly, that protests would arise if the Christian rulers of the Twentieth Century, approximating in compassion certain generals of antiquity, were to call a truce, the while they composed their differences; or, even from no higher motive than a sense of burning shame that the bloody arbitrament they have provoked should be prosecuted during the celebration of the advent of the Prince of Peace.

No! It is not on the battlefield, but in the council chambers of the nations where the directing wills preside of those whose collective wisdom and forbearance, whose collective understanding and tolerance, whose collective conception of the God they profess to worship, have brought humanity to this pass. Here, indeed, is the spirit of hate, a potent influence.

It finds expression, on either side, in the talk of "crushing," of annihilation, of reducing the foe to ever-lasting impotence.

That way madness lies. If hate is to be the last word in this unholy business; if hate is to be the dominating inspiration of the terms of settlement, then the settlement will be no settlement, the peace will be no peace.

A few years, it may be a decade or two, and once again will the peasant be called from the plough, the artisan from the workshop, the clerk from his desk. Once again will the prophets cry from the council chambers their devilish appeal. "If ye would secure peace, prepare for war!" Once again will the high-priests in every land convert their pulpits into Pagan shrines and trample under foot the Christ.

But will the people "love to have it so"—again? Do they "love to have it so" to-day? I do not believe it. The people acquiesce. They do not love. How can they love the pestilence which sweeps from their lives the most precious gifts of life, which plunges them into the storms of grief, smites them with the paralysis of desolation, drives them into poverty and misery?

Did the people, the masses of the people, on either side desire this war? Would the atmosphere which made war possible have been produced but for the poison distilled, month by month, year by year, into their minds by the professional non-combatant libertines of the pen; but for the insanity of the monstrous expansion of armaments, bleeding white the peoples for their own ultimate destruction, which was all that the genius of statesmen could evolve in response to increasing manifestations, everywhere, in favour of a peaceful settlement of international disputes? The toiling millions in our great cities, the peasants and labourers of the countryside, whose capacities, in vast majority, are concentrated upon securing the wherewithal to feed and clothe and house themselves, and upon catching such stray beams of sunlight as may haply come their way—what part or lot have *they* in checking or controlling, or even understanding the forces which hurl them into the abyss of war, changing the greyness of their lives to the blackest darkness?

That fatal Sunday of August 2 found me in a small Continental town. Its irregular, ill-paved streets were full of men and women and children, mostly weeping; though the younger children only wondered. At every door stood little groups of people with faces drawn and pitiful. Reservists uttering their last farewells, putting gently aside encircling arms, taking the last pledge from quiver-

ing lips. Above all, permeating all, a consciousness of
some invisible, irresistible presence, inhuman, pitiless;
some monstrous, unseen hand stretched out, tearing son
from mother, husband from wife, father from children.
And one realised with an icy chill at one's heart that the
inevitable had really happened; that because one of the
great ones of the earth had fallen beneath the hand of the
assassin in a far-distant country, because the other great
ones of the earth had quarrelled as the result of that
crime, because the rulers of Christian Europe had for
years been squandering the substance of their peoples
in piling up weapons destructive of human life until all
Europe was one vast arsenal, and had planned and
schemed against one another through their appointed
agents; that because of such things, these humble folk in
this small town in which I moved were stricken down,
their lives rent and shattered.

Twenty-four hours later I passed through the empty
House of Commons, a short hour before those fateful
words were to be spoken—wisely or unwisely, I argue not
to-night—which have already resulted in the loss of
thousands of British lives, in sorrow crossing the thresh-
hold of tens of thousands of British homes. And, here
again, the hand of death seemed to hover, outstretched,
menacing, prophetic in the dim recesses of the silent
Chamber. Outside—you will remember it was Bank
Holiday, black Monday our posterity will call it—a crowd
filled the streets, interested but uncomprehending, laugh-
ing, joking, chatting, gazing at the buildings which,
doubtless, some of them were seeing for the first time,
thoroughly enjoying themselves, while, a few yards away,
their destinies hung in the balance.

No. It is not true. The mass of the people do not
"love to have it so."

Kept in ignorance until the quarrels of their governors
have passed the limits of adjustment, they are stung to
fear, lashed into fury, flogged into hatred by the potent
machinery existing for this purpose.

Against such a combination they are helpless.

And what have we done in the past, you and I, who,
compared with them, have leisure for constructive thought
and constructive action, what have we done to stand
between their helplessness and the forces making for war?
What are we doing to-day to stand between their help-
lessness and the forces, now so strongly in the ascendant,

making for a perpetuation of the evils which generate war?

To-night we pray. But when we leave this hall, what then? What of the morrow and the to-morrows? We may construct some tiny oasis in this desert of human suffering. We may alleviate some private grief. We may remove some trifling effect of this immense disaster.

But what are we prepared to do, what are we prepared to sacrifice, to make a return of such disaster impossible? To save the next generation from what this generation has not been spared? To save the people from their help-lessness? To make them understand that they have the power to help themselves if they will but exercise it? What part are we prepared to play in the greatest work which lies open to human endeavour in the world to-day?

Let us pray for sound judgment. Let us pray for courage to denounce and expose what may be faulty and wrong and in need of reform in our own records and pro-cedure. It is cheap to denounce the shortcomings of others. Let us pray to be delivered from unctuous rectitude, from cant and hypocrisy, from smug self-righteousness and self-satisfaction.

Let us so labour and strive for humanity in this, humanity's dark hour, that, if not we ourselves, then our sons, building upon the foundations we have laid, shall, despite the prophets, contribute in giving to the world a variant from the old despairing message, a variant which shall contribute a new message, a new message of assured hope, pointing to a certain goal.

And that message shall be this : " The prophets may prophesy falsely, but the priests heed them not, and the people reject their teaching, and the end thereof shall be peace among the children of men.''

So be it.

CHAPTER VI.

France and Germany before the War[1]

WITH the Triple Alliance the German felt safe for a long while. There was a time when the German deemed himself, thanks to it, in perfect security. . . . He does not feel nearly so safe now. Facing the Triple Alliance, the Franco-Russian Alliance has come into existence, then the Triple Entente. The encircling manœuvres of Delcassé took place. All this has got on his nerves. And let us not forget that he is profoundly convinced that he—the German—can remain secure and pacific, but that the Frenchman on the other hand becomes aggressive as soon as he feels himself secure. . . Hitherto we have desired two contradictory things : on the one hand to keep the peace. . . On the other we have never consented to admit, even to ourselves, much less to declare publicly that we accept the Treaty of Frankfurt or the territorial *statu quo.* We accepted and indirectly recognised the accomplished fact in signing an alliance which implied it. But at the same time we hailed that alliance as making the *Revanche* certain. . . The Germans conclude that France desires the *Revanche,* and that prudence alone prevents us from saying so right out. They feel that we are on the watch, ready to profit from the opportunity which ensures us the victory. I ask every honest Frenchman, are they wrong? Would you in your inmost soul assert that they are wrong?—*"Faites un roi sinon faites la paix,"* by Marcel Sembat. (*Paris, Eugène Figuière et cie.* 12th *edition,* 1913.)

Thus, we see, when the time comes, and it may come soon, when Slavism desires to make an end of Germanism, the friendship of Russia can save us if we are fully determined to fulfil all our duties towards her. Germany does not doubt that France, remaining immutably attached to her treaties, would support her ally with all her strength, choosing, however, the most favourable moment for intervention.—(*L'Allemagne en péril,"* by *Colonel Arthur Boucher,* 1914 ; *op. cit.*)

SLOWLY, but surely, the international conditions existing before the war are revealed, and their connection with the great catastrophe becomes clear to the dullest understanding.

How often have we heard and read the phrase "Germany's unprovoked attack upon France "? How persistent has been the attempt to suggest that France would not have dreamed of a military offensive against Germany if the German Government had not initiated the offensive against her !

[1] *The Labour Leader,* March 11, 1915.

47

What is the story incessantly dinned into the ears of our people? Is not this a fair summarised version of it?

"Germany has been preparing for this war for forty years, waiting for the psychological moment to declare it. In the opening days of August the moment came. With a cynicism which has never been equalled she immediately rushed upon France. What had France done to her? Nothing. Did the French desire war? They were the most peaceable people in Europe. Could Germany have had any other motive for this monstrous act of aggression than sheer greed of conquest? She had plotted for decades to strike at France successfully, and when the time seemed to her ripe she made her onslaught without the ghost of an excuse."

And do not innumerable Frenchmen hold the same view—the view that France would have remained neutral if Germany had left France alone and confined her attention to Russia? Did not my good friend Peaix-Séailles endeavour to sustain that thesis in the last issue of the *Socialist Review?*

Well, what remains of it now, after Sir Edward Grey's reply to Mr. Jowett's second question? Sir Edward Grey informed Mr. Jowett that although His Majesty's Government did not know the terms of the Franco-Russian Alliance, they did know :—

"that the French Government could not contemplate an attitude of neutrality in the event of Russia being attacked by Germany as well as by Austria."

Let us then in common decency consign the untruth of a France wantonly attacked by Germany with no excuse to the lethal chamber, where, in company with so many others, it can find oblivion.

Germany attacked France because, if she had not done so, France would have attacked her. That is the truth. Does it exonerate Germany for her share in building up the system which has led to eighteen millions of men being whirled into mutual destruction because one man was shot in the streets of a Bosnian town? Assuredly not. But then, neither does it absolve other Governments from *their* share in that abomination. Does it exonerate Germany from launching her legions at France through Belgian territory, after having first asked for a peaceful passage, which, apparently, we did not officially regard as especially diabolical in 1887? Assuredly not. But then neither does it exonerate the diplomatists of other countries who have since told us that they were thoroughly aware that Belgium would fall a victim to the European group system in the event of a war between the two groups, and who did not stir a finger to save her from that fate.

What this categorical statement of Sir Edward Grey's does, however, bring home to all that have ears to hear and eyes to see is the absurdity of attempting any longer to describe the extension of a Balkan squabble to the West of Europe—involving the Belgian, British, and French peoples in the calamity of war—as the outcome of German determination to subjugate Europe.

And what it does further suggest is the absurdity of imagining that the "crushing" of Germany, if by that phrase is meant the attempted "dismemberment" or national extinction of Germany, is calculated to eliminate the diplomatic cult of the "Balance of Power," which is now clearly seen to be the snag upon which European civilisation has split.

What Sir Edward Grey's reply to Mr. Jowett does demonstrate beyond all question is that the German Government and the German people (for, apparently, they speak with one voice) *are* expressing their real conviction when they state that they, too, are fighting for their national existence; that they *are* just as sincere in their belief as other Governments and peoples may be, that th's war is, for them, a defensive and not an offensive one.

That the German Government would have performed an act of the highest political wisdom in maintaining a strict military defensive on the Franco-German frontier, and thereby refrained from perpetrating the grave immorality of an invasion of Belgium is my belief. But was such an act, under such circumstances, humanly possible? It would not have saved Germany from a French attack, nor from British attack if Germany had ventured to use her Fleet against the French, for on August 2 Sir Edward Grey gave the French Ambassador the assurance that if the German Fleet attacked French coasts or shipping the British Fleet would intervene.

The German Government was thus faced with this situation : (a) That of maintaining a military defensive against France (for all the military experts were in agreement that an invasion of France *via* the Franco-German frontier was a virtual impossibility), thus throwing to the winds the entire strategic plans of its military advisers; (b) That of foregoing the use of its navy.

Does anyone believe that any Government in such circumstances would, or could, have consented to such a course? How could it have faced the agitation led by the heads of its fighting Services; an agitation which would have been based upon the cry that Germany, confronted with two powerful antagonists, was being betrayed at the supreme hour of peril by its rulers? Is it exhibiting bias, or pro-Germanism, or anti-patriotism, or any of the other 'isms, to describe Germany's position and France's position at the height of the crisis as having been, in effect and respectively this :—

Germany : Compelled to a military defensive, fatal to the national security in the opinion of its military advisers, (a) owing to the invulnerability of the French frontier ; (b) owing to Belgian neutrality : Compelled to abandon any idea of using her Fleet against France owing to the British threat.

France : (a) Free to adopt a military offensive or defensive ; to choose the psychological moment when Russian pressure had paved the way for a French assault upon the German lines, against which the entire French military strength would have been massed; (b) Free to dispose of her Fleet as she listed; to use it against German shipping; to use it against Germany's ally in the Adriatic —with complete immunity, owing to British support.

I continue to think that the German Government would have been wiser from the point of view of its own interests in facing these odds and in running these risks, because, had it done so, French public opinion and British public opinion would have split in two, neutral opinion would have been strongly on Germany's side, and I doubt whether the French and British Foreign Offices could have sustained their respective parts.

Even setting aside, for the sake of argument merely, the influence of fear, which, as we know, swept through Berlin when the news of the Russian general mobilisation arrived, I ask once more : Could the German Government, or *any* Government, have had the courage or, indeed, the power, to have taken such a line under such circumstances?

I am not concerned with defending the German Government; its many precedent diplomatic follies and the aggressive language of its militarists were largely responsible for the situation in which it found itself in the opening days of August. All I am concerned with is to picture to myself, and to try to induce others to picture to themselves, what that situation at that moment was, and what were the alternatives with which the German Government was faced.

And my object in doing so is to suggest two things, which, if they came to be believed by the public of this country, would necessarily affect the public view as to the extent of German culpability, and would strengthen opinion in favour—as Professor Pigou put it the other day—of an honourable and not a penal settlement; and this, in turn, would be calculated to save innumerable lives.

My suggestions, then, are these : First, that the increasing light which is being thrown on the *pre*-war situation must strengthen conviction in all minds capable of rational thought that the genesis of this war is to be sought, not in original sin grafted on the German Government or nation, but in a universal reign of fear, produced by the imbecilities of international diplomacy, ostensibly pursuing an ideal of "Balance" which is as unexplainable as it is unattainable, and doing so by means of a militarism which, from being the handmaiden, has become the master of the diplomatists themselves.

Secondly, that this increasing light must strengthen the conviction of all whom the blood-lust does not blind, that humanity can advance not one single step nearer the goal of its emancipation from the errors of the past by the massacre of another million or two of human beings.

CHAPTER VII.

The "pro-German" Taunt[1]

THE speech of my noble friend, with all the authority of the name he bears and with all the weight of his own character and position in the country, will be read with delight by all the partisans of Russia throughout Europe; and at the same time not without regret by those who are allied to us in opposing that Power. I say that my noble friend has, as far as in him lies, this night rendered signal service to the Emperor of Russia by aiding him in this war with the Allies. ˌHe has done his utmost to encourage the Emperor of Russia to resist a compliance with those demands which England, France, and Austria consider just.—(*Lord Clarendon on Earl Grey's peace speech in the Lords' debate of May 25, 1855*).

If he—Lord Malmesbury—might be permitted to speak of the right hon. gentleman as an abstraction, he would say that no longer ago than the preceding night he dreamed he heard a man, whom all his admirers said was the greatest orator of the day, address an august assembly in a tone and manner, with a force of words, with a colouring of expression, and, he might add, with a distortion of facts, which were worthy of any Russian Minister, and which would have gained such Minister every Cross of St. Andrew that the Russian Government has to bestow. When he awoke in the morning after his dream, he felt so humiliated as an Englishman that he would not believe what he had heard, until he read it first in the morning newspapers—(*Lord Malmesbury, referring in the Lords' debate of May 25, 1855, to Gladstone's peace speech in the Commons.*)

LET us face quite frankly this charge of being "pro-German" (or, as Mr. Perris puts it in his letter to you, of endeavouring "to excuse the ways of the Prussian Junker") which is levelled at anyone who attempts to re-establish a sense of perspective in the public mind in regard to this war; whether the charge be conveyed in the form adopted by the anonymous gentlemen of the "anti-German League" who write from Southampton or in the "more-in-sorrow-than-in-anger" form of Mr. Perris, whose interesting little volume, "Our Foreign Policy and Sir Edward Grey's Failure," stands on my bookshelves. I dissent altogether from the view that it is in the highest

---

[1] *The Labour Leader*, March 25, 1915. Written in connection with an attack upon the Author by Mr. G. H. Perris.

degree injudicious to pen a line or to say a word which
suggests that Germany is not the sole responsible author
of the war.

I dissent for three reasons, all of which appear to me
closely concerned with the interests of the British people
and not at all with the interests of the "Prussian Junker."
First, because it is not true that Germany is the sole
responsible author of this war, although her governing
classes possess a considerable measure of responsibility
for it.   The interests of the British people are not
permanently served by the propagation of an untruth,
however popular it may be at the moment.   Secondly,
because the more deeply rooted becomes the belief that
Germany is the sole responsible author of this war, initiated
by her in order to "subjugate Europe," the more will
public opinion gravitate towards the "unconditional
surrender" policy; and that policy means an indefinite
prolongation of the war and, consequently, an immense
additional loss of life.   And this appals me very much,
whereas the charge of being "pro-German" does not appal
me in the least.   Thirdly, because the policy of "unconditional surrender" is a policy which means a bad settlement; a settlement which would settle nothing, even if
it could be enforced, which would pave the way for fresh
convulsions, and which, both in its external and internal
implications, would, in the ultimate resort, bring disaster
upon the British Commonwealth.   It is not, therefore, to
serve the interests of the "Prussian Junker," but to serve
the interests of the British people that some of us feel
constrained to urge upon our countrymen that the enemy
is not the monster of popular caricature.   Apparently there
are men in Germany who are acting precisely as we are :
who are reacting, as we are endeavouring to do, against
the doctrine of blind hate of Britain.   Their efforts are
lauded in our patriotic Press.   Ours are denounced as
"pro-German."

I wonder whether those who abjure us to tread as
delicately as any Agag lest we be called "pro-German"
and, therefore, run the risk of impairing what little
influence we may possess, realise the illogicality of their
advice? If Germany is the *sole* responsible author of the
war, and started it in order to "subjugate Europe," why
in the world are we bothering our heads about secret
diplomacy and democratic control of foreign policy; about
the "Balance of Power," the study of international

relations, the private armament interest and so forth? Does not the fact that a growing multitude in these Islands is troubling itself about these things prove conclusively that many of us do NOT believe that responsibility for the war is *solely* attributable to the "Prussian Junker," but that it is attributable to a universal system of statecraft conducted behind the back of the peoples, rooted in a false philosophy, and reposing upon the universal fallacy that national security is obtainable only through gigantic armament? Very well. Why, then, having attained this degree of sanity, should we shrink from the next step; from examining how Germany's position, as well as the position of other Powers, was affected by that universal system both before and during the crisis of last July? Why should we shrink from trying, as Marcel Sembat puts it in his famous book, to place ourselves in the "skin of a German"? Shall we ever be in a position to contribute towards the building up of a happier, saner, Europe if, while working not only for general reforms, but for British reforms and, thereby, implicitly admitting that both are required, we keep up the pretence that Germany is the sole villain of the piece? The two things are incompatible. You cannot at the one and the same time (*i.e.,* if your argument is a stage towards effective action) maintain (*a*) that the ruling classes of Europe, including those of your own country, are partners in responsibility for this System which you desire to overthrow, and (*b*) that the governing classes of all Europe were lambs and Germany alone the ravening wolf; that all, save the rulers of Germany, had but one desire, to live in harmony and preserve the peace of the world.

Now if Germany was not the sole responsible author of the war she *must* have a case, and if we wish to construct for the future we *must* understand that case. If it is in the interest of the British people that Germany should be crushed and pulverised, dismembered, reduced to impotence nationally and economically—all of which courses are daily being recommended and all of which may be comprised in the policy of "unconditional surrender"; then, of course, it is no use trying to understand what Germany's position was in the "Balance" prior to the outbreak of war, what were her national necessities, what her fears. Let us, clothed in the mantle of our own impeccability, turn a blind eye to all but her visible faults and punish her for those faults to the utter-

most. But is it? I contend that it can never be to the
interest of any civilised people that another civilised
people should be so treated, whatever may be the faults
that the rulers of the latter have committed. In the case
of Britain and Germany, I contend that, apart from moral
considerations, it would be national insanity were such a
policy to receive national endorsement.

I imagine there are a great many people at present
who, for the satisfaction of grinding Germany to powder,
are prepared to contemplate with relative equanimity Japan
forcing a defensive and offensive alliance upon China
which would leave her mistress of China's external and
internal policy, as the preliminary step to converting
China's fabulous millions of human material into a vast
host equipped with all the modern engines of human
destruction, the secret of whose manufacture has been
obligingly furnished to the Japanese by the Anglo-German
armament ring. I imagine there are a great many people
at present who, provided Germany may be stamped flat,
are prepared cheerfully to acquiesce in a settlement which
would find Russia with the whole of Poland as a Russian
satrapy, Danzig a Russian port, Russia installed at
Constantinople, from thence dictating the destinies of the
Levant, commanding all the overland routes to India; a
Russia possessed of an army of ten million men, partly
equipped with British, and largely with French, money,
and with a powerful fleet in the Black Sea built by British
firms. But that there are such people is no valid reason
why we should all be required to qualify for a lunatic
asylum. .

When our Foreign Office revived the "Balance of
Power," so far as England was concerned, it threw in its
lot UNCONDITIONALLY (the characteristic of our foreign
policy during the past decade has been the wholesale
surrender of national assets without adequate compensating advantages) with Russia and France against
the central European Powers; above all, when it invited
the Japanese to join in the struggles of Europe, our
Foreign Office successfully manœuvred the British people
within the portals of the aforesaid asylum. But that is no
reason why the British people should persist in remaining
permanent inmates of that building. If they do not wish
to be so they must resolutely make up their minds to
examine the German case with honesty and fairness;
realise that it cannot be disposed of by military defeat;

realise, too, that the river of blood which now separates
the two peoples must be bridged.

What was Germany's position in the "Balance of
Power" system before the war? It was this. She had
an alliance with Austria and with Italy. But it had long
been notorious (except, apparently, to Mr. Perris) that
Italy's interest in the *triplice* had become purely formal.
It had decayed with the modification of the causes which
originated it, and with Delcassé's pledge of a free hand in
Tripoli, latterly taken advantage of. Facing her were
Russia and France. Far from being in a condition to
dictate to Europe, she was strategically very vulnerable;
and, with an unfriendly Britain, the "Balance," instead
of being in her favour, was tilted against her. In the
last ten years the military and naval expenditure of France
and Russia in combination has largely exceeded the
military and naval expenditure of Germany and Austria
in combination. The naval question had embittered Anglo-
German relations. British official policy became pro-
nouncedly hostile over the Morocco affair—no conceivable
British interest or compensating advantage being thereby
secured : that by the way. Thereafter British official
policy, although outwardly the relations of the two
Governments had improved, was a doubtful element in
Germany's calculations. I am not here discussing the
extent to which the policy of Germany's rulers were
responsible for the dangerous position in which she found
herself; whether she was justified in building a fleet or
not. I am simply stating what that position was. The
element in the situation dominating all others was the
growing Russian menace. In the two years preceding the
war it had become acute, and Germany's fears were
genuine. Our mentors in the Press affect to ridicule that
feeling, forgetting that for the best part of half a century
British foreign policy was wholly inspired by fear of
Russia—although, unlike the Germans, we have never had
the felicity of Russia as a next-door neighbour. If we
could feel fear of Russia because of India, why not
Germany because of Germany? Germany's fears were well
founded. The Pan-Slavists and the Grand Ducal Party
had triumphed over the Peace Party (it was largely, almost
entirely, an affair of warring personalities and personal
grudges prevailing in the diplomatic world), including the
elements in the Imperial household favourable to peace. I
have no space to set out the story here, but it has been

a commonplace in the Chancelleries since the spring of
1912 that the War Party in Russia had gained the
ascendancy and that a collision with Austria, and
consequently with Germany, to whom the annihilation of
Austria would have been the death warrant, was merely
a matter of time.

From that period onwards the whole question has
been : Would the three eagles tear and rend one another
alone, or would the Western Powers be dragged in? The
key to the situation was France—nationally pacific in the
main, governmentally under the heel of Russia, and
clinging to the "revanche." Could France be induced,
like Italy,[1] to stand aside in a quarrel not her own, or
would the French Government—which has never disclosed
the terms of its treaty with Russia to the French people
—be involved? If the former, then there would be no
German attack upon France or, *a fortiori,* upon Belgium.
If the latter, Germany would strike first at the foe whose
rapidity of mobilisation more nearly approximated to her
own. These were commonplaces *before* the war. Why
affect ignorance of them now?

And this brings me to Mr. Perris' letter. What is the
use of Mr. Perris telling me that I am defending a
"preventive war"? A "preventive war" is a mere phrase.
You might just as well apply it to *official* Britain's policy
as to *official* Germany's policy in the catastrophe which
has overwhelmed Europe. What is *official* Britain waging
but a preventive war : a "Balance of Power" war as the
Times keeps on reminding us at intervals—speaking, of
course, for the Foreign Office? What is a "Balance of
Power" war but a "preventive" war? What I said in my
article was that France would have attacked Germany if
Germany, thanks to her more rapid mobilisation and her
more efficient preparations, had not taken the initiative.
But that is no "dogmatic" assertion of my own. France
made it clear from the first that she would not remain
neutral. (I have set out the official quotations in detail
before and may be excused from doing so again.) Sir
Edward Grey confirmed the fact in his reply to Mr. Jowett
the other day. What does a country do when it is not
neutral? It joins in the fray, choosing, if it is allowed to
do so, the psychological moment best suited to its
interests. France was not allowed to choose that moment,
and no one ever supposed she would be. Mr. Perris seems

---

[1] Italy had not then come in.

to think that the "aggressor" in a war is *necessarily* the party who fires the first shot. But this is by no means the case, and the history of many wars disprove it. Was Japan the "aggressor" in her war with Russia because she opened the ball before even declaring war? Again, it is not I who am talking "solemn nonsense" when I state that the German Staff was convinced that a military defensive in a general European war—*i.e.,* a war which found Germany faced with Russia on one side and France on the other—would have been fatal to German national security. I merely state a fact—the fact that that was the opinion of the German Staff : that their whole strategy was founded on that belief. I am not qualified to criticise that opinion from a military point of view; but such an authority as Colonel Repington —from what I have read of his writings—does not appear to have thought that it was "nonsense."

To conclude. I was concerned to show that Sir E. Grey's reply to Mr. Jowett provided the final proof that France did not intend to remain neutral in a Russo-German war : in other words, that France would have intervened on behalf of Russia when the moment was ripe in the judgment of her military advisers. I endeavoured to make it clear that, such being the case, the fact of Germany having initiated the military offensive instead of waiting for the military offensive to be taken against her, was *not* evidence of a desire on Germany's part to "subjugate Europe," and could not honestly be described as constituting a "wanton aggression" upon France, but was the axiomatic outcome of Germany's position in the "Balance."

I might, of course, have added a great deal more on that point. I might have added that when the still unexplained mystery of the misunderstood telephone conversation between Sir Edward Grey and the German Ambassador occurred, as the result of which the latter imagined that the British Government proposed using its good offices to press neutrality upon France, the rulers of Germany clutched at the opportunity of leaving France alone, as a strong swimmer in a current clutches at a friendly log, the Kaiser immediately telegraphing to King George, and the Chancellor to the German Ambassador, that the western progress of their military machine would be stayed if Britain guaranteed French neutrality. Was that action reconcilable with a plot to "subjugate Europe"?

The authenticity of these telegrams has never been questioned to my knowledge. Their text is to be found in Price's "Diplomatic History of the War."

Let me repeat, then, once again, that my object in calling attention to these things is the object stated in the earlier part of this article, and no other. I have no friends among "Prussian Junkers." I have not, like a number of men prominent in British public life have done, dined at the Kaiser's table or hobnobbed with the Kaiser at teaparties or reviews. I have not even a financial interest in the armament ring. What I do possess is a profound conviction that an ultimate reconciliation between Britain and Germany is essential to the future peace of the world, and to the truest interests of this country.

Ministering to that conviction, I intend to do my little best to urge the necessity for the exercise of common sense and common fairness on this side, if that result is to be attained.

CHAPTER VIII.

Militarism and the Beast of the Apocalypse[1]

I HAVE said that to attribute the sole responsibility for this war to Germany was to perpetrate an injustice and an untruth. I have also said that the French Government was resolved not to remain neutral in the event of a Russo-German war. I contended that such being the case the German military offensive against France last August could not honestly be described as wanton aggression, and furnished no evidence *per se* of a desire on Germany's part, "to subjugate Europe." I also explained that in my judgment the truth ought to be insisted upon, not in the interests of "Prussian Junkers," but in the interests of the British people; and I gave the reasons which led me to form that judgment.

Since then two Ministerial utterances bearing upon the subject have been made; one by Sir Edward Grey,[2] the other by Lord Haldane.[3] In both statements Germany's sole responsibility for the war has been reiterated. In particular her antecedent military preparations have been pointed to as something peculiar and special to Germany and as providing conclusive proof of premeditation. We have had presented to us once again the familiar picture of the ravening wolf of German militarism, set in the midst of a flock of meek pacifist sheep—the other European Powers. It is only the psychology of a state of war which permits of such statements passing muster for an instant. Of the intelligent people—as distinct from the people who allow others to do their thinking for them—who accept these statements, I make bold to say that a considerable number hypnotise themselves into believing them because they wish to believe them. But the danger is that the constant beating of this particular drum will strengthen all the elements in British civilian life which, inspired by the anger and grief resultant from the loss of loved ones

[1] *The Labour Leader,* April 15, 1915.
[2] March 22, 1915.
[3] *Daily Chronicle,* April 1, 1915.

in the field, by blind sentiments of revenge, and by policy, are pressing for the infliction of such terms upon Germany as the price of peace, as would defeat the very ends proclaimed to be those of the Government when it joined in the war; prepare the way for fresh convulsions and perpetuate the armaments of Europe. That is why an effort must be made to deal with these statements.

Not only has Germany been making formidable preparations for war for a considerable time past, but she has made them with that meticulous thoroughness which the Germans import into all their activities. This is not in itself a proof of premeditation. It is a proof of efficiency. German militarism is militarism carried to the highest point of efficiency. It does not differentiate otherwise from the militarism of other nations. What is "militarism"? It is the product of a statecraft rooted in a philosophy which regards nations as antagonistic units and which imposes upon the peoples the burden of armed force. That armed force may be concentrated upon land or upon the sea. But whether upon land or upon the sea its justification is defended on the ground that to secure peace each State must be stronger than its neighbour. As German militarism is the most efficiently organised, so it is probably the most ruthless, for ruthlessness and efficiency in militarism go hand in hand. The more efficient the militarism the more ruthless its action, because *inter alia* every fresh invention of man which can be applied to the destruction of man will be developed to its utmost capacity by the efficient militarist. Our own First Sea Lord has recognised very clearly that modern war must be ruthless. In an interview accorded in 1910[1] to his friend, the late Mr. W. T. Stead, he declared : "The humanising of war ! You might as well talk of humanising hell ! . . . If I am in command when war breaks out I shall issue as my orders : 'The essence of war is violence. Moderation in war is imbecility. Hit first, hit hard, and hit anywhere.' " Barely a fortnight before the outbreak of this war Sir Percy Scott justified from the same point of view the action which Germany is now adopting in sinking ships, other than ships of war, by means of submarines and mines. Discussing the potentiality of a proclamation to that effect on the part of a Continental Power at war with an island Power, he said :—

"Such a proclamation would, in my opinion, be

[1] *Review of Reviews*, February, 1910.

perfectly in order, and, once it had been made, if any
British or neutral ships disregarded it and attempted to
run the blockade, they could not be held to be engaged in
the peaceful avocations, referred to by Lord Sydenham, and
if they were sunk in the attempt, it could not be described
as a relapse into savagery or piracy in its blackest form."[1]

It was not a German who wrote :—

"War is the divinely appointed means by which
environment may be readjusted until ethically fitted and
best becomes synonymous."

It was a well-known British military writer, Colonel
Maude.[2] It was not a German who wrote :—

"The worst of all errors in war is a mistaken spirit of
benevolence."

It was an equally well-known British military writer,
Major Stewart Murray.[3] It was not a German who
wrote :—

"The proper strategy consists in the first place of inflicting as terrible blows as possible upon the enemy's army,
and then in causing the inhabitants so much suffering that
they must long for peace and force their Government to
demand it."

It was a well-known British military critic, Dr. Miller
Maguire.[4]

"Militarism" is not a German product. It is just as
much a British product. But in our case it finds, owing
to geographical position, its chief expression on the sea.[5]
The plain fact of the matter is that a systematic endeavour
to represent your enemy, whoever he may be, as outside
the pale of human kind, is an absolute necessity to-day
for any Government which has involved its people in war.
It is only by such means that the willingness of millions
of people who have nothing to gain and everything to lose
by war can be induced to tolerate war. And so God and
the humanities are alternately invoked to describe the
enemy as a fiend among the nations, and fear and hatred
act as chief recruiting sergeants.

Germany prepared for this war. She carried her preparations to the highest maximum of efficiency, and she

---

[1] *Times,* July 16, 1914.
[2] "Armaments and Arbitration."
[3] "The Future Peace of the Anglo-Saxons."
[4] *Times,* July 12, 1900.
[5] This was written before Great Britain had also become a
conscript Power.

is waging war with the ruthlessness which modern war, in the opinion of prominent men of other nations, demands. All that is self-evident. But that does not in the least degree fasten upon Germany sole responsibility for the outbreak of war, nor does it in the least degree prove that Germany in going to war did so in order to "subjugate Europe." And this for quite a number of reasons, the first of which is palpable to all those whose mental condition remains normal.

It is not only Germany that has been preparing for war, but all *Europe*—France, Russia, Britain. The only difference in actual fact between Germany's conduct in the past forty years and the conduct of the other Powers mentioned, is that the latter have not only been preparing for war, but have *waged* war, whereas Germany has been content with preparation.[1] France has been waging war continuously for the past quarter of a century. She has conquered Tonquin, Madagascar, Morocco, Tunis, together with enormous tracts of country in West and West-Central Africa. Russia has waged a great war against Japan. The British Government has conquered the South African Republics and incorporated them within the British Empire.

And, I repeat, all Europe has been *preparing* for war. The history of the last decade is a history of constantly increasing preparation for war on the part of *all* the Powers, coupled with a steadily-growing apprehension at these preparations on the part of *all* the peoples concerned. It is often stated that Britain alone was unprepared. Britain was not unprepared on the basis of the national policy precedently accepted by both parties in the State, *i.e.,* a paramount navy and a small expeditionary force for use on the Continent. The British Navy was fully prepared. Mr. Churchill has told us in minute detail the extent of our pre-war preparations.

"The German Army was not more ready for an offensive war on a gigantic scale than was the British Fleet for national defence."

That the Germans may have regarded their Army in the same light as we regard our Navy as an instrument of national defence does not, of course, figure in Mr. Churchill's presentation.

[1] With the single exception of the guerilla warfare against the Hottentots and half-breeds in German S.W. Africa.

But, it is said Germany's preparations were made for the purpose of provoking war, and the preparations of all the other Powers—upon some of which I shall dwell later—were made in order to prevent war. How comes it, then, that the other Powers have not only prepared but waged war, and that Germany has not? How comes it that Germany did not wage war upon her neighbours whom she desired to subjugate when she could have done so with every guarantee of military success? She could have smashed France with ease in 1887, and our official classes, judging from statements in such papers as the *Standard* and the *Spectator,* would have been rather pleased than otherwise.[1] It was in the *Nineteenth Century* for March of that year that Professor Edward Dicey wrote :

"The German Empire, as we know it now, came into existence with the Franco-German War. In the course of seventeen years it has become very strong and very formidable, not only as a military but as a political power. That it may become yet more strong and more formidable is my heartfelt wish as it must be that of every Englishman who understands the conditions of our own tenure of power, and who realises the dangers to which Europe is exposed by the aggrandisement of Russia."

Germany could have smashed France with equal ease when Russia, exhausted by the Japanese War, was incapable of stirring a finger to help her. Germany could have smashed France with equal ease when we were engaged in annexing the South African Republics. I do not know whether it be true that the Kaiser resisted suggestions from Russia and France to form a coalition against us at that time; but I have met British people who believed it, and the statement has been made in print in this country more than once. "A friend in need is a friend indeed" was the letterpress figuring above a photograph of the Kaiser in the *Daily Mail* of November 11, 1899. Why, if Germany desired to "subjugate Europe" did she wait until August, 1914, when her military supremacy, as I shall show later on, was less assured than at any period during the previous thirty years? How can these things be reconciled with the present charge against Germany of having bided her time and deliberately provoked a war when she thought the psychological moment had come? They cannot be.

[1] *Vide* Chapter II.

The curious thing is that from the very circles whence these charges emanate come assertions which entirely dispose of them. Our patriotic Press has conjured up a Kaiser on all fours with "Boney," a sinister, implacable plotter, who concealed unholy ambitions beneath a spurious mask of good-will. They want to send him to St. Helena; to try him for murder; to expel his dynasty from Europe. But that is not the opinion of Lord Haldane, and it is not the opinion of the French either. Lord Haldane, in the course of an interview with an American journalist, has recently delivered himself of the following utterance :

"In past years I think the Kaiser undoubtedly opposed war. But I am afraid his opposition to it gradually weakened. He appears to have settled into the war mood two years ago."[1]

Of singular interest this statement. Up to two years ago, then, the conspiring Kaiser conspired for peace. That is said by a British Cabinet Minister who knew the Kaiser personally and has eaten of the salt at his table. Let us retain the declaration in our minds. Lord Haldane's statement is the more interesting for his subsequent reference to Document No. 6 of the Yellow Book, in which is recorded a conversation said to have taken place between the Kaiser, the King of the Belgians, and General Von Moltke in the early part of November, 1913. The conversation is reported by the French Ambassador at Berlin. The accuracy of its transcription has been denied in Germany. We need not attach overmuch importance either to the conversation or to the denial; for obviously we can check neither the one nor the other. But for the sake of argument let us admit that it did take place, and that it is truthfully transcribed. The conversation is less important than the statement of the French Ambassador, who goes quite as far as Lord Haldane, for he speaks of

"William the Second, whose personal influence has been exerted in many critical circumstances in favour of the maintenance of peace. . . ."[2]

Like Lord Haldane, the French Ambassador declares (on the strength of the conversation he reports) that these pacific sentiments had changed. But that is not the only

[1] *Daily Chronicle,* April 1, 1915.

[2] *Vide* similar French statements in Chapter XI.

statement in the Yellow Book corroborative of Lord Haldane. We are told in Document 5 that if war did not break out in 1911 over Morocco it was largely because of the "pacific desires of the Emperor and the Chancellor."

Thus far, then, our examination establishes that the Beast of the Apocalypse, otherwise the German Emperor —and we are told that who says Kaiser says German officialdom—was, until quite recently, a powerful factor for the preservation of the peace of the world. We are told so in the French Government's official publication on the war, and by a British Cabinet Minister, with exceptional advantages of knowing the truth. What is left of the "forty years' preparation" legend?

But when did the Kaiser abandon that rôle, and why? These questions remain to be examined. The date is of importance. Two years ago, says Lord Haldane. That would take us back to April, 1913. But another document in the French Yellow Book suggests an earlier period. *Annexe* I. to Document 1 contains an extract from the French military *attaché* in Berlin written (apparently) in the early part of 1912, and describing the effect of the Morocco affair upon the mind of Germany. He says :—

"We discover every day how deep and lasting are the sentiments of wounded rancour against us provoked by the events of last year."

The "events of last year" were the events connected with the Morocco dispute, when the French Government, with the assistance of British officialdom, tore up the Treaty of Algeciras, filled Morocco with French troops, and defied Germany. The French military *attaché* continues :—

"The resentment felt in every part of the country is the same. . . . The Emperor and the Government yielded; public opinion has neither forgiven them nor us. Public opinion does not intend that such a thing shall occur again."

It would seem, then, from the above that the Kaiser's "pacifist desires" which contributed so largely to preventing war over Morocco were adversely affected by what is admitted to have been a widespread national resentment at the manner in which Germany considered she had been treated over Morocco. And this should be of interest to all British people.

But we may let that pass, for although important assuredly, it is not the most important conclusion derivable

from what precedes. The point of really capital importance
is this. Throughout the lengthy period during which
Germany considered herself safe, owing to her military
strength, Germany was pacific, and the German Emperor's
influence was exerted in the interests of peace, "in many
critical circumstances." That is vouched by the French
Yellow Book and by Lord Haldane, in official statements,
published and delivered—bear this in mind—while war is
actually raging. If one desired to cite statements to the
same effect made by British and French Authorities, before
the war broke out, one could fill an issue of the *Labour
Leader* with comparative ease. It was only when, in the
opinion (rightly or wrongly) of the rulers of Germany,
Germany's position in Europe was no longer safe owing
to the proportionate growth in the striking forces and in
the disposition of her potential foes, *i.e.,* during the past
three or four years—that, according to those French and
British statements, official Germany ceased to be pacific.

The significance of these conclusions is immense. If
the French Yellow Book and Lord Haldane are, in this
particular, recording the truth, the charge of decades of
premeditation and of a blow struck when it was most likely
to succeed—timed with that intent—can no longer be
sustained if we have regard for truth and honesty. But
that is not all. If Germany was pacific when she deemed
herself secure, and ceased to be so when she deemed herself
insecure, this war, so far as Germany's part in it is concerned, is a war not due to vile and disorderly ambitions,
but is a war due to *fear.*

Let us see what light can be derived from official figures
and from non-German publications in this regard.

But before doing so it is essential that we should refer
once again to the Morocco affair in the light of what has
transpired since. On February 29, 1912, I penned these
concluding sentences to the Introduction of my book on
Morocco :—

"The Morocco problem is not settled. In one sense
it may be said to be only beginning. It will loom largely
on the horizon during the lifetime of the present
generation."

. . . .

A year has passed since the contents of the above
chapter appeared, and the interval has seen a continuance
of the systematic effort to ascribe the "armed peace" of
Europe solely to Germany's ambitions and to her

Emperor's Machiavellism. The following Notes may, therefore, be usefully added to what precedes.

I. *Europe's universal preparation for war.* The famous Note to the Powers of August 24, 1898, which will always redound to the credit of the Tsar, is the clearest avowal of *all* Europe's folly.

In proportion—the Imperial circular reads—as the armaments of each Power increase, so they less and less fulfil the objects which the Governments have set before themselves. Economic crises, due in great part to the system of armaments à outrance and the continual danger which lies in this accumulation of war-material, are transforming the armed peace of our days into a crushing burden which the people have more and more difficulty in bearing. It appears evident, then, that if this state of things continues, it will inevitably lead to the very cataclysm which it is desired to avert, and the horrors of which make every thinking being shudder in anticipation.

But can a solitary human being, knowing anything at all of contemporary history, contend that Germany had been solely, or even prominently, responsible for the condition of affairs lamented by the Tsar in 1898? Which were the three Governments that had filled the world with the clamour of their disputes in the twenty odd years preceding the Tsar's circular, keeping all Europe on tenterhooks and incurring chief responsibility for the enormous increase in armaments—the subject of the Imperial lamentations? They were the Governments of Britain, Russia, and France. The Russo-Turkish war of 1877; the acute Anglo-Russian friction arising therefrom in 1878; the bitter quarrels between those two Powers resulting from Russia's advance into Asia, culminating in the Pendjeh affair in 1885; the kidnapping of the Prince of Bulgaria by Russian agents in 1886; the Franco-Italian dispute over Tunis in 1881; Anglo-French rivalry in Egypt, in Siam, in West Africa, and on the Nile—these had been the chief contributory causes of the "armed peace" and world ferment which had converted Europe, even at that period, into an arsenal. It is a ridiculous and puerile distortion of history to pretend otherwise. As a matter of fact you will hardly pick up a volume of European history, or a treatise on Germany, written before the war by English authors, which does not fully recognise that the creation of modern Germany has been one of the most powerful factors making for peace in Europe.

II. *Did the Kaiser propose or oppose a European coalition against Britain at the time of the Boer war?* Shortly after the contents of this Chapter had appeared in the *Labour Leader,* I received, in connection with my reference to this subject (*supra*) the following comments from a correspondent, who is one of the best informed authorities on foreign affairs in this country :—

In March, 1914, the *Novoe Vremya* (the organ of the Pan-Slavist Party) published an interview with an anonymous Russian statesman (who was none other than Count Witte, Russia's famous Finance Minister) suggesting that, in the past, a Russo-German agreement could easily have been achieved on the basis of a partition of the Austrian Empire. The interview was, no doubt, intended as a kite, but the *Pesther Lloyd* (the official organ of the Austrian Government) replied in its issue of March 29, confirming the statement that such an agreement had been ventilated between Russia and Germany. It then said : "It is true that this coalition between Russia and Germany was to be directed against a third Power, but that Power was not Austria-Hungary, *but England*. The inspirer of the scheme was Count Lobanoff, the then Russian Foreign Minister, and Count Witte, then Minister of Finance, who both worked at the realisation of the plan. Prince Lobanoff was a convinced friend of the Dual Monarchy, and a passionate enemy of England, against whom it had been his life's object to get up a Continental coalition. . . *The plan broke down against the opposition of Austro-Hungary and Germany, who did not want to take part in any action directed against England.*

My correspondent adds an equally interesting item of French testimony :—

"We have also a reference from the French side in M. Réné Pinon's book, "France and Germany," published in 1913. M. Pinon says : 'History will inquire how it was that, so short a time after Fashoda, Franco-Russian policy was not able to wrest some advantages from England's embarrassments, and in deciding upon neutrality did not succeed in getting a full price for its neutrality. It is possible that the explanation must be sought in the contradictions of German policy. *If Germany had really wished for a rapprochement with France and Russia for an active collaboration outside Europe, she could have seized the tempting opportunity.*' "

Further light has now been thrown upon this matter in a speech delivered last autumn by General Botha. On September 3, 1915, the *Daily News* published a cable from Johannesburg recording a speech by General Botha. No contradiction has since appeared so far as I know. The speech had reference to an alleged offer from Germany to recognise the independence of the *ex*-Boer republics if the South African rebellion proved successful; and General Botha's speech was, very naturally and properly, directed to an indignant denunciation of the alleged offer.

But, with the apparent intention of lending further point to his denunciation, General Botha made a very remarkable statement, so remarkable indeed that the *Daily News,* in publishing the despatch, headed it, "An historic refusal of assistance." The essential passage in the statement was this :—

(7)

"At the time of the South African War, other nations were prepared to assist the Boers, but they stipulated that Germany should do likewise. *The Kaiser refused.*"

Six weeks after the publication of this utterance, the *Times,* commenting editorially upon M. Delcassé's resignation, declared (October 14) that the latter :—

"with the help of the Tsar, thrust aside German proposals for a Continental combination against us during the Boer War."

Where lies the truth—with General Botha or the *Times*, with the Northcliffian *Daily Mail* in 1899 or with the Northcliffian *Times* in 1915? The day has gone by when any serious student of international politics can accept the *obiter dictum* of Printing House Square without the most ample reservations. It is otherwise with General Botha. No man living is in a better position to know the facts. Subject to authoritative contradiction, his statement stands.

CHAPTER IX.

The Morocco Intrigue

IN so grave an hour, so full of peril for all of us, for all our countries, I shall not indulge in an elaborate search after responsibilities. We have ours, and I claim before history that we (Jaurès and the French Socialist Party) had foreseen them and announced them. When we said that to penetrate into Morocco by violence, by arms, was to inaugurate in Europe an era of ambitions, covetousness and conflicts, we were denounced as bad Frenchmen; but it is we who were concerned for France. There, alas! lies our national share of responsibility. It acquires precision if you recall that the Bosnian-Herzgovinian question is the occasion of the present struggle between Austria and Serbia, and that we Frenchmen were not entitled to utter, and were unable to utter, the least remonstrance when Austria annexed Bosnia-Herzegovina, because we were committed in Morocco, and because we desired that our own sin should be forgiven us by forgiving, on our part, the sins of others. And so our Foreign Minister said to Austria : "You can take Bosnia-Herzegovina, provided you let us take Morocco." We hawked our offers of penitence from capital to capital, from nation to nation. We said to Italy : "You can go to Tripoli, seeing that I am in Morocco. You can steal at one end of the street, seeing that I have stolen at the other end."—*Jean Jaurès, speaking at Vaise a fortnight before the outbreak of war and his own assassination.*

The clash between the Entente and the Central Empires was brought about by a series of steps, some great and some small. Some of those steps were taken by one side, some by the other. One of the longest steps towards war was taken by the British Government's action during the Agadir crisis, culminating in Mr. Lloyd George's diatribe at the Mansion House.—*Hon. Bertrand Russell in "The Policy of the Entente, 1904-14."*

But this long series of duplicities and repudiated undertakings naturally embittered Germany against both France and England. It is enough to make one despair that humanity will ever evolve far enough to deserve—by honest use—its one supreme gift of reason, to see how blind animal passion still renders the majority incapable of even the elements of justice when considering any, opponent's position.—*Mr. Charles Hayward in "What Is Diplomacy?"*

THE quarrel which arose between Britain and Germany in 1905, and again more acutely in 1911, over the affairs of Morocco, will be regarded by future generations as one of those episodes in a nation's history which leave indelible traces upon its destinies, forging links of inter-connected circumstances affecting a remote

71

posterity.   By Britons the episode will be remembered in time to come with amazement, anger, and shame.

To the British *people*, the importance of the episode was transcendental, and the persistent attempt by certain, not all, British historians and writers in the Press and magazines to pass on, even now, to future generations the utterly distorted narration of the facts which did duty in 1911 and 1912, is a monstrous perversion of patriotism.

For the Morocco quarrel marked a turning point in British history.   It was Morocco which caused the initiation of those secret Franco-British naval and military "conversations" which, by imperceptible degrees, and without the knowledge of the Cabinet, let alone Parliament and the nation, committed us to a course of policy which immensely increased the dangers of war in Europe, and made our participation therein practically inevitable.[1]

It was Morocco which gave a definitely hostile character to our relations with Germany.

It was Morocco which gave the influences in Britain favouring a war with Germany their signal opportunity to inflame public sentiment against Germany—and to inflame it through the withholding of facts essential to knowledge.

It was Morocco which, as Mr. Ramsay Macdonald has truly said, "slammed the doors in the face of the peace-makers in Europe."[2]

It was Morocco which inaugurated the veritable holocaust of Treaty obligations culminating in the invasion of Belgium.   No doubt the long immunity enjoyed by Leopold II. in breaking the Congo Treaty set the first immoral example.   But that was the case of an individual, and not of a European Government, defying the public law of Europe.

It cannot be too often insisted upon that the violation of honourable bonds, which disgraced Europe in the decade before the war, and which is now ministering to Europe's destruction, began with the attempt of the Foreign Offices of France and England to set aside the public law of Europe in the matter of Morocco.   The attempt achieved success by threatening the Power which protested with war.

The violation of the Treaty of Berlin by Austria followed the violation of the Act of Algeciras, and, as in the former case, was successfully accomplished by the

---

[1] *Vide* Chapters XXXIII. and XXXIV.
[2] Foreword to "Ten Years of Secret Diplomacy" : *op. cit.*

same method. Austria's offence, morally blameworthy, was ethically venal by comparison; for Austria had preceded her action by decades of administrative effort in the territories she wrongfully annexed, and she accompanied her annexation by substantial monetary compensation to Turkey; while all the Moors got were bullets. Tripoli followed Bosnia. In the Tripoli case the Treaties of Paris and Berlin were both violated. After Tripoli, Persia. Finally, Belgium. A veritable basketfull of scraps of paper.

.   .   .   .

The story of the long Morocco intrigue cannot be fully grasped unless it is studied in detail. No summary can convey its full implications. The detailed story is given in my book. I shall only recall it here in outline. To make the story intelligible thus treated, it is necessary to indicate the international framework in which the intrigue was set up.

In the last quarter of the nineteenth century, a number of events contributed to make Morocco an object of interest to four European Powers. These four Powers were Britain, France, Spain, and Germany. Spain, of course, had a very long historical connéction with Morocco. The British interest was commercial and strategic. The British strategic interest was concerned in preventing any first-class Power from acquiring a footing on the Mediterranean coast-line of Morocco, thereby neutralising the commanding position of Gibraltar, and threatening the ascendancy which Great Britain enjoys through possession of the Rock. British policy did not aim at securing political rights in Morocco. The French interest was of a different character. It was purely Imperialistic. The ambitions of the French Imperialists in the early part of the period we are discussing were only nascent. But they were unmistakable, and from the Imperial point of view comprehensible, French Imperialism coveted Tunisia on the east and Morocco on the West of Algeria, in order to form a great North African Empire under the French flag. Spain's interest was sentimental. Germany's interest was wholly economic. Germany's industrial development was beginning. German explorers had visited several parts of interior Morocco and seen in it a rich field for trade and industrial enterprise.

In 1880 these four Powers, and other Powers indirectly
interested, came to the conclusion that an International
Conference ought to be convened in the general interest
of Europe's relations with this semi-barbarous African
State. The Conference was held at Madrid. The
Sultan's representatives took part in it and, with their
concurrence, various resolutions were adopted. The most
important was that all nations should in future enjoy
equality of commercial treatment in Morocco—the "most
favoured nation" clause having been until that moment
enjoyed by Britain alone.

During the next two decades—1880 to 1900—the
policy of the four interested Powers preserved the
character described above. An attempt by Lord
Salisbury to induce the Moorish Government to bring
about some much needed reforms met with failure, owing
to the local opposition of the French official representatives, supported from Paris. The representatives of the
German Government, on the other hand, supported the
British mission. The dream of a French North African
Empire had, in part, materialised. French control had
been established in Tunis at the price of a bitter quarrel
with Italy, which almost led to war, and did lead to Italy
joining the Teutonic combination—thus was born the
Triple Alliance.[1] Having absorbed Tunis, French
Imperialism was busily engaged in seeking for pretexts
to interfere with Morocco, and a long coterminous frontier
with Algeria, passing through wild and desert country,
gave many openings for diplomatic and military intervention. Germany was developing her trade with
Morocco. Her Consul at Fez had succeeded in negotiating a commercial Treaty with the Sultan, and a Moorish
embassy had been received at Berlin. The German
Government refused to ratify the Treaty until the
signatory powers to the Madrid Conference had been
consulted and had signified their assent thereto.

The opening years of the new century saw the birth
of the intrigue.

French foreign policy was then in the hands of M.
Delcassé—ambitious, impulsive, a very stormy petrel of
international politics, violently Anglophobe one moment
and Germanophobe the next. His personality has been one

[1] Crispi's Memoirs can be usefully consulted in this connection.
("The Memoirs of Francesco Crispi": Hodder and Stoughton).

of the most disturbing influences in Europe. M. Delcassé sought to clear the approaches to Morocco from two directions. He made a bargain with Italy, and sought to make one with Spain. Baulked of Tunis, Italian Imperialism looked towards Tripoli, and was assured that France would not oppose an eventual Italian occupation of Tripoli, if Italy placed no obstacle in the path of France in Morocco. To Spain M. Delcassé turned with a proposal for a Franco-Spanish partition of Morocco. The negotiations dragged on for a considerable time, and were on the eve of conclusion when, apparently, the British Foreign Office heard of them. The upshot was that the Spanish Government refused to ratify.

Meantime, events were pointing to a new re-shuffling in the eternal game of beggar-my-neighbour, which diplomatists call the "Balance of Power." The prolonged friction between Britain and France was to make way for accommodation, only to be replaced by an even deadlier friction between Britain and Germany.

In 1904 the British and French Governments agreed to compose their differences all over the globe. Not one of their differences was worth the bones of a single British or French soldier, or the tears of a single British or French widow. But one or the other of them had repeatedly brought both nations to the very brink of war —twice in connection with West Africa, once about Nilotic swamps, once over Siam, while the Egyptian squabble was of long standing, and the dispute about Newfoundland coufish was a hardy perennial. When, therefore, the average Englishman and the average Frenchman heard that their Governments had at last acquired a modicum of common sense, they were genuinely delighted. And the simple soul, if cast in a British mould, took rapidly enough to the new doctrine, which bade him believe that the Frenchman might become a reformed character without being "rolled in blood and mud." And the simple soul, if located in a French frame, was equally pleased to think that the perfidiousness of Albion had been over-rated.

Simple souls both. For under cover of an amicable settlement the seeds of the mightiest war of all time were being sown.

. . . .

By one of the several published arrangements, the French Government agreed to leave us alone in Egypt.

In return for this concession the British Government recognised that France, owing to the proximity of Algeria to Morocco, had special interests in the latter country.   The reference to Morocco was ambiguously worded except in one particular.   Both Governments declared they had no intention of altering the "political status" of that country.

That was "diplomacy."

Shortly afterwards the French and Spanish Governments issued a joint Declaration, asserting that they remained "firmly attached" to the integrity and independence of Morocco.

That, too, was "diplomacy."

. . . .

Secret articles were attached to the Anglo-French agreement, and a secret convention was attached to the Franco-Spanish "Declaration."

These provided, in effect, for the realisation of the ambitions of M. Delcassé and the French Imperialists. At last Morocco was within their grasp.   France and Spain were to divide Morocco between them.   One important proviso was, however, insisted upon by the British Government, in accordance with its traditional strategic policy, already described.   France was to be excluded from the Mediterranean coast-line, which was to fall to Spain. This was a fly in the ointment from the French Imperialistic point of view, and accounted, no doubt, for the fact that M. Delcassé concealed the secret clauses even from some of his Cabinet colleagues.   Throughout the years that followed, French public opinion allowed itself to be dragged along by the French Imperialists in the belief that France was securing, not "a mutilated Morocco," as was later to be realised, *but the whole of Morocco*.   And that is not the least of the deceptions practised upon the French people by its Foreign Office, with the connivance of the British Foreign Office.

Apart from the territorial rights they had so calmly attributed to themselves, the French and Spanish Governments had also arranged to share the economic spoils of Morocco between them.   As Spain had no money, this side of the arrangement virtually gave France a lien over every enterprise connected with the economic development of the country.

This dishonest triangular robbery at the expense of a weak native State, and at the expense of the rest of the world, was, of course, concealed from the Parliaments and peoples of Britain, France, and Spain. Spain, indeed, was a decoy duck.

But there was Germany to reckon with.

. . . .

The German Government had at first declared that it saw nothing inimical to German interests in the Anglo-French published agreement. This statement was made a few days after the publication of the latter, and six months before the completion of its complement, the secret convention between France and Spain. When the Franco-Spanish "Declaration" was published, Germany, already resenting M. Delcassé's breach of diplomatic etiquette in not officially notifying the Anglo-French published agreement, saw in this further announcement what appeared to be a studied intention to shut her out altogether from a say in Moroccan affairs, to which her position as a participant of the Madrid Conference, and her interests in the country, entitled her. She began to suspect the character of the deal. Suspicion changed to certainty when Parisian indiscretions hinted at the existence of "secret articles" and at Britain's knowledge of them; and when M. Delcassé suddenly pitched a veritable cargo of reforms at the head of the Sultan, and peremptorily demanded immediate compliance. Thereupon the German Government decided to make it clear that Germany had no intention of being excluded from the field. The Kaiser went to Tangier, and in a speech to the Sultan's deputation declared that he looked upon the Sultan as an entirely independent Sovereign. At the same time the Sultan, doubtless at Germany's suggestion, issued a Note to all the signatory Powers of the Madrid Convention, suggesting a further international Conference upon the affairs of his country and Europe's connection therewith. This the German Government promptly accepted.

The attitude of the German Government was legally unassailable. Its argument, as officially put forward, may be paraphrased thus : "The future of Morocco is an international matter, not a Franco-British matter. France and Britain have come to an agreement amongst themselves about Morocco. But this does not dispose of the question so far as we are concerned. Under cover of that agreement France is making demands upon the Sultan, and making them in a tone which amounts to the assertion of a mandate to interfere permanently with the government of Morocco. Such a mandate she can receive only from the signatory Powers of the Madrid Convention. We have given her no such mandate. Our interests in Morocco are important and growing. But even if they were not we could not allow ourselves to be elbowed roughly out of the way in this fashion. We have a right to be consulted about Morocco, and we do not intend to be jockeyed out of this right simply because it has suited England and France in their own interests to make a deal about a country which, in point of fact, belongs to neither of them." The man in the street may say: "Why did not the German Government avow that it knew all about the secret arrangements and denounce them at the bar of European public opinion?" The reason is not far to seek. Governments do not act in that way. They cannot. Such action on the part of the German Government would have meant an open breach with France and England, and if France and England had declared themselves prepared to stand by what they had done, Germany would have had to choose between war and an ignominious retreat, although she was morally and legally in the right. The first lesson of diplomacy is that you must never speak the truth. You must proceed by subterfuge. You must pretend you do not know, when you know all the time. You must profess to believe that the other party is playing straight, and that the only difference between you and him is a matter of interpretation, whereas you are well aware that he has tricked you; so you trick him into believing you do not know you have been tricked. All this is of the essence of "diplomacy."

. . . .

So once again the British people and the French people were deceived. The German Government's action was denounced by the inspired organs of the British and French Foreign Offices as grossly provocative and designed to test the solidity of the Anglo-French *entente*. *The Times* easily out-Heroded Herod. Its personal attacks upon the Emperor were particularly violent. After refusing to go to the Conference, the British and French Governments finally consented. Indeed the French Government, having got rid of M. Delcassé, was anxious to smooth things over as far as it could. The Conference met at Algeciras. It was protracted and stormy. In the end it drew up a plan of reforms, con-

ferred certain strictly limited police powers upon France
and Spain, provided for the international capitalisation of
certain European enterprises in Morocco, *and affirmed
once more the integrity and independence of the Sultan.*

. . . .

Here was Sir E. Grey's chance.   He was not responsible for the secret arrangements.   The Algeciras Act
might, and should, have inaugurated an entirely new
chapter.   Sir E. Grey could have said to France:
"The Act of Algeciras makes the secret treaties null and
void.   But you have got a footing.   If you play your cards
tactfully with Germany, she will recognise your Protectorate in course of time.   Our diplomacy will help you.
But if you rush matters and proceed as though the
Algeciras Act did not exist, we shall not support you.   It
is an International Act, which lays down that the Sultan
of Morocco is independent, and that the integrity of his
country must be respected.   Our signature is at the foot
of that Act, and we cannot in honour help you to break it.
But go slowly, carry the Germans with you, and we will do
our best to make your path an easy one."   It would not
have been a strictly moral course—towards Morocco—
but it would have been at least infinitely better than the
course actually adopted.

Instead, the British Foreign Office chose to regard the
Algeciras Act as a diplomatic defeat, and plunged deeper
into the morass.   While the Conference was actually being
held, or immediately after, Sir E. Grey was approached by
the French Ambassador in London, and consented to the
initiation of those secret military and naval "conversations," which were to have so fatal a sequel.[1]

. . . .

The result of the intrigue up to this point (1906) had
been as follows :—

The British people had been committed, without
knowing it, to diplomatic support of the secret ambitions
of the French Foreign Office, in other words to a potential
French Protectorate over Morocco.

They were supporting, without knowing it, a dishonest
Treaty which said one thing and meant another.

They were committed to supporting the quarrel of their
Government with Germany, but, owing to essential facts
being withheld from them, their support was based upon

[1] *Vide* Chapters XXXIII. and XXXIV.

a complete misunderstanding and misapprehension of the German case.

Diplomatic support of France was in process of being converted, without their knowing it, into a potential *material* support—*i.e.,* the British people were in the process of being committed to war with Germany on behalf of France.

Incidentally it may be recalled that *five years were to pass* before the British people became first acquainted—in the columns of a couple of Parisian newspapers—with the existence of the secret Morocco arrangements, and *eight years were to pass before they learned that, arising out of those secret agreements, they were morally pledged to support France in a European war.*

. . . .

The five years which followed Algeciras witnessed the intrigue following the course of its logical development; the original lie gathering around in a maze of other lies; the secret commitments dragging the country nearer and nearer to the abyss; unavowed and unavowable liabilities paralyzing our diplomatic action, rendering abortive any attempt to straighten out Anglo-German relations, deflecting our national policy into all sorts of unnatural channels, and poisoning the diplomatic wells of Europe.

The French Imperialists treated the Algeciras Act like waste paper. They proceeded systematically to conquer and absorb Morocco, by direct military action and piece-meal occupation, by fomenting internal discord, and by financial combinations which strangled the revenues of the Moorish Government. Every step they took was applauded, and every criticism thereon in Germany was denounced, by the officially-inspired British Press. Of their culminating action, the march upon Fez, Sir E. Grey hastened to express his official approval in Parliament. During the whole course of these proceedings the French Chamber, profoundly uneasy at the turn events were taking, registered again and again the determination of France to uphold the Algeciras Act.   But in the then condition of France, with short-lived Cabinet succeeding short-lived Cabinet, at intervals of six months or less, and with the militarists and Imperialists steadily working to the desired end, the Chamber was powerless to stay the progress of events, or put on the brake.

. . . .

The German Government was resentful, but embarrassed. It sought steadily to avoid a rupture, and appeared to aim at producing a state of affairs, through successful bargaining with France in other directions, which would have enabled it to prepare the way for acquiescing in a French Protectorate, provided the French Government would allow it to save its own face with its own public opinion and to placate its own Imperialists. This the French Government, owing in part to perpetual changes in the *personnel* of Ministers, was either unwilling or unable to do. The running comments of a neutral diplomatist present as true a general picture of what was passing in Berlin during these years as we are ever likely to get, although the specific efforts to reach an accommodation are discussed in detail in my book. The following extracts are from the despatches of the Belgian Minister at Berlin, Baron Greindl :—

May 6, 1908.—" The most interesting feature of the White Book I had the honour of enclosing in my yesterday's report is the forbearance with which the German Government pretends to ignore the flagrant contradiction between the uniformly correct declarations of the French Government, and the conquest of Morocco which France is carrying on, on the strength of a so-called European mandate which no one has given her, and professing to be swept along by circumstances which she calls fortuitous, but which, in point of fact, she has carefully provoked. . . Germany tolerates. She cannot do otherwise. The time for diplomatic negotiations has gone by. She can only choose between pretending not to see, and war, which the Emperor will not have, and which would be condemned by German public opinion.

April 20, 1911.—" I do not think there is the least desire here to play an active part in the Morocco affair. Any illusions must have disappeared long ago, if they were ever entertained, as to the value of the Act of Algeciras, which France signed with the firm intention of never observing   But the policy of standing aside does not solely depend upon the Imperial Government. It must be helped from outside. It is perfectly true that public opinion is uneasy. . . The Imperial Government has been criticised for its undue toleration towards France in the matter of Morocco. . . . . If the French Government really desires to avoid the chance of a conflict, it is that Government's turn to manage affairs with sufficient prudence and pretended moderation; not to force Germany to abandon her inaction.

May 1, 1911.—" The anxiety of German public opinion is real . . . the Imperial Government has long been criticised for shutting its eyes to France's failure to observe the Act of Algeciras. . . . What is the significance of the semi-official warning conveyed to Paris? Does the present Foreign Secretary, who is much more energetic than his predecessor, mean to convey that he is not prepared to tolerate any further French encroachments? . . . Despite the tendency of the semi-official article, the position remains a very delicate one. A mistake may force Germany to take action. Much, too, depends upon the Press. Some French newspapers show much too openly that it is intended to make Morocco another Tunisia. The attitude of the German papers is, generally speaking, very reserved; but those inspired by the Pan-Germanists put forward notions which are most embarrassing to the Imperial policy.''

When the intention to occupy Fez was being openly discussed by the French Press, the same Belgian diplomatist, and also his colleague in London, the Count de Lalaing, wrote expressing their fear that if that event should take place, Germany would be compelled to intervene, as the violation of the Algeciras Act would then be too flagrant and open, to be ignored.

Baron Greindl writes under date of *May* 10, 1911 :—

"France began by making arrangements with England and Spain in 1904 without taking the trouble to consult, or even to advise, the other interested Powers. Until Germany objected it was openly stated that Morocco would become another Tunis. Alongside the public arrangement, France signed a secret Treaty with Spain (a secret very badly kept) for the partition of Morocco. The Act of Algeciras wrought no change in French projects. It only compelled France to carry them out more slowly, step by step, instead of in a single stride, like the Bardo Treaty was extorted from the Bey of Tunis. Since then the progressive invasion of Morocco has been methodically pursued. . . . I remain persuaded that Germany desires to avoid entangling herself irremediably in this Moroccan affair. But I must repeat what I wrote in my report of May 1, that the situation is a delicate one. Indeed it is becoming so more and more. If the Imperial Government is to justify its inaction in the eyes of German public opinion, it is essential that the French Government should not compel the German Government to abandon that line.

June 17, 1911.—"The Imperial Government maintains, therefore, its original standpoint. It is playing the part of mere spectator, reserving its liberty of action in the event of the essential clauses of the Act of Algeciras, *i.e.,* the sovereignty of the Sultan, and the integrity of Morocco ceasing to exist owing to French action. There remains nothing of either. When will Germany think it advisable to say so, and what use will she make of her recovered liberty? I am persuaded that her chief desire is to avoid a war which Morocco is not worth, and which France can spare Europe by putting into the conquest of Morocco the dose of hypocrisy which is necessary in order that public opinion in Germany shall not become excited. Everyone does not share my opinion ; some of my colleagues are astonished at the forbearance of Germany.''

. . . .

When it became clear that the French army, after "relieving" Fez, had no intention of departing therefrom, Germany sent a gunboat to Agadir to intimate that she was at the end of her patience, and that the Morocco question should not be settled without her. Her action, morally significant, was materially insignificant. The *Panther* only carried a complement of 125 men. Moreover, Germany's action had been preceded by a much more vigorous demonstration on the part of Spain, whose Government took umbrage at what it deemed the high-handed action of the French. Thinking Spain was to be deprived of its advantages under the secret convention, the Spanish Government sent a large body of troops to occupy the areas allotted to Spain under the Treaty. When the little German gunboat anchored off Agadir, there were 100,000 French and Spanish troops in Morocco, France was in actual military occupation of a considerable proportion of the country, the authority of the Sultan's Government had entirely disappeared, and the Act of Algeciras existed—as a memory.

. . . .

What followed has passed into history and left an indelible mark upon it. Sir E. Grey's attitude was more French than the French, more "royalist than the King." He professed to see in Germany's action a menace to

British interests and, *mirabile dictu*, a "reopening" of
the Morocco question ! What the Foreign Office saw in
Germany's action, of course, was a challenge to the secret
arrangement with France, now coming to fruition despite
the Algeciras Act. Sir E. Grey insisted that the British
Government must be a party to the Franco-German
negotiations. However, negotiations began between the
two Governments without the British Government
becoming a party to them. *The Times* fulminated
daily. Suddenly, in the midst of the negotiations, on July
20, *1 he Times*, whose editorials and Paris despatches had
been characterised by almost incredible violence, announced
that Germany was making outrageous " demands " upon
France. It specified those alleged " demands." It
*declared that no British Government would tolerate them,
even if a French Government were found feeble enough to
do so* ! It pressed for the despatch of warships to Agadir.
The next day Sir E. Grey sent for the German Ambassador.
He adopted *The Times'* tone and *The Times'* "facts," and
he hinted that it might be necessary to take steps to protect
British interests. The German Ambassador angrily protested. The same evening Mr. Lloyd George was put up
by the Foreign Office to make a speech at the Mansion
House. It virtually amounted to a threat of war, should
Germany press her "demands." In its editorial next
morning *The Times* hailed Mr. Lloyd George as a sort of
national saviour, emphasised in insulting language the
significance of the speech, and compared Germany to Dick
Turpin. Public opinion in all three countries reached fever-
heat and for a few days war seemed imminent.

It was avoided by the pacific elements in the French
Government, headed by M. Caillaux, the French Premier,
who played much the same part in the crisis as M. Rouvier,
the then French Premier, played in the 1905 crisis; by the
German Emperor and by the pacific elements in the German
Government. Rumour has it that Lord Morley took a
vigorous line on behalf of peace at British Cabinet Councils.
Both the German and French Governments encouraged
and, indeed, invited the Socialists and the Social Democrats respectively to organise immense peace demonstrations in Paris and Berlin.

Meantime the Franco-German negotiations continued
and reached a solution in November. Germany recognized
a French Protectorate over Morocco, but bound down
France to observe the open-door for trade and capital

investments in Morocco; received a portion of French equatorial Africa and ceded a small section of German equatorial Africa by way of exchange.

.   .   .   .

The whole story of the intrigue was subsequently dragged into the light in a series of debates which took place in the French Chamber, and in the Senate. The secret treaties were denounced in scathing terms, and the duplicity of the policy followed was condemned by some of France's most distinguished public men.

In the course of the debate it transpired that negotiations covering a wide field of Franco-German colonial interests in Africa, had been proceeding for several months between the two Governments before the march upon Fez. They had not reached a conclusion owing in large measure to the constant changes of Cabinet in France. It transpired that when the French occupied Fez, the German Government had given the French Government the clearest warning that it could no longer remain passive in view of what Germany regarded as the culminating destruction of the Algeciras Act; and *had there and then intimated its willingness to treat on the basis of a German recognition of a French Protectorate,* provided that Germany received compensation elsewhere, even as Britain, Spain, and Italy had received compensation. The French Foreign Minister's statement to the Chamber completely disposed of the notion —which was the basis of all the British Press attacks upon Germany, and which even to-day is still repeated with astounding ignorance or wilful perversion—that the German Government, in sending a gunboat of 1,000 tons and 125 men to the most God-forsaken part of the Atlantic coastline of Morocco, intended to seize a portion of the country itself.

The French Foreign Minister was equally categorical as to the character of the so-called "demands" upon France, as reported in *The Times* of July 20, and so precipitately endorsed by Sir E. Grey. There were never "demands" in the sense suggested by *The Times*, and the statement of that paper that the "demands" included the reversion to Germany of France's right of pre-emption over the Belgian Congo was a fabrication.

In short, the French Foreign Minister's revelations disposed of the whole structure erected by Sir E. Grey in the House of Commons in November, when justifying his

(8)

attitude in July.   They also disposed of the malevolent
charges of *The Times*.   Unfortunately, these revelations
came one month too late to affect the debate in the House
of Commons.   The French Yellow Book, issued at a
much later stage, showed that the famous *Times'*
despatch could only have been based upon a distorted
account of a confidential conversation which had taken
place between the German Foreign Secretary and the
French Ambassador.

. . . .

The effect in Germany and in France of the line of action
pursued by our Foreign Office, and of Mr. Lloyd George's
speech, was disastrous from the point of view of the
preservation of European peace.   It strengthened the
hands of the French Imperialists and Jingoes and,
generally, of all the influences in France belonging to the
revanche school.   It convinced even the most pacific
German Social Democrats, in the words of Mr. Ramsay
Macdonald,[1] that "Germany was the victim of an evil
conspiracy, and that our friendship was merely feigned."
Upon the German Jingoes it acted like champagne.   Upon
the German governing classes, and upon the German
Emperor, it had a profound effect, as is admitted in the
French Yellow Book on the War without its compilers
realising, apparently, all the significance of their
admission.   If it be true, as the French Yellow Book
asserts, that from thence onwards the German Emperor
became convinced that war was inevitable, how many
of those who accept that view have ever paused to inquire
into the circumstances which brought about the conviction?

It is impossible to doubt, especially when we bear
in mind the menacing aspect the near Eastern problem
was then assuming,[2] that *from this moment* the military
party in Germany acquired enormous strength, and that
the military point of view was given additional weight
in the councils of the Empire.   Nor can one affect
surprise that it should have been so.

For what was the paramount lesson to be learned
from this episode?   It was that Great Britain was
prepared to go all lengths in support of France on an
issue in which French diplomacy—as honourable Frenchmen recognised and deplored—had behaved dishonestly;
dishonestly to the French people and dishonestly to

[1] Foreword to "Ten Years of Secret Diplomacy": *op. cit.*
[2] *Vide* Chapter XV.

Europe; and had trampled upon an international agreement in order to secure its own ends.

.   .   .   .

German feelings after Agadir can be more readily understood when we observe the impression which British diplomacy, and the utterances of the most powerful section of the British Press, made upon the minds of neutral diplomatists in the various capitals of Europe. We may regard their impressions as ill-founded. We cannot disregard the fact that they did form those impressions.

In a despatch, dated Berlin, September 23, 1905, Baron Greindl refers to the "astounding efforts made by the British Press to prevent a peaceful settlement of the Morocco affair. . . ." He argues therefrom that British public opinion is *"prepared to welcome any combination hostile to Germany."*

In a long despatch dated October 24, 1905, M. Leghait, the Belgian Minister in Paris, discusses the European situation, and that of France in particular, in grave terms. He expresses the belief that Britain desires "to avoid a conflict," but doubts whether "her selfish aspirations are not leading us towards one." Reporting on July 14, 1906, M. E. van Grootven, Belgian chargé d'affaires in London, states :—

"Latterly the Foreign Secretary has repeated on several occasions to the various ambassadors accredited to London, that Great Britain is bound to France in regard to Morocco, and that she will fulfil her engagements to the end, even in the event of a Franco-German war, and at whatever cost."

From Baron Greindl, April 5, 1906 :—

"The British Press did all that it could to prevent the Algeciras conference from coming to a head. It has shown itself more uncompromising than the French newspapers, and has ceaselessly propagated alleged plans of German aggression which have never existed. It does not seem that the British Ambassador at Algeciras made the slightest effort to find a solution which should conciliate the views of Germany with those of France. It was, of course, anticipated that England would uphold French policy; but her engagements in no way prevented her from playing the part of moderator."

From the Count de Lalaing, Belgian Minister in London, June 23, 1906, in reference to the efforts of Lord

Avebury and others to improve Anglo-German relations :

"The real effect is virtually *nil*. The siege of public opinion has been carried out. The British Press has so overdone the attacks upon the Emperor, his Government, and his people that the public remains suspicious."

Reporting from Paris, on February 10, 1907, M. Leghait speaks of his fear that Germany may risk all : "to free herself from the grip in which British policy is squeezing her." M. Cartier, chargé d'affaires, writing from London under date of March 28, 1907, talks in almost identical language of "British diplomacy, whose entire resources tend towards the isolation of Germany." The allusions to the evil consequences of British Press attacks upon Germany are numerous in subsequent despatches. Writing from London on May 24, 1907, the Count de Lalaing particularly censures the Northcliffe Press. He accuses it of "warping the spirit of a whole people." He adds :—

"It is evident that official England is secretly pursuing a hostile policy which aims at the isolation of Germany . . . but there is an obvious danger in thus openly embittering public opinion as the aforesaid irresponsible Press is doing."

Baron Greindl, reporting from Berlin on May 30, 1907, pays a glowing tribute to the efforts of Sir Frank Lascelles (then British Ambassador in Berlin, afterwards playing a leading part as Chairman of the Anglo-German Friendship Society to promote good feeling between the two countries) to improve relations, but is sceptical of the result.

It is exasperating and melancholy to read in despatch after despatch, year after year, the same conviction animating the entire Belgian diplomatic corps as to the character of British diplomacy. If the view were confined to the Belgian Embassy in Berlin, one could put it down to pro-German prejudice. But exactly the same impression is seen to prevail at the Belgian Embassies in Paris and in London. If these Belgian diplomatists were hopelessly wrong in their estimates, then how hopelessly incompetent must our diplomacy have been to produce the impression they formed of it. The cumulative significance of their judgment cannot be gleaned from mere extracts. Extracts do not heighten the adverse judgment. They minimise its comprehensiveness. Yet in the event of a European war, the Belgians had obviously most to fear from Germany.

Passing to the events of 1911, we find Baron Guillaume, Belgian Minister in Paris, writing on April 29 of that year, remarking in connection with the confusion reigning in many French Government departments over Moroccan affairs :—

"England, which thrust France into the Moroccan morass, contemplates her work with satisfaction."

The Count de Lalaing, writing from London on May 9, 1911, thinks, on the other hand, that official quarters in England are becoming anxious lest France should commit some imprudence which would give Germany a pretext for intervention. He refers to the frequent visits of the French Ambassador to the Foreign Office. Reporting on May 22, he testifies to the excellent impression made by the visit of the German Emperor and Empress, who went about in homely fashion without any fuss or pomp. It was short-lived.

We come to the occupation of Fez, the despatch of numerous Spanish troops to Morocco, and the arrival of the *Panther* at Agadir. A despatch from Baron Guillaume, dated Paris, July 8, 1911, serves to explain the attacks of the British officially inspired Press upon M. Caillaux, the French Premier. After describing the chaos in French official circles and explaining that recourse had been had to British advice, he says :—

"I have reason to believe that M. Caillaux has, perhaps reached the point of regretting the insistence placed upon this step, and the attitude taken up by the British Cabinet. There will be much less chance of reaching an understanding with Germany if England takes part in the discussion, and I feel confident M. Caillaux and M. de Selves[1] regret the complexion which was given to the Morocco affair by their predecessors. They were ready to retreat if they could do so without humiliation."

The Count de Lalaing, writing from London under date of July 24, calls particular attention to the famous article in *The Times* of July 20, and to Mr. Lloyd George's speech. Baron Guillaume sums up the situation as it appeared to him from Paris on July 28. He thinks that France is against a final rupture. He expresses great confidence in the pacific sentiments of the German

[1] French Foreign Minister.

Emperor, "notwithstanding the rather frequent exuberance of some of his actions." He adds :—

"I feel, speaking generally, less faith in the peaceful desires of Great Britain, who does not dislike to see other parties devour one another. But in these circumstances it would be difficult—I will say impossible—not to intervene *manu militari*. . . As I thought from the first day, the key of the situation is in London. It is only there that it can assume gravity."

. . . .

The crisis over, the peril escaped, British sentiment underwent a notable change. One gathered the impression, even in circles to which Cabinet opinion was accessible, that in many quarters, and although the full facts were not then known, the idea was current that the Foreign Office had not been very wisely directed. The Haldane mission was doubtless the outcome of this feeling. On both sides of the North Sea disinterested and distinguished men put out great efforts to heal the breach.

Why these various efforts failed, and were bound to fail, is told in Chapters XXXIII. and XXXIV.

CHAPTER X.

European Militarism, 1905-1914[1]

THE German Army is vital, not merely to the existence of the German Empire, but to the very life and independence of the nation itself, surrounded as Germany is by other nations, each of which possesses armies about as powerful as her own. We forget that, while we insist upon a 60 per cent. superiority (so far as our naval strength is concerned) over Germany being essential to guarantee the integrity of our own shores—Germany herself has nothing like that superiority over France alone, and she has, of course, in addition to reckon with Russia on her eastern frontier. Germany has nothing which approximates to a two-Power standard. She has, therefore, become alarmed by recent events, and is spending huge sums of money on the expansion of her military resources.—*Mr. Lloyd George in the "Daily Chronicle," January 1, 1914.*

I T has been shown that, according to Lord Haldane and the French Yellow Book, the German Emperor had consistently worked to preserve the peace of Europe until within the last three or four years (or, possibly, as Lord Haldane opines, the last' two), when, according to Lord Haldane, his opposition to war "gradually weakened." It has been further shown that this official British and French testimony to the pacific efforts of the German Emperor, coupled with the theory universally held here that the national policy of Germany is directed by and incarnated in the person of the Emperor, indicates that, until three or four years ago, official Germany was pacific. The deduction to be drawn from these officially promulgated premises is that official Germany's pacific policy coincided with the period during which Germany's rulers considered Germany's position in Europe to be nationally secure, and that the alleged abandonment of that policy coincided with the period during which Germany's rulers considered that Germany's position in Europe was no longer nationally secure. The only conclusion possible from these premises is that if, as alleged, Germany's official policy ceased to be inspired with pacific intentions during the past three or four years, the cause thereof was not a desire to "subjugate" Europe

[1] *The Labour Leader,* April 29, 1915.

—which would have been attempted when Germany's proportionate strength was greatest—but was inspired by *fear,* fear of being "subjugated."

I now wish to quote certain figures which, I am inclined to think, will support the conclusions above indicated, and will throw a curious light upon Sir Edward Grey's statement the other day to the effect that : "We now know that the German Government had prepared for war as only people who plan can prepare."[1]

It will, I suppose, be universally conceded that military expenditure is a fair test of military preparedness. The postulate we are asked to accept—nay, that we are told we have accepted—is that the Teutonic Powers, Germany especially, of course, have been preparing and planning for a great war against the other European "group," to which, under the senseless system of Statecraft shared in and praised on numerous occasions by our own diplomacy, Europe has been divided. Very well. Let us test that statement by the amount of money the Powers concerned have spent upon their armies. The issue is a square one.

TABLE I.

MILITARY EXPENDITURE IN THE DECADE 1905-14.

Austro-Hungary.	Germany.	France.	Russia.
£	£	£	£
234,668,407	448,025,543	347,348,259	495,144,622

It will be observed that, in the period named, military preparedness has been expressed by the Teutonic Powers in an expenditure of £682,693,950, and by France and Russia in an expenditure of £842,492,881. In other words, *France and Russia in combination have, during the past ten years, spent £159,798,931 more than Austria and Germany in preparing for war.*

These figures give furiously to think as they stand. But if we sectionalise them and present them in two quinquennial periods, *i.e.,* if we show what the military expenditure of these four Powers was in the period 1905-9, and in the period 1910-14 respectively, the significance of these figures will be enhanced. This I will now proceed to do.

[1] March 22, 1915.

TABLE II.

MILITARY EXPENDITURE IN THE PERIOD 1905-9.

£

Austro-Hungary 105,962,783
Germany 195,647,224

Total £301,610,007

France 150,530,462
Russia 215,485,152

Total £366,015,614

MILITARY EXPENDITURE IN THE PERIOD 1910-14.

Austro-Hungary 128,705,624
Germany 252,378,319

Total £381,083,943

France 196,817,797
Russia 279,659,470

Total £476,477,267

It will be remarked that the first period, 1905-9—during which British and French official authorities declare that official Germany's policy was pacific—the military expenditure of France and Russia was already considerably in excess of that of Germany and her Austrian ally. But not so considerable, apparently—other factors being taken into consideration—as to cause the rulers of Germany serious uneasiness. During the second period, however, that excess progressively increased from £64,405,607, its amount at the close of the first period, to £95,393,324. Put otherwise, *France and Russia have spent during the past five years* £95,393,324 *more than the Teutonic Powers in preparing for war,* which works out at an average of excess just under £20,000,000 *per annum,* not far short of the entire cost of our own army. During this latter period it was that Germany's rulers became really alarmed. With what justification we shall perceive when we examine the figures in detail.

In 1908 Russia's military expenditure made a tremendous leap forward, rising from £40,913,653 to £45,227,850, and the same phenomenon was observable the next year, when another five million pounds was added, the total for 1909 amounting to £50,416,915. In 1909-10 the German figures, which had risen from £37,122,582 in

1906-7 to £42,719,612 in 1908-9, fell to £40,604,764. But Russia's rose again that year to £51,140,034, despite the huge increase in the two former years, and France added, for her part, another two and a half million pounds. Next year (1910-11) Germany's figures showed another slight decrease (£40,347,037), but Russia maintained and slightly exceeded the previous year's (£51,349,332), while France added a further two million and a half pounds. The position which had been reached in 1912, the year preceding Germany's immense increase, when, according to Lord Haldane, the German Emperor's opposition to war "weakened," was this: Russia and France in combination were devoting in that single year £89,259,671 to military preparations, while Germany and Austria were spending £67,254,555. *In other words, the process of yearly increase maintained by the first two named Powers had attained such proportions that, in a single year, Russia and France were spending £22,000,000 more than Germany and Austria.*

Then it was that *fear* gripped the vitals of the rulers of Germany, and at a single bound the German estimates went up from £42,389,775 to £68,434,262.[1] The estimates of the four Powers for the catastrophic year of 1914 stood as follows :—

TABLE IV.
MILITARY EXPENDITURE IN 1914.

Austro-Hungary and Germany £92,865,354
Russia and France £114,270,338

These figures tell their own tale. They reduce to absolute absurdity the legend of a Germany arming to the teeth in order to overawe her innocent and peaceable neighbours.

Let us, then, summarise the conclusions to be derived from these researches. First, what is the premise we are asked to accept and upon which we are asked to base our whole intellectual approach? It is that Germany has been the sole responsible author of this war, which was undertaken by her rulers to "subjugate Europe." And, further, that the truth of the premise is to be sought in Germany's preparations for war, which preparations were on such a scale and of such a character as to furnish unmistakable evidence that her rulers deliberately planned and plotted

[1] A very large proportion of this expenditure was ear-marked for fortifications, especially in Silesia, evidence of the fear of Russian aggression and of the desire to guard against it.

this war and launched it upon Europe when, in their
opinion, the psychological moment had arrived.   To
express any doubt as to the accuracy of the premise is to
be a "pro-German."   But surely we have the right to
examine the accuracy of the premise?   We are not children
incapable of reasoning powers.   Are we not entitled to
look into matters for ourselves?   What is one test which
any of us can apply, without any special knowledge or any
special training, provided we give ourselves the trouble?
Obviously one of the very first ways of testing the premise
we are invited to accept is to make an investigation into
the national expenditure upon armaments—*i.e.*, to say
upon preparations for war—of Germany and her ally on
the one part and their potential foes, Russia and France,
on the other.   Well, what do we find as a result of this
examination?   We find this :—

MILITARY EXPENDITURE OF THE TEUTONIC POWERS AND OF
THE FRANCO-RUSSIAN COMBINATION RESPECTIVELY.

From 1905 to 1909.

The Teutonic Powers £301,610,007
The Franco-Russian Combination ... £366,015,614

From 1910 to 1914.

The Teutonic Powers £381,083,943
The Franco-Russian Combination ... £476,477,267

EXCESS OF WAR-PREPARATION-EXPENDITURE BY THE
FRANCO-RUSSIAN COMBINATION OVER THE TEUTONIC
POWERS IN THE DECADE 1905-14,
£159,798,931.

I close this article by recalling that Germany's
fears, for which these figures supply an eloquent
explanation, have been understood and, what is more,
freely and publicly acknowledged, by leading British
statesmen in the course of the past decade.   Here, for
instance, is another extract from a speech by Mr. Lloyd
George, delivered at the Queen's Hall on July 28, 1908 :—

"Look at the position of Germany.   Her army is to
her what our navy is to us—her sole defence against
invasion.   She has not got a two-Power standard.   She
may have a stronger army than France, than Russia, than
Italy, than Austria, but she is between two great Powers
who, in combination, could pour in a vastly greater
number of troops than she has.   Don't forget that when
you wonder why Germany is frightened at alliances and

understandings and some sort of mysterious workings
which appear in the Press, and hints in the *Times* and
Daily Mail. . . . Here is Germany, in the middle of
Europe, with France and Russia on either side, and with
a combination of their armies greater than hers. Suppose
we had here a possible combination which would lay us
open to invasion—suppose Germany and France, or
Germany and Russia, or Germany and Austria, had fleets
which, in combination, would be stronger than ours, would
not we be frightened? Would we not arm? Of course we
should."

The year 1909—six months after Mr. Lloyd George's
speech—opened   with   France   and   Russia   voting
£82,411,963 for their combined armies against Germany's
and Austria's £54,562,094. But Germany, it seems, is
the only Power which has been preparing for war, and in
so comprehensive a manner that her intention to
"subjugate Europe" is now clearly apparent! And yet,
according to Lord Haldane and the French Yellow Book,
official Germany was working for peace in 1909, although
her potential foes were devoting sums enormously larger
than she was upon military preparations.[1]

[1] In connection with the figures given above, I desire to express
my indebtedness to Mr. Carl Heath, Secretary of the National Peace
Council. The figures are extracted from the Budgets of the respective Powers, and they can be checked from the International Peace
Year Book for 1915, published by the National Peace Council. In
the case of the Austro-Hungarian returns, a sum of eight millions
sterling has been added for each year under review, to cover the
expenses of Austria's and of Hungary's "National defence" troops,
the accounts of which are rendered separately from the expenditure
upon the Monarchy's "Common Army," *i.e.*, first line troops.
    It has been suggested to me that the Italian figures ought to be
added to the German and Austrian. I disagree. It would be as
logical to add the British figures to the French and Russian. As
already stated, the *raison d'être* of Italy's accession to the Teutonic
Powers disappeared years ago, while in Balkan affairs the antagonism
of interests between Austria and Italy had been steadily growing.
But even if the Italian figures were thrown into the scale—
£141,518,105 in the decade 1905-14—the expenditure of the Teutonic
Powers plus that of Italy, would still show a slightly smaller total
than that of the Franco-Russian combination, which total would, of
course, be swelled were the British figures to be added to it. Italy's
intervention on Austria's behalf in any Balkan dispute had of late
years become unthinkable, as unthinkable as her participation
in a war against Great Britain. The main point to bear in mind,
however, is not that the Franco-Russian combination spent enormously larger sums on military preparations than did the Teutonic
Powers in the decade preceding the war ; but, in view of that fact,
the palpable absurdity of the attempt to saddle Germany with a
responsibility which was collective.

CHAPTER XI.

Germany's position before the War judged by Frenchmen[1]

WE who live behind the rampart of the sea know but little (save in times of panic) of the fear that besets a State which has no natural frontiers. . . . Germany accomplished a wonderful work in unifying her people (or, rather, Bismarck and his compeers did it for her); but, even so, she has not escaped from the disadvantages of her situation; by land she is easily assailable on three sides. . . . .—*The Political History of Germany. By J. Holland Rose. "Germany in the Nineteenth Century." (University Press, Manchester,* 1915.)

For Germany, the presence of France on one frontier and Russia on the other creates a crisis that is constant and unchanging.—*The naval and military situation of the British Isles. By "An Islander" (London: John Murray,* 1913).

CONVINCING proof has now been given of the absurdity of attributing to Germany the desire of "subjugating Europe" in the face of a military expenditure by Germany's potential foes in Europe, *i.e.*, the Russo-French combination, during the past ten years exceeding hers and her ally, Austria, by more than £150,000,000 sterling. Mr. Lloyd George's speeches show that six years ago, *when the proportionate excess of military expenditure by Germany's potential foes was not so large as it afterwards became,* the British Government was fully alive to the vulnerability of Germany's position and of Germany's fears; and that her largely increased expenditure in recent years was natural. I now propose to deal with some French testimony on that point.

One need not refer to any *post-bellum* statements by German public men to appreciate how substantial and how well founded was the element of *fear*—fear for the national safety, which has weighed upon the rulers of Germany with increasing intensity for the last few years. Surely we, who until last year had never crossed swords with the German race, cannot fail to be impressed by the testimony of military writers belonging to a nation which only forty-

[1] *The Labour Leader,* May 13, 1915.

five years ago was engaged in a life and death struggle with Germany, when we find such writers freely admitting the perilous position in which Germany stood before the war? If *they* could be honest enough to admit the fact immediately before the war, surely it is puerile for us to pretend to ignore it now that the war has come?

One of the most popular military writers in France is Colonel Arthur Boucher. His three books—"France Victorious in the War of To-Morrow," "The Offensive Against Germany," and "Germany in Peril," ran to many editions. The last was published early last year. Observe its title, "Germany in Peril" (*"L'Allemagne en Péril"*). Colonel Boucher is imbued with all the military spirit of his race. But he is no blind fanatic. He is a generous foe. He thinks that Germany should have restored Alsace-Lorraine to France. That, in a French officer, is natural enough. He looks forward to war with Germany on that account; but on that account alone. He is not anxious for war in itself. One gathers that he would infinitely prefer the "restoration" of Alsace-Lorraine without a war. He would like to shake hands with Germany and to see Germany entering a Franco-Russian alliance.

"Forming a group so strong that no country, no coalition, could think of struggling against it, they (the three Powers) could forbid war throughout the world."

He deems it "monstrous" that the three nations should be thinking of war instead of peace. Incidentally, he pays the German Emperor a warm tribute as a peacemaker, which may be read in conjunction with Lord Haldane's declaration and with the contents of the French Yellow Book referred to in the last chapter.

"The German Emperor has given positive proof within recent years of his desire to maintain peace. If a number of his subjects push for war, a still more considerable number bless him as the Sovereign of Peace."[1]

As the title of his book indicates, Colonel Boucher was fully alive—as a Frenchman—to Germany's peril, and

---

[1] *Vide* also this passage in Marcel Sembat (*op. cit.*) :—

"Conditions are sometimes stronger than the wills of men and even of Emperors. Do not let us neglect, that is my advice, that precious element of peace, the Imperial will. If the Emperor William had been differently inspired, we should have had war already, and—let us be just—he has allowed some fine opportunities of laying us out to go by. If, instead of making a speech at Tangier, he had made war, where should we have been?

the conclusions of his book are wholly directed to telling the Germans how foolish they are to retain Alsace-Lorraine, and how their obstinacy—as he puts it—in doing so is their principal source of danger, seeing that France :—

"is unalterably determined to wrest the people of those provinces from the yoke of their invaders and to see the French flag floating once more from the summit of their public buildings."

Here are some notable passages from the book :—

"Germany is threatened to-day on all her frontiers, and finds herself in such a position that she can only ensure her future and face all her foes by seeking first of all to eliminate us from their number by concentrating, from the beginning, all her forces against us."

So much for the "wanton aggression" upon France. One can imagine the contempt with which French military men must read the diatribes in our "patriotic" newspapers.

"To be in a position to resist attacks which menace her on all sides Germany is compelled to develop her military powers to the supreme degree. . . . It was to guard against the Russian danger that Germany made her (Military) law of 1913."

The latter avowal is particularly noteworthy in view of the successful attempt to represent to the British public the German military increases of that year as purely provocative. But I shall have more to say on that score when I come to examine the Russian preparations in 1912-14.

Of course, so long as Germany will not give up Alsace and Lorraine, our French military authority is well content that France should take the utmost advantage of Germany's "Russian peril."

"Thus, we see, when the time comes, and it may come soon, when Slavism desires to make an end of Germanism, the friendship of Russia can serve us if we are fully decided to fulfil all our duties towards her. *Germany does not doubt that France, remaining immutably attached to her treaties, would support her ally with all her strength, choosing, however, the most favourable moment for intervention.*"

Precisely. Colonel Boucher continues :—

"If Russia attacks Germany, France becomes mistress of the situation. It will be sufficient for France to draw her sword at the opportune moment to make it impossible for Germany to defend the provinces she took from us."

Indeed, Colonel Boucher is all for a French military offensive in the event of a Russo-German war. He argues that the French soldier is always at his best in attacking. He thinks it bad strategy to wait for the adversary to attack you; and his second book, "The Offensive Against Germany," is devoted to discussing the ways and means of a resolute French military offensive upon the outbreak of the war. In this respect he is in full agreement with Lieut.-Colonel Grouard, who, in his "The Ultimate War" (published in 1913), envisaging a Franco-German war as the result of the Franco-Russian alliance, strongly pleads for a French offensive upon the outbreak of war :—

. "In these circumstances the defensive would no longer be imposed upon us; on the contrary, we should profit by our numerical superiority[1] and take the offensive as rapidly as possible."

Why do our statesmen and "patriotic" newspapers persist in holding us up to the world as hypocrites, by reiterating that Germany's offensive against France was "wanton"? Do they imagine that such an attitude deceives anyone—outside Britain?

The last quotation from Boucher's book which I will give is this :—

"From whatever aspect Germany's position is studied it will be realised that her future is of the darkest, and that she has placed herself in the most perilous situation. Now of all the factors which contribute towards compromising the destinies of this great Power, the chief factor is certainly the hostility of France. To what might Germany not aspire if she were assured merely of our neutrality?

In the French Ambassador's despatch recording the alleged conversation between the Kaiser,. the King of the Belgians, and General Von Moltke, the French Ambassador reports—at second hand, of course—that "William II. has been brought to think that war with France is inevitable, and that it will have to come to it one day or other." During the conversation the Emperor is described as having "appeared over-wrought and irritable." The frank and outspoken writing of our French military author would seem to indicate other considerations than a desire to "subjugate Europe" for this reported attitude of the Emperor's! Germany could have peace—but only by an act which no one but an

[1] *I.e.*, in the immediate theatre of hostilities.

impulsive Frenchman could imagine to be possible. Otherwise, war—France using Russia for her ends as Russia was using France; the two lambs on one side, the ravening wolf on the other ! Directly Russia was prepared to "make an end of Germanism" the French armies would be in readiness to fall upon Germany's flank "at the most opportune moment." For that moment military and Chauvinist France had been longing for forty years—and preparing. As Lieut.-Colonel Grouard puts it :—

"In no army has greater work been accomplished during the last thirty years than in the French army. Both as regards the improvement of our armament and in studying the best conditions for its usage, daily and incessant progress has been made in every branch of the military art."

That is true, and if the degree of general efficiency has been less than in Germany, it has been due, not to lack of interest or inferior capacity for hard work among French officers, but to the differences of the national temperament; to the superior capacity of German organisation, and to the corruption and intrigues of French political life and their reaction upon the army, which were so startlingly exemplified in the Dreyfus case.

Colonel Boucher's testimony is, of course, especially significant because it is the testimony of a soldier who, writing in the very year of the war, tells us with complete frankness, first that Germany's position in Europe is one of the utmost danger; secondly, that unless Germany will restore Alsace-Lorraine to France, France is fully determined to assist Russia to the uttermost in "making an end of Germanism." What adds to the interest of Colonel Boucher's writings is the honesty with which he recognises the efforts made by the German Emperor to preserve peace and the obvious reluctance with which he himself contemplates a further war with Germany.

A pendant to Colonel Boucher's book is Marcel Sembat's. I call it a pendant for this reason—illogical, I admit—that the two writers are at the poles in political thought and everything else. Sembat's book (it appeared in 1913, I believe, and my copy bears the imprint, "twelfth edition") is a striking illustration of the best side of the French character (that strange medley of contradictions, immortalised by de Toqueville), civic courage. No Englishman, in similar circumstances, would have dared to talk to his countrymen with such directness as did

Sembat to his about Alsace-Lorraine. Instead of tearing
him to pieces, they read his book. However, what I
particularly wish to bring out in connection with Sembat's
volume is the further light it throws upon the position of
Germany just before the war, and upon German
psychology. It is extraordinary that one should be driven
to bring to the notice of British readers the sanity of a
distinguished Frenchman in order to counteract the
insanity of the British newspaper talk of the present day.
For the nonce Sembat imagines himself a German, and
thus describes his sentiments :—

"I experience the sensation of a full national existence
only since the victory of 1870 and the unity of the Empire.
Since then I count for something in the universe, and I
am sheltered. For nothing in the world, you understand;
at no price, will I allow my unity to be touched. Directly
I am told that German unity is threatened I rise, ready to
sacrifice everything. Am I a Socialist, a Catholic, a
Liberal, a Conservative, I am there if anyone threatens
German unity."

Sembat goes on to show how real in the German mind
had become the Russian menace.

"The German obsession of Russia does not correspond
at all with the hostility, born of their defeat, which many
Frenchmen entertain for Germany. It originates from
bitterness of yesterday, and anxiety for to-morrow. . . .
The German has grown up under the overshadowing threat
of a formidable avalanche suspended over his head; an
avalanche always ready to become detached, to roll down
upon him; an avalanche of immense savagery, of barbarous
and brutal multitudes threatening to cover his soil, to
swallow up his civilisation and his society."

Sembat remarks that the Russian of *his* imagination is
the Russian of Tolstoy, Gorki, Turguenieff; not the
autocratic Russia commanding its legions of Asiatic
hordes. But, he adds :—

"If I fail to understand the Russia which haunts
Germany I shall be incapable of understanding the effect
which the Russo-French alliance produces upon the mind
of the Germans."

And he drives home the distinction in its practical
aspects :—

"And, after all, does not the Tsar possess within his
dominions all the barbarians of Turkestan and Central
Asia? Conquered? What nonsense! The day when

European Russians, too Liberal-minded or too Socialistic, cause the Tsar inconvenience, will he hesitate to lead against them his *sotnias* of Cossacks and Turkomans? That day, it will be Asia, the barbarous Orient, which will be at the doors of Europe and on the threshold of Germany. The Franco-Russian Alliance, and the Triple *Entente,* appear, therefore, to the German as a compact between two civilised peoples and barbarism."

Then Sembat goes on to show how the anxiety of the German *people* with regard to Russia is increasing, how it is even outpacing *official* German anxiety; and, with great courage, to show how the contradictory attitude of France must increase that anxiety.

In 1908 Lloyd George, in effect, asked his countrymen —those same countrymen who are now told to believe that Germany is the sole responsible author of this war, undertaken by her "to subjugate Europe," and that the surest proof of it is to be sought in her great military preparations :—

"Can't you understand how reasonable are Germany's fears? If you were placed as Germany is placed, with Russia on one side and France on the other, her enemies in the event of a European war, would not you arm, would not you build?"

And he answered his question himself.

"Of course you would."

Now, looking back at the record of the past ten years we find that Germany armed, and armed heavily, but that the Russo-French combination spent 159 million pounds sterling more upon its armies than Germany and her ally upon theirs'; and we find French authors of repute, writing on the very eve of the war, fully acknowledging, from their respective points of view, the naturalness of Germany's FEARS and the dangers of her position.

We have now cleared the ground for a further examination of the causes of Germany's anxiety in regard to the "Russian menace," which will lead us to glance at the naval expenditure of the Teutonic Powers and of the Russo-French combination.

Meantime, let me reiterate once more that my object is to assist in destroying the legend that Germany was the sole responsible author of this war, undertaken by her to "subjugate Europe." And that my object in assisting to destroy this legend is concern, not for the Prussian Junker, but for the future interests of the British people.

CHAPTER XII.

Secret Diplomacy[1]

When a small number of statesmen, conducting the intercourse of nations in secrecy, have to confess their inability to preserve good relations, it is not an extravagant proposal to suggest that their isolated action should be supplemented and reinforced by the intelligent and well-informed assistance of the peoples themselves.—*Arthur Ponsonby, in "Democracy and Diplomacy" (Methuen and Co., 1916).*

Wars are made by Governments acting under the influence of the governmental theory. And of this fact . . . . no better example could be given than the present war. Before it broke out nobody outside governmental and journalistic circles was expecting it. Nobody desired it. And though, now that it is being waged, all the nations concerned are passionately interested in it, and all believe themselves to be fighting in a righteous cause, yet no ordinary citizens in the days preceding the outbreak would have maintained that there was any good reason for war, and few even knew what the reasons alleged were or might have been. Even now the nations have quite opposite views as to which Government was responsible. We believe it was the German Government; and with equal conviction, Germans believe it was the British. But nobody believes it was the mass of the people in any nation. The nations who are carrying on the war, at the cost of incalculable suffering, would never have made it if the decision had rested with them. That is the one indisputable fact. How can such a fact occur? How is it possible for Governments to drag into war peoples who did not desire war and who have no quarrel with one another? The immediate answer is simple enough. In no country is there any effective control by the peoples over foreign policy. That is clear in the case of the great military Empires. But it is true also of France and of England, where in other respects Government is more or less under popular control. The country has no real choice, for it only gets its information after the decisive action has been taken.—*Mr. G. Lowes Dickinson in "The War and the Way Out" (1914).*

I sometimes ask myself whether in the future it will not be necessary and, indeed, if it would not be a good thing, that the Foreign Secretary should take the House of Commons in the first instance, and his countrymen at large in the second, much more into his confidence than he has done in the past. We have passed in recent years through European crises, the full gravity of which was not realised by our people, if realised at all, until after they had passed into history. I ask myself, can you conduct democratic government on these principles?—*Mr. Austen Chamberlain, February 8, 1914.*

[1] Speech delivered at Devonshire House, Bishopsgate, May 14, 1915.

It seems contrary to the fundamental principles of a Parliamentary Constitution that a nation should be bound by obligations, upon the policy or impolicy of which its representatives have had no power of pronouncing an opinion, since they have been kept in absolute ignorance of their existence.—*Lord Courtney of Penwith, in "The Working Constitution of the United Kingdom and its Outgrowth."* (1901.)

I am disposed to deny entirely that there can be any treaty for which adequate reasons cannot be given to the English people, which the English people ought to make. A great deal of the reticence of diplomacy had, I think history shows, much better be spoken out.—*Walter Bagehot, in "The English Constitution."* (1872.)

"Everyone may remark what a hope animates the eyes of any circle, when it is reported, or even confidentially asserted, that Sir Robert Peel has in his mind privately resolved to go, one day, into that stable of King Augeas which appals human hearts, so rich is it, high-piled with the droppings of two hundred years; and, Hercules-like, to load a thousand night wagons with it, and turn running water into it, and swash and shovel at it, and never leave it till the antique pavement and real basis of the matter show itself clean again! . . . To clean out the dead pedantries, unveracities, indolent somnolent impotencies, and accumulated dung-mountains there, is the beginning of all practical good whatsoever. . . . Political reform, if this be not reformed, is naught and a mere mockery. . . . Nay, there are men now current in political society, men of weight, though also of wit, who have been heard to say, 'That there was but one reform for the Foreign Office—to set a live coal under it,' and with, of course, a fire brigade which could prevent the undue spread of the devouring element into neighbouring houses, let that reform it! In such odour is the Foreign Office, too, if it were not that the public, oppressed and nearly stifled with a mere infinitude of bad odours, neglects this one—in fact, being able nearly always to avoid the street where it is, *escapes* this one, and (except as a passing curse once in the quarter or so) as good as forgets the existence of it."—*Carlyle on the Foreign Office.—"Latter-Day Pamphlets."* (1850.)

WAR is anarchy, and armed peace is anarchy. And the true anarchists of our time are not the crazy individuals who imagine they can reform society by removing the figureheads that strut across its stage. They are the so-called statesmen and leaders of the nations who, for decades past in every land, have directed man's increasing ingenuity in arts and crafts, his inventive genius and his triumph over the forces of nature—to preparations for his own destruction; who have filled the world with the clamour of their insensate boasting whenever some new and still more formidable development in the art of killing has been perfected in their respective countries; who, while prating of their love of peace, have bidden their misguided and unhappy peoples to conspire for the more efficient slaughter of their neighbours by land and sea, beneath the sea and from the skies above; and who appear,

even now, incapable of perceiving that if they make not
haste by a collective effort to arrest and control the
elements they have unchained, they risk dragging down
the civilised world about their ears and of being themselves
overwhelmed in the ruins.

We thrill when we read of the deeds of patient heroism
of our men at the front. But we believe, with an intensity
of conviction that nothing can shake, that they were not
created to be slain and mutilated in the flower of their
youth. We do not rejoice with easy and vicarious pride
as we see them pouring down that valley of misery and
abomination. We long with an immensity of longing to
remove them from it. Meanwhile, we labour to ensure
that the settlement, when it does come, of this war shall
be of such a kind, and that changes of such a character
in the official intercourse between Governments shall follow
this war as will prevent the next and succeeding
generations from being swallowed up in the abyss of
desolation which has been dug for the present generation
by the systems to which the peoples have so long been
fettered.

Now there are two main avenues along which we can
advance for the attainment of the end we have in view.
It is essential that both should be used simultaneously,
and that every track which leads into them should be used
also. For there is no royal road to any reform.

These two main avenues I may call the subjective and
objective : the one—if I may express myself thus
crudely—approachable through internal consciousness, the
other through the consideration of external factors. Upon
some of us will fall naturally the task of attempting to
create something like a thought-revolution on the subject
of war; of attempting to infuse the spiritual forces in our
midst with constructive strength for the deliverance of
mankind from the forces of destruction; of attempting to
inculcate the truth that if war does and can call forth noble
sentiments—as every cataclysm in human affairs is bound
to do—it is a false philosophy which teaches that those
noble sentiments can only be called forth by war, and it is
a mental confusion which can even momentarily regard the
calling forth of such sentiments as compensation for the
odious barbarity of war itself, or for the hypocrisy, the
lying and falsification, the disappearance of all sense of
fairness, generosity, and perspective, the almost incredible
ethical degradation and the moral and spiritual collapse

which accompany a state of war. Upon some of us, I say, will fall naturally that task—the task of appealing to the subjective sense in man. And to none more than the Friends who—as a body—in the midst of the universal *débâcle,* keep the light of the spirit burning brightly, and keep alive within us the Divine figure, that but for them, almost, would be totally eclipsed by the pagan deity which casts its sinister shadow over Christian altars in every belligerent land.

Upon others will devolve the task of endeavouring to concentrate men's minds on those positive factors in the life of States—constitutional, organic, economic—which constitute the propelling causes of war : with a view to their reform or removal. Amongst those causes none is more potent, none more elusive, none more difficult to present in such form as will carry comprehension of its subtle dangers than secret diplomacy.

Men at all times have been the patient slaves of words and phrases. The word "diplomacy" conjures up something mysterious, a sort of official holy of holies, of which the ordinary mortal must speak with bated breath.

And yet all that diplomacy really means, in its practical application, is the way in which the particular department of Government entrusted with the duty of conducting the official relations of the State with other States does its work.

The affairs of a nation, like the affairs of a commercial undertaking, are committed to various departments to look after. In the case of a nation one department of Government pays the national bills—I fear with alacrity if it be question of an increase in armaments, with reluctance if it be question of improving the housing accommodation of the working classes. That by the way. Another deals with local administration, another with education, and so on. Just so the Foreign Department is charged with the regulation of the nation's official intercourse with other nations. Pardon my being so elementary, but, indeed, it is through slurring over this simple fact that a plain issue comes to wear an aspect of mystery and complication.

In discussing "diplomacy" we must begin by grasping the simple fact that what we are really discussing is not an abstruse science, a complicated chess gambit, a Chinese puzzle, or a problem of higher mathematics—although the diplomats would like us to think that it is all this rolled

into one—but the methods and systems of work of the
Foreign Department of this nation and of other nations.

Now, while the management of the Foreign Departments of other nations is necessarily interesting and
important to us, I submit that the management of our own
is infinitely more interesting and more important to us.
Our primary interest and our primary duty is, therefore,
to make ourselves thoroughly acquainted with the manner
in which our own Foreign Department is carried on, what
its composition is, what powers it possesses or has
usurped, what facilities we have for checking and
controlling it.

The Foreign Department of this nation consists of a
Foreign Secretary, who is a member of the Government
of the day—elected on purely domestic issues. His
responsibility is covered by the principle of Cabinet
solidarity, a principle for which there is a good deal to be
said for and against. The Foreign Secretary is assisted
by forty first-class clerks in the Foreign Office and by 120
representatives abroad, consisting of ambassadors,
ministers, councillors, first, second, and third secretaries
and attachés. Of these 161 gentlemen perhaps twelve at
the outside are in a position to exercise a decisive influence
upon the Department's actions. They are the Foreign
Secretary, the Under-Secretaries at the Foreign Office, and
the Ambassadors. We may say, therefore, that the
Foreign Department of this country is managed, and the
foreign relations of this nation are conducted, in all
essential respects by twelve gentlemen.

The next point to consider is this : By whom is the
work of this Department regulated and directed? By
Parliament and the nation? In theory : yes. In practice :
no. Does the nation collaborate in the Department's
work and control its decisions? In practice : not at all.
Has the nation any means of estimating the mental
processes and material facts by which the decisions of the
Department are arrived at? The nation has not. Can the
nation ascertain as a regular course or at a given moment
what the Department is doing, what action it is contemplating, or has adopted, on any particular problem affecting
national interest? Not unless the Department is willing
to impart the information—and it is usually unwilling. Is
the nation consulted upon the arrangements which the
Department concludes with foreign States? No. Is
Parliament enabled to examine and debate the treaties,

conventions, or understandings which the Department has negotiated with Foreign Powers before the Government is committed to their adoption? No. Can the Department commit the nation to treaties, conventions, and understandings with foreign States, involving the potential use of the armed forces of the Crown, without informing the nation, through Parliament, that it has done so? Yes, the Department can and does.

Now consider what this means. The work of the Foreign Department affects the nation more vitally than does the work of the whole of the other departments of the State put together. The Department's proceedings determine the extent of, and the expenditure upon, the armed forces of the Crown. If the Foreign Department has committed the nation, without its knowledge, in liabilities towards foreign Powers, and if the extent of, and the expenditure upon, the armed forces of the Crown do not keep pace with the character of the obligations thus incurred, the nation may suddenly find itself confronted with a position which may lead to irremediable disaster.

The issue with which the Foreign Department deals, in the ultimate resort, is the issue of peace and war; and the issue of peace and war is the issue of national life and death. There is not a home in this country, there is not a family, there is not an individual, man, woman, or child, whose interests, whose life, whose future are not intimately concerned with the character and conduct of our official relations with foreign States—*i.e.*, with the conduct of our Foreign Department. The evolution of our social problems, the improvement in the conditions of masses of our population—these things may be arrested and jeopardised for years by war, and war or peace are largely determined by the conduct of our own Foreign Department. And it is not only the interests of the present generation which are at stake; the future of our children and of our children's children may be profoundly affected by the peculiarities, temperamental and otherwise, the outlook, the mode of thought influencing the positive actions of the dozen gentlemen who control the Foreign Department.

And yet, by some mental aberration, by some vice of national slackness and looseness of thought, this nation, which imagines itself to be living under a democratic constitution, has allowed its Foreign Department to become, in effect, an autocratic institution conducting its operations in silence and in secrecy behind the back of the nation, and utterly contemptuous of public opinion (except when public opinion is too strong for it), which it moulds into a condition of receptivity to its decisions through the columns of an inspired and, I fear, largely unscrupulous popular Press. Moreover, it is a singular fact—to which I venture to draw your special attention—that the last decade, which has witnessed so remarkable a democratic advance in this country, has also witnessed a notable accentuation of autocracy in the management of our Foreign Department.

Many factors have contributed to bring about this state of affairs. On the pretext of removing the functions and the conduct of the Foreign Department from Party controversy, anything in the nature of real Parliamentary discussion on foreign affairs—of such debates on foreign policy as characterised the days of our fathers and grandfathers—has virtually disappeared. The hollowness of the pretext is apparent directly you test it. First, because foreign policy has not, in point of fact, been an issue in our elections for many years past; secondly, because such rare discussions and criticism of foreign policy as has been heard in the House since the present Government took office has come either from members of its own party or from members of the parties associated with its fortunes; thirdly, because the Government in meeting those criticisms has been invariably able to rely upon the uncritical support of the Opposition. The withdrawal of the issues of our foreign policy from so-called party controversy has, therefore, come to be something quite different from what it professes to be. It has come to mean the suppression of Parliamentary discussion of any kind, and the country has been kept more than ever in the dark as to the conduct of its Foreign Department. I doubt if at any period in the last one hundred years the country has been kept so much in the dark as during the last ten.

The natural result has been a decay of the sense of Parliamentary responsibility for, and Parliamentary interest in, foreign policy, and this has had its counterpart in the country. In the course of the last ten years Parliament has been moved to real and fruitful activity only on one particular problem of foreign policy—and that entirely because pressure upon individual members of Parliament from their constituencies was such that it broke down all obstacles and let in a rush of healthy democratic air, not only into the lobbies, but even into the musty, stuffy atmosphere of Downing Street.   On that particular problem the nation became fully informed by agencies operating outside the official world, and the nation resolved that the known and publicly contracted treaty obligations of this country should be adhered to, and that a great wrong, for the existence of which we were partly responsible, should be set right.   The nation determined that Parliament should discuss the Congo question, and in eight years there were seventeen debates upon it in Parliament, more time being devoted to that one question than to any other single problem of foreign policy for fifty years. There is a moral in that episode which we may do well not to lose sight of in the work which lies before us in the future.   There is one other factor which testifies to the utterly undemocratic character of our Foreign Department.   The Department is run exclusively by members of the aristocracy and landed gentry.   It is the last stronghold of aristocracy, monopoly, and privilege in the public service.   How is it that, while the increasing democratisation of the public services has marked the rise of Democracy in this country, the Foreign Department has remained untouched by the process?   It is because British Democracy, in its climb to power, has totally neglected this branch of the public service; has failed to realise how inextricably interwoven is the character, conduct, and inspiration of our foreign policy with the ordinary, everyday life of the nation; has looked upon foreign policy as something occult and outside its ken—and, I may add, has been encouraged to do so, especially of recent years, in all sorts of ways?   British Democracy is paying for that mistake to-day, but, as yet, it has no conception of how heavy the bill will in any case be, or how stupendous it may become.

I referred a moment ago to the fact that there are 120 representatives of the Foreign Office abroad.   And there you have the vice of the whole system.   These 120 gentlemen, who have many virtues and not a few defects—the virtues and the defects of their caste—are not the representatives of the nation in fact, although they are in name. They are the representatives of a Department, and the proceedings of that Department are withheld from the knowledge of the nation and conducted outside the great arteries of the national life.   Until the nation insists that the men it sends abroad ostensibly to represent its interests are selected by merit and competition, and not by nomination and favouritism; that wealth and position shall not be the determining factors in their appointment; that they shall not be chosen exclusively from the aristocracy, but from the best which every class in the community can produce; above all, that the Department which they serve shall work in the light and not in darkness, the national destinies, and the happiness and welfare of every one of us —rich and poor, high and lowly—will remain as they are to-day, at the mercy of a particular Department in the State.

It will be a long fight and a stern one, because just as at one time English monarchs and their political supporters, while conceding to the people the right of making laws, denied to their representatives the right of controlling the administration of those laws, so do there exist among us to-day influences, not, indeed, royal influences, but influences far more powerful, which are resolved to oppose to their utmost capacity any real and effective national control over the Department which determines the national issues of life and death—which they regard as their own special preserve and co-existent with the supreme power they wield over the national destinies.

It will be a long fight and a stern one; and if we do not prepare for it now, lay our plans now, organise now, not only shall we have no voice in the character of the settlement which will close the war, but when the war is over we shall be more helpless than before.

For of this let us be well persuaded :—

"The substitution—to use the words of the Prime Minister—for force, for the class of competing ambitions, for groupings and alliances and a precarious equipoise of a real European partnership, based on the recognition of equal right and established and enforced by the common will."

That substitution will never come about until the peoples have won control over the conduct of their relations with other peoples.

A secret and autocratic diplomacy stands between the peoples and the mutual comprehension of each other's needs. It is the greatest obstacle to the emancipation of the peoples from the shackles of militarism and war. It is the greatest obstacle to the solidarity of the human race. The British people have led the way in many of the reforms which have powerfully contributed to enlarge the boundaries of human freedom. If they have the will they can lead the world in the greatest of all reforms which lies open to human endeavour to-day.

CHAPTER XIII.

An Appeal to President Wilson[1]

THERE have been occasions in the life of peoples when the national soul, bewildered and stricken, has been saved by a single individual possessing in himself the combination of qualities which enabled him to adopt a clear and definite line of conduct, and to give to his fellow-countrymen at the psychological moment just that inspiration and that lead required by the circumstances.

There has never been, until to-day, an occasion when the international soul, labouring in agony, cried out for a man to succour it.

But that situation has now arisen, and in the two hemispheres there is one man, and only one man, who, by his character and through the great position he enjoys, can save the soul of the peoples and of the Governments of Europe.

That man is President Wilson.

. . . .

I write to the sound of the measured tramp of armed men. The confused clamour rising from the streets is shattered by the roll of drums. The martial setting cannot obliterate the haunting melancholy conveyed by the shrill whistling of the fifes. It even permeates the sunshine, and robs it of its balm. For the message of the fifes is the piercing homage to Death. Death is in the very air we breathe, we Europeans. Its outstretched wings beat against the mansion of the rich and the cottage of the lowly. Death on land and on the sea. Death emerging, implacable and sinister, from the bowels of the deep. Death falling, swift and relentless, from the blue vault of heaven. Death in all the hideous and revolting forms with which modern man and modern science have equipped it.

Presently these strong, clean-limbed young fellows, the flower of our people, the hope of our future, who a moment

[1] Written in May, 1915; published in the *New York Tribune*, July 4, 1915.

114

ago swung past to the sound of the fifes, will be burrowing
in the ground like rodents, slaughtering and being
slaughtered; covered with vermin; the festering bodies of
days-dead men at their feet, in front of them, behind them,
huddled in shapeless masses, grotesquely stretching rigid
limbs skyward. The foul smell of burnt and decomposing
flesh will be in their nostrils by day and by night. Flies
in myriads will be settling about them, pumping putridity
into their undressed wounds. They will be foul and mad
with the blood-lust; their bodies repulsive to them; their
nerves shattered by the everlasting roar of the hurtling
shells; their souls blunted and scarred.

Thus, in a hundred cities of Europe to-day. Tramp,
tramp, tramp. The march of death to the sound of the
fife and drum, in the genial sunshine of declining May.
Thus, too, in the far-flung battle lines. Millions of men
who had no quarrel until their rulers invented one, living
like brute-beasts, acting like brute-beasts; fly-blown,
verminous, stinking with uncleansed wounds; physically,
mentally, morally thrown back a thousand years. In the
plains and valleys, on the mountain slopes, multitudes of
corpses, uncovered by the stoppage of the floods and the
melting of the snows, fill the air with the germs of disease.
And that other army grows and grows—the army of the
widows and the orphans; the army of the bereft and
destitute, of the broken-hearted, of those for whom life
henceforth is but a vale of tears.

And still the rulers will not speak.

The war has lasted ten months. It is roughly computed
that three and a half million men—the pick of European
manhood—have been killed outright and as many more
permanently disabled. It cannot be said that any one of
the belligerent States is nearer the accomplishment of the
professed aims of its rulers when they entered the war, as
the outcome of this unprecedented human holocaust and
the colossal wastage of economic resources which has
accompanied it. But of far greater importance is the
question : "What are the various belligerent States fighting
for now? What vital issue to the peoples concerned
could not now be secured by negotiation?"

And that is what no Government will state in explicit
and authoritative terms. No Government will do so, lest,
if it did, its enemies should imagine that the national
interests it supposedly represents would suffer. "The
enemy would conclude that we were weakening" is the

parrot cry in every capital. No Government will assume the responsibility of uttering a word which would permit of the enemy imagining that it is anxious for peace. Yet the rulers of every belligerent State must be anxious for peace in their hearts; if only because they must begin to realise that the edifice of civilisation is tumbling about their ears and that dynasties and castes run a considerable risk of being buried in the ruins.

That there is an intense longing for peace among the peoples—especially among the working classes and the peasantry—cannot be questioned. But 'as the entire machinery at the disposal of the Governments for influencing public opinion is engaged in fomenting national passions to the highest pitch of intensity, by representing the enemy-country as the embodiment of evil and treachery and by crediting the enemy-country with the purpose of utterly destroying its adversaries, the very longing for peace becomes a spur to national fury. Indeed, the Governments recognise the popular desire for peace and cunningly pander to it. A "lasting peace," they cry, "can only be secured by the complete pulverisation of the enemy"—whereas they know full well that that would mean the indefinite prolongation of the war and its renewal at no distant date : for you cannot pulverise a people. Here in England the very recruiting placards with which our cities and towns are plastered almost invariably urge men to join the colours in order to hasten the advent of peace. It is everywhere the same, in one form or another. The admitted desire of the peoples for peace is used to exploit them for prolonging the war. The Governments decline even to hint at the terms upon which they would be mutually prepared to discuss the basis of a possible settlement. And so the slaughter continues on an even vaster scale. Yet, some day, the Governments will have to discuss or perish. Meantime they are blind leaders of the blind; straws upon the elements, they, in their folly, have unchained; incapable of controlling them; knowing not whither they are drifting.

Every belligerent people—except the Italian—believes that it is fighting, and every Government asserts that it is fighting, in self-defence, for national existence, for the right to preserve its own traditions, its own modes of life, its own homesteads. If what the Governments assert be true, then each and all of them are suffering from hallucination; for assuredly it is in the interest of no single people that its adversaries should lose their national existence and be destroyed—since civilised life is built upon foundations of human exchange, and the lack of clients with whom to exchange would spell national bankruptcy. And the truth lies just here. All the belligerent Governments ARE under the spell of an hallucination, the hallucination of fear. The driving force of fear, it was, which made possible this wicked and suicidal struggle. I am not in the majority, with those who maintain that the rulers of Germany deliberately planned this war and are wholly responsible for it. That they have a large measure of responsibility for it is patent. That others share responsibility with them can be gainsaid only by such as have come under the spell of the hallucination. Fear caused this war. Fear is prolonging it. Fear is aggravating its natural bestialities. Fear is making every chemical laboratory into a chamber for the concoction of new and more terrifying modes of human destruction. It may yet evolve some substance capable of destroying an army corps or of firing a city in a few moments. The end might thereby be hastened, it is true.

The fear of the Governments is communicated to the peoples, and millions who are not engaged in killing are employed in manufacturing implements to kill. To such a pass has come our civilisation. The civilian population in every belligerent State is becoming drunken and maddened by fear. For it is the support by the civilian population of its rulers which prolongs the war. It is the civilian population that fears; not the men who fight. They do not fear. Neither do they hate with the same intensity, because, being inured by their occupation to physical bravery, they respect it in their foes. They respect, too, the keen competition in brains behind the firing lines. And respect chases out hatred. Moreover, they know that what the papers print of their adversaries are mostly lies; and that sickens them. Every day some incident occurs, even in the hours of carnage, that helps them to remember that those to whom they are opposed are men like themselves, full of courage and resource as themselves, obeying orders even as they themselves, suffering even as they themselves must suffer. If it rested with them the war would not last long.

From the civilian population this deep, underlying fraternity of suffering and a common discipline is hidden. Fed every day upon the lowest garbage of sensational

(10)

journalism, its passions stimulated by every imaginable device, torn by the cruellest tremors for loved ones in the field and rooted in dull revenge under the stress of bereavement, the civilian population hates with a hatred unknown to most soldiers. And so in blind fear, in blind hate, the peoples stumble forward along the valley of abomination and despair, behind their infatuated and insensate leaders.

No force, it would seem, which either the belligerent peoples or their Governments can evolve will arrest the madness which is destroying civilisation. And yet if it be not arrested disaster beyond the imagination of brain to grasp will overwhelm Europe. That force must come from without, and there is but one man who can wield it—President Wilson.

. . . .

Rash, impertinent, it may appear for a foreigner to write thus of your First Citizen, to raise an unknown voice in hearing of the accumulated cares which weigh so heavily upon the leading representative of a neutral State—upon one who is the living embodiment of your true dignity and your true greatness. Yet in countless European hearts there beats the hope—the pathetic trust—that in him humanity may find its saviour—that there may be granted unto him a message from the Cross. I do but express feebly enough, what multitudes are thinking, hoping, awaiting. Formless, vague is the hope. Nevertheless it is very real. Can shape and substance be given to it?

The belligerent Governments have for decades encouraged man's progress in invention, his triumphs over nature in the direction of man's destruction; and now they have unloosed all the factors of primal savagery armed with these terrible powers. They see the work of decades crumbling before their eyes. They shudder at the ethical degradation; the spiritual collapse which is overwhelming society. They recoil with horror at the abyss of economic ruin, of disease and want, of social tumult which yawns wider at their feet as month follows month, each month a catastrophe in itself.

And yet each fears to be the first to tread the path which leads to the international Council Chamber. Each bases its resolve to go on to the bitter end. Each repudiates every suggestion to state the terms upon which it would consent to discuss. None dare take the initiative.

But if they will not speak to one another, would they severally refuse to lay their views before your President on the understanding that the collective expression of those views should be communicated by the President to them all in a public dispatch? In so doing they would sacrifice none of their "prestige," to which they cling and which each deems would be jeopardised if it opened communication with the others. Did they respond to that invitation, they would not necessarily, thereby, commit themselves to acceptance of the President's ultimate mediation. But it would be a step on that road; or at least a step toward an armistice.

The essential is that the peoples in each belligerent State should be in a position to know what at this moment the Governments are fighting to attain—not in vague, but in precise terms. This they cannot now learn because the Governments will not tell them, save in rhetoric capable of an infinite variety of interpretation. This, through the President's initiative, they might ascertain, and they have suffered and are suffering so greatly, the future outlook for them is so appalling, that it would be incredible if in each belligerent State there were not set up, as the result of that knowledge, currents of opinion sane enough to endorse what was reasonable in the desires of their adversaries, and formidable enough to correct what might be unreasonable in the demands of their own rulers.

For example, despite the clamour of our own Jingo publicists, literary men and politicians—and do not forget on your side that we, too, like you, have such elements among us : that we have our class which wishes for its own ends to "Prussianise" the nation, and that we, too, have our unscrupulous and powerful journalists who constitute the mouthpiece of that class, and who are prepared, even in the midst of this desperate struggle in which we are engaged, to throw mud at any and every Minister of the Crown whom they believe to be opposed to their policy—despite these "Prussians in our midst," were the people of this country to learn through such a *démarche* on the part of your President that Germany was prepared to evacuate Belgium and the North of France as a result of a compromise which would restore her oversea possessions or pave the way for her acquisition by negotiation of similar outlets elsewhere; and if they were to learn that on the strength of assurances such as Sir Edward Grey offered her on July 30—when the tramp of

armed legions was already shaking the plains of Europe—
that the British Government "would endeavour to promote
some arrangement, to which Germany could be a party,
by which she could be assured that no aggressive or hostile
policy would be pursued against her or her allies by France,
Russia, and ourselves (Britain), jointly or separately";
were the British people assured that Germany—on this
basis—was prepared to discuss a cessation of the strife;
were the British people assured of this, I believe there
would arise a popular movement in favour of the conclusion
of peace strong enough to sweep everything before it.

I believe that, because, for the British *people* this was
a war entered upon on behalf of Belgium; because the
inspiration which moved tens of thousands of young
Britishers to offer up their bodies to Moloch, was
indignation at the violation of Belgium and pity for the
wrongs inflicted upon her; and because the alternative to
such a German offer would mean, in any event, the
continued sacrifice of Belgium, the prolongation of the
German grip upon her if the Franco-British armies could
not break the German line, her utter destruction if,
breaking that line, the Franco-British armies contested,
as they needs must, every yard of Belgian soil with a
desperate energy and with annihilating effects for Belgium.
Indeed, were the interests of Belgium alone at stake, every
humane man and woman on both sides of the Atlantic
should ardently wish that her liberation might come by
negotiation, and not at a price which would leave her one
"vast ruin and cemetery combined."

I would even go so far as to express the conviction that
if the British people became aware through the inter-
mediary of President Wilson that Germany were willing
to accept in principle the creation of an International
Council, upon which both the belligerent and the neutral
Powers would be represented, and before which the
Governments would undertake to bring all their disputes
for adjudication, binding themselves to give publicity to
the Council's proceedings and to exercise diplomatic,
economic and in the ultimate restore coercive action in
support of the Council's decisions; a principle which would
automatically involve the gradual disappearance of
militarism and colossal armaments as the dominant
factors in international politics, and, eventually, the
internationalisation of land armaments and armies; the
British people would, if Germany were thus minded, be

brought to reconsider that claim to absolute dominion over the natural highways of the globe which has been hitherto the basis of their foreign policy and the bulwark of their national freedom, but which cannot in itself alone continue to be so, in any event, for long, in view of the development of submarine powers of offence and of airism, the advent of which have—although we perceive it not in the fury of the combat—totally altered the British national and imperial problem.   Moreover, it is self-evident that there can be no internationalisation of land power, if there be none of sea power.

And is it inconceivable that Germany should be so minded? No doubt, if you take the view that Germany cynically planned and executed this war for the purpose of "subjugating Europe," striking when she thought the hour had come; it is inconceivable. But not only will posterity reject that legend; when the mists of passion have cleared, and when things reassume their true perspective, when men of the present generation once again see themselves as they really are, they will wonder how they came to credit it. That legend will perish, just as surely as Germany's crime in her relentless treatment of a small people who had done her no wrong and did but defend what they had a right to defend, will ring down the centuries to the detriment of the German name.

If you do not take that view, but place yourself, as well as a foreigner can with no other sources of information than those accessible to all men, "in the skin of a German," to use the expression employed by Marcel Sembat, the leader of the French Socialists and a member of the French War Cabinet, in the famous treatise "Faites la Paix : sinon faites un Roi," which he addressed to his countrymen a few months before the war, you will discover manifold reasons why Germany should be willing to make peace on some such terms as those indicated. If fear, as I contend, has been at the bottom of the great catastrophe —fear common to all the Powers which plunged into the war last August—an "arrangement," to which Germany would be a party, "by which she could be assured that no aggressive or hostile policy would be pursued against her and her allies" by France, Russia, and Great Britain, jointly or separately, such an arrangement would remove those fears from the future. And if the British Government realised the practical impossibility and, from the point of view of the British national interest, the undesirability of excluding Germany from a place in the sun commensurate with her legitimate requirements, I cannot conceive that a single German possessed of common sense would desire the retention of either Belgium or Northern France, and I do conceive it likely that tens of thousands of Germans, smitten with remorse attendant upon the saner vision ensuing from the advent of peace, would eagerly co-operate in healing the wounds of that unhappy land.

For the rest, Germany's supreme interest is peace, and when you have said all there is to be said of her national faults and of her conduct of the war, the solid fact remains that this powerful nation had for forty and four years kept the peace when war broke out last August. Attention has, of course, been drawn to this many times; but, considered in the light of international reconstruction and Germany's attitude thereto, it is a fact of cardinal importance. No other great Power can boast such a record. With the sole exception of the guerilla campaign with a Hottentot tribe in South-West Africa and sundry skirmishes with primitive tribes in German East Africa, against which we can set a dozen far more comprehensive campaigns of a similar kind, Germany had kept her sword in the scabbard, while her neighbours had been drawing theirs and laying about them with great energy. She had rattled it loudly and offensively often enough, especially when she became nervous at her position in the "balance of power," as the man who is apprehensive of his neighbour's intent puffs out his chest and assumes a fierce expression. But she had not drawn it. She could have drawn it with every chance of success again and again had the desire of her rulers been the "subjugation" of Europe, or even of a part of Europe, in the years when her military strength was incomparably superior to every possible combination against her. She could have drawn it on a Balkan issue when Russia, crippled by her war with Japan, was helpless; she did no more than support her one real ally in Europe in an offence, but a technical one, against the sovereignty of the Porte, whose sovereignty, guaranteed by all the Powers, has been flouted by each in turn with absolute cynicism whenever it suited their interests to flout it. Had she desired to crush France she could have done so in the 'eighties, when the British official world would have been rather pleased than otherwise. She could have done so when, embarrassed by the Boer war, we were incapable of helping France, even had we wished to do so; or, again, when freed from any danger from the Russian side after Mukden. She did not do so. Why? She was proportionately far stronger as a land Power in the 'eighties, the 'nineties, and in the first five years of the present century than in 1914. For just upon half a century Germany had waged no war. Neither had her Austrian ally. The personal influence of their rulers had been exerted time and again, as eminent politicians and writers in the countries of their present foes have borne witness, in the cause of peace. Germany's oversea possessions had been acquired not by wars of conquest, but by treaty arrangements. Her ally had never been attracted by the oversea imperialist mirage. During that period Russian imperialism had waged a sanguinary war with Japan; British imperialism with the Dutch republics which had been absorbed in the British Empire; France had been indulging in wars of conquest against coloured peoples all over the globe, and as a result had annexed an area of territory as large as the United States; Italy had embarked upon two formidable campaigns, the latter of which was the most cynically immoral venture of our time. While her neighbours were fighting, Germany was building up a marvellous industrial edifice, which had everything to lose by war, and a great overseas trade, which was bound to be temporarily ruined by war.

When these facts are borne in mind—and none can gainsay them—when it is considered that even Germany's enormous expenditure upon armaments during the last ten years falls short by hundreds of millions of the expenditure of her potential foes under the European "balance of power" system—that "foul idol," as Bright once called it—and that she has never once put forth her great strength, the presumption is that, judging from her own past conduct, Germany would welcome an honourable peace, and that if this be denied her she will drag down the civilised world with her in her fall. In her position Britishers would do the same.

Were President Wilson able to lay even the first foundations of the future bridge across the gulf of existent Anglo-German enmity the end of this awful tragedy would be in sight. For Anglo-German enmity has become the key of the situation. The Balkan question, and with it the problem of Austro-Russian rivalry, is not insoluble on the basis of a settlement founded upon nationality, of home rule within home rule. We owe the origins of this war not to the insolubility of Austro-Russian contentions, but to the seeds of strife sown by two rival diplomatists—Aerenthal[1] and Iswolski[2]—watered by the subsequent intrigues of Hartwig[3] and von Tschirsky,[4] just as we owe its world-wide extension to the intrigues, ignorances and incompatibilities of temper of half a dozen rulers and diplomats operating in an atmosphere of mutual fears and concealing their manœuvres from the gaze of their peoples, thus giving free rein to the criminal enterprise of a few powerful publicists and an internationalised armament ring. Neither are the problems of Alsace-Lorraine or of Poland insoluble if a solution be sought in the ascertained desires of the peoples of those disputed areas, and not on the basis of military considerations, which have never settled any problem of international politics. The real problem which faces the world to-day is none of these. *Anglo-German enmity is the real problem.*

Neither people can destroy the other, whatever the politicians or the papers say.

Every belligerent Government must make sacrifices for peace; must be compelled to do so by its peoples if it will not of its own accord. But it is at least probable that elements in the ruling classes of all the belligerent countries are looking for a golden bridge. And after all it is the peoples, not the diplomats who blundered them into war or the publicists who hounded them at each others' throats, trading on their fears, that are paying with blood and tears.

Once again, then, the essential is that the Peoples should mutually and severally be in a position to know the nature of the adversary's claim. If the Peoples have the right to make war they also have the right to make peace.

. . . .

It is a great thing to ask of President Wilson that he should endeavour to make himself the medium through which that knowledge can be acquired. But he is the only personal force in this distracted planet to whom we can

[1] Formerly Austrian Foreign Minister.
[2] Formerly Russian Foreign Minister.
[3] Russian Minister at Belgrade.
[4] German Ambassador at Vienna.

turn. Supported by the American people, fortified by the deep humanities which inspire him and by the wide and penetrating grasp of men and things which he possesses —if he could bring himself to make this effort he would be the saviour of the world, and his name would be blessed from generation unto generation.

CHAPTER XIV.

Is Truth or is Fiction the greater National Interest?[1]

I HAVE received a considerable number of letters in connection with this series of writings, and their general tenour convinces me that the latter are serving a useful purpose. One valued correspondent, however, thinks that the ordinary man will conclude that I am seeking "not only to defend Germany, but to defend Germany at the expense of England." I have greater faith in the ordinary man. In my own belief those abstract entities known as "Germany" and "England" have had little or nothing to do with this war. To defend Germany's rulers from the charge of having deliberately brought about this war for the sake of world-dominion and to "subjugate Europe," is not to defend them from their share of responsibility in the catastrophe, or for their methods, and it is not to defend Germany at the expense of England. It is to defend Germany against a charge whose untenability becomes patent when the records and the acts of the other great European Powers, in the matter of war preparations and the waging of wars, and in the matter of a long series of proceedings anterior to the war, are examined. And to do that is not to do anything detrimental to the British national interest. It is to do something which, on the contrary, serves the British national interest. It is to do something which, in all humility one may claim, is calculated to serve the interests of all the peoples of Europe.

For if it can be demonstrated that this charge against Germany is untrue and that Germany had real cause to fear aggression, this war is seen to be the outcome, not of the inherent wickedness of one particular ruler, or group, or nation, but of a system of Statecraft common to

[1] The *Labour Leader,* May 13, 1915.

all Governments, a system of official intercourse between
Governments, in which all the peoples have helplessly
acquiesced and for which all Governments are directly, and
all peoples indirectly, responsible.   And it is only when,
and if, all Governments and all peoples have realised that
the truth lies *here* that these systems can be overthrown
and the conception of a real union between the nations
can evolve. So long as one particular nation is credited
with special and peculiar vices by the others, so long will
the others remain blind to the part played by their own
rulers in producing the situation out of which the war
arose, and *so long will every practical effort at the
re-establishment of public law in Europe be doomed to
death in birth.* We must build a new structure and we
must use new material. *We cannot build a new structure
in Europe without Germany.*   If, therefore, we do not
build upon a foundation of truth, the Europe which
emerges from this war will be even more unstable than
the Europe produced by the Treaty of Vienna a century
ago.   If, therefore, the attempt to make British people
visualise the real position of Germany in the system of
European Statecraft known as the "Balance of Power" as
it existed in the decade preceding the war, involves running
counter to certain current public utterances by individuals
who constitute the British Government for the time being,
or by individual British publicists, that is merely incidental
and unavoidable, and is not pursued as an end in itself
by the writer.

    And now to return to the main purport of these
articles. For some years previous to the war, Germany's
chief cause of apprehension lay in the growing ascendency
in Russia of just those very forces, Jingoism (Pan-Slavism)
and Militarism, which we are asked to regard as peculiar
to Germany herself. The recent growth of these forces in
Russia had been principally attributable to three main
factors : the shaky position of the governing autocracy,
driven to seek popularity among the noisy and Jingo
elements in Russian society, in order to stem the rising
tide of social discontent and democratic aspirations; the
restlessness of the fighting services, smarting under the
blow to their prestige inflicted by the war with Japan; the
diplomatic defeat sustained by Russia in the quarrel with
Austria over the annexation of Bosnia and Herzegovina
in 1908-9, which diplomatic defeat had been finally
consummated by Germany's uncompromising support of

her ally on that occasion. These factors in combination
had given an immense impetus to the reactionary elements
in Russia. The fears engendered thereby in Germany were
shared equally by the mass of the people—it is essential
to bear this clearly in mind—and by the official classes,
and under cover of this fear the reactionary elements in
Germany acquired additional influence, and the General
Staff additional arrogance and power. The more tense
became the situation, the more did the German people in
the mass forget their domestic grievances against the
harsh officialdom   and   the   undemocratic   tendencies
characteristic of the dominant partner in the Empire—
Prussia; the more did they rally round the organising
genius of Prussia as the bulwark of their national liberties
and the symbol of their national unity.

The storm clouds on Germany's eastern frontiers
loomed the heavier owing to the attitude of France, the
foreign policy of whose rulers had become notoriously
subservient to the Russian autocracy, and where a
recrudescence of the Chauvinist military spirit among the
rising middle-class generation had been specially marked
—as impartial Frenchmen admit and well-informed
Frenchmen know—since the Morocco quarrel had revealed
a disposition on the part of official Britain to give to the
entente with France the complexion of a virtual offensive
and defensive alliance. Add to this the strained relations
with Britain; the naval rivalry; the determination of official
Britain to look upon the growth of the German navy as
a cause of offence in itself; the boastings of official
Germany about the "trident"; the boastings of official
Britain when the Dreadnought era was ushered in; the
incessant public bickerings of rival Navy Leagues and of
the incendiary Press on both sides—and the genuineness
of Germany's fears can only be denied by those who insist
upon shutting their eyes and closing their ears to the
truth. Germany had substantially contributed to creating
the situation giving rise to her own fears and the fears of
all   Europe.   But   other   Powers   had   substantially
contributed, too. To attempt to strike a balance of
responsibility would be futile. It is sufficient to insist that
Germany feared; that she had good reasons to fear; that
the reasonableness of her fears was admitted by our public
men and by French public men and writers of repute—even
military writers—and that to sweep all this aside on the
pretext that Germany suddenly plunged Europe into war

of diabolical set purpose and for purely selfish aims, is a perversion of the facts of which history offers few parallels, and which cannot in the end survive, but which will, if we persist in being slaves to it, lead this nation stumbling along an interminable vista of woe into an unfathomable pit of disaster.

Before dealing more specifically with the causes, other than those furnished in the statistical and other data touched upon in these articles, why the situation in Russia should have been a matter of increasing uneasiness in Germany, there is one point which it is necessary to touch upon, for none is more misunderstood. Comprehension of Germany's true position in Europe before the war is impossible unless we fix firmly in our minds that a violent disruption of the Austro-Hungarian monarchy represented for Germany just one of those few really vital dangers which—given the existing division of Europe into groups —a nation cannot afford to run. From the moment that Bismarck's long and successful policy of maintaining friendly relations with Russia became seriously impaired (the cooling process began in his lifetime and dates from Russia's disappointment at the result of the Berlin Congress) the preservation of the Dual Monarchy became for Germany synonymous with her own preservation. The consummation of the Russo-French alliance, which was the consequence of the Russo-German breach, bound up Germany's fortunes with those of the Dual Monarchy absolutely. Thenceforth Austria could not be imperilled without Germany being imperilled. A stricken Austro-Hungary meant a Germany completely isolated in Europe, for to Italy's notorious political fickleness had been added, from the practical point of view, her military weakening through the bad and mad Tripoli adventure. A glance at the map will convey a clearer appreciation of this elementary verity than reams of disquisition. Hence the internal and external concerns of the Dual Monarchy were of capital import to Germany, and Germany's intervention in Austria's favour over the Bosnian crisis of 1908-9, directly Russia's attitude became openly threatening, was natural and inevitable—however brutal and crude in its manifestation.

To assume, as is now currently assumed, that Germany had become the virtual dictator of Austro-Hungarian policy, is not warranted by the facts as publicly accessible. On the contrary, the presumption would seem to be that

the very obligation under which Germany found herself
tc support the Dual Monarchy compelled her to defend
her ally's policy regardless of its wisdom.   That a self-
villed and dominating personality like Count Tisza, the
Hungarian Premier, who has played so conspicuous a part
ir the policy of the Dual Monarchy, would submit to a
Potsdam dictatorship, is absurd on the face of it.   Indeed,
the notion of a meek and placid Austria-Hungary, clay in
tht hands of the potters at the Wilhelmstrasse, argues a
complete   ignorance   of   the   relative   situations   and
relationships of the Teutonic Powers, and of the character
of their respective governing classes.   (A perusal of the
Austrian   Red   Book   in   the   second   edition   of   Price's
invaluable "Diplomatic History of the War," and of the
interesting volume on the Balkans recently issued by the
Buxton Brothers, should correct the impression.)   It has
only taken root here owing to the clumsy and, so to speak,
post-prandial attempt to ignore and set aside, and even
to suppress, the sudden general mobilisation of all the
Russian armies in the very midst of the resumed Austro-
Russian discussions in the last days of July, which swept
Berlin off its feet.   The well-informed writer in *The Round
Table* for September last is much nearer the truth when
he says that Germany had "in a sense lost control over
her ally," and when he speaks of the German Emperor
having become in a measure "the catspaw of Viennese
intrigue."   The fact is that Germany had axiomatically to
pay the piper for her ally's mistakes and for those incessant
fluctuations in her policy which, as in Russia, characterised
the rise and fall of this or that set of influences—male and
female—struggling for mastery at the Viennese Court.
Nationally speaking, Germany's position in the balance
impelled her to support the one ally left to her in Europe,
whatever **the** circumstances, and whether that ally was
right or wrong, wise or unwise.

Indeed,   the   more   contemporary   documents   are
examined, the more untenable becomes the argument that
Austro-Hungarian policy has been subservient to German
direction, and that, in the crisis of 1914, the Kaiser had
onlv to lift his little finger to ensure obedience to his wishes
.at Vienna.   If, for example, that very valuable volume,
"The Inner History of the Balkan War," written by a
British officer with peculiar qualifications for the task, be
studied,[1] it cannot but induce the conviction that Germany

[1] By Lieutenant-Colonel Reginald Rankin.   (Constable.)

had the very greatest difficulty in preventing her ally from kicking over the traces at that time—1912-13. As the author himself puts it, Germany did her best to "hold back Austria from a policy of violence." That Austrian statesmen, exasperated by the support given to Serbia, at least by unofficial Russia, sounded both Germany and Italy with a view to securing their support of an Austrian declaration of war against Serbia, we know from the statement made by Signor Giolitti, on August 9, 1913. Curiously enough, that statement has been interpreted as a further proof of German plotting. In point of fact, it is proof that the Austrian proposal was turned down by Germany and Italy together. Signor Giolitti says distinctly that Italy *joined with the German Government* to restrain Austria.

Baron Beyens, then Belgian Minister at Berlin, now Belgian Minister for Foreign Affairs, has also recorded in his recent book that the :—

"diplomacy of the Wilhelmstrasse (*i.e.,* Berlin) applied itself, above all, to calm the exasperation and the desire for intervention at the Ballplatz (*i.e.,* Vienna)."[1]

More significant still is Baron Beyens' despatch to his Government on November 30, 1912, in connection with the visit of the Archduke Ferdinand (heir to the Austrian throne, afterwards murdered at Sarajevo). The Belgian diplomatist writes :—

"The Archduke stated at Berlin that the Austro-Hungarian monarchy had come to an end of the concessions it could make to its neighbour. The Emperor and his councillors showered upon him, none the less, counsels of moderation which William II., when conducting his guest to the railway station, summarised in the homely language which is habitual to him, and in these expressive words : 'Above all, no foolishness !' There is no doubt that the Emperor, the Chancellor, and the Foreign Secretary are passionately pacific."[2]

But the very success achieved by German diplomacy in 1912-13 militated against similar success in 1914. Counsels of moderation had averted a European war then ; but they

[1] "L'allemagne avant la guerre."
[2] The Belgian Diplomatic Despatches : *op cit.*

had been followed by an intensification of Austro-Serbian friction, by an even graver strain ·in Austro-Russian relations, and in the assassination of Austria's heir and the Emperor's personal friend, the Archduke. Moreover, the whole situation in Europe had worsened. I am not arguing that Germany put all the pressure she might have placed upon Austria in July, 1914. I do not know, and I do not suppose there is a solitary human being in this country who does. But what I do say is that in the very nature of the case, it was no longer possible for the German Government to assume so emphatic an attitude in 1914 as it did in 1912 and 1913; and what I do say is that I have, for my part, seen not one scintilla of documentary evidence showing that Germany instigated the Dual Monarchy to take up an intransigent position. The attitude of the German Government appears to have been that Austria was justified in coercing Serbia; and that Russia would not go to extreme lengths in supporting Serbia against Austria. When later on the German Government perceived that Russia did intend to go to all lengths in support of Serbia the German Government went as far as it dared go without risking to rupture the alliance, in restraining Austria. I am not discussing the rights and wrongs of the three Governments concerned. I am merely endeavouring to disentangle the truth from the coating of prejudice and passion under which, for British understanding, it has been concealed. Let us imagine a broadly parallel case.

Supposing that, after years of friction—friction due to faults on both sides—between the Indian Government and Afghanistan, the Prince of Wales had been murdered in the streets of an Indian town close to the Afghan border, and supposing the Indian Government, convinced, rightly or wrongly, that Afghan agents had inspired the crime; British public opinion, it may safely be asserted, would have been as convulsed with rage as was public opinion in Austria-Hungary after Sarajevo. Would the British Government have gone to a Conference under such circumstances? And would an ally of Great Britain, dependent upon Great Britain for its own security, have risked a rupture with Great Britain by insisting that Great Britain should do so, especially when the Power, believed by both Great Britain and her ally to be morally responsible for Afghanistan's general attitude, interfered menacingly on Afghanistan's behalf, on the ground that the inhabitants of Afghanistan were of the same race as its own subjects?

Wherever in this volume I am concerned with the attempt to make my countrymen take a juster view, in the interests of a permanent peace, of German actions and of German policy, I have scrupulously refrained from reinforcing my arguments by citing German authorities. I have invariably relied upon the statements of our own authorities, or of authorities in allied and friendly countries. But in this particular matter of Germany's support to Austria in her quarrel with Serbia after the murder of the Archduke, it seems to me impossible to leave uncited the despatch of the German Chancellor to the German Ambassador at Vienna on July 30, 1914. This despatch, or what purported to be a copy of it, was shown by the German Foreign Secretary to Mr. Crozier Long, the correspondent of the *Westminster Gazette,* and appeared in that paper on August 1. Its genuineness has since been vouched for by the German Chancellor in the course of one of his speeches in the Reichstag. It reads as under : the italics are mine :—

"The report of Count Pourtalès (German Ambassador at Petrograd) does not harmonise with the account which your Excellency has given of the attitude of the Austro-Hungarian Government. Apparently there is a misunderstanding, which I beg you to clear up. We cannot expect Austria-Hungary to negotiate with Serbia, with which she is in a state of war. The refusal, however, to exchange views with St. Petersburg would be a grave mistake. We are, indeed, ready to fulfil our duty. *As an Ally we must, however, refuse to be drawn into a world conflagration through Austria-Hungary not respecting our advice. Your Excellency will express this to Count Berchtold with all emphasis and great seriousness."*

An ally in Germany's position, confronted with powerful potential foes on east and west, could hardly have gone further.

July 30 was the crucial day in the whole maze of confused negotiations which the Russian *general* mobilisation order (*vide* Chapter III. and foot-note thereto) smashed for good and all. This can be seen at a glance. On that day the German Ambassador—in response to a suggestion made to him the previous day by Sir Edward Grey, and communicated by him to Berlin—informed Sir

E. Grey that the German Government would endeavour to influence the Austrian Government not to continue its operations in Serbia after the occupation of Belgrade and its vicinity. (White Book No. 103.) Thereupon the German Ambassador telegraphed to Berlin that Sir E. Grey would make representations to Russia in that sense, and the German Government communicated with Vienna. Sir E. Grey wired Petrograd, expressing the earnest hope that if this solution were obtainable it might be possible to suspend military preparations on all sides. The situation thus appeared to admit of a compromise at the last moment, although the fact that Russia had partially mobilised—*i.e.,* had mobilised against Austria—was an awkward obstacle.

King George showed himself no less eager to bring his royal influence to bear upon this hopeful suggestion. He also wired—to Prince Henry—in part as follows : the italics are mine :—

"My Government is doing all that is possible to induce Russia and France *to stop their military preparations, if Austria would content herself with occupying Belgrade and the adjacent portions of Serbian territory as a pledge for the conclusion of an agreement satisfying her claims, while at the same time other countries stop their preparations for war.* I count upon the great influence of the Emperor to obtain from Austria the acceptance of this proposal. He will thereby prove that Germany and England are working together for the prevention of an international calamity. Please assure William that I am doing all that lies in my power to do in order to preserve the peace of Europe."

All this, let it be repeated, took place on the morning and afternoon of July 30, *and we know now that Austria accepted the proposal King George and the British Government were so anxious she should accept.* (No. 50 Austrian Red Book.)

But what was Russia's reply to the proposal? Her reply was to issue a midnight general mobilisation order —*i.e,* mobilisation against Germany—for she had already mobilised against Austria.

If her Government had waited only twenty-four hours, the situation was saved, for, in the nature of things, Austria's reply to the proposal could not have become known until the 31st.

But, as Mr. Phillips Price remarks, the military party at Petrograd triumphed on the 30th, and "cut the ground from under the feet of the diplomats, by the precipitate issuing of mobilisation orders," just as the military party triumphed at Berlin on the 31st when Russia's action became known.

Again, on the 31st, a delay of twenty-four hours might have saved Europe—and this time the blame was Germany's.

Russia's fatal order for a general mobilisation at midnight on the 30th, without even waiting for the Austrian reply to the Anglo-German proposals—which reply, as we have seen, was an acceptance—at once enlarged the area of immediate tension. It produced a genuine popular panic in Berlin—all the British and American correspondents who were in Berlin at the time are agreed on that. That the Russian general mobilisation did not necessarily mean that Russia had decided upon war, could not weigh against the sentiment provoked by the fact that the order had gone forth for a general mobilisation of all the Russian armies. It was that *fact,* and the deadly fears conjured up by past memories, which governed the entire situation. It was that *fact* which gave the military party in Berlin its chance. At 2 p.m. on the 31st "Kreigzustand," the military state preceding mobilisation, was proclaimed in Berlin. At midnight Berlin issued its fatal summons to Petrograd to demobilise in twelve hours. At 5.30 on August 1 the general German mobilisation was announced. At 7 p.m. the declaration of war on Russia was handed in.

. . . .

Rash and precipitate as it was, the action of Germany had not been as rash and precipitate as the British Ambassador to Russia had warned the Russian Government it would be, as early as July 25, in the event of Russian mobilisation. On July 25 Sir George Buchanan told the Russian Foreign Minister that in his opinion : "If Russia mobilises Germany would not be content with mere mobilisation or give Russia time to carry our hers, *but would probably declare war at once."* (White Book No. 17.)

As a matter of fact, the actual declaration of war was issued some thirty hours after the general Russian mobilisation became known in Berlin.

Why did the British Ambassador to Russia believe that a general Russian mobilisation would lead to an immediate German declaration of war?

It could only have been because he thought that the effect of such action on the part of the Russian Government would enable the German Military Staff to present to the German Government such an overwhelming case, based upon military exigencies, as the German Government would be incapable of resisting without imperilling its position and endangering the throne.

We have been taught to believe that the case of military exigency which the German military authorities did, in fact, present, was purely mythical.

But however we may condemn the German ultimatum to Russia, following the Russian general mobilisation, events which none can gainsay have proved that there was nothing mythical in the German military case. So advanced were the Russian preparations on the German frontier that on August 3 the Russians attacked Memel; on August 5 the Russian covering troops crossed the German frontier near Lyck; on August 7 Rennenkampf's main army crossed the German frontier at Suwalki, while Samsonov, one of the most popular generals in the Russian army, with five army corps, was advancing from Mlawa. On the 20th the Germans were routed at Gumbinnen after a four days' battle; on the 21st they were again heavily defeated between Frankenau and Orlau. By the 25th the whole of East Prussia up to the Vistula was in Russian occupation.

The alleged results of that occupation were given in the Manifesto[1] issued last summer by the National Executive of the German Social Democratic Party, which, before the war, represented five million German voters, as follows :—

"Four hundred thousand people in East Prussia have been forced to flee as refugees; 1,620 civilians have been murdered, and 433 wounded; 5,410 male civilians (amongst them helpless old men), 2,587 women, and 2,719 children have been removed to Russia; 24 towns, 572 villages, and 236 farms, totalling 36,553 buildings, have been entirely or partly destroyed, and about 200,000 homes have been entirely or partly plundered and devastated."

[1] Published in the *Labour Leader* and some other papers, July 8, 1915.

It is, of course, impossible to check or verify these detailed statements. They may be exaggerated. All one can say is that the history of all wars records broadly similar results following in the wake of an invading army. Belgium, Poland, Galicia, and East Prussia are not exceptions to the melancholy rule.

But the military occurrences in East Prussia which followed so rapidly the outbreak of war lend additional significance to the warning of the British Ambassador on July 25, and place the midnight order for the general mobilisation of the Russian armies in its true perspective among the events which have brought Europe to its present pass.

CHAPTER XV.

Russia's Military Preparations[1]

EVERYBODY knows that hitherto our war plans always bore a defensive character, but even foreign countries are well aware that the idea of defensive tactics has now been abandoned, and that the Russian Army will be active. . . . Russian public opinion has a great interest in knowing that our country is ready for all eventualities. *Si vis pacem para bellum.* Russia, in complete union with her Supreme Leader, wants peace, but she is ready.—*"Bourse Gazette of Petrograd," March 13, 1914, in the course of an article commonly attributed to General Sukhomlinoff, then Russian Minister of War.*

The hatred towards Austria, which has accumulated in the heart of the Russian nation, has long been seeking an outlet in war, and is only being kept back within the limits of the last degree of patience by the Russian Government with the utmost difficulty. But there is an end to all things. A moment may arrive when even the Russian Government will prove impotent to fight down the hatred towards Austria-Hungary, which fills the Russian people, and then the crossing of the Austrian frontier by the Russian Army will become an unavoidable decision.—*The "Golos Moskvy," March 12, 1914—one of the most influential of Russian Conservative papers.*

The extension southwards is for Russia an historical, political, and economic necessity, and the foreign Power which stands in the way to this expansion is *eo ipso* an enemy Power. . . . I say quite briefly and precisely : everywhere at every spot throughout the Levant, Russia has been, and is still, meeting, in trying to solve her most vital problem, the Eastern question, the resistance of Germany, acting either alone or as the Ally of Austria. Hence it has become quite clear to the Russians that if everything remains as it is, the road to Constantinople will have to be carried through Berlin. Even Vienna is but of secondary moment.—*Dr. Paul Mitrofanoff—a Russian professor well known in political circles—in the "Preussische jahrbucher," May, 1914.*

In an article published only two months before the war, the military correspondent of *The Times* explained how well founded were the German fears of Russian aggression. He explained that Russia had raised her peace effectives by 150,000 men, "making a total peace strength of about 1,700,000, or approximately double that of Germany." He added : "The Russian reply to Germany is next door to a mobilization in time of peace, and it quite accounts for the embittered outburst of the *Cologne Gazette*, and for the German pot calling the Russian kettle black. . . . There are signs that Russia has done with defensive strategy. . . . The increased number of guns in the Russian Army Corps, the growing efficiency of the Army, and the improvements made or planned in strategic railways

[1] The *Labour Leader*, June 24, 1915.

138

are, again, matters which cannot be left out of account. These things are well calculated to make the Germans anxious."—*Times*, *June 3, 1914.*

For Englishmen, this war is primarily a struggle between Germany and France. For the Germans it is emphatically a Russo-German war. . . . The politics which made the war and the sentiment that supported it had reference exclusively to Russia. . . . It is for us in this country of the first importance to follow the direction of German thought. . . . It is not merely a tie of sentiment or kinship which unites Germany to Austria. Austria is the flying buttress of her own Imperial fabric. Cut the buttress and the fabric itself will fall.—*Mr. H. N. Brailsford in the "Contemporary Review," September, 1914.*

INTO the merits and demerits of the Austro-Russian quarrel I do not propose to enter. The origin of the dispute lay in the personal rivalries and mutual trickeries of the Austrian and Russian Foreign Offices which culminated in the formal act of annexation by Austria (under Aerenthal) of Bosnia and Herzegovina, without the compensating advantage of an agitation in Russia's favour, backed by Austria, for the reopening of the Dardanelles problem, for which the Russian Foreign Office had been prepared to acquiesce in Austria's technical breach of the Berlin Treaty. I say "technical," because Austria had been in occupation of Bosnia and Herzegovina for thirty years, and the sovereignty of the Porte in those old Turkish provinces had become even more nominal than, for instance, in Egypt. A community of interests was thenceforth established between Russian diplomacy and Serbia. Serbia had grievances against Austria apart from the Bosnian annexation, but her *essential case* was —we are prone to forget it— that of a small kingdom desirous of becoming a large one at the expense of the territory of a powerful neighbour; an ambition which, in analogous cases, has been represented to the wider public as respectable or as disreputable according to the interests furthered or hindered by such ambition. In lending her occult influence to the Serbian propaganda aiming at the dismemberment of the Austro-Hungarian State—its avowed purpose—and in carrying out to the same end elaborate intrigues in Galicia, as to which I recommend a perusal of Stepankowsky's pamphlet[1] (it has the great

¹ "The Russian Plot to Seize Galicia" (Henry James Hall and Co., 25 South Molton Street, London. Price, 6d.). As to Russia's treatment of Poles and Ruthenians alike in the portions of Galicia which she has occupied since the war, I suggest a reference to the pamphlet entitled "The Resurrection of Poland" (Paris: 71 Rue de Rennes. Price, 6d.).

merit of having been published a few months before the war), Russian Imperialism may be regarded as justified by way of reprisals for the Bosnian affair, or it may not. That must be a matter of opinion. The fact remains that the future of the Dual Monarchy was unquestionably involved by these actions of the Russian Government and its agents, avowed or unavowed, and, such being the case, Germany's position in the "Balance" became vitally affected, as already explained.

There was, however, a peace party at Potsdam and at Petrograd. At the end of 1910 a meeting had been arranged between the Kaiser and the Tsar, and the outcome of it was an agreement settling the vexed Bagdad railway question, so far as Russia and Germany were concerned. With that one specific cause of Russo-German difference removed, it might have been thought that the way was clear for an eventual Russo-Austrian accommodation through German auspices. But the bitterness of the Russo-Austrian quarrel—I repeat, an affair, in the main, of personalities moving like sinister shadows behind the screen of international politics—did not lessen. It became more intense. The formation of a Balkan alliance under Russian *ægis* occasioned much alarm in Vienna and disquietude in Berlin. The Serbian propaganda against the Dual Monarchy became even more virulent. The German military mission to Turkey—not the first, and an Englishman was in command of the Turkish fleet—caused a furious outcry in the Pan-Slavist Press of Russia. A campaign of invective raged in the Russian, Austrian, and German Press. These years, 1911-12, were booming ones for the international "death providers"; the vultures gathered together, visualising death and decomposition from afar.

And now, pursuing our investigations into the cause of German fears, let us glance at the war preparations of her mighty neighbour, the Colossus which haunted the imagination of our own governing classes for fifty years, although *our* homesteads and *our* civilisation were far removed from the shadow of its presence, while Germany lived beneath it. And my readers, as they peruse the story, will be careful, I trust, to repeat to themselves : "We are told that Germany alone made preparations for war; that Germany's attitude was alone provocative; that Germany alone planned and schemed; that Germany alone, and deliberately, set out to fling Europe into the maëlstrom of war, with the fixed intention of 'subjugating' her neighbours; that German 'militarism' is a disease peculiar to Germany; that Germany is and has always been the ravening wolf in the sheep-pen of European harmony and sweet reasonableness.''

With the opening of 1913 there came an immense increase in the already notable recrudescence of Russian military activity, which *The Times* and other Tory newspapers have been good enough to record for us, and to record with an appearance of glee, eloquent of their own desires. Synchronising with these symptoms across her borders, Germany became more and more alarmed and disturbed. Writing as far back as 1911, the famous "Military Correspondent" of *The Times* remarked :—

"The possibility of a war on two fronts is the nightmare of German strategists and, considering the pace at which Russia has been building up her field armies since 1905, *the nightmare is not likely to be soon conjured away.''*

The underlying note of satisfaction is interesting and characteristic. I have already dealt with this "building up" as expressed in £ s. d. Its significance is not fully translatable by merely quoting figures of expenditure. I propose to confine myself largely to *The Times*. In the Russian supplement (March 28) an article, entitled "The Russian Army : The New National Spirit,'' by Lieut.-Colonel Arivenko, was given much prominence. In it we were told that :—

"Not only foreign, but even Russian opinion, has but a vague idea of the profound changes that have taken place in the Russian Army since the war of 1904-5.''

These changes were enumerated. In 1905, service reduced from four to two and three-quarter years, securing an increase of 200,000 reservists; 1907, "Reserve units" transformed; 1907-9, military schools amended and enlarged, corps of time-expired non-commissioned officers created (20,000); 1910, new equipment with heavy guns and new transport, wireless stations, automobiles, aeroplanes, etc. Arivenko assured us that Russia was pacific, but it would be a mistake to suppose that this tendency argued an "unpreparedness for war." The "blending of the new and the old" had given the Russian Army "a strength perhaps greater than it ever had before" : "in a possible future conflict it may be hoped that we shall not see a repetition of the reverses of 1904-5." A special ukase maintained on a war footing the mobilisation of half the Russian Army on the Austrian frontier, set up in 1912. Another confirmed the Compulsory Service Amendment Act of 1912, providing that all persons born in the last quarter of 1892 should join the colours in 1913 instead of 1914.—(*The Times*, April 11.) *The Times* "Military Correspondent" states as a "rumour" (August 22) that the Army is to be raised to 41 army corps; the artillery is being increased :

"New formations *in the West* seem destined to strengthen the covering troops at least, *if not to advance the line of concentration of the main armies,* and there is talk of seven new cavalry regiments, of improved cadres for the reserves, and of a transformation of the strategic railway system."

These measures are given in greater detail in the Russian Red Book, to wit : three new army corps, a division of sharpshooters, and two divisions of infantry—to be quartered in the *Western provinces;* the artillery to be increased to 15,000 guns; the regular cavalry to be strengthened by the addition of a cavalry division to each army corps; the entire system governing the reserves to be modified in order to make them "a much more powerful, numerous, and serviceable unit." The St. Petersburg correspondent states (*The Times*, September 10) :—

"The degree to which the war strength of the Russian Army will be affected by the changes now coming into force is not known, but competent observers who put the peace footing at 1,400,000 are inclined to name 3,500,000 men as the greatest possible war strength. That Russia has unlimited reserves of untrained men capable of creating a still vaster army if necessary is, of course, beyond doubt. . . . . *By general consent the Russian Army* has never been in better condition. It is well clothed, well fed, and while the evidence as to the state of its artillery is inconclusive, its musketry training has been greatly improved."

Meantime the military relations between Russia and France were close and continuous. The Grand Duke Nicholas, who had attended the French manœuvres in 1912, telegraphed to General Joffre to represent the French Army at the Russian manœuvres (*The Times*, June 17).

Alluding to these intimate relations, *The Times* St. Petersburg correspondent remarks (September 10) :—

"It is also clear that, although for many years past Staff visits have been interchanged, at no period has there been such close co-operation on military matters between the two countries or has each army watched so closely the development of the other as at present."

It was—as sundry revelations in the French newspapers subsequently established—owing to Russian pressure during M. Poincaré's visit to Petrograd in August, 1912, that the Three Years' Law for the French Army had been decided upon in principle.([1]) Of course, all these Russian and French preparations have been represented here as the result of German action. The quotation in Chapter XI. from Colonel Boucher's book disposes of the fiction. But the real point is—and this has been my central argument—that preparations for war were being carried on by both rival groups, and not by Germany alone. In his speech in the Reichstag on April 8, 1913, introducing the new Army Estimates, the German Chancellor remarked :—

"Germany was like no other country . . . wedged in between the Slav world and the French."

Much what Mr. Lloyd George had been impressing upon a British audience five years before. He continued :—

"Germany could never compete with Russia, whose Emperor could always call out more men than Germany. In any war Germany would stake her confidence upon the courage and the spirit of the people, but it was necessary to give figures to show what extraordinary military efforts Germany's neighbours were making. In Russia there was a most marvellous economic development of the giant Empire, with its inexhaustible natural resources, and an Army reorganisation such as Russia had never known, as regarded the excellence of the material, the organisation, and the speed of conversion from peace to war strength."

That was symptomatic of German feeling.

A necessarily brief reference to accessible information in 1913 would be incomplete without recalling Colonel

[1] *Vide* Chapter XVI.

Seely's reply to Mr. Hunt's question in the House on
June 5. Mr. Hunt asked :—

"What additions had been made during the last two
years to the peace strength of the armies of Russia,
Austria-Hungary, Germany, and France. . . . ?

The reply was as follows :—

RUSSIA.

Additions made	75,000
Present Peace Establishment ...	1,284,000
Future : not yet ascertained.	

FRANCE.

Additions proposed	183,715
Future Peace Establishment ...	741,572

GERMANY.

Additions made	38,373
Additions proposed	136,000
Future Peace Establishment ...	821,964

AUSTRO-HUNGARY.

Additions made	58,505
Present Peace Establishment ...	473,643
Future : not yet ascertained.	

The figures, as will be seen, are incomplete, but their
very incompleteness adds eloquence to the totals. Even
on the strength of these incomplete figures, and taking
the Russian and Austrian "present" peace establishments
as the basis of reckoning, we see an enormous numerical
preponderance of units in favour of the Franco-Russian
combination as against the Teutonic Powers; in other
words, we get the same result as when applying the test
of military expenditure. Thus :—

FRANCO-RUSSIAN COMBINATION : 2,025,572.

TEUTONIC POWERS : 1,295,607.

The fatal year 1914 began with an intensification, if
possible, of the Russian preparations, accompanied by
much less reticence in the Russian Press. In March
Russia answered the question which Colonel Seely had
been unable to do the previous June (see above), as to her
"future peace establishment," by extending the period
of service for recruits and by increasing the annual

contingent to 130,000, which increased the permament peace footing by 500,000 men. On March 12 the *Golos Moskvy,* an influential Conservative organ, wrote :—

"The hatred towards Austria which has accumulated in the hearts of the Russian nation has long been seeking an outlet in war, and is only being kept back within the limits of the last degree of patience by the Russian Government with the utmost difficulty. But there is an end to all things. A moment may arrive when even the Russian Government will prove impotent to fight down the hatred towards Austro-Hungary which fills the Russian people, and then the crossing of the Austrian frontiers by the Russian Army will become an unavoidable decision."

The *Novoe Vremya*—the organ of the Pan-Slavists— had already stated (March 7) : "The hour is approaching. . . . It is necessary to work on the Army from top to bottom, day and night." That same month was notable for the introduction of a Bill into the Duma imposing heavy duties upon imported flour and rye from Germany. The incendiary utterances of the Russian Press *were studiously kept from British readers,* and the retaliatory utterances of the German Press were given the widest publicity, especially in *The Times* and its compeers—thus continuing to foster the impression here that the recrimination and intolerance were all on the German side (see, for example, *The Times* of March 5 and 6). In March came the announcement of the forthcoming visits by King George to Paris and by President Poincaré to Petrograd. On March 12 the St. Petersburg correspondent of *The Times* reports :—

"According to the newspapers large extraordinary military and naval credits have been discussed in a secret sitting of the Duma."

On March 19 we have a further telegram from the same source, headed by *The Times* thus : "Russia's Giant Army. Unprecedented Peace Effectives," and containing the following paragraphs :—

"I understand that the Duma Committee has agreed to the Bill of Indemnity retrospecfively sanctioning the prolongation of the service of time-expired men for three months after the legal limit. The fourth class, which should have returned home on January 14, is, therefore, due to be released on April 14. As the conscripts forming the first class have been with the Colours since last August and are now able, if necessary, to take the field, the Russian Army has now attained an effective numerical strength hitherto unprecedented, being not far short of 1,700,000. . . . There is not the slightest difficulty in providing an additional 150,000 conscripts this year."

A further telegram, on March 29, states :—

"The Russian Government has drawn up a programme which provides that orders shall be placed for 330 aeroplanes."

On April 6 the same correspondent announces the "Russian test mobilisation."

In July President Poincaré went to Petrograd. On the 19th *The Times* Petrograd correspondent telegraphed :—

"Frequent discussion of European problems is a necessity of the alliance—no less than naval and military preparations. Naturally, it is the progress of the Russian Army which most concerns France, but the naval *renaissance* indicated by the approaching entry into commission of the first two of the eight large ships of the Russian naval programme is by no means the least interesting political event since President Poincaré's last visit to Russia."

On July 20 the *Novoe Vremya,* discussing the merits of the Triple Entente, remarked that "ITS SUPERIORITY ON LAND AND SEA JUSTIFIES MORE ENERGETIC LANGUAGE IN THE COUNCILS OF EUROPE."

The British Ambassador at Vienna had ascertained on July 15 what the character of the Austro-Hungarian Note to Serbia would be.[1]   He advised the Foreign Office

---

[1] The following foot-note appeared in the *Labour Leader* of September 30, 1915 :—

A correspondent, who is a diligent student of the Continental Press, draws my attention to a controversy in *Die Neue Zeit* between two prominent Socialists, David and Kautsky, over this statement. As the point raised is of very considerable historic importance, it may be well to throw light upon the matter. The passage alluded to reads as under, and the italicised sentences are those which have occasioned the controversy :—

The British Ambassador at Vienna had ascertained on July 15 what the character of the Austro-Hungarian Note to Servia would be. He advised the Foreign Office on July 16.

on July 16. It is reasonable to assume that the Foreign Office communicated its information to the British Ambassador at Petrograd. On July 21 President Poincaré and the French Premier and Foreign Minister were in Petrograd, and the decision of the Franco-Russian combination was then, no doubt, arrived at.

I have made it clear, I think, why, from a military point of view, Germany had reasons for anxiety for her safety, and how the element of fear in her case cannot be dismissed as idle fiction. I have written enough from that standpoint—and quoted enough—to demonstrate the untenability of the popular idea which ascribes sole responsibility for this war to Germany.

It is reasonable to assume that the Foreign Office communicated its information to the British Ambassador at Petrograd. On July 21, President Poincaré and the French Premier and Foreign Minister were in Petrograd, and the decision of the Franco-Russian combination was then, no doubt, arrived at.

This passage is specially emphasised by David in reply to a criticism by Kautsky on David's book on the war—a book, by the way, which I have not seen.

In rejoinder, Kautsky impugns the accuracy of my statement about the British Ambassador at Vienna. He points out that the British White Book opens on July 20, with a despatch dated that day from Sir E. Grey to the British Ambassador at Berlin, in which Sir E. Grey stated that he told the German Ambassador in London on that day (July 20) that he "had not heard anything recently" (i.e., anything about Vienna's intentions towards Serbia). Kautsky naturally concludes—being insufficiently informed—that my statement as to our Ambassador at Vienna having ascertained the character of the impending Austro-Hungarian Note to Serbia on July 15, and having telegraphed his information to the Foreign Office on July 16 is nothing but a "surmise."

But Kautsky is wrong. I made no surmise. I stated the facts. Kautsky has evidently not read the later despatch from the British Ambassador at Vienna dated September 1, and published by the Foreign Office as a separate publication after the issue of the White Book. This later despatch now forms No. 161 of the 1d. White Book. If he will turn to that despatch Kautsky will find the following passage :—

As for myself, no indication was given me by Count Berchtold of the impending storm, *and it was from a private source that I received on 15th July the forecast of what was about to happen, which I telegraphed to you the following day.*

We have it, therefore, on Sir Maurice de Bunsen's own admission, that on July 15 he became aware of the impending Note to Servia, and that he telegraphed his information to the Foreign Office on July 16.

How this is to be reconciled with Sir Edward Grey's despatch to our Ambassador at Berlin on July 20 it is not my business to inquire. Diplomacy is a fearful and wonderful thing, and it is not surprising if, in the maze of tergiversations, the parties responsible for editing official despatches should sometimes inadvertently contrive to let out the truth.

CHAPTER XVI.

Russia and the French Three Years' Military Service Law

BEFORE I deal with the naval expenditure of the rival European groups, it would seem advisable to refer in greater detail to the statement in the previous chapter relating to Russia's connection with the revival in 1913 of the French "Three Years' Law" for military service.

The situation in which France found herself in the opening months of 1912 was this. The entire nation was militarised. By this I mean that *every adult male not physically unfit* was compelled to serve *two* years in the army at a stretch, and so many weeks or days in every subsequent year until the age of 45. In this respect the situation of France was unique among the Great Powers. That is a very important point which is sometimes forgotten.

Now a permanent situation of that kind constitutes a terrific burden upon any nation. The fundamental cause of it was the retention by the Republican Government of *la revanche* as the foundation for all French foreign policy. With the abandonment of that policy the burden would fall, but so long as the Republican Government's fixed resolution to regain Alsace-Lorraine governed the external policy of France, the burden was there. Of late years it had reached the intensity above described, owing to the growth in the German population, so that while a numerous section of German citizens escaped a prolonged term of military service, Germany could still maintain an army which, on its peace footing, was sufficiently large to compel France—given her foreign policy—to levy this tribute on *all* her sons, in order to keep pace with her Eastern neighbour.

And even so, in a decade or two, France's capacity to keep pace would automatically disappear through the mere factor of population.

This cruel dilemma it was which had persuaded many

patriotic Frenchmen that the policy of *la revanche* must in the national interest be given up. They were fortified in their view by the marked change which had come over public sentiment in the annexed provinces. Forty years of increasing material prosperity and inter-marriages had wrought a profound modification in popular feeling. But for the blundering brutality and stupidity displayed by the German military on several occasions this sentiment would have become even more generalised in a territory whose inhabitants are, and have always been, mainly of German stock. Except in certain localised areas, public opinion was verging more and more towards *full* autonomy within the German Empire.

It is, I think, no exaggeration to say that an actual *party* had come into existence in France with the definite purpose of working for a gradual acceptance of the inevitable, and a burial of the hatchet. It was, in short, a peace party; but it had no exclusive political complexion. Men bitterly opposed to one another on domestic affairs—like Jaurès and Caillaux—led it in their respective ways. The books of Marcel Sembat,[1] Georges Bourdon,[2] and others, ministered to it amongst the general public. The movement was gaining steadily, despite the formidable obstacles it had to contend against on both sides of the frontier . . . . and elsewhere. It is idle, alas ! to deny that the British Foreign Office view contemplated any genuine accommodation between France and Germany with alarm, and during the Morocco crisis of 1911 *The Times*, the *Spectator*, and other organs which express that view, went astonishing lengths in their covert threats to the Caillaux Cabinet for its pacific tendencies, while *The Times'* habitual sneers at Jaurès—the only great political figure whom the Republic has thrown up since Gambetta, and unquestionably the most honest and far-seeing of French politicians—took on a more acrid note. The despatch to *The Times*, published from Paris on July 20th of that year (1911), and to which it gave editorial support, reveals as no accessible contemporary document (except the Belgian diplomatic despatches) reveals, the attitude of the British diplomatic world towards the prospect of a Franco-German reconciliation.[3]

[1] *Op. cit.*
[2] *L'Enigme Allemand.*
[3] *Vide* "Ten Years' Secret Diplomacy" : *op. cit.*, and "The Policy of the Entente" : *op. cit.*

Needless to say, such a consummation was as distasteful to the Pan-Slavist elements in Russian foreign policy as it was to *The Times* and to those whose views *The Times* expressed.

. . . .

Such, then, was the position of France when, in the spring of 1913, the French Government brought forward a proposal to increase the term of military service to *three years—i.e.,* to require *every adult Frenchman* to serve three consecutive years in the army. This converted the existing burden, already grievous, into an unbearable one, and those who opposed it in France did so from the intimate conviction that if this burden were imposed, war or revolution must ensue.

How came the French Government to take this step?

. . . .

The statement that Russia pressed the French Government to adopt the *Three Years' Law* was repeatedly made by the French Radicals and Socialists during the passionate discussions which that measure provoked in France. The struggle which raged around it became a trial of strength between the peace party in France and the war party; between those who were averse to a war with Germany and those who were anxious for it; between those who objected to France becoming the catspaw of Russia and those who were willing to go to any lengths to meet Russia's exigencies, in order to bring about an opportunity for the *revanche.* I invite the reader to peruse the columns of *The Times* in this connection. During the whole period covered by this desperate struggle between opposing forces in France *The Times* supported the Chauvinistic elements in the French nation.

It not only supported them—that would have been natural enough in view of the bitter detestation of Germany and her Emperor which inspired those who directed the foreign department of *The Times.* But it supported them with a concentrated fury, with a frenzy of zeal, with an invective against the other side so great, that the battle which was being fought might have been one between British political parties rather than French. As in 1905-6, when the first Morocco crisis occurred, as in 1911 during the second crisis, so in 1912-13-14 over the *Three Years' Law, The Times* was to all intents and purposes the organ of the French extremists. It is absolutely impossible that *The Times* should have steered this course without the tacit—to put it no higher—approval of the Foreign Office, not necessarily of the Foreign Minister, but assuredly of the Department itself and of the British Embassy in Paris.

The charge made by the French Socialists received a "sort of" denial by the French Premier (M. Barthou) in the Chamber on July 16, 1913, whereupon several Deputies shouted that the Finance Minister had himself admitted the truth of it. A curious scene ensued. M. Dumont (the Finance Minister) declared that what he had said was, that he would accept the *Three Years' Law* rather than expose the French Ambassador at Petrograd "to humiliation." This ingenuous explanation evoked the natural retort that if the project for the restoration of a law which ensured a three years' instead of a two years' service with the colours for all Frenchmen was a spontaneous act of the French Government, why should the French Ambassador at Petrograd be "humiliated" if the French Chamber rejected the project? The charge was persisted in and, indeed, maintained after the Bill became law, and on June 6, 1914, *Le Temps*—which plays the part in French foreign politics that *The Times* plays with us—found it necessary to insert a denial from its Petrograd correspondent. The amusing sequel was, of course, concealed from public opinion over here. *Le Temps* was compelled to print a denial of the denial by stating in its issue of June 8 that the French Ambassador at Petrograd (M. Paléologue) had only accepted the post on the explicit condition that the *Three Years' Law* should be maintained in its integrity as "being accurately informed of the sentiments of the Russian Court and Government, he was in a position to inform the French Government that the controversies raised in France by the Law were being closely followed," and that "if the Law were in the least impaired he (M. Paléologue) would be compelled to resign."

Further evidence is not lacking. On August 4, 1912, the foreign affairs writer on the Paris paper, *Le Gaulois,* stated that, "it was by no means impossible that new military, as well as naval arrangements, between Russia and France might be under consideration, although it was unlikely that the public would learn anything about them until they were ready for practical execution." This was written on the eve of the President's departure for Petrograd, and the anticipation proved, so far as the naval arrangement was concerned, so remarkably accurate that the conclusion of a Franco-Russian naval convention was announced immediately after the President's return. This convention, as *The Times'* Paris correspondent was again good enough to inform us, had been "preceded by an exchange of views—perhaps I ought to say by arrangements—between the British and French naval authorities." In the case of the military arrangements, the writer in *Le Gaulois* was equally accurate when he prophesied that the public would know nothing about them until they were ready for practical execution. For the French public *was* allowed to know nothing about them until they became embodied in the *Three Years' Law*.

When, finally, the *Three Years' Law* was brought forward, it was vigorously opposed by the redoubtable M. Clémenceau, who, in the course of his meteoric career, has overturned more French Governments than any other living French politician. This was a serious matter, and an interview between M. Clémenceau and the President (M. Poincaré) was, therefore, arranged. The confidential conversation which took place leaked out. These things invariably do in France. Several French papers (*L'Humanité* and *Gil Blas* amongst them) published detailed accounts of the President's arguments to M. Clémenceau. The accounts concurred. Here is *L'Humanité's* :—

"He, M. Poincaré (the President), reminded his visitor of the visit he had made to St. Petersburg the preceding summer, when he was still Minister for Foreign Affairs. He apprised him of the very clear impressions he had formed during his sojourn among our Allies. The President gave him (M. Clémenceau) to understand that *grave events are about to take place, that sooner or later the question of Austria will undoubtedly be raised and that serious international complications would not fail to arise.* . . . Doubts had been expressed (in Petrograd) as to the state of preparations in France, whose military situation since the *Two Years' Law* had been far from favourable as compared with the situation when the Alliance had been concluded. He (the President) had been given to understand in a friendly way that there was at St. Petersburg a Germanophil party which constantly insinuated—not without some show of reason—that there was no longer any equality between the military strength of Germany and France. That is why he (the President) and his Ministry had decided to re-introduce the *Three Years'*

Law, whose object was to produce abroad the effect desired by France's Allies. That was also why M. Delcassé had been sent to Russia. In fact, the Franco-Russian Alliance was threatened with disruption, because France was not sufficiently strong, or, at least, did not appear to be so.''

The accuracy of this account of the Clémenceau-Poincaré conversation, so pregnant of what lay ahead, was never denied. Only five weeks before the war—June 23, 1914—M. Justin de Godart, who afterwards became one of the Under-Secretaries at the French War Office, wrote a vehement article in *Le Courrier Européen* (Paris), in the course of which he said : "I am perfectly convinced that we have abandoned our freedom, so far as our military organisation is concerned.'' He went on to say that it was an open secret that the President had brought back with him from Petrograd two years before, an order, or at least a suggestion, that France should re-enact the *Three Years' Law.* We are no longer masters of our defence strategy. . . . Our patriotism rebels when we are told that the Three Years' service is France's only means of protection. Has the Republic really become the slave of Russia ?''

.   .   .   .

This summary would be incomplete without a reference to the striking despatches of the Belgian diplomatic representative in Paris (Baron Guillaume)[1] in connection with the events summarised in the President's interview with M. Clémenceau. Baron Guillaume reports from Paris (February 21, 1913) that M. Delcassé's nomination to the post of French Ambassador to Russia burst upon Paris "like a bombshell.'' On April 17 the same diplomatist reports the "increasingly bellicose and imprudent'' character of French public opinion. On June 12 he refers as follows to the *Three Years' Law :*—

"It is, therefore, practically certain that French legislation will adopt a measure that the country is unlikely to be able to bear for long. The obligations of the new law will be so heavy for the population, the expenses it will involve will be so exorbitant that the country will soon protest, and France will be confronted with this dilemma; either an abdication which she could not bear, or speedy war. The responsibility of those who have dragged the nation into this situation will be heavy. . . . The propa-

[1] *Op. cit.*

ganda in favour of the *Three Years' Law,* which was bound
to lead to a revival of Chauvinism, has been admirably
prepared and staged. It paved the way for M. Poincaré's
election to the Presidency. It is being pursued to-day
without caring for the dangers to which it gives rise.
Uneasiness is general in the country."

As the months went on, Baron Guillaume's anxiety
increased. Writing on January 16, 1914, he reports :—

"I have already had the honour of informing you that
it is Messrs. Poincaré, Delcassé, Millerand and their
friends who have invented and pursued the nationalist,
boastful and jingoistic policy, whose revival we have
witnessed. It is a danger for Europe—and for Belgium.
I see in it the greatest peril which threatens the peace of
Europe to-day. Not that I am entitled to suppose that
the Government of the Republic is disposed to trouble the
peace of Europe deliberately—I think rather the contrary
—but because the attitude which the Barthou party has
taken up is, in my judgment, the determining cause of the
increase of military tendencies in Germany. The bellicose
follies of the Turks and the *Three Years' Law* appear to me
to constitute the only dangers to be feared from the point
of view of European peace. I feel able to indicate the
perils which the present military legislation of France have
created. France, weakened by the decrease in her nativity,
cannot long support the three years' system of military
service. The effort is too considerable, financially, and
as regards personal burdens. France cannot sustain such
an effort, and what will she do to escape from the position
in which she will have placed herself?"

Writing on May 8, 1914, he says :—

"It is incontestable that during the past few months
the French nation has become more Chauvinistic and more
confident in itself. The same men, instructed and competent, who, two years ago, showed lively anxiety at the
mere mention of possible difficulties between France and
Germany, have changed their tone. They now say they
are certain of victory. They dwell largely on the progress,
which is truly very real, accomplished in the army of the
Republic, and contend that they could at least hold the
German army in check sufficiently long to enable Russia
to mobilise, to concentrate her troops and to fling herself
upon her Western neighbour. One of the most dangerous

elements in the situation is the re-enactment in France of the *Three Years' Law*. It was imposed light-heartedly by the militarist party, and the country cannot sustain it. Two years from now it will either have to be abrogated or war must ensue."

His final warning is conveyed on June 9 :—

"The Press campaign of the last few days in favour of the *Three Years' Law* has been one of extreme violence. Every possible means has been adopted to influence public opinion, and it has even been sought to involve the personality of General Joffre. We have witnessed, too, the French Ambassador at St. Petersburg taking, contrary to all usage, a somewhat dangerous initiative for the future of France. Is it true that the St. Petersburg Cabinet imposed the adoption of the *Three Years' Law* upon this country and is pressing to-day with all its weight to secure the maintenance of that law? I have not succeeded in obtaining light upon this delicate point, but it would be the graver, seeing that those who direct the destinies of the Empire of the Tsars cannot be ignorant of the fact that the effort which is thus demanded of the French nation is excessive and cannot long be sustained. Is the attitude of the Cabinet of St. Petersburg based, then, upon the conviction that events are so near that the tool it proposes to place in the hands of its ally can be used?"

As Mr. Lowes Dickinson remarks,[1] "what a sinister vista is opened up by this passage." He adds : "I have no wish to insinuate that the suspicion here expressed was justified. It is the suspicion itself that is the point." Yes, but when Mr. Lowes Dickinson wrote that, the French evidence summarised above was not at his disposal. Can any sane man doubt the real facts after perusing it?

Surely hypocrisy has reached its apotheosis when, in face of this history, *The Times,* of all papers, remarks in its leading article of May 15, 1916 :—

"Her (Germany's) onslaught upon her neighbours was wanton. Nobody thought of attacking her; there was no coalition against her; and she knew there was none. Relying upon her preparedness and upon the unpreparedness of her neighbours, she suddenly assailed them."

[1] "The European Anarchy" (*op. cit.*).

CHAPTER XVII.

European Navalism[1]

IN June, 1900, Germany issued her famous " Navy Act," providing for the reconstruction and a large increase, of her naval armament which at that time, for a nation dependent so greatly upon imported raw material for her industries, was relatively insignificant. What, at that period, were Germany's potential foes, France and Russia, spending on their navies compared with her own expenditure? It is interesting to recall the figures because the relative positions of the rival groups before the "Naval Act" have been lost sight of in the increasing virulence of the Anglo-German controversy as the execution of the German programme proceeded.

TABLE I.

NAVAL EXPENDITURE OF FRANCE, RUSSIA, AND GERMANY IN THE FIVE YEARS 1897-1901.

Years.	France. £	Russia. £	Germany. £
1897	10,444,000	6,239,000	6,467,000
1898	11,716,000	7,089,000	5,972,000
1899	12,081,000	8,652,000	6,485,000
1900	12,511,000	9,962,000	7,472,000
1901	13,107,000	11,659,000	9,642,000

Germany's naval programme was deliberate and open. It was adhered to with one exception. An amendment publicly issued in 1908 provided that battleships and cruisers were to be replaced after 20 years, instead of after 25 years, as stipulated in the Act. Various attempts were made at various times in this country to establish that, side by side with her open and avowed programme, Germany was pursuing a secret programme of accelerated construction. These attempts culminated in 1909 in one of the most discreditable Parliamentary episodes of recent

[1] The *Labour Leader*, July 15, 1915.

years; what Mr. Alan Burgoyne, M.P., editor of the *Navy League Annual,* and in some measure the chief of the "Big Navy" men (and, consequently, not suspect of pacifism, "little Englandism," or any of the other "isms") described as "one of the most portentous pieces of Parliamentary humbug ever practised upon the electorate." I shall not revive it here. Those who wish to re-familiarise themselves with its unsavoury features may be referred to Mr. Hirst's volume.[1] But when the history of Anglo-German relations during the past decade is impartially written, the part which this episode played in embittering those relations will be adjudged as it deserves, and the historian will note that the gross deception practised upon Parliament remained uncensured. It is, however, well to recall these words pronounced by Mr. Churchill after the great "scare":—

"That law (the Navy Act) as fixed by Parliament, has not in any way been exceeded, and I gladly bear witness to the fact that the statements of the German Ministers about it have been strictly borne out by events."

Following the precedent employed in regard to military expenditure, I will now give the figures of naval expenditure for the ten years preceding the war on the part of Germany and Austria, and of the Franco-Russian combination respectively.

TABLE II.

TOTAL NAVAL EXPENDITURE IN THE DECADE 1905-14 (15).

The Teutonic Powers—
Germany £185,205,164
Austro-Hungary £50,692,814

The Franco-Russian Combination—
France £161,721,387
Russia £144,246,513

Total expenditure by the Teutonic Powers £235,897,978
Total expenditure by the Franco-Russian
Combination £305,967,900

Thus we find that in these last ten years the naval expenditure of France and Russia *actually exceeded that of Germany and Austria by* £70,069,922.

The Russian figures must naturally be read in conjunction with the fact that the destruction of Russia's most powerful ships in the war with Japan (1904-5) necessitated fresh construction. No such argument applies, of course,

---

[1] "The Six Panics" (Methuen).

to the French Navy, which, after a period of decline, began to revive once more. It is surprising to note that in the last ten years France alone has spent only £24,383,777 less than Germany on her navy; more than ever surprising when one bears in mind that France's naval expenditure showed an enormous increase in the second period of the decade (*i.e.*, 1910-14), or, in other words, since—as we learned last year—British support was virtually assured to her in the event of a general European conflagration. Moreover, if we take into account the effect of the Japanese war upon the Russian naval position, we must also take into account the character of Russia's recent naval expenditure and the interpretation consistently placed upon it by the mouthpieces in the British press of the British governing class.

In June, 1912, eight years after the Japanese War, the Duma voted a sum of £43,000,000 for the navy, to be spent over a period of five years, but the Russian Year Book of 1914 mentions that five years hence, and perhaps "even sooner," a further demand would be made upon the Duma for £78,300,000 more. We must go to *The Times* to get the ever-faithful reflection of the Russian official mind and its interpretation by the British official mind. We read in the issue of that journal for June 24, 1912 :—

"But however significant the attitude of the Government on the Navy Bill may appear in respect of internal policy, it is vastly more important in respect of foreign policy. In his preamble to the Bill, Admiral Grogorovitch repeatedly dwelt on the respective relations of Russia and Germany as a fundamental reason for the revival of Russia's naval power. . . . These statements in themselves suffice to indicate the course to *which Russia's foreign policy has been irrevocably committed,* and for this reason the Navy Bill should finally allay all suspicions and remove any doubt which may arise, both in this country and abroad as to the fidelity of Russia to her alliances and agreements. The details of the shipbuilding programme itself are, if anything, still more convincing. The type of vessel selected for the future battle squadrons shows that they are not exclusively intended for operations within the narrow waters of the Baltic. *All the Dreadnoughts, whether building or projected, are to have a large coal capacity, which would enable them to operate either in the North Sea or in the Mediterranean. . . . Although the programme approved by the Duma is to be carried out in*

*five years its effect cannot fail to make itself felt long before
that time and to stiffen the foreign policy of this country
in regard to neighbouring Powers."*

There could hardly have been a more direct threat !

In estimating how far the element of fear has been the
most powerful factor in Germany's military and naval preparations and in the series of events culminating in this
war (and my fundamental contention is that mutual fear
has been at the bottom of the whole tragedy), we are
bound—in this matter of naval expenditure—to take into
account the naval expenditure of Great Britain. Obviously,
Britain's naval preparations could not be left out of the
German reckoning, since not only the British official case,
but the British popular case for viewing Germany with
distrust, suspicion, and alarm, was Germany's determination to carry out the provisions of the Naval Act of 1900
—in other words, to have a strong navy. Moreover, the
close connection between Russia's increased naval expenditure and Russian and British foreign policy was becoming
visible to the naked eye, let alone to official sources of information. The arrangement between Messrs. Vickers,
Ltd., and the Russian Government was public property.
The *Times* announced (June 25, 1913) with visible satisfaction that British shipbuilding knowledge and technical
advice had been secured for Russia's need. We were told
of special factories, large orders for new guns, and so
forth. Six months later *The Times* was again chronicling
a combination between Vickers, Ltd., and the leading
banks of St. Petersburg for the establishment of "extensive gunworks" in Russia—this was considered of "great
importance" to Anglo-Russian relations. A month before
the tragedy at Sarajevo, we find *The Times'* St. Petersburg
correspondent reporting Russia's Foreign Minister (M.
Sazonoff) as stating in the Duma :—

"The establishment of a sound friendship between
France and Great Britain and also between Great Britain
and Russia had brought Great Britain within the sphere of
political communion previously existing between Russia
and France. . . ."

Referring to the discussions concerning the conversion of
the Triple *Entente* into a formal Alliance (mooted by Lord
Esher—a member of the Committee of Imperial Defence—
in *The Times*), M. Sazonoff went on to say :—

"It seems to me a somewhat exaggerated importance
has been attributed to a *mere matter of form.* There may

be a formal alliance not based on real community of interests and not supported by the reciprocal sentiments of the peoples. On the other hand there may be political combinations of Powers imposed by unity of aims. In the latter case friendly co-operation is assured, *irrespective of the form and scope of the written word.* The important thing is that we should not stand still."

What, then, was Britain's naval expenditure in the decade 1905-14, the period under review?

TABLE III.

British naval expenditure, 1905-14 ... £391,916,470[1]

We find, then, that in the event of a European war Germany had to reckon upon meeting on the sea a combination of possible foemen—two of them certain, one problematical, but having to be taken into account—who in ten years had spent in preparations for a naval war a total sum of £697,884,370, against her own and her Ally's expenditure on such preparations in the same period amounting to £235,897,978 : *a combination, in other words, which had spent £461,986,392 more than Germany and Austria combined, and £512,697,206 more than Germany alone on naval equipment—for war.*[2]

Say anything you like about Germany and the Germans, but can you, in the face of these naval figures and in the face of the military figures precedently given and by none challenged, continue to say, with due regard to truth and honesty, that Germany's preparations for war, compared with the preparations of her enemies, were such as to make it unquestionable that she was hatching a vast conspiracy to subjugate Europe?

[1] Less some 40 millions under Pensions, Coast-Guard, Reserves, and Steamship subsidies, for which no corresponding provision exists in the votes of foreign Powers, except France and Italy. (House of Commons return, August, 1914.)

[2] The Peace Society—47 New Bond Street, E.C.—has issued this year (1916) a detailed table entitled "The Armed Peace of Europe, 1914." In this table the "annual cost of the Army and Navy" of the Russo-French Combination and the Austro-German combination is given as follows :—

Russia	£105,955,980	Austro-Hungary...	£24,992,000
France	81,065,967	Germany	59,034,770
Total	£187,021,947	Total	£84,026,770

According to the same table, Great Britain's expenditure was £80,430,000.

CHAPTER XVIII.

The Spectre of Fear[1]

IT IS the universal reign of Fear which has caused the system of alliances, believed to be a guarantee of peace, but now proved to be the cause of world-wide disaster. . . . And this universal Fear has at last produced a cataclysm far greater than any of those which it was hoped to avert.—*Hon. Bertrand Russell in "War the Offspring of Fear" (Union of Democratic Control publications: September, 1914.)*

I WOULD suggest, then, that this charge of "pro-German be squarely faced. What was, and is, the basis of that charge? It is that some of us decline to juggle with our reasoning powers to the extent of accepting as accurate the popular view attributing to Germany *sole* responsibility for this war, undertaken by her with the deliberate intention of " subjugating Europe." It is that some of us realise how short-sighted is the view which bids us keep silent on that issue, because not to keep silent is to incur unpopularity. What does unpopularity matter when everything that we hold dear, nationally and individually, depends, in the ultimate resort, upon the nation seeing straight on that issue?

At the present moment, if we are to judge by the utterances of several members of the Government, of the Press, and of publicists and literary men who have the public ear, these charges against Germany are universally accepted as axioms, axioms which must govern the national war-policy and—never let it be forgotten for one instant—the national war-policy is not only a military and naval question *but a political question.* These axioms are held to justify and make intelligible the policy, more and more loudly proclaimed, that this war must be prosecuted until Germany "surrenders unconditionally"; until she proclaims herself ready to submit to any and every humiliation the Allies choose to inflict upon her in the hour of complete victory. They are held to justify the denunciation of "traitorous" applied to any suggestion for mediation by

[1] *The Labour Leader,* July 22, 1915.

neutral Powers to arrest this stupendous slaughter or to the acceptance of any possible openings for reasonable discussion between the belligerents. From these axioms the civilian spirit of hatred and revenge draws its inspiration. These axioms are trumpeted on the housetops in order to sweep aside all the professions made by our official classes upon the outbreak of the war. While they stand unchallenged, what really effective and practical countervailing weapon remains for those who believe that these axioms are erected upon false premises, and that the road to which their acceptance tends is the road, not to national and international salvation, but to national and international disaster?

My object is to shake these axioms from the hold they have acquired over the national mind, and to do so not by elaborating opinions or indulging in rhetoric, but by recalling concrete facts. What are the facts I have endeavoured to recall? They may be classified under three main heads :

I.—GERMANY'S POSITION IN THE "BALANCE."

In the event of war arising out of Russo-Austrian rivalry in the Balkans it was common knowledge that (a) France would join Russia against Germany, choosing the moment best suited to her interests—if she were allowed to choose it; (b) Germany would thus be compelled to fight on two fronts; (c) Germany would take the military offensive against France at once, which her greater powers of rapid mobilisation enabled her to do; (d) Germany would probably seek to use Belgian territory for the purpose.

Conclusion: Germany's attack upon France was not "wanton" nor "unprovoked," and was no proof in itself of a desire to subjugate Europe. It was the inevitable opening stage in a general European war waged on the existing system of alliances and groups which divided Europe into two hostile camps. It had been known and proclaimed to be inevitable years before the war broke out. Morally indefensible, the occupation of Belgium by the German armies was a virtual certainty.

Belgium was the predestined victim of a general European war which should find Britain entangled with one or other of the two rival groups.

II.—Germany's War Preparations.

(a) Militarism is not an exclusively German product. (b) With the single exception of a guerilla warfare against a Hottentot tribe in S.W. Africa, Germany had kept her sword in its scabbard for 45 years—with all her militarism; while *all* her present foes have within that period indulged in the pastime of war, and acquired, or endeavoured to acquire, extensive over-sea possessions in so doing. (c) Germany prepared for war and carried her preparations to the highest pitch of efficiency, which has been equally characteristic of the industrial and scientific branches of her national organisation. (d) On the assumption that preparations for war are indicative of a desire and intention to go to war, there is no case against Germany which will not apply equally to her neighbours. For Germany's potential foes had been spending even more—far more—than she had in war preparations during the decade immediately preceding the war—the decade marking the gradually increasing tension in Europe. (e) In that period the Russo-French combination spent £159,798,931 more on its armies than the Teutonic Powers spent on theirs, and the military effectives of the former largely exceeded the military effectives of the latter. (f) In the same period the Franco-Russian combination spent £70,069,922 more than the Teutonic Powers on its navies, while if it be conceded—and it cannot well be denied—that the possible use of the British Fleet against Germany in the event of a general European war was envisaged by the rulers of Germany, the naval expenditure of Germany's potential foes exceeded her own expenditure and that of her ally in that period by £461,986,392. (g) Taking military and naval armament together, Germany's potential foes, Russia and France, had between them spent on preparations for war, in the decade 1905-14, £229,868,853 more than Germany and her ally, and if the factor of Britain's naval strength were thrown in the scale, £621,785,323 more than Germany and her ally.

Conclusion: The argument that Germany's war preparations were directed to the "subjugation" of Europe will not bear examination. You do not undertake to "subjugate" nations, vastly exceeding your own nation in numbers, when those nations are spending hundreds of millions more than you are spending on preparations for war! The German argument is that the war preparations of Germany's potential foes were directed to the subjugation of Germany. In the face of these figures it is at least as plausible. The truth is that each "Group" was terrified of the other "Group," and that, to quote an old declaration of Sir E. Grey:

"If this tremendous expenditure on armaments goes on it must, in the long run, break down civilisation. You are having this great burden of force piled up in times of peace, and if it goes on increasing by leaps and bounds as it has done in the last generation, in time it will become intolerable. There are those who think it will lead to war, precisely because it is becoming intolerable. I think it is much more likely the burden will be dissipated by internal revolution—not by nations fighting against each other, but by revolt of masses of men against taxation. . . . The great nations of the world are in bondage to their armies and navies at the present moment—increasing bondage."

Just so. But it is a little late in the day to tell us *now*—now that, unfortunately, the above prediction has been falsified—that the German expenditure has been the sole cause of all the mischief, when the expenditure of the Triple *Entente* has vastly exceeded the German.

III.—Germany's Fears.

(*a*) Germany's fears were genuine and natural, **and** were admitted to be so by British and French statesmen and military writers long before the outbreak of war. (*b*) They increased proportionately with the relative decrease in Germany's military power in relation to that of her neighbours. (*c*) Had Germany's desire been to "subjugate" Europe she would have struck at France and at Russia when her superior armament ensured her the certainty of prompt success on several occasions within the past twenty years. Had Germany's supreme aim been the conquest of the British Empire, she would have disposed of France with ease during the Boer War, or have joined that Power and Russia in a hostile coalition against us, which there is good reason to believe was urged upon her at that time.

Conclusion: The charge against Germany that she has been alone responsible for this war and has plunged the world in strife to minister to detestable ambitions will be ridiculed by the next generation. The war is fundamentally the outcome of fears of one another entertained by the governing classes in either "Group," fears produced by the vicious philosophy which lies at the root of European state-craft. That these fears have been able to mature into fate-ful consummation is due to the fact that the Governments have been wholly uncontrolled by the democracy and have carried out their secret rivalries and intrigues behind the backs of the peoples, concealing the truth from their Par-liaments and surrounding their obscure and unintelligible aims in a network of secret manœuvres. The peoples have been helpless to save themselves, because they have been lacking in combination, organisation, and effective co-operation.

.   .   .   .

The question which confronts the democracies is to-day a plain one. Are the causes which have produced this war to be perpetuated? If so, the course of the peoples is clear. *They must continue to take the advice of those who have led them to this pass.* It is quite easy and simple to do so. It requires no mental exercise, no moral courage. It is the line of least resistance. The British and French peoples must continue to lend ear to those who tell them that Ger-many must be "crushed," who demand Germany's "un-conditional surrender." And the German people must continue to hearken to those who tell them that Britain must be "crushed." They must continue to regard those who preach this doctrine, at a comfortable distance from the bestialities to which it has given rise, as "patriots," and those who differ as "traitors." But they must not deceive themselves. If they do follow this advice it is the young children of to-day who will pay the price of the fatuous arrogance and criminal vindictiveness of their elders; for the horror will begin all over again. The course must be steered with eyes wide open—with the certainty that the "crushing" policy will bleed us all whiter and whiter and that the fruit of "victory" on those lines will be putrid in the mouth. It is better to be called "pro-German" and "traitor" than to bow the knee to that advice.

And we need not unless we will. For there is another way; another policy; another creed.

PART II

CHAPTER XIX.

The Union of Democratic Control[1]

I HAVE never been more deeply convinced of anything than I am of the urgent necessity of working, and working now, more especially when so many are distracted by the turmoil of battle, to prevent my fellow-countrymen from being misled, to strive for the attainment of great ideals, and to keep my country's honour free from corruption by the evil influences of debased and vicious doctrines.—*Mr. Arthur Ponsonby in a letter to his constituents.*

DURING the fatal opening days of last August, when the hopes of a generation withered before our eyes and civilisation plunged back into barbarism, a small group of men met together in the house of one of them. For years they had shared a common conviction that Europe's statesmen were drifting to a catastrophe which, if it eventuated, would overwhelm mankind. In their several ways they had endeavoured to rouse public opinion to the terrible gravity of the situation; and they had failed. The monster of militarism had mastered the diplomats whose tortuous evolutions and mediæval proceedings had done so much to create it. The peoples, dominated by fear and panic, neither informed nor consulted, had been whirled—after a few short weeks of confused and secret negotiations between their rulers—into a maëlstrom of passions and mutual slaughter. Was anything left for this small group of men to do? Should they confine themselves to the facile and popular task of denouncing the enemy and giving such assistance as it might be in their power to render to works of charity or relief for the victims of the war? Or should they attempt to evolve some constructive programme; to indicate some definite line of thought, to provide some rallying centre for future political action—national in its inception, international in its ultimate aims—around which men and women holding, it might be, divers and even contradictory views as to the origins of the war, could, nevertheless, gather, restore their shattered faiths, and strive to lay the foundations of a more enduring edifice?

[1] Published in the *Contemporary Review*, July, 1915.

With no light heart, assuredly, could such a step be contemplated. When discussion reached the point of decision, just five individuals in the group felt that the effort must be made. Fully conscious of their own deficiencies and shortcomings, but confident alike in one another's integrity, and in the righteousness of the cause they espoused, they launched their frail barque upon the troubled seas.

Thus was conceived the Union of Democratic Control, in circumstances of painful difficulty, without organisation, without funds, without support. To-day, the Union is solidly entrenched. Its rapid expansion has astonished none more than its founders. Fifty[1] branches, directed by purely voluntary local endeavour, united to the parent body as to policy and common action, and represented on its councils, but otherwise conducting their propaganda in accordance with local conditions and wholly self-supporting, are established throughout England, Scotland, Wales, and Ireland. The individuals forming the Committees of these auxiliary organisations are usually, and sometimes prominently, associated with the social life of the community. Adherents daily swell the Union's ranks from all sections of society. As its name implies, the Union directs its appeal to the Democracy—to the people as a whole—and Labour organisations in considerable numbers have officially joined the Union, paying its affiliation fees and receiving and distributing its literature. The Independent Labour Party has virtually adopted the Union's four cardinal points of policy, and supports them actively and whole-heartedly. But the Independent Labour Party does not stand alone in this respect. Trades and Labour Councils and Trade Unions are affiliating in increasing numbers, and the literature of the Union is gradually permeating the labour world. The public desire for information as to the Union's objects may be gathered from the fact that within the area of greater London alone between 300 and 400 addresses and lectures have been delivered by Union speakers in the last five months to Adult Schools, Trade Unions, Brotherhoods, Co-operative Societies and Guilds, and various ethical societies.[2] The demands upon the Union are, moreover, continuously increasing, and the staff of 45 lecturers attached to the London branch—all of whose services are given free of charge—can with difficulty meet the calls upon their activities. This process is being dupli-

[1] Now eighty.
[2] These figures have since been enormously increased.

cated in many provincial cities where the Union has an established branch. As for the Union's literature, it is more and more in request, alike in this country and in neutral States.

It must be evident that a movement of this kind, which yesterday was not, and to-day is already becoming a power in the land despite the efforts of the London Press to boycott or misrepresent it; which is steadily forging its way into the public mind, not in this country alone, but in other lands; which is already known in the five Continents, and which is only in its infancy and has nothing ephemeral about its programme and nothing secret about its methods —it must, I say, be evident to all reasonable human beings that this movement deserves at least to be understood. For its growth is so remarkable that if it be wisely guided it seems destined to become a factor in national politics and in international relations with which the reactionary elements in every Government will have to reckon, and from which the democratic elements in every Government may derive strength.

What then are the convictions which inspire the Union of Democratic Control? What are its objects? By what means and by what methods is the Union prosecuting those objects? We believe that the Ordeal by War as a method of determining disputes between civilised States has become an absurdity and a criminal absurdity, possessing even less relevance to the removal of the causes of the dispute and offering even less hope of obviating future disputes, than the Ordeal by Poison, or the Ordeal by Fire, by which both individuals and communities were wont, and in primitive society are still accustomed, to adjust their immediate differences. We believe that the Ordeal by War between civilised States is a criminal absurdity because we do not believe that it is able to provide a solution for any single problem, or combination of problems, which may give rise from time to time to international friction. The Union seeks to permeate the public mind with that belief by every means in its power—not as a theoretical proposition, but with the force of a living and practical truth for which humanity should labour, strive, and consent to sacrifice its thought, its energy, and its means.

Concurrently with the presentation of the general argument, the Union urges that public opinion, in this land primarily, and in so far as its example and teaching may be followed and shared by similar movements of opinion in other lands, throughout the world, should concentrate upon the main factors—mechanical, constitutional, traditional, and so on—which lead Governments to force their peoples to have recourse to the Ordeal by War, and which lead the peoples to support the Governments in their action. It is of the essence of these aims that the Union's appeal to national and international sanity should be uttered and presented *now,* while the horrors of this desolating war absorb us all. For the Union contends that if the peoples of the belligerent States are desirous—as we believe them to be—that their successors, the younger children not yet fit for cannon fodder, should not be immolated upon the same altar; the peoples must not leave the Settlement to be dictated by the rulers, the diplomatists, and the professional men of war in the higher command, whose clashing ambitions, incompatibilities of temper, incapacity of judgment, ignorance of national needs and aspirations, and whose secret manœuvres have, in the opinion of the Union, brought the world to the present pass. For the peoples to give *carte blanche* to the diplomatists would be, in our view, to place a premium upon an international Settlement calculated to perpetuate the vicious errors of the past and to sow the seeds of future wars.

To the extent in which it is possible to crystallise these convictions and objects in a number of *formulæ*—and it is, of course, not possible to do so in a completely satisfactory manner—the Union of Democratic Control has adopted as the backbone of its constitution four cardinal points[1] embodying the policy which should inspire the future Settlement, and which should dominate the national and international situation after peace has been declared. I will deal with these points *seriatim.* The first clause in the charter —so to speak—of the Union reads as follows :—No province shall be transferred from one Government to another without the consent, by *plébiscite* or otherwise, of the population of such province."

In postulating that no province shall be transferred from one Government to another without the inhabitants thereof being consulted, we formulate a desire which is essentially democratic and essentially just, but which, unfortunately, has not guided the Governments in previous *post-bellum*

[1] A fifth point has now been added, reading as follows : "The European conflict shall not be continued by economic war after the military operations have ceased. British policy shall be directed towards promoting free commercial intercourse between all nations and the preservation and extension of the open door."

Settlements. It has been wittily said that every war waged in the past century has been made ridiculous by the next, and the practice of diplomats to treat the peoples—in peace and in war—as pawns in a game of chess is largely account- able for the truism. Shortly after the present war broke out, several Ministers of the Liberal Cabinet placed a very different ideal before the public. I may cite, in particular, Mr. Churchill's utterances in this regard :—

"Let us, whatever we do, fight for and work towards great and sound principles for the European system. The first of these principles which we should keep before us is the principle of nationality—that is to say, not the conquest or subjugation of any great community, or of any strong race of men, but the setting free of those races which have been subjugated and conquered. And if doubt arises about disputed areas of country, we should try and settle their ultimate destination in the reconstruction of Europe which must follow from this war, with a fair regard to the wishes and feelings of the people who live in them."[1]

And, again :—

"We want this war to settle the map of Europe on national lines, and according to the true wishes of the people who dwell in the disputed areas. After all the blood that is being shed, we want a natural and harmonious settlement, which liberates races, restores the integrity of nations, subjugates no one, and permits a genuine and lasting relief from the waste and tension of armaments under which we have suffered so long."[2]

To enunciate such principles is one thing; to give prac- tical effect to them is a very different thing. It is useless disguising from ourselves that powerful influences are now at work, and will be exerted when the belligerents have severally laid down their arms, to settle the destinies of the inhabitants of "disputed areas" in accordance with the accidents of military conquest, and not in accordance with the principles enunciated by Mr. Churchill and others of his colleagues. The cases of Poland and Alsace-Lorraine are classic examples of the diplomatist's art in this respect. If the influence of Great Britain at the Settlement is to be exerted in favour of the principles so warmly endorsed by

[1] At the London Opera House, September 11. (*Morning Post*, September 12.)

[2] In the *Giornale d'Italia.*—Text issued by the Official Press Bureau. September 25.

Mr. Churchill, the British people must face the facts in advance, and understand them.   The future destinies of the Poles and of the inhabitants of Alsace-Lorraine must be decided by themselves, and must not depend upon the military results of war.   Machinery must be evolved not only by the belligerent States, but by the neutral States—whose interests in securing a stable Settlement are obvious —to ensure that the wishes of the people concerned shall be honestly ascertained and honestly recorded, and that their verdict, whatever it may be, shall be regarded as binding upon the Governments affected.   By our national attitude towards this problem will the professions, officially and unofficially made on behalf of Great Britain at the outbreak of war, be tested.   The restoration of Belgium to the Belgians is but one aspect of it.   A Settlement based upon the recognition that the inhabitants of "disputed areas" are not movable goods, but human beings with traditions, aspirations, and economic interests of their own, is the only Settlement which offers any prospects of permanence, and it must be universally and impartially enforced.

It would, for instance, be a bitter satire upon the generous impulses which have moved the people of Great Britain in this war, and upon the professions of British statesmen, if the struggle resulted in a Settlement under which the opportunities for national development of any section of the Polish population in Europe (which numbered 23 millions in the opening years of the present century) fell short of those which, in increasing measure since 1866, the Galician Poles have enjoyed under the much-abused rule of the Dual Monarchy.   This consideration applies equally to the Ruthenian (Ukrainian) population of Eastern Galicia, which, with the support of the Polish democracy of the province, secured early last year many of the reforms for which it had been agitating, if, to quote Mr. Asquith, "room" is to be "found and kept for the independent existence and free development of the smaller nationalities —each with a corporate consciousness of its own."   I will not on this occasion attempt to discuss the problem of Alsace-Lorraine in any detail.   I will merely remark that the principle set forth by Mr. Churchill and Mr. Asquith, and embodied in Clause I. in the constitution of the Union of Democratic Control, applies with equal force to the inhabitants of those provinces, and can no more be honestly or safely departed from in their case than in the case of the Belgians, the Serbians, the Poles, and, for that matter, the Bulgars, the Finns, and the Persians.

The second and third clauses in the constitution of the Union may be treated conjointly. They read as follows :—

"No treaty, arrangement, or undertaking shall be entered into in the name of Great Britain without the sanction of Parliament. Adequate machinery for ensuring democratic control of foreign policy shall be created.

"The foreign policy of Great Britain shall not be aimed at creating alliances for the purpose of maintaining the balance of power, but shall be directed to concerted action between the Powers, and the setting up of an International Council, whose deliberations and decisions shall be public, with such machinery for securing international agreement as shall be the guarantee of an abiding peace."

I suppose most people will concede that the present condition of Europe provides a conclusive demonstration that the machinery regulating the official intercourse between States has broken down. At this moment passions necessarily run high and judgment is obscured. But, even so, no man who preserves any sense of perspective at all but realises that the element of fear has been a powerful, if not the predominating, element in producing at once the moral atmosphere which has made this convulsion possible, and the material factors thereof in the shape of enormous and perfected armaments which are being used by the belligerents for one another's destruction. The last quarter of a century has witnessed an astonishing advance in the arts of peace. Great forces, some measurable, some intangible, have been operating to draw the civilised peoples closer to one another, to accentuate the mutuality of human needs, to reduce the significance of political frontiers as an obstacle to community of effort. The whole tendency of modern development emphasises the interdependence of civilised peoples. But over this natural and healthy growth a parasitic growth has flung its tentacles, stunting normal expansion. Side by side with the elements of co-operation have risen the elements of potential destruction. The fairer the promise the more over-shadowing the menace. While innumerable demonstrations have testified to the spread of the idea of human solidarity among the *peoples,* the *Governments* have been steadily increasing their armaments, applying the triumphs of human science over nature to preparations for the swift annihilation of man, levying increased toll upon the communally-earned wealth of the nations in order to perfect and multiply engines for their extermination. Fear, and a belief in the assurance of their governors that only by such means could national safety be secured and peace maintained, has induced the peoples to acquiesce; but, while acquiescing, the manifestations in favour of international solidarity have multiplied, inspired by the pathetic hope that in due course they would succeed in purging fears and removing the burden of armaments which constituted the material expressions of those fears. But the odds were too heavy. The forces working for peace have lacked cohesion, organisation, and concentration of purpose.

Now, the problem for humanity to-day and to-morrow is this. Have the peoples the will, the determination, the resolve to work constructively, each within its own frontiers and as far as possible in co-operation with one another, for the elimination of the fundamental causes conducive to the creation of mutual fears; for the removal of the factors in the national life which occasion those fears and which attain supremacy over the destinies of countless millions as the outcome of those fears? If so, the peoples must *organise*. *We must organise against war.* We have been faced with a vast organisation for the promotion of war, not in one country only, but in all countries. If we imagine that the close of the present war will automatically destroy that organisation, we are preparing for ourselves the most bitter of delusions. The possibilities—nay, the probabilities—are that it will be stronger at the end of the war than it was at the beginning. However that may be, it will assuredly exist, and those who incarnate it will dominate the Governments. *We must evolve a vaster organisation to oppose it.* We can do so if we will, for the entire mechanism of war is of our own tolerating. If we ceased to tolerate it, it would cease to be. Our future is in our own hands.

To achieve this end we must revolutionise the proceedings of diplomacy, and we must convert Mr. Asquith's verbal expression into a positive policy, a policy which shall substitute "for force, for the clash of competing ambitions, for groupings and a precarious equipoise," a "real European partnership based on the recognition of equal right and established and enforced by the common will."

In other words, we must get rid of secret diplomacy and the fetish of the "Balance of Power" which defies analysis and means precisely what the diplomats desire that it shall mean at a particular moment. And each people must begin at home. If each waits for the other to move, all will be equally helpless in the future, as they have been in the past. *And the key-note to action must be Organise, still Organise, again Organise!*

The Union of Democratic Control combines, in the clauses quoted further back, both the national and the international aim. Prominent personalities, differing so widely in their political ideals, as Lord Bryce, Lord Rosebery, and Mr. Austen Chamberlain, have severally, within recent years, drawn attention to the secrecy of our own diplomacy, and to the almost unlimited powers of the Cabinet in determining our foreign policy. The report of the recent Royal Commission has partially lifted the veil from the totally undemocratic character of our diplomatic machinery. Some of the most respected names in French political life—M. Ribot, Baron d'Estournelles de Constant, Senator de Lamarzelle—protested in the French Legislature against the secrecy of Anglo-French diplomacy in the Morocco affair. No one who has really studied the evidence available will deny that the last decade has witnessed a marked tendency towards increased secrecy in the handling of our foreign policy, together with a steady decrease in the facilities for Parliamentary and public discussion. The virtual withdrawal of foreign affairs from national debate has, strangely enough, synchronised with the spread of educational opportunities among the great mass of the people. This state of affairs cannot continue in a community such as ours without the gravest danger to the British Commonwealth. A democracy upon whose shoulders reposes in the ultimate resort the burden of sustaining the greatest Empire the world has ever known, cannot be kept in perpetual ignorance of its Government's relations with foreign Powers—which we term foreign policy. The conduct of our foreign policy involves the most vital of all issues to the life of the nation, the issue of peace and war, which is the issue of individual and national life and death. The Union of Democratic Control labours under the deepest conviction that one of the greatest needs of the hour and of the future consists in a systematised effort to drive this elementary truth into the minds of the masses in this country—to demonstrate the indissoluble connection between the management of our foreign affairs and the daily life, the welfare, the happiness of every individual in the land.

If it be right and proper—and none will gainsay it—that the self-governing Dominions should be consulted as to the terms of Settlement which will eventuate from this war, and should share in the counsels of the Mother Country with regard to the direction of our foreign policy in the future, *a fortiori* are the people of these islands entitled to be taken into the confidence of the Government. It is their right. They must be quickened in their appreciation of it, and when they are so quickened that right can only be denied them at the risk of imperilling the safety of the State.

But the necessity for fundamental reform goes far deeper than that, and in opposing it the pedagogues are, all unconsciously, playing with fire. For there is a new spirit abroad, and those who affect contemptuous indifference to it tread in dangerous paths. Tens of thousands of young men have flung themselves into the field of battle to-day, inspired by a double sentiment—to help the weak and to assist in bringing wars to an end. Is the nation which accepts their sacrifice to treat them as unworthy of consultation on the causes, the events, the rivalries which lead to war? Again, do the politicians who during the past five years have been engaged in familiarising the masses with their just grievances, and bringing home to their understanding that those grievances are not necessary and ordained, but preventable—do they ever consider whether they will not one day be asked: "Who made this war? What had we to do with it? Were we consulted? Did you tell us this and that?" It is no use pretending to believe that it will be for ever possible to persuade the nation that the war is explainable by the events of the six weeks which preceded it. More and more will it become apparent that the war has been the inevitable outcome of a universal system; that its true origins must be sought in that system, and that one of the most potential factors in that system is a Statecraft which, in all lands, in this land as in others, carries on its evolutions behind the peoples' backs and pursues ends remote from the "things that really matter" to the lives of the mass of the people. For those feelings a safety valve will have to be found, and the only possible safety valve is to prove to the people

that henceforth the foreign policy of this country shall be
a really national foreign policy; that the people shall be
fully acquainted with the nature of their liabilities, and
shall clearly perceive where they stand and whither they
are being led.

Among the organic reforms to ensure greater national
control of foreign policy which the Union of Democratic
Control advocates are these : The complete reform of our
diplomatic service, carrying with it the abolition of the
income test and the substitution of competition and merit
for nomination, privilege, and class distinction.   No
Treaty, alliance, or understanding of any sort, contract,
obligation, or liability involving national responsibilities
to be entered upon without the consent of Parliament :
Parliament to have the additional opportunity of discussing
every treaty in detail before being asked formally to ratify
it.   The Foreign Office vote to be discussed annually in
the House of Commons as a matter of regular procedure;
the vote to occupy two days, and to be treated like the
army and navy estimates.   Periodical pronouncements on
foreign policy in the country to be the recognised duty of
a Foreign Secretary.   A Foreign Affairs Committee of the
House to be formed for purposes of deliberation on points
of detail and with the object of further strengthening
Parliamentary control, knowledge and sense of responsibility.   All treaties to be periodically submitted to discussion with a view to amendment, confirmation, or can-
cellation.   All these organic reforms can be secured without
drastic constitutional changes.   Indeed, they would go far
to make of democratic government a reality, and not what
it is at present, so far as the conduct of the foreign policy
of the country is concerned, a sham.   Taken in combination they would operate in the direction of diminishing the
autocratic position of the Foreign Secretary, who, to-day,
owing to the congestion of Parliamentary business, to the
enormous labours devolving upon Cabinet Ministers, the
curtailment of Parliamentary privileges, and the ensuing
decay of interest in the House on foreign affairs due to
increasing lack of responsibility, escapes in practice all
effective control, and is entirely dependent upon his permanent officials, selected from one particular class in the
State, and imbued with all the virtues, but also with all
the prejudices and narrowness of outlook inherent in that
class.

But these organic reforms will not in themselves suffice to secure real national control of foreign policy. They will have to be accompanied and stimulated by an awakening of the nation as a whole, both to its interests and to its rights. One will be the complement of the other. In advocating these reforms and in making of them a conspicuous feature of its propaganda, the Union of Democratic Control is chiefly concerned with the interests of the people of these Islands, as is natural. It maintains that the democracy of the United Kingdom may fairly lay claim to the sympathy and moral support of the democracies of the Self-governing Dominions in its efforts to strengthen the national control over foreign policy. But it would be idle to suggest that the democracies of the Self-governing Dominions are not also entitled to claim the sympathy and assistance of the British democracy in any attempt they may be led, severally or collectively, to put forward in favour of the wider problem of Imperial control. It is now clearly apparent that under the system obtaining it is possible not only for the Cabinet, but for a section of the Cabinet to contract obligations of honour towards foreign Powers involving the potential use, not only of the armed forces of these islands, but of the Empire. This is the second occasion within a comparatively short period that Canadian, Australian, New Zealand, and South African blood has been shed as the result of policies in the formation of which none of the Self-governing Dominions have had a share. The situation is obviously an impossible one. Upon a solution being found for it—and the case of India is, in principle at least, analogous—depends the preservation of the British Empire. Personally, I find it difficult to apprehend how the *national* democratic claim and the *Imperial* democratic claim can be satisfied by a Legislature and a Government elected at the heart of the Empire on purely domestic issues, but responsible in fact for, and directing in practice, the conduct of foreign policy, the administration of the fighting services, and the administration of the vast tropical Dependencies of the Crown whose social and economic problems are inextricably interwoven with the destinies of European States.

"For groupings and alliances and a precarious equipoise—a real European partnership." In those words is embodied the policy of the Union of Democratic Control. Mr. Asquith is not a sentimentalist. But that utterance is his. Neither are we sentimentalists, and whatever steps

Mr. Asquith and his colleagues, and their successors, whoever they may be, intend to take in that connection, the Union of Democratic Control intends to work for the policy which that utterance embodies. We are doing so. And in this case, again, the people of every State must concentrate primarily upon instructing and impregnating the public mind within their particular State. Moreover, initiative must come from somewhere. Great Britain has led the world in so many reforms making for human liberties that she may well take the lead in an effort to rid humanity of a conception of Statecraft which no longer responds to the needs of civilised men. The pursuit of the "Balance of Power" is a diplomatic will-o'-the-wisp hovering over the graves of innumerable victims. By the statesmen of no country has it been erected into a cult to a greater extent than by our own. This is an additional reason why the attempt to substitute "a real European partnership" should come from us. The vagaries of the "Balance of Power" led us in 1854 to espouse the cause of the Turk in a quarrel which was not of Russia's seeking; in 1878 to regard national "honour" as compatible with reinstating Ottoman despotism over Christian populations; in the 'seventies and 'eighties to see in what was then currently described as the German "hegemony" in Europe, a cause for eminent national satisfaction; in 1900 to contemplate war with France over some West African jungle, Nilotic swamp, or Siamese river; in 1910 to regard Germany as the potential foe. And if, as the outcome of a complete victory of the Allies, it were considered desirable to inflict upon Germany one tithe of the pains and penalties recommended by the *Morning Post* school, by the distinguished gentlemen who write letters to *The Times*, and by a notorious section of the press (which is able to command an enormous publicity), it is absolutely certain that the Franco-Russian combination would be regarded on the morrow of the war as the disturber of the "Balance" and the future enemy. The pursuit of the "Balance" has now reached the apotheosis of its monstrous imbecility. It has conducted us to the most colossal failure of human wisdom in the history of the world. Is Armageddon to be followed by a renewal of the policy of the "Balance," or by some new conception of international policy and statecraft?

The Union of Democratic Control believes that in all countries where public opinion is articulate there exists an intense desire for the creation of international machinery supported by the collective will of Europe, which would adjudicate upon disputes between States of a character not susceptible of treatment by the Hague Court, and which would be invested with the necessary power to enforce its decisions in the ultimate resort. We believe that the creation of such machinery is practicable and not Utopian if public opinion in favour of it in every land is *organised*.

Among the vested interests concerned in keeping Europe in a condition of fear and apprehension, none perhaps are more insidious and more dangerous than the interests bound up with the armament industry; *and in no country are they more powerful than in our own*. The Union of Democratic Control puts forward, therefore, as its fourth *desideratum* that : "Great Britain shall propose as a part of the Peace Settlement a plan for the drastic reduction, by consent, of the armaments of all the belligerent Powers, and to facilitate that policy shall attempt to secure the nationalisation of the manufacture of armaments and the control of the export of armaments by one country to another."

It is a self-evident proposition that so long as the influence of militarist ideas within each State is buttressed by the material factor, represented by gigantic armament, the organised growth of the forces of Pacifism will be faced with a formidable obstacle. The reduction of armaments must accompany any real change in the relationship between States, and that is why we ask that Great Britain should take the lead in making proposals, whose effective realisation, however, must depend upon the success of the other proposals which have been discussed above. The reduction of armaments involves, or should involve, the abolition of the internationalised private interest in the manufacture of armaments, which is, perhaps, the greatest of all scandals of our time.

Such are the chief ends and aims of the Union of Democratic Control. Each part of the programme we put forward for the consideration of our fellow-countrymen is linked up with the others. By the steady prosecution of the whole we believe that a happier and a more secure Britain will result, and that the mutual fears and suspicions which have hung like a nightmare over the civilised peoples of Europe, finally culminating in this terrible catastrophe, can be removed and their repetition **avoided.**

CHAPTER XX.

A Plea for Sanity of Thought[1]

PEACE, say we, by crushing Germany, since she is the only disturber of the peace. Peace, say the Germans, by crushing the Allies, since they are the only disturbers of the peace. But how does this view of the Germans look to us? Does it look like peace? Do we imagine ourselves lying down for ever, beaten, humbled, and repentant, under the protection of an armed Germany? Well, as we feel about the German idea, so, we may be sure, do they feel about ours. That route does not and cannot lead to peace. . . . We can no more crush her (Germany) than she can crush us. And the attempt to do so can only lead to a new war.—*Mr. G. Lowes Dickinson ("After the War," A. C. Fifield. 6d.).*

If you were to ask privately all those who do not provide implements of war, or edit patriotic papers, or belong to the intellectual victims of these papers, whether they would not gladly undo this war if they could, you would find it easy to accommodate in one single sanatorium the whole lot of those who would answer in the negative. . . . . An invisible army will arise from the souls of the victims of this self-killing war, and with this army we shall conquer all the others that have gone so far astray."—*Mr. von Tepper-Laski, President of the "New Fatherland League," in "Das Freie Wort."*

WHILE our gallant soldiers are laying down their lives in the marshes of Flanders, in the Gallipoli Peninsula, in the Persian Gulf, in the Cameroons, and in East Africa, ideas are fermenting, policies are in the making, elements are contending which will determine whether their collective sacrifice will have been vain or fruitful. I say collective sacrifice, for sacrifice in the individual, whatever form it may take, can never be fruitless. But the outcome of collective sacrifice may be, and frequently has been, in war. Just as the present war commands an unprecedented collective sacrifice, so will its consequences be unprecedented. Does it mark the final convulsions ushering in the birth of a new era, setting free a new spirit which has been striving for light and utterance? Or will the fetters that bind humanity be riveted but the tighter for it, the struggling masses flung back, the artificial barriers which separate the peoples from one another strengthened with

[1] The *Labour Leader*, August 26, 1915.

additional buttresses? Are the peoples to mingle in peaceful intercourse, knitting closer links of mutual comprehension; or will the frontiers still grin with countless cannon; the ocean highways still be cleft with monsters of destruction above and beneath the depths; the sky still be polluted by whirring engines of death?

"Is it to be hate?" as Mr. Harold Picton asks.[1] The people of this country have an enormous share in determining these questions. which for them have not merely an ethical value, but a most practical and utilitarian significance, considered nationally and individually. There are some, it is true, to whom nationality makes but scant appeal. The sentiment for land of birth, for the body of history, custom, and tradition, which through the centuries has moulded certain types in a certain setting and produced broadly defined characteristics and ideals—that sentiment awakens little echo in some breasts. To their owners nationalism has had its day; for them the lamp of hope shines in a wider sphere, a more catholic outlook. They long for the time and anticipate it, when man shall have but one cradle and one country—the universe; shall own allegiance to none but Universal Law. In the internal unification of States, laboriously achieved, they see but the prelude to that comprehensive unification which shall abolish political frontiers and weld humanity into one universal commonwealth. For them internationalism is the goal, and they find no place for nationalism within it. Theirs, intrinsically, the more splendid vision if the religion we profess has any significance at all. But all its perspectives may not harmonise. Internationalism of a kind which shall bring the world at least measurably nearer the Christ philosophy may not of necessity involve the disappearance of nationalism, except in its aggressive and intolerant form. It is an obstacle to the growth of a great ideal to make its acceptance dependent upon the abandonment of an existing one, passionately clung to by the bulk of humanity, and not proven incompatible with the former. Moreover, the horizon open to the best of us is pitifully limited, and dogmatism on such a theme is worse than useless.

For my part, I write as one who believes that the British commonwealth has evolved ideals in the art of

[1] By Harold Picton. London : George Allen and Unwin, Ltd. Price, 3d.

Imperial Government which have generated a greater measure of human liberty for a greater aggregate of the human race than any system which the Continent of Europe has created or could by any possibility have created, given geographical conditions; as one who believes that were the ideals of political freedom, which after much travail the British genius has crystallised into definite institutions, to be overthrown, the world would be immeasurably the poorer. But I write, too, as one who believes that these achievements have been performed at the price of weakening the nerve centre of the Imperial edifice. The very virtues which have produced a race of Imperial statesmen with large ideas marked by political sagacity have led here at home to an indifference towards and neglect of social problems and to a blind and partly unconscious selfishness which are undermining the whole structure, and constitute the flaw in the foundations of a very splendid edifice. That flaw the democracy, in my judgment, can alone remove. We stand to-day at the parting of the ways.

We are in the grip of a conspiracy against truth in this country. To speak truth is to be unpatriotic. To bid the nation weigh carefully the outlook and think for itself is to be "pro-German." And the misfortune is that a great many—a vast mass—of reasonable people, belonging to all classes, are allowing themselves to be hypnotised, do not realise the profound modifications of thought which this war is creating, and are, by their blindness, bringing down upon the British commonwealth those very dangers which they dread. Take, for instance, this vision of an internationalism which shall replace nationalism. The people who most declaim against it are doing most to spread it. Why? Because they see in it nought but the mutterings of a soulless proletariat. Do they ever ask themselves what the governing classes have done for the masses that the latter should be led to regard death and mutilation on the field of battle as the sublimest manifestation of human worth, the supreme achievement of human duty? Do they, ready as they have ever proved themselves to be to consent to such sacrifice when called upon—and none can justly dispute that claim—ever take the trouble to inquire why incentives to similar action may be lacking in the lives of millions of their countrymen? For them, "patriotism" has but one meaning. But for them country, home, history are tangible realities, fibres which permeate their being, cords responding instantly to the touch—and

with reason. But what are country, home, history to numbers in those crowds they all uncomprehendingly jostle in
the busy thoroughfares of life? For them prowess in arms
means a social halo; and often more material gains. But
for those others—what? In one case substance worth the
risk; the risk itself framed in irridescent hues of excite-
ment and glory. In the other sterility, the goal of risk;
beyond the goal, submergence in the drudgery and precariousness of the heretofore. What reward was meted out
to the conquerors of Waterloo? The rulers whom they
served completed the process of reducing them to the most
pitiable of all situations to which a people can be reduced
—the situation of a landless proletariat. The conquerors
of Waterloo became the serfs of the aristocracy and landed
gentry. The termination of a protracted struggle "for the
liberties of Europe" found the mass of the people of England irremediably divorced from their land, degraded and
poverty stricken. The degradation still subsists in our
Poor Laws. Where in Europe will you see the like? What
benefit did the British people derive from the two and a
half millions which Pitt presented to the King of Prussia,
or from the million expended annually on the German
legion in order to keep order in England? What was
given them in return for fertilising the mountains of Spain
and Portugal with their blood? Did that particular war
of liberation liberate *them?* It did usher in a notable era
of improvement for the French and Prussian peasants.
But the conquerors of Waterloo were bereft of all. Since
then their descendants have been struggling hard and are
still struggling to obtain a measure of justice under changed
economic conditions.

But they have never won back their heritage—the land.
Our Junkers have clung fast to it. It can be legitimately
said of the classes whose power is so largely based to-day
upon that dispossession that if they are brave and fearless,
as they have always been, their patriotism has, nevertheless, a silver lining. To-day these same classes, slavishly
adulated and emulated by a new-sprung hybrid type
deficient in the virtues which characterised and still in some
measure characterise those they ape and are, in part, sup-
planting, but opulent and commanding publicity; take little
trouble to conceal their hopes that the aftermath of this
war of liberation will be conscription, Protection, and the
final burial for this generation of urgent social reforms.
And it is from them that emanate the counsel of a war of

extermination and strangulation towards our present enemies—even though it last a decade and sweeps the very breath of liberty from our land. It is from them that came the arrogant "Thou shalt not grow," which is one of the root causes of this war. It is from their organs that come the epithets of "traitorous," levelled at those who bid the people think out the aftermath of such a policy in the light of what has gone before. Among the vice-presidents of the Anti-German Union are a marquis and two belted earls, who between them own 300,000 acres of British soil, to say nothing of the proprietor of a certain London newspaper which is frankly Militarist, Conscriptionist, and Protectionist.

When we are faced, as we are to-day, by the clatter of certain politicians and by the Tory Press (supported by a number of "intellectuals," who seem to have exchanged a certificate of lunacy with their German colleagues) in favour of a "war of attrition" which is to last three, five, ten years if need be; when we are faced with this, and when we realise the immense powers behind the appeal, it appears to me that some of us are bound to put the other side of the picture. And for this reason : that persistent neglect of the other side of the picture, the neglect involved in this proclaimed policy, will in the ultimate resort destroy the British Commonwealth.

A few months before the war, statistics were placed before us. They apprised us, did these statistics, that in the majority of English counties our agricultural population was permanently underfed, and that 60 per cent. of our agricultural labourers between the ages of 20 and 65 were receiving wages below the standard required to maintain health. They told us that the housing conditions of our working classes in most of our great cities and in very many parts of rural England were a disgrace to a State calling itself enlightened; that the slum areas of our cities alone sheltered between two and three million citizens of this proud Empire. They told us that here in wealthy England half a million people were dying yearly from preventable disease; that infantile mortality in our manufacturing centres marked a higher percentage than prevails among the primitive races we are so anxious to proselytise; that a vast host was living, through no fault of the units composing it, just on the poverty line, in the midst of the ostentatiously displayed wealth of the richest State in Christendom; that the mass of the people were enjoying but a fractional part of the national income—built up by their muscles and their sweat—and that half the acreage of the United Kingdom is held by 10,000 persons out of a population of 45 millions.

Do those who have spread these facts before us in official documents; do the prelates, and the well-fed and comfortable (the battalions that possess reserves to stave off the pinch of economic stress), who fling up their hands in horror at the conception of political internationalism— do they ever contemplate, one wonders, that some day they may be faced, not merely by the sullen mutterings of the cowed and starved, but by questions clamoured from the throats of multitudes? Questions they would find it hard to answer and to meet. Questions such as these :"What is the 'security' you offer me in exchange for my blood and that of my sons?" "What is the 'home' I am asked to defend?" "Where is my 'land' which you tell me is in peril?"

CHAPTER XXI.

The Interests of Belgium[1]

THE *a priori* refusal of the Allies to negotiate a general European settlement permitting a peaceful evacuation of Belgium would be for my country the equivalent of a death warrant. Such a refusal would also constitute a great crime—the greatest crime indeed which human history has ever known.—*M. Henri Lambert (ex-Member of the Commission for the reform of the Belgian electoral laws, Member of the Société d'economic politique, etc.), in the "U.D.C." for December, 1915.*

BROADLY speaking, there are two alternate lines of policy upon which the people of this country have to make up their minds. If, and when, the opportunity presents itself to discuss a termination of the war, either through the good offices of Neutral Powers, or in some other fashion, will they insist that it shall be taken? Or if that opportunity occurs will they actively approve of, or tacitly acquiesce in, its rejection? In other words, will they be disposed to consider a settlement not dishonourable to them; or will they decline, and if they decline, why will they decline? The answer to the question, one assumes, depends upon what the British people, not merely the British Government, not merely the British governing classes, but the British people, really want.

Do they want to "crush" Germany, or do they want what Mr. Churchill said the Government wanted last September?[2]

"We want a natural and harmonious settlement which liberates races, restores the integrity of nations, subjugates no one, and permits a genuine and lasting relief from the waste and tension of armaments under which we have suffered so long."

That is what the British people have got to decide, and the sooner they set about making up their minds the better.

It is true that Mr. Churchill has talked since about the "unconditional surrender" of Germany. It is for the British people to choose whether the first or the second edition

[1] The *Labour Leader*, September 9, 1915.
[2] 1914.

of Mr. Churchill suits them best. There is an ethical side
and a strictly utilitarian side. When we consider the
ethical side, Belgium is naturally the chief figure in the
picture. Let us, then, look at the ethical side a moment.
No one will gainsay that what stirred the generous
emotions of the mass of the British people was the in-
famous invasion of Belgium, and her treatment by the invaders. If the invasion of Belgium had not occurred and
the Government had decided to go to war with Germany
because a state of war existed between Germany, France,
and Russia, there would have been a complete split in the
Cabinet, and an immediate "stop-the-war" movement
would have been the outcome. It was Belgium that made
the appeal to British hearts. It is of our duty towards
Belgium that the British Government has continually
spoken. "Remember Belgium" has been the main
theme in recruiting propaganda. It is true that *The Times*
and other papers, annoyed when Mr. Lloyd George recently
declared that but for Belgium he would not have supported
the war (or words to that effect), hastened to state that
while Belgium's case was a sad one, we were really at
war to maintain the "balance of power"; and it is true
that *The Times* spoke the truth when it made that declaration. It spoke for the Tory Party as a whole, for the
most influential section of the governing class, for the
militarists and Jingoes; and it said quite accurately, so
far as those forces in the nation are concerned, that we
are at war for the "balance of power."

To do it justice, *The Times* revealed the inner mind of
the classes who have hitherto directed the foreign policy
of this country quite early in the day, for on December
4[1] it wrote: "We have always fought for the balance of
power. We are fighting for it to-day." The then existing interpretation of the "balance of power" by those
classes was specified with blunt emphasis by the *Spectator*
a few days afterwards, when it remarked:

"If Germany had tried to invade France by the direct
route instead of by way of Belgium, we should still have
been under a profound obligation to help France and
Russia. It is useless to tell us that we were free to act
as we pleased. . . All our dealings with France—our
sanction of her line of policy, our military conversations
with her Staff, our definite association with her acts abroad
—had committed us to her cause as plainly as though we

[1] 1914.

had entered into a binding alliance with her.   And what is true of our understanding with France is true in a scarcely less degree of our understanding with Russia.''

But the British *people* did not support the war, the bulk of the Cabinet did not support the war, and would not have supported the war, to fight the battle of France and Russia alone; in other words, for the "balance of power." The British *people* supported the war out of pity and indignation for Belgium.

If the British people still feel pity and indignation for Belgium, then it is time they faced honestly what the effect upon Belgium would be of a refusal on our part to consider a settlement which would restore her territorial integrity and compensate her (so far as it is possible to compensate her) for the material damage she has suffered. I am assuming, for the purposes of the argument, that such a settlement may be, or may become, within the bounds of practical politics. I will deal further with that assumption later on. What, then, would be the result for Belgium of a refusal on our part to discuss terms of peace of which the evacuation of Belgium would be an integral part? Well, the first and palpable result would be a prolongation of the German occupation of Belgium; a postponement of Belgium's liberation. What would ensue? Obviously, an intensified renewal of (*a*) the German attempt to break our line, (*b*) our attempt to break the German line. If the Germans succeeded in breaking our line, Belgium would cease to occupy much place in our thoughts, for obvious reasons. Simultaneously with a changed perspective of Belgium in *our* thoughts, the "annexation" party in Germany would be immensely strengthened. Belgium's future would be one of exceeding blackness from whatever standpoint examined. If we succeeded in breaking the German line, the Anglo-French armies would dispute with the German for every square yard of Belgian soil, destroying with shell-fire, as they would be compelled to do for military reasons, every town, village, homestead, and public building which sheltered the German troops. What would remain of Belgium at the end?

The man who does not face these questions is not being honest with himself; nor is he being honest towards Belgium. So far as Belgium's interests are concerned, her most vital interest is a settlement which shall, as speedily as may be, restore her integrity, enable her, with help, to build up once more her industrial and agricultural life,

and give her a greater measure of security for the future
than she has had in the past. The latter can only come as
the result of the destruction of the theory of the "balance
of power," and with it the abandonment by the Governments of the group system of international relationships.
And that can only be achieved by a process of international
reconstruction which it will be the task of every true demo-
crat in every country to labour for unceasingly after the
war. If we are to consider Belgium's interest, Belgium's
interest clearly does not lie in having the whole of her
territory converted into one vast ruin.

But it may be said, "If Belgium's interest is as you
set it forth, why does not the Belgian Government make
some sort of statement in that sense?" A moment's consideration will show that it would be impossible for the
Belgian Government to make any such statement. Belgium is, virtually, one of the Allies. She is the last of
them that could put forth an independent wish at this
moment. Her Government is enjoying the hospitality of
French soil; hundreds of thousands of Belgian refugees
are established in France and England. Well, if not the
Belgian Government, then, at least, some Belgian newspaper or public man? How? I believe there are still
papers published in Belgium. What they are saying I do
not know, but we cannot accept as genuine Belgian opinion
any printed expression of opinion in a Belgian newspaper
which passes the German censors. *Le Vingtième Siècle*
is printed at Havre, and the *Indépendance Belge,* I believe,
in London. But these are merely Government organs so
far as any expression of public policy is concerned. As for
individuals—other than members of the Belgian Government—the only statements I have seen are those of M.
Henri Lambert and M. Paul Otlet, and there is certainly
nothing in what they have written which suggests that my
view of Belgium's interests is not the right view. Both
these distinguished Belgians have written with sound sense
and a practical appreciation of the underlying issues of
the war and of the fate of their country. M. Henri Lambert owns a big industrial establishment at Charleroi, and
is an honorary member of the Society of Political Economy
of Paris. He is an Economist of repute, a man of wide
reading and much experience, of sterling honesty and strong
character. His letter in the *Nation* the other day, his
letters in the *Westminster Gazette,* and two remarkable

pamphlets, one of which has been translated into English,[1] are familiar, I dare say, to some of my readers. As a Belgian he might be excused for taking a view of the war which excludes sanity of judgment. I do not know, but I suppose he must be a great material loser from it, apart from his feelings of belonging to a small nationality shamefully used. But he does not think, apparently, that true patriotism for a Belgian civilian consists in adding his voice to the sterile declamations against the enemy. He realises that the Germans are not naturally endowed with a double dose of original sin, and that the origin of the war did not start with the bombardment of Liège.

"The international situation to-day—he writes—is due to a series of special circumstances affecting the interests of nationalities. National psychology is a factor which has played in it a part, the importance of which neither is, nor can be, contested. But the real 'causes,' the original and deep-seated causes, were of a far more general character, connected with the very nature and necessity of things. . . .

"The war will of necessity be followed by a peace, but the universal and permanent peace that each of the belligerents declares to be the supreme result to be attained by this war will not be the achievement of superiority of arms, nor of skilful strategy, nor, alas! of the bravery of soldiers : these forces will only be capable of imposing a temporary peace, consisting in the subjection and oppression of the conquered. A peace worthy of the name and worthy of true civilisation will be the achievement of the thought of those who shall succeed in furnishing a conception of the mutual rights of nations, in accordance with true justice."

And for Henri Lambert—and I very largely agree with him—one of the fundamental "causes" of this war is the protectionist and monopolistic policy adopted in economic matters by many of the Governments; by all, in a certain measure, though by Britain herself, hitherto, least of all —since Bright and Cobden's great achievement. Freedom of trade is for Henri Lambert the true road to a permanent peace among the nations. He does not discard other avenues of approach, but he says, in effect, "Neglect

[1] "The Ethics of International Trade" (Oxford University Press. Price, 2d., June).

this one, and your efforts are vain." And here I am in complete accord with him.

Here, then, is a well-known citizen of a country which has suffered much and grievously at German hands. You do not, however, find him demanding that Germany shall be crushed. He implores the European Governments to remove one of the most potent causes of international disputes, from which small countries like his own become, in the ultimate resort of war arising from those disputes, the victims, and freely admitting the "precarious position" of Germany, economically speaking, before the war.

M. Paul Otlet is the director of the Bibliographical Institute of Brussels, and Secretary of the Union of International Associations. In his thoughtful paper published last month, "Les conditions de la paix et de la sauvegarde de l'humanité" (*Les documents du Progrès, Lausanne*), he strikes the same note substantially as M. Henri Lambert. He does not see in this war Teutonic demonology triumphing over an international company of angels. He, too, goes to the root of things.

"The present war—he writes—if not in its origin, at least in the actual condition of its development and in its continuation is due not to one cause alone, but to a number of causes, which can be classified in the following manner."

He classifies his "causes" under seven heads, and to the economic cause he attributes primary importance. He thus defines it :

"Obstacles to expansion owing to the lack of colonies, the closing of markets as the result of protectionist or prohibitionist measures, unfair competition, export rebates, and 'dumping,' brought about by trusts sheltered by customs tariffs."

I do not propose to go into the arguments of these two Belgian gentlemen at any length at this moment. I shall, indeed, have myself to deal here with the enormously important problem of which they treat. What it behoved to place on record was their opinion as Belgians considering first the welfare of their country and not their own individual feelings of anger against its invaders. They see in a peace resulting from military victory on either side no future security for Belgium. They see in a negotiated settlement which shall take into account the national necessities of the various belligerents the only avenue through

which security for Belgium can come. And that, needless
to say, is the view of the Union of Democratic Control,
of the Independent Labour Party, of all men who decline to
let themselves be driven like cattle by newspaper bullies
into approval of courses which would be fatal, not for
Belgium only, but for Britain and for Europe as a whole.

CHAPTER XXII.

What is the War's Object?[1]

THEY (the people of England) might be misled for a time by passion, or duped by political intrigue; but ere long the sound practical good sense of the nation re-asserted itself; and he believed that a year would not pass before the country would ask with one voice: "Tell us for what we are fighting; tell us, if we are victorious, what will be the results of victory; tell us what recompense we may expect, except barren wreaths of glory, for a sacrifice of uncounted treasure and for mourning and misery in a hundred thousand English homes."
—*Lord Stanley on the Crimean War (Annual Register, 1855).*

PERHAPS the determined efforts of certain individuals and certain influences to establish a Cæsarism in our midst and, as a short cut to this goal, tŏ force Conscription upon us (not on the merits of the case, but as the result of an intrigue in which political and personal ambitions and great vested interests are leagued); perhaps this menace, which threatens dire consequences to our national efficiency, will prove to be a blessing in disguise. For it seems that only a momentous event will wrench the nation out of its mental lethargy, compel it to mobilise its brains, to think out clearly whither it is being led. In many respects the nation is living in a fool's paradise: in no respect more completely than in the surrender of its powers of constructive thought, in allowing its faculty of critical judgment to be atrophied, and in becoming the slave of phrases without inquiry as to their purport and significance. For what objects is the nation striving? What results does it hope to obtain from the "utter and complete defeat" of Germany? Is "utter and complete defeat" a realisable achievement in terms of modern warfare? Is a "war of attrition," upon which the nation is invited to pin its hopes, other than a mere collection of words devoid of practicable import?

The people are not thinking out these questions for themselves. They are allowing the "Government" to do their thinking for them, and publicists, every one of whose

[1] The *Labour Leader,* September 23, 1915.

predictions have been falsified in the last twelve months.

So long as the Government presented to the world a united front, "trust the Government" was at least an invocation which could reasonably be uttered. But what is there in the spectacle which the Government presents to-day to justify a demand for the continued paralysis of constructive criticism, not only as regards the conduct of the war—and here criticism has not lacked—but as regards the infinitely graver problem of the ultimate objects with which the war is being waged? Is the surrender of the national judgment with regard to the Government's policy, or lack of policy, concerning that supreme issue wise or even safe, when the very Ministers who demand it are engaged in washing the national dirty linen in public for the enemy's edification, and by their intrigues and plots against one another are convulsing the nation in the face of the enemy? Can the nation suffer itself to be led blindfold in respect of the war by Ministers who proclaim the profound animosities and divergencies which separate them as to the methods of prosecuting the war, and who summon to the support of their contending ambitions the most powerful organs of the public Press?

The time has come for asking some plain questions. The agitation for Conscription, violently thrust upon the country, raises the entire question of the ends for which the war, now thirteen months old, is being waged. For what *ultimate* purpose does an important section of the Government agitate for Conscription? What is the goal at which Ministers—Conscriptionist and anti-Conscriptionist —are aiming? Do they aim at securing an honourable peace; a peace which would liberate Belgium and Northern France from the invader; lead to the adjustment of the Alsace-Lorraine trouble on the basis of a *plébiscite* or of racial affinity; to the reconstitution of an independent Polish kingdom; to a federated Austria; to a Balkan settlement conceived as far as possible on the lines of nationality and a common tariff from which could evolve in the fulness of time a true Balkan Federation containing within itself sufficient vitality and coherence to make it independent of Austrian and Russian intrigue; to the "open door" for trade in over-sea possessions; to the abolition of the right of capture of private property at sea, and the recognition, by territorial readjustments in Africa and economic facilities in the near East, that the energies of a great nation of 65 millions, increasing at the rate of three-quarters of a million *per annum,* represents an element in the world which cannot be denied its fair share of opportunities in the development of the universe. Is it, as we were assured when it broke out, a war which, in the conscious purpose of those who direct our national policy, shall, out of the wreckage of human hopes and the desolation of human homes, give birth to international machinery for the future settlement of disputes between States, thus registering this war as the final spasm of a perverted statecraft?

Or is it a war of destruction and extermination that we are now waging? A war to which those in authority refuse to contemplate any conceivable limit of time in the endeavour to reduce the enemy to absolute impotence? A war in which those in authority decline to consider any negotiations for a settlement not preceded by an unconditional surrender of the enemy? If it is *not* such a war as this, why does not the Government indicate in other than rhetorical language capable of sinister interpretation the policy it is in reality pursuing, and the national aims it has in view? If it is not a war of destruction and extermination, why does not the Government dissociate itself from the utterances which emanate day by day from organisations and individuals claiming to speak for the nation; utterances which thereby strengthen the reactionary elements in the enemy countries, proportionately weaken the elements favouring an honourable peace, and prolong the holocaust?

"Some honourable gentlemen," Bright once remarked in a famous House of Commons speech, "talk as if Russia were a Power which you could take to Bow Street and bind over before some stipendiary magistrate to keep the peace for six months." Are we fighting to-day under the same delusion with regard to Germany? Are we fighting that British troops may march along the *Unter den Linden* in Berlin? If not, why cannot the Government say so? Are we fighting to seize and to retain all the German Colonies and to prevent Germany from ever holding oversea possessions in the future? If not, why cannot the Government say so? Are we fighting to shatter the political unity of Germany and violently to split up the Germanic Federation? If not, why cannot the Government say so? Are we fighting to dismember Germany, to reduce her territory in Europe by an extension of the Russian territorial area westwards, and the French and Belgian territorial area eastwards? If not, why cannot the Government say so? Are we fighting to build up an economic fence round Germany in the future, to differentiate against her trade throughout one-fifth of the habitable globe over which flies our flag, and to induce our Allies to act similarly; permanently to cripple her industrial activities, her foreign trade and shipping; to make deserts of her ports? Is the blood of the most virile in our land being spilled for these purposes ? If not, why cannot the Government say so?

For one and all of these objects are constantly proclaimed by pen and voice in this country to be the firm purpose of the nation to achieve. *And these statements are believed in Germany.* Just as the British newspapers publish the ravings against England of incendiary publicists and tub-thumping politicians in Germany; just as those British newspapers who advocate the crushing policy towards Germany lay stress upon these ravings and conceal from us the counsels of moderation which are also printed on the other side of the North Sea; so do the German newspapers reproduce the alleged designs of the British Government and people, conveyed in the intentions advertised here, and not repudiated by the British Government. And as these utterances with us are numerous and incessant, so are the German people, from the bottom to the top, persuaded that the fixed and unalterable purpose of the British nation is to shatter the German Empire, destroy the national integrity of Germany and reduce the German nation to political and economic paralysis.

They are wrong, of course. The British nation wants none of these things. The British people, like the German people, like all the belligerent peoples, want security; and it is only in the measure in which they refuse to think for themselves and listen to the voices of false prophets that they can be led to believe that security is obtainable by an "utter and complete" military defeat of the foe. Nor can any elements of sanity contained in the British Government desire these things. Such elements will intellectually reject them, not out of consideration for the German Government—the German methods of warfare are not conducive to rouse such sentiments—but from considerations of national self-interest. But no single member of the British Cabinet has publicly repudiated any of these proclaimed intentions. Why not? What could Britain lose in power and prestige by an official repudiation of purposes attributed to her by irresponsible speakers and writers, whose utterances fan the flames of hate and fear, and assist to perpetuate the massacre of the innocent?

For let us realise the truth. This war in its dominating and precipitating origin was a struggle for mastery between the Russian and Teutonic autocracies. *To-day it has become an Anglo-German war.* Mr. A. G. Gardiner is right when he says that without us the war would have been over long ago, in the sense, of course, that British gold and the command of the sea by the British fleet jointly enable our Allies to receive the cash sinews of war and an uninterrupted flow of American ammunition. It is equally true to say that if the ruling classes of Britain and of Germany would consent to negotiate, ten millions of men would escape the horrors of another winter campaign. I can fancy the Pan-German editor and the Tory Conscriptionist exclaiming as they read that sentence : "The people would not allow them to negotiate." The *people!* What people? Who are they who talk so glibly of "the people"? Do they mean the soldiers? Do they mean that the soldiers, the men living and dying daily in the Hell which the Statecraft of the great has brought upon them—that these men, involved in a common suffering, would prevent the Governments from negotiating? Do they mean that the workers in Germany and Britain would besiege the Reichstag and Westminster . . . to prevent the Governments from negotiating? Are they quite sure that the day may not come when, if the Governments will not negotiate, the democracies will compel them to do so?

The peoples in every land may be as persuaded to-day as they were thirteen months ago that the cause of their respective countries is the just cause and the only just cause. How could they believe otherwise, seeing that the entire mechanism of the Governments has been working full time to persuade them in those beliefs, and when the stress of cruel bereavements and the tremors of apprehension for beloved ones in daily danger of death provide an unlimited supply of lubricant for that mechanism? Nevertheless, the peoples want peace. In millions of hearts throughout Europe to-day there beats a passionate desire for a cessation of this senseless slaughter. Millions of lips in Europe are framing to-day prayers for the deliverance of humanity from the fiend of war, from another winter campaign. Is there a home in

France, in Germany, in Belgium, in Russia, across whose threshold the angel of death has not passed?

When will the Parliaments come to the rescue of the peoples and force the Governments to negotiate?

This war has become an Anglo-German war. The nature of the settlement which shall terminate the war will depend primarily upon the temper of Berlin and London. The delay within which the beginning of a settlement may be discussed depends primarily upon the temper of Berlin and London. Those who revile us for preaching the gospel of reason as opposed to the gospel of hate, point to France. "Go and preach it there," they sneer, "and see where you will find yourself." Little do they know of the French mind and soul outside Paris! France is supporting with a heroism and a dignity beyond compare the adverse decrees of Fate. *But France is slowly bleeding to death.* For France, even more, perhaps, than for Belgium herself, peace, and an early peace, is essential—even from the point of view of those who believe in the future maintenance of the policy of the "balance of power."

This war has become an Anglo-German war. In the Reichstag voices have been raised to protest against the policy of plunder and annexation on the Continent; to reject the doctrine of hate; to proclaim the true interests of Germany to lie in an honourable and just settlement.

But in the British Parliament no voice has yet been raised in similar strains; no utterance has yet been heard in repudiation of the doctrine of destruction, colonial annexation, and economic strangulation.

At a moment when a section of the Government is endeavouring to stampede the country into Conscription, there is the more urgent need for the note of statesmanship on the wider and fundamental issue—the policy and ultimate objects of the war—to be sounded.

CHAPTER XXIII.

Reactionaries in Germany and Britain[1]

THE idea of conquering foreign lands must be discarded, since nowadays the incorporation of an entire people, or the mutilation of an ancient State, which is a pillar of cultural power, can only be undertaken if there be a firm intention in the near future to risk another general war to maintain such a conquest. . . . The independence and freedom of the European nations, the German as well as the others, is the indispensable condition, without which there can be no peace and no peaceful work.—*Extract from pamphlet issued by the "Bund des Neues Vaterland" ("Society of the New Fatherland").*

Even, therefore, if we assign to Germany a monopoly of the spirit of aggressive militarism, European peace is not secured by crushing Germany.—*Mr. J. A. Hobson in "Towards International Government." (George Allen and Unwin, Ltd.)*

IT is clear that a bitter struggle is now raging in Germany, between the forces of reaction and of reason, on the subject of Belgium and the invaded portion of Northern France. With a brutal cynicism, the German militarists and Chauvinists are clamouring for the annexation, absorption, and assimilation of these European areas. Their attitude is on all fours with the utterances of Russian reactionaries in connection with Galicia before the war and with their acts during the occupation of that country—as to which the British public is allowed to know nothing. These gentle Teutons proclaim their ideal of a predatory empire and seek to lure their countrymen to fatal courses in the name of national safety; in reality, on behalf of national vanity in its most detestable form, and on behalf of material interests of class, naked and unashamed. But they are confronted by powerful influences working against them; influences which include personalities in the closest touch with the throne (and, it is stated, by the Kaiser himself) and with the official world, as well as the Social-Democrats. In this struggle the future destinies not of Belgium only, but of Germany herself and of Civilisation are involved.

[1] The *Labour Leader*, September 30, 1915.

A variety of circumstances will, no doubt, combine to determine which side shall eventually triumph. But among those circumstances the attitude of Great Britain will count as one of great, and, perhaps, capital importance. We can assist the German party of reaction and embarrass the party of reason—in effect, the party which aims at an honourable settlement of the war—in two ways. We can refuse to entertain the very idea of peace negotiations until the Germans have been driven from French and Belgian soil *manu militari*. We can characterise all German feelers towards peace negotiations thrown out from German sources as "intrigues"; describing them at one moment as an acknowledgment of approaching collapse and calling, therefore, for scornful rejection, and the next moment as impossible of consideration, on the ground that consideration would be tantamount to an admission that Germany had not been and could not be "crushed." That is one method, and the policy which underlies it is, of course, the "crushing" policy, advocated by some in the genuine belief that the national safety demands a Germany crushed and dismembered, by others from much the same motives as animate the German reactionaries in their proposals with regard to Belgium and Northern France. The latter point needs emphasising.

What are the elements in Germany which demand the subjugation and spoliation of Belgium and France? Possibly some of the Generals, although on that point we have no information; while from neutral sources it is rumoured that Von Moltke and Von Hindenburg (whose collective influence at this moment must be enormous) are averse to the annexationist policy. Setting the Generals on one side, we find in the annexationist camp the agrarians—*i.e.*, the ultra-protectionists, the enemies of democracy and freedom not only beyond but, and especially, within the borders of their own country; certain big industrial interests; certain "intellectuals" bemused with arrogance and suffering from that lack of a sense of modern perspective which appears to be an effect of a surfeit of historical reading; the type best described as the "civilian-militarists," of all types floating on the war-scum the most odious, "lip-heroes" as Professor Foerster[1] dubs them; the colonial Chauvinists—*i.e.*, the men who covet a large colonial empire by fair means or by foul; the

---

[1] In the *Forum* of Munich.

Jingo journalist and, we may be sure, working in the background, the armament interest.

And what are the elements here at home corresponding to the above, our "Prussians," so to speak (although, really it is becoming a little ridiculous to talk about "Prussian militarism," seeing that the King of Bavaria is the greatest Jingo of them all; "Bavarian militarism" would be a welcome change); the people who seek in every conceivable manner to assure the British public that the true voice of Germany is the voice of the German annexationist, tear a passion to tatters in their denunciation of it and then go on to urge that precisely the same policy they condemn as "German" should be adopted towards Germany by the victorious Allies! What our Generals are thinking the "man in the street" has no means of ascertaining. But in my experience, and in the experience of every one of my friends without exception, not a solitary military man of any standing at all, supports in private conversation the "crushing" of Germany—in the sense intended by our reactionaries—as either feasible or desirable. Setting, then, as in the case of Germany, military opinion aside, we find in the British reactionary camp the industrial and agrarian protectionists, many of the great landowners and monopolists, and the Conscriptionists, whom the *Globe* appropriately enough divides into two camps :—

"Those who wish to use the war to secure military conscription; those who hope to secure compulsory labour by obtaining national military service."[1]

And, again, as in Germany, the intellectuals afflicted with historical gangrene, the "lip-heroes," the Jingo-journalist (much more powerful here), and the aggressive Imperialists corresponding to the German colonial Chauvinists, but differing somewhat from their Teutonic prototypes insomuch as they do not avow their intentions on the trombone, but utilise the more subtle strains of the harmonium to convey their sentiments. Their sentiments are that Germany's sins are such that we can only punish her adequately by adding her colonial domains to our own Imperial heritage; naturally in a spirit of pure altruism, as a duty laid upon our shoulders by Providence, accepted with patient humility and resignation. Lastly, the armament interest keeping, for the nonce, discreetly in the background.

[1] Issue of August 30.

Such, then, is one method whereby Public Opinion is this country can play into the hands of the reactionaries in Germany, by playing the game of the reactionaries at home, between whom there is little to choose, save that the former are less cultured (for all their appeals to "Kultur") than the latter in the art of cloaking reaction in the garb of respectability; and who are, in both cases, *working for ends identical in principle, antagonistic to the interests and rights of the mass of their countrymen respectively.*

The other method would consist in allowing the German reactionaries to imagine that those Englishmen and Scotsmen who are incurring the wrath of their own Jingoes by appealing to the national sense of judgment, fairness and reason, are imbued with anything but detestation for their German prototypes, or are in the least degree less opposed to the predatory policy which the latter proclaim. No terms of settlement which included a German annexation of Belgium and of the invaded districts of France would find backers in this country. No section in Britain would acquiesce in a peace on those lines. Only a Britain utterly defeated, extenuated, and compelled to an unconditional abandonment of the struggle would consent to such a peace as that. And this calamity it is not within the power of Germany to inflict. Moreover, did it lie within her power, she would not secure *peace* thereby; but only a temporary cessation of hostilities. Those who are opposed to a policy which urges the prosecution of the war to the point of a German "unconditional surrender" (I am not concerned with discussing the practicability of the idea) because they think it insane from the standpoint of the British national interest, morally wrong and fatal to all hopes of international reconstruction, would be among the first to declare that the adoption by official Germany of the policy of the "Plunder-Party" would blend every shade and section of British thought into a unity of uncompromising resistance.

But at present there is no proof that the "Plunder-Party" has captured the German official machine, still less the majority of Public Opinion. There is good reason to suppose that it has done neither, and will do neither unless our reactionaries here persist in giving their German prototypes the chance of advancing the one and only card which might enable them, after all, to win the day—the card of a Germany whom the ruling class in Great Britain was implacably resolved to crush, despoil, pulverise economically, and reduce to a position of permanent inferiority in the councils of the nations. That, in effect, is what the British reactionaries *are* preaching. Let us see to it that they do not capture *our* official machine. For if the reactionaries on the other side were able to show that their card was not a *marked* one, they would proceed to argue that a Germany thus threatened must in self-preservation disable at least one of her foes for generations, and buttress her defences and powers of material recuperation by the annexation of territory, and the seizure of ports and coal and iron fields, evoking the spectre of fear by way of justification, which, in nations as in individuals, beckons along the road of savagery and stupidity.

The question, then for the British and for the German people alike is whether their collective sacrifices and sufferings are to be exploited by the selfish ambitions or stupidity of certain classes; whether their collective sacrifices and sufferings are to lead them, not up the slopes of the mountain of hope, but into the marshes of the valley of despair; whether the end of this infernal slaughter is to be, not mutual security and opportunity to build up their shattered lives afresh and prepare a brighter heritage for their children, but a perpetuation of unrest and an immeasurable aggravation of economic and social evils, cursing the rising generation and generations yet unborn.

CHAPTER XXIV.

The Penal Policy[1]

"BEFORE peace can come Germany must accept complete and utter destruction of her whole racial ideal and submit to be put into the tightest of leading strings."—*Mr. John Buchan, at the Bechstein Hall (Mr. Balfour in the chair). "The Times," April 27, 1915.*

"From this consideration there follows the conclusion which many people, including ourselves, have been extremely reluctant to adopt, but which seems to be irresistible—namely, at the end of the war Germany must cease to exist. . . . It is the State that must be destroyed. . . . . Not only can we not grant such a State an honourable peace, we cannot grant it peace at all."—*"New Statesman, May 15, 1915.*

"The German must be broken to pieces before there can ever be peace or safety."—*"Morning Post," May 12, 1915.*

"The Kaiser, his system, his sham culture, and the nation which follows him in reckless cruelties, must be crushed : the dynasty must be blotted out.—*Sir W. B. Richmond, "Daily Mail," September 15, 1914.*

"Sweep away the whole of the over-sea possessions of Germany, and whatever the cost of this war may be to us in men and money we shall breathe freely for generations to come."—*Sir R. Edgcumbe, "Daily News," August 25, 1914.*

"Territory must be taken from Germany to weaken her power." —*Mr. J. M. Robertson, the then Parliamentary Secretary to Board of Trade. "Manchester Guardian," October 23, 1914.*

"It is necessary to humble and humiliate the German Empire." —*Lord Charles Beresford, "Morning Post," November 5, 1914.*

"A steady war of attrition must be waged against German commerce, finance, credit and means of livelihood."—*"Times" Military Correspondent, December 13, 1914.*

"But, however the world pretends to divide itself there are only two divisions in the world to-day—human beings and Germans.—*Mr. Rudyard Kipling, "Morning Post," June 22, 1915.*

"Germany must be got out of France and Belgium by direct force of arms. Austria and the Balkans should be permanently with-

[1] The *Labour Leader,* October 14, 1915.

drawn from German influence and German soil must be occupied, and we must refuse to re-open the sea to German purposes until we have made the future secure."—*Mr. J. L. Garvin, National Liberal Club: "Westminster Gazette," October 12, 1915.*

THE overpowering need of the moment is that the belligerent Governments should, in some form or another, become acquainted with the views entertained by each as to the terms upon which they would negotiate; that, in short, the first stage in the bargaining bout should begin. It matters little how the initiatory steps are taken. The most practicable method would consist in a declaration conveyed to mediatory Powers. [It is known that several of the neutral Powers are ready and anxious to mediate.] But it does matter that the peoples in each of the belligerent States should be taken into the confidence of the Governments; that the Parliaments should be informed, at any rate of the broad lines of the settlement envisaged by the Governments as honourable and reasonable. For if in one sense this war is not, and never has been, the "Peoples' war" it is described as being by the apologists of diplomatic incompetence, in another, and a very grim sense, it is a Peoples' war, and the Peoples have the right to see that it shall be a Peoples' peace and not a diplomatists' juggle concluded behind the Peoples' backs. In *that* sense the war is for us particularly a Peoples' war, and the People are entitled to know the real and ultimate aims of their Government. These the people do not at present know. That is why I appealed the other day to those members of Parliament who have retained their civic courage, their independence of judgment, and their sense of perspective, to press, in effect, for a Ministerial declaration and a Ministerial repudiation of the "crushing" policy, pointing out that the party of reaction and conquest in Germany was proportionately strengthened, and the party favouring reasonable terms of settlement proportionately weakened, by the conviction—which the German papers of all shades reflect—that the British Government and nation are intent upon reducing Germany to political and economic impotence.

No doubt it is legitimate to argue that Ministers have never said, in so many words, that their desire is to crush Germany; but only to crush "Prussian militarism," or to "destroy the military domination of Prussia." But these expressions, which Ministers have used, are either mere rhetoric—and rhetoric in such a case is a dangerous thing

—or it is something even more mischievous. We cannot, therefore, understand too clearly that the rest of Germany stands or falls with Prussia. Many liberal-minded men in Britain think differently because they establish a correlation between "Prussianism" as a force in German normal political life, and "Prussianism" as a factor in a Germany struggling against a world in arms. They are thinking all the time in terms of franchise and "bureaucracies," and such like. They, or many of them, are so temperamentally predisposed to crusades against reactionaries of the hearth that they are intellectually incapable at this moment of realising the profound abyss which separates the feelings of non-Prussian Germany towards Prussia in peace, and those feelings to-day. Apart from the fact that the domestic side of "Prussianism" is an issue which the German people themselves can alone work out, "Prussia" to-day, considered in terms of the war now raging, is indistinguishable from the other States of the Germanic Federation; indeed, one might say, indistinguishable from the Teutonic race as a whole—the Bavarian, for example, being ethically and spiritually far more drawn towards Austria than towards Prussia, but just as great a "Prussian" (in the sense used by our coiners of catch-phrases) for the needs of this war as the most Prussian of Prussians. The vast amount of nonsense which centres round the phrase "Prussian militarism" is reinforced by quotations from the effusions lauding force as a sort of national cult, obligingly provided by certain German intellectuals and philosophers and even military men. I say "even" military men, for while we can argue with justice that the philosophers ,so-called, are atrocious; we can only denounce the militarist as montrous by the exercise of an hypocrisy which, if it be unconscious, is a reflection upon our intelligence. Militarism *per se IS* the cult of force in human affairs, and the professional militarist must be a believer in that cult. That he should rush into print to proclaim the fact adds nothing to our knowledge. Allowing for crudity of expression and brutality of diction, which the stern physiography of Prussia and its sinister experiences at the hands of more favoured peoples have evolved, there is little substantial difference between the philosophy of Cramb or even of Carlyle (in some moods) and Kipling (in others) and the particular brand of Teutonic philosophy now held to single out the Germans as pertaining to a lower strata of humanity. As to the German professional militarists, the Keims, the Bernhardis, and the rest, if you read their pre-war writings otherwise than superficially and with the fixed determination to discover therein the "mark of the beast," you will not only find in them that glorification of war which—unless you are very simple—you would expect to find. You will also find running through them the conviction that sooner or later, and sooner rather than later, Germany would be called upon to fight for her life against a host of enemies. And when you bear in mind even the very limited selection of utterances from the lips and pens of British, French, and Russian politicians, military men, and journalists during the past ten years, which I have quoted in this volume, you cannot but recognise that these German "political Generals," as Dr. Nippold[1] calls them, had no difficulty whatever in making out a case for the consumption of the German public, whatever their own motives may have been in doing so; and they were probably mixed, like the motives of most human beings.

To call attention to these things is not to minimise the share of responsibility borne by these elements in the life of Germany in building the European powder magazine, and in helping to explode it; still less to palliate the German treatment of Belgium, which will ring down the ages to the detriment of the German name. But it is only by bringing to a proper focus this whole field of considerations, and keeping the focus, that such phrases as "crushing Prussian militarism" can be adjudged at their true worth.

Neither must it be overlooked that since the war broke out events have been conspiring to fuse all sections from the Emperor to the working man.

It is not merely the shedding of torrents of German blood and the plunge into mourning of all classes in Germany which is accountable for the fusing process. It is the belief which *events arising out of the war* have caused to become universal in Germany, that the German people WERE the predestined objects of coalesced attack; and that the motive thereof was their destruction. And this, not because they were more bellicose than their neigh-bours—that in the past forty-five years they had proved

[1] *Op. cit.*

themselves less bellicose in action than any of their great
neighbours is a material fact absolutely conclusive on the
point to any German—but because they were becoming
steadily greater and more prosperous, more dreaded as
competitors in art and crafts.   What has occasioned that
belief which we may deem erroneous, but which to-day is
one of the dominating elements in the international
situation?   It has been determined in chief by : (a) The
British "blockade" policy; (b) the loudly-advertised
intentions of powerful sections of the community here, in
regard to Germany's economic and political future; (c) the
reports of Belgian Ministers abroad to their Government,
discovered in the archives of the Belgian Foreign Office
and distributed broadcast throughout Germany by the
Government.   On the "blockade" policy, viewed from the
standpoint of strategic necessity, or in relation to
Germany's submarine policy, or as a legitimate act of war,
I am not competent to pass an opinion.   Moreover, I am
concerned now only with its psychological effect upon the
German mind.   What that effect is may be judged, not
from extraneous sources, but simply from what the Press
here has published as to the confidently anticipated results
which would ensue from the policy, viz., the restriction of
a substantial portion of the necessary food supply of the
German population.   The anticipation may correspond
with fact, or it may not—I do not know—but the
psychological effect is bound up with the advertised
intention. "England wants to starve us out; to strike at
us through our women and children," could hardly be
surpassed as a battle-cry creative of the cement of national
unity.   As to (b), it will be recalled that steel had hardly
clashed when the most powerful newspaper Trust in this
country started, with the warm approval of certain commercial and politico-commercial bodies, its "War on
German trade."   While our soldiers were dying for a
great ideal, these civilian patriots were manufacturing
schemes for increasing their business profits.   The
agitation in due course died down—in the particular
form in which it was first manifested.   But it has
been revived and, as I shall show in my next
article, exists among us now as an organised movement, with powerful financial and "high society" support.
It is accompanied by incessant pronouncements by men
prominent in the life of the nation, as to the "punishment"
we purpose inflicting upon Germany when we have brought

her to that "unconditional surrender," which the Government indirectly (except in the case of Mr. Churchill, who used the actual words) allows it to be assumed is the Government's penultimate object.   The "punishment" takes many forms, varying from territorial mutilation in Europe to economic strangulation, from political disintegration to a permanent veto upon the holding of over-sea possessions.   The last-named "punishment," which a completely victorious alliance could impose with greater facility than it could the other items in the programme, is now being endorsed by no less an authority than Sir Harry Johnston, whose name carries weight in Germany, and who pleads for it with almost fanatical passion in the columns of the *New Statesman.*

As to (c), it would need a special study adequately to convey the impression which the reports from Belgian Ministers alluded to above must be making upon the psychology of the German people.   The authenticity of these documents is not questioned.   The time will come when they will be regarded as, perhaps the most important contribution to our knowledge of *pre*-war conditions, and a complete vindication of those who have condemned the secrecy of British diplomacy.   A brief indication of the character and scope of these documents has already been given.   They show, with a unanimity whose cumulative effect is staggering, that, in the eyes of all these Belgian diplomats stationed in the various capitals and charged with the duty of conveying to their Government the impressions the·· formed of the character and objects of the foreign policy pursued by the various Governments to which they were accredited, the policy pursued by the diplomacy of England and France, sustained by influential Press agitations, had every appearance of being directed to the isolation and discomfiture of Germany; that it was, in short, aggressively and deliberately anti-German.   It may not have been—all this will have to be threshed out later on.   But that is what *seemed* to be its character to these trained observers [who, being neutral, may be assumed to have been impartial] noting its evolution from those inner sanctuaries where the fate of peoples is lightly decided in darkness and in secrecy.   And if Anglo-French diplomacy *seemed* thus inspired to these neutral observers, what must it have seemed to the diplomatic representatives of Germany in foreign capitals and, consequently, to the German Government?

Possess yourself, then, of the mind of the average intelligent German citizen and you will find that, under the influence of these events, it must work like this :—

"We are to be starved into surrender. After our surrender, which is to be unconditional, our trade is to be throttled by combinations and differentiations. That was the object of our enemies all along. They proclaimed it almost as soon as the war started. Our commercial access to foreign markets over-seas is to be hampered and restricted. Territorial areas over-seas are to be wrenched from us. We are not to be allowed to possess colonies or dependencies. As our industrial population must have raw material to be kept in employment, these concerted measures will mean for us economic paralysis. Britain means to stifle us and to use the French and Russian armies for the achievement of her purpose. That it has been her fixed intention is now made evident by this long series of Belgian diplomatic reports which our Government has found. We are the victims of a diabolical conspiracy."

I am not asserting that this frame of mind reflects the true facts of the case. But I do assert that the principal events I have examined *must* appear to the German mind to embody the true facts of the case. And I do assert that to talk of "Prussian militarism" and "Prussian domination" as factors which can be isolated and "destroyed," in connection with the ultimate aims of our policy towards Germany, is to display a superficial and even a frivolous mentality unworthy of the name of statesmanship, and calculated to lead the nation into a quagmire of political error—the same sort of *intellectual* mistake which lost us the American Colonies. To tell the average German that you intend to "crush Prussian militarism" is to tell him that you intend to crush Germany : her commerce, her shipping, her prosperity, her competition in the markets of the world, her colonial enterprise.

I have said before that I am persuaded the British people have not this end in view, and that I do not believe the sane elements in the British Government have this end in view. But that powerful, organised forces in this country have this end in view, are endeavouring to super-

(16

impose it upon the national mind and, by the advertisement which is given to them in the Press, are strengthening the Germans in their conviction that this is, indeed, the fixed purpose of the British Government and nation, thereby prolonging the war, I shall now show.

CHAPTER XXV.

Hate as a Creed[1]

FROM henceforward the Germans are to the English an accursed race. We will not buy from them, sell to them, eat with them, drink with them, nor pray with them.—The *Globe,* October 7, 1915.

"Everything German taboo."—*Motto of the Anti-German League.*

"No German labour, no German goods, no German influence; Britain for the British."—*Motto of the Anti-German Union.*

"Germany under all."—*Motto of the Imperial Maritime League.*

THE two most prominent organisations which devote their energies to the propagation of the policy which may be described as "crushing Germany" and which advocate it, in effect, as desirable in the national interest and as the supreme end and aim of the war, are the anti-German League and the Anti-German Union. The significance of such organisations is that they crystallise, as it were, all the looseness of thought which has gathered round the phrase "Prussian militarism," all the passions incidental to a state of war, all the natural bitterness, the unreason, the intolerance and unfairness which curse humanity in war time, into a perfectly definite and deliberate purpose. They seek to direct the piteous aberrations from which an afflicted humanity suffers in a period of war, for the pursuance of aims which in themselves are ignoble and sordid. They take advantage of the mental dislocation which war brings and, coldly, with calculation, trade upon hate and fear, orienting these elements towards ends frankly material. They are the exploiters of hate, analogous to the ghouls of the battlefield. We shall see as we dissect their manifestoes that were this attempt to impregnate the national policy with the virus of an enduring hatred; were this appeal to the lowest human instincts to succeed in its objects, the *nation* in whose interest they are said to be put forward would lose by every test—ethical, economic, or political—which can be applied. Certain classes, certain vested interests, would, however, gain,

---

[1] The *Labour Leader,* October 21, 1915.

and gain largely—for a time at all events. The proposals set out by these organisations would hit the consumer all round—the poor especially—but they would put money into the pockets of certain kinds of producers. They would raise the value of his lands to the great landlord. They would impoverish the needy man still further and increase the revenues of the rich. Such is the species of spurious patriotism which flaunts itself in war time and seeks to identify itself with the spirit of self-sacrifice. All wars have produced it, and sometimes Governments and peoples have been led grievously astray by it.

Both the Anti-German League and the Anti-German Union appear particularly desirous of capturing the working man. Curiously enough, they have neglected to include representatives of the working class among their patrons and committees. More curious still, these are exclusively drawn from a class which—as a class— abominates the claims of Labour, and in peace time, utilises the whole machinery at its disposal to counteract them. "Everything German taboo." That is the motto of the Anti-German League, whose committee is headed by the Marquis of Hertford (whom "Who's Who" indicates as former Captain in the Grenadier Guards and the proud possessor of 12,300 acres of British soil), and is under "the distinguished patronage" of Lord Frederick Fitzroy (also late of the Grenadier Guards); a number of ladies of title and a number of military and naval officers— presumably retired. The League desires, above all things, to "Smash the Germans commercially." Mark that. That amiable intention is in the forefront of the League's programme. Fighting for the "liberties of Europe"? Ah! that is well enough for the men who are laying down their lives in Flanders, in the Gallipoli Peninsula, in the burning sands of Mesopotamia, in the jungles of West Africa. But your aristocratic patriot of the Anti-German League brand is much more utilitarian. It is the *trade* of the Teuton he is after, not the Teuton's blood. For this purpose—the purpose of smashing the Germans com- mercially—the League invites its adherents to take the pledge—I mean, of course, the Anti-German pledge. The Anti-German League promises, amongst other things :—

"Not to purchase, use, or consume German or Austrian goods whatsoever. Not to employ a German for either domestic or commercial purposes. Not to place contracts with any German-owned or controlled Company, Trust, or Corporation. or to send goods by, or travel in, German ships."

No doubt German armament trusts are included in this interdict, but there is no special reference to them—a regrettable omission. Among the far-seeing objects the League has in view is to "legislate for a protective and, if necessary, a prohibitive tariff on all German and Austrian made goods." (One seems to detect here a far-off echo of the familiar Pipes of Pan!) In the document which accompanies its pledge form, and which is described as an "Introduction by the Founder," one reads such Tariff Reform, new style, as this :—

"Thirty years ago we were miles ahead of all our competitors in manufacturing, in trade, in finance, and in labour, but what have we done to maintain that premier position among the great nations? We have, alas, permitted foreigners, particularly Germans, to dump their goods at the very gates of our great works, while our own men have starved or emigrated. We have to our own lasting disgrace readily purchased German produce to the detriment of our industries."

And so on. It seems that the Germans have had the astounding impudence, without even a "By your leave," to increase their merchant shipping "from 500,000 tons to 5,000,000 tons" in the last thirty years. Clearly a nation that can act thus is past reforming. There is much talk about "Made in Germany, the mark of the Beast," the "Butcher of Berlin," and so forth. In short, the programme of the League is a repulsive and vulgar appeal to national cupidity. This precious society asks for a million subscribers at one shilling a head; in other words, for an income of £50,000 a year, "not a large income certainly to exploit the aims we have in view."

At first sight it may seem queer that there should be necessity for an Anti-German Union as well as an Anti-German League. Perhaps it is an illustration of the Quaker saying : "All the world is queer but thee and me, dear; and thou art a little bit queer." Anyway, "you pays your money and you takes your choice." The Union is specially favoured by the *Daily Express* and the *Morning Post*. The Editor of the *Daily Express* is a celebrity who once wrote a book entitled "Exiled in England." His

name is Blumenfeld. It is a very patriotic paper, the
Daily Express. That is why it thinks so highly of the
Anti-German Union.   As for the *Morning Post,* so
attached is it to the Union that its proprietor figures among
the Union's vice-presidents.   The *Morning Post* preaches
the Union's policy in its leading articles with punctilious
regularity.   It also makes a speciality of insinuating that
those who combat its doctrines are rewarded for so doing
with German gold.   It opens its columns to the Secretary
of the Union for the diffusion of similar insinuations, and
declines to insert replies on the ground of insufficiency of
space.   I used to be a little puzzled as to why the directing
minds of the *Morning Post* seemed so bent upon this
particular style of public controversy.   But I now understand that it must be a case of inherited mentality, on the
"judge others by what you once were" attitude.   I am
indebted to a correspondent for the revelation.   The
correspondent obligingly forwarded me a copy of Lord
Malmesbury's memoirs[1] the other. day, and suggested that
I should therein find the key to the *Morning Post's* mentality.   Now, Lord Malmesbury, you will remember—
and if you don't remember you may be forgiven—was
Foreign Minister in the Derby Cabinet (1852), and I very
much regret to say that in those days the *Morning Post*
was in the pay of a foreign Government—a Government
with which we were on the worst of terms.   That is
vouched for by Britain's Foreign Minister of the day.   Here
is the passage :—

"November 4. An article in the *Morning Post* from
its correspondent in Paris on the title of Napoleon III.,
retailing nearly every word of my last conversation with
Walewski (the French Ambassador)."

"November 5. Sent for Walewski. He confirms that
the French Government paid the *Morning Post,* and that
he saw Borthwick, the editor, every day."[2]

Very sad !

With these distinguished backers in the Press, the
Anti-German Union fills the atmosphere with its patriotic

---

[1] "Memoirs of an Ex-Minister." By the Earl of Malmesbury.
(Longmans, Green and Co., 1884.)   Vol. I., p. 362.

[2] See, too, passages in Vol. II., p. 107, as to the *Post,* which
"obeys the orders of the Emperor to write one down." And (p. 151) :
"The *Morning Post* has received orders from the French Emperor to
attack me on every possible occasion. Mr. Borthwick, the editor,
saw him at Paris and got his orders from himself."

vibrations. Its personnel, you will concede, is well fitted
to make a special appeal to the intelligence of the working
man, being so eminently qualified, by sympathy with the
latter's aspirations, knowledge of his needs, and understanding of his claims, to be his guide, counsellor, and
familiar friend in these dark and troublous days. For
is not its president the Earl of Euston, and do not its
seventeen vice-presidents include the Marquis of Sligo,
the Earls of Egmont, Kenmore, Kilmory, and Oxford,
Lord Headley, Lord Leith of Fyvie, and a bevy of
Peeresses? In fact, but for Mr. Ronald McNeill, M.P.,
and the Right Hon. Sir F. Milner, Bart. (at one time—
horresco referens !—on the General Council of the Anglo-
German Friendship Society[1]), the whole of the *Union's*
seventeen vice-presidents are ornaments of the Peerage.
The *Union's* motto is more ornate than the *League's* :—

"No German labour, no German goods, no German
influence. Britain for the British."

In short, the Chinese wall within which the British
people shall in future be cribbed, crabbed, and confined
for the greater benefit of Tariff Reform manufacturers
and rural landlords.

From the *Union's* "Aims and Objects " and from its
"Policy" I extract the following items :—

"To defend British industry and British labour against
German competition. To fight against German influence
in our social, financial, industrial, and political life. To
expel Germans from our industries and commerce. 'To
explain the folly of granting peace on terms so easy as to
make it possible for the Germans again to disturb the peace
of Europe and the world.' "

The world has, you observe, ever been a peaceful one
until the wicked Teuton disturbed its blissful repose. The
Union proposes to discourage the use of German shipping
lines by English passengers and merchandise; to form a
register of traders who will undertake not to buy or to sell
German goods, and to take sundry other steps of a similar
character. The *Union,* as I have remarked before, is
being well boomed in the Press. But it is being advertised
in other and more subtle ways. *Its leaflets and subscription forms may be seen displayed on the counter of one
at least of the best known of London Banks.*

[1] *Vide* "Report of the Inaugural Meeting held at the Mansion
House, May 1, 1911."

This glance at the chief hate-mongers and their ideals and methods would be incomplete without a passing reference to the Imperial Maritime League, whose motto (these people cannot get along without mottoes) is, "Germany under all." It seems, according to the *Imperial Maritime League* that "we have got to smash them (the Germans) now once and for ever that they rise not again." The League has a partiality for the word "smash." It has issued a "Smashing the enemy declaration," which demands—after Mr. Churchill's and the *New Statesman's* own hearts—the "unconditional surrender" of the enemy :

"Germany must be left at the close of this titanic struggle—so firmly fettered that she may never rise again in the panoply of war."

All the other belligerents, apparently, may retain that panoply. But Germany, it appears, must not even wear the panoply of trade :

"The sun has got to set now, once and for all, either on the British or German Empires."

Such is the articulated policy the *working classes* are asked to endorse by the "Prussians in our midst." These organisations and their organs in the Press are typical of the influences and forces in our social system which are fatally, necessarily, inevitably inimical to the interests of the workers—so long as our social system reposes upon its present bases. Yet they appeal to the working men of Britain to support them. They incarnate, do these elements, all that is intolerable and intolerant, selfish, and short-sighted in our national life. It is these elements which have controlled hitherto the entire course of our foreign policy; which compose to-day our diplomatic service, and which will go on doing both if we allow them. Do not, I beg of you, minimise their power for mischief. It is not for nothing that a man in this country sports a coronet and flaunts armorial bearings. They can organise. They can lead. They have the governing instinct. They are wealthy. They are provided with keys which unlock the council chambers of the State. Through their power over the Press they can play a ponderating part in "national" decisions. They do not monopolise the spirit of hatred and revenge among us to-day, but they *organise* it. The more the workers fall under the spell of their doctrines, the bigger the price the latter will have to pay

in the end.   For the policy they preach is—Death;
physical death for multitudes, for it prolongs the war;
social and economic death for multitudes, because the
longer the war lasts the greater the social misery and
suffering which will follow it.

I now propose to examine some of the specific proposals
which the policy of hate contains.   The purpose which will
inspire me in so doing will be the dual one of (a), demonstrating their ineptitude from the point of view of practical
politics; (b), setting forth what I conceive to be the true
national necessities of Britain and Germany, from the
standpoint of the future of Anglo-German relations.   In
this examination I shall be guided by the conviction that
an understanding of their mutual needs by the British and
German peoples is the keynote to any possible reconstruction of Europe, of escape from a repetition of the armed
peace of the last twenty years, and from a repetition of its
inevitable sequel, attended by consequences even more
cataclysmic for humanity.   My conviction is based upon
the incontestable fact that the British and German peoples
have got to go on living on the same planet; that they
cannot do so as permanent foes; that they cannot suffer an
indefinite prolongation of mutual hatred without mutual
disaster, and hence that they must discover the way out,
and, having discovered it, pursue it to their mutual
salvation.

CHAPTER XXVI.

The "Trade War"[1]

IT is no exaggeration to say that if this conflict goes on indefinitely, revolution and anarchy may well follow; and unless the collective common-sense of mankind prevents it before the worst comes, great portions of the Continent of Europe will be little better than a wilderness, peopled by old men, women, and children.—*Lord Loreburn, in the House of Lords, November* 8, 1915.

I only wish to draw you to this conclusion, that the war has resulted in something like a deadlock of force and has operated to diminish the standard of our civilisation, to take away the guarantees of liberty, to diminish the trustworthiness of law, and to endanger the situation amongst nations, neutrals as well as combatants. If that is so, surely it is not surprising that one should begin to ask, Is any escape possible from this rake's progress upon which we have entered? Must we go on to witness a continually extending panorama of war? Is there no alternative? I believe there is. The passion of national independence is glorious and well worthy of any sacrifice. I recognise all its claims. But the passion of national independence must in some way be reconciled, if civilisation is to continue, with the possibility of international friendship, and unless you can see out of this war something which will lead to international friendship, coming into alliance with, and being supported by, national independence, you have nothing before you but a continued series of wars, hate after hate, extermination after extermination, from which, indeed, you may well recoil.—*Lord Courtney of Penwith, in the House of Lords, November* 8, 1915.

We are told we are fighting for liberty and democracy against tyranny, but gradually we have seen the very system we abominate, whose very existence we detest, instituted in our midst, and in setting out to destroy it in the enemy, we are creating it at home.—*Mr. Arthur Ponsonby, in the House of Commons, November* 11, 1915.

I have been violently abused for using the word "peace." I am not going to allow myself to be charged with saying out of this House what I dare not say inside it. I have never, nor, so far as I know, have any of the friends who are associated with me, spoken of "peace at any price" or of "peace at any time." For my part, I have always said precisely and absolutely the opposite. I have said that I thought there were certain things that we ought to want and without which this war could not end. . . . But I have said . . . that there is nothing inherently disgraceful or humiliating in attaining these things by negotiation, and not by fighting. It is just as honourable, and it is less disastrous. It avoids incalculable human suffering, and it is more effective if what you want is a permanent peace. . . .—*Mr. Charles Trevelyan, in the House of Commons, November* 11, 1915.

[1] The *Labour Leader*, October 28, 1915.

222

OUR national capacity to judge sanely of the present situation must be guided, as I have sought to emphasise throughout, by some clear conception of the ultimate aims we are pursuing in this war. At present we possess no such clear conception. The terrible events which are convulsing Europe and the confusion which reigns in our own national Councils alike militate against it, and there appears no constructive force, articulate in the nation at this moment, to visualise beyond the present and to detach the national mind from the mirage provoked by catch-phrases, such as come glibly to the lips of those who have spent most of their lives in talk.

A monster styled "Prussian militarism" is enthroned before the national imagination; and that its overthrow alone is needed to re-establish peace and good-will on earth is so persistently taught, that to question it is denounced as virtual treason. That the German military machine is utterly ruthless and that some of its operators are deaf both to pity and to policy, is true enough—the odious tragedy perpetrated last week in Brussels is but an additional proof.[1] But the myth which, because of this, portrays "Prussian militarism" as a sort of entity in itself, a something wholly exceptional and peculiar, is not less fabulous, or less calculated to distort the national sense of perspective in regard to the character of the European struggle, or to blind the national judgment to the nature of the elements which have been let loose by the rulers of the world. Those who reiterate incessantly that we are fighting "Prussian militarism" delude the nation. We are fighting a people of 65 millions, or, if you reckon in the Austro-Hungarians, of over 100 millions, who believe that we seek their destruction as a people. And it is the daily statements made by those who command the avenues of publicity among their foes, and who claim to represent the intentions of their foes; it is these, far more than any statements of their own Governors, which continually strengthen these people in that belief. *That* is the truth.

The noblest utterance which this war has yet elicited has been given to the world by Miss Cavell herself :—"But this I would say, standing as I do before God and eternity, I realise that patriotism is not enough. I must have no hatred or bitterness towards anyone." To her, indeed, in that supreme hour there seems to have come a Divine message. Herself a victim to the barbarous insensibility

[1] The Execution of Miss Cavell.

that war engenders, her dying words were not an incite-
ment to hate and revenge, but an appeal to the Christ ideal
which the statesmen of Europe are trampling in the blood
of the peoples, calling the while upon some Pagan deity to
justify their hideous work.

I have said that the Parliaments are guilty, although
in a lesser degree. Parliament here is ready to debate the
details of a Budget, to listen to platitudes about the
Balkans, to wrangle fiercely over conscription, to make
unkind remarks about the censorship. It is capable of
becoming annoyed over a variety of matters connected
with the management of the war. But so far it has shown
no sign of grappling with the fundamental issue—the
object and purpose with which the war is now being waged.
From Parliament has come hitherto no lead, no guidance,
no ray of light sweeping aside the comparative unessentials
and throwing the essentials into bold relief. Some organs
of the Press are beginning to clamour for the "truth."
But the truths for which they agitate are the lesser truths,
and when Ministers have been driven to speak more openly
of the military outlook in the various theatres of war;
when, perchance, this or that Minister has paid the penalty
attaching to a foolish boast, or has succumbed to the
personal animosities which this demand for "truth," in
part at least, conceals; or when some strategical success
comes to relieve the monotony of gloom, all this insistence
upon the "truth" will fade away, to be presently renewed
when, and if, a further period of military ill-success sets in.

For those who would say to the nation :—"The truth
which you need to apprehend lies not there, but in the
interminable march of your youth to the shambles, in the
mortgaging of your children's patrimony, in the growing
irritation of neutral Powers at your maritime policy,
casting, as it does, new and sinister shadows upon the
international screen, in the increasingly alarming inroads
upon your financial stability, in the fearful future preparing
for your posterity; it is in these portents, whose cumulative significance escapes you, that reside the truths you
must realise; it is that you incur these ills *with no distinct
conception of the goal you seek, without measuring the
consequences by a conscious effort of the will"* : for those
who would say this to the nation, the Legislature has,
apparently, no liking. So, in the absence of Governmental
and Parliamentary leadership and in the functional abdication of the Press, are we reduced to pursue the search

for truth by such lights as we individually possess, and to proclaim it in the measure of our understanding and our opportunities.

And our vision, I think, will be contained within the boundary of the verities if it be inspired by the conviction that the *essential* problems peculiar to the belligerent States before the war, and which affected their mutual relations, will survive the war. The working out of these problems may be modified by the war, but their constituent factors will remain unaltered. Fundamentally the war is an attempt to solve these problems by the stupidest and most inconclusive of all means. But they will not and cannot yield to that treatment, because that treatment ignores growth, and growth is indestructible. The essential problems, then, which confronted the nations in their international relationships before the war will confront them at the settlement, and after the settlement. The war will not solve them, and the antiquated mechanism in vogue before the war will not solve them. A new mechanism must be created, and the peoples themselves must create it. The lubricant of that mechanism must be mutual comprehension. There must be, on the part of each belligerent people, a conscious and sustained effort of the will to understand the nature of these problems as they affect its own destinies, and as they affect the destinies of its neighbours. And the starting point of that intellectual process must be a firm grasp of the first principle in the life of the modern State, viz., the *common interests* which unite the people of each belligerent State to its neighbours. When that principle is clearly apprehended war is seen in its true perspective—an outrage perpetrated upon the community by a restricted section thereof, an outrage rendered possible only through the intellectual failure of the community as a whole to appreciate the truth of that first principle.

Let us apply this first principle to the problem of Anglo-German relations, upon whose future adjustment on a basis of mutual comprehension depends the realisation of that "New Europe" for which the belligerent peoples are told by their Governments they are striving, and for which the mass of them believe, more or less vaguely, themselves to be so striving. And let us apply it first to the problem of commercial intercourse, which is at once the most visible test of those *common interests* of which I have spoken and the most powerful

medium to heal the wounds and bitterness engendered by
war. And here we are faced immediately with the
trail of the exploiters of war. To follow that trail, to
expose the exploiter in his haunts, must be our purpose.
He calls himself a German, a Briton, an Italian, a Frenchman, a Russian, according to the community to which
he belongs. In reality he is neither one nor the other
and he is all in one. He is just an exploiter. His
purposes are selfish, and his selfishness is cosmopolitan.
To him the buying and selling of commodities between
peoples is beneficial to the extent in which he profits by it.
If his competitors in other lands, by better organisation
or ingenuity reduce his profits, trade to him becomes a
"war," his competitors become enemies, and as he is
extremely noisy, and often influential, bitterness arises
through his laments between the mass of consumers and
producers in the country in which he lives, and in the
country whence proceeds the competition to which he
objects. We have seen that the proclaimed object of the
organisations for the stereotyping of Anglo-German hatred
and the newspapers which support them is to destroy
German trade. The *Morning Post* puts the matter quite
baldly :—

"Our aims should be to destroy German trade because
by trade a nation lives."

This scheme to destroy German trade is to be all-
embracing. Sixty-five millions of Germans are, henceforth, to be artificially forbidden to sell goods to the British
Empire, the French and Russian Empires, and Japan, with
Italy and the smaller fry thrown in. This is the "trade
war" for which the *Morning Post* and other papers and
numerous influential bodies here are preparing, and which
they are urging shall follow the holocaust of human life.
Hatred must survive in the counting-house.

Now a "trade war" is, intrinsically, as great an outrage
upon the peoples as a war of armaments and a war of men,
of which latter it is, indeed, often the forerunner and
contributor, as Mr. Brailsford has so powerfully portrayed
in his "War of Steel and Gold."[1] It is an outrage
upon the peoples on that account; and also because it seeks
to interfere violently with the first principle of international
relationship, the *common interest* between peoples. The
influences which would impose this new form of warfare

[1] G. Bell and Son.

upon humanity at the close of a desolating war are the most dangerous enemies of the peoples among whom they are established. To prevent the Germans from selling to us by the erection of "penal tariffs" is to lay plans for the further impoverishment of the British people when the latter, after the war, are struggling with unemployment, lowered wages, immense rise in the cost of living, depreciation of monetary values, and the hundred vicissitudes war brings in its train. It involves and necessitates its complement. If the Germans cannot sell to us neither can they buy from us, and the exclusion of 65 millions of people from active commercial intercourse with their neighbours means a penalisation, not of them alone, but of their neighbours too. This advertised war upon the German producer and consumer is, therefore, the intimation of a coming war upon all British consumers, and upon a very considerable proportion of British producers; and, obviously, the section of the community which will be hardest hit by that war is the British working class. The employment, and, therefore, the means of livelihood which the British workers enjoyed through the labours of German workers will disappear : by restricting competition in the production of manufactured goods, and by narrowing the market, the British working man will be called upon to pay more for what he uses. Every restriction placed upon the free circulation of produce and manufactures, even in normal times, is really an invasion of the rights of mankind in the interests of private individuals connected with some particular branch of production or manufacture. The interest of the overwhelming mass of peoples in the freedom of commercial intercourse is common and universal. It holds good in the case of the relationship between civilised (so-called) peoples and between civilised peoples and uncivilised (so-called). Deliberately under cover of the passions of war, to prepare a future in which 65 millions of people in Central Europe are to be debarred from trading with their neighbours is in itself a crime. It is doubly a crime, because it is also to prepare the way for future wars, of the sort we are experiencing to-day. The British Empire, grandiloquently exclaims the *Morning Post,* can do without Germany, but Germany cannot do without the British Empire.

Let us see.

CHAPTER XXVII.

German Competition[1]

"HERE is a low political economy, plotting to cut the throat of foreign competition, and establish our own; excluding others by force or making war on them; or, by cunning tariffs, giving preference to worse wares of ours. But the real and lasting victories are those of peace and not of war. The way to conquer the foreign artisan is not to kill him, but to beat his work."—*Emerson.*

"The trade which we can only capture by throttling Germany with the aid of the British Fleet will not long be ours when normal conditions recur; and then what will become of the capital which we are adjured to put into it? How did Germany originally secure this trade? She won it fairly by science, intelligence, hard work, and adaptability. Only by those qualities can we recover and keep it."—*The Times* (September 24, 1914).

STATISTICS are never stimulating. But it is only by a reference to statistics that we can appreciate the importance to the British people of the labour and enterprise of the people of Germany and *vice-versa.* In 1911 the total value of the direct trade between the British Empire and Germany amounted to £160,640,000. In the list of foreign countries and British possessions from which we imported and retained merchandise in 1912, Germany figures second. The net value of that merchandise amounted in that year to £65,841,000. We bought £25,000,000 more from Germany than from France, £27,000,000 more from Germany than from Russia, and £25,000,000 more from Germany than from India. We sold Germany £40,362,000 of produce and manufactures; £10,000,000 more than we sold to the United States, £15,000,000 more than we sold to France, and £27,000,000 more than we sold to Russia. Germany supplied us with 10.4 per cent. of our total imports, and she absorbed a greater proportion of our total exports (8.2 per cent.) than any country in the world except India. How can an attempt to "destroy" a commercial connec-

---

[1] The *Labour Leader,* November 4, 1915.

tion of that kind be undertaken without causing an immense amount of distress to the people of these Islands?

From whatever aspect this problem of Anglo-German commercial relationship is examined, the more inimical to the interests of the masses of the British people, and the more inherently fallacious does the policy propounded by the Anti-German organisations and the so-called Imperial newspapers appear. To read their outpourings you would imagine that all we have to do is to replace the £70,000,000 of goods which Germany and Austria sent us annually before the war, by producing the articles at home, and that in so doing we should not only be as well off, but even better off. This calculation, of course, overlooks the fact that even if we could perform this miracle we should not be as well off or better off, for the very simple reason that the disappearance of that *import* trade would involve the corresponding disappearance of an *export* of British produce, manufactures, and services to pay for it. Again, to close our markets to German trade after the war would not merely involve the direct loss of the national transactions with Germany; for the policy, it seems, is to be a sort of joint combination on the part of the Allies. It would, thus, involve a further loss for the British people in the decreased purchasing power of the Allied States, consequent upon the self-inflicted loss imposed upon them by their rulers arising out of the disappearance of the volume of trade carried on between those States and Germany before the war. No State can shut out its people from so immense a market as that which the Central European Powers provide without inflicting grievous disabilities upon its own people. No commercial firm can suddenly strike off a large proportion of its *clientèle* without heavy loss resulting from the inevitably ensuing restriction of transactions. And the same thing holds good with nations. The people of each State are the clients of their neighbours. These, if you like, are commonplace truisms. But when we see how they are overlooked in the collapse of the reasoning faculty which is to be observed all around us, it may not be inappropriate to call attention to them.

The same absence of rudimentary common-sense can be noted in other branches of the professional hate-monger's business. Germany, as we have seen, is to be faced at the close of the war with a trade boycott extending through five-sixths of Europe, the whole of Africa, and

(17)

virtually the whole of Asia if, as is firmly hoped, Japanese political pressure can forcibly close the Chinese market to her[1] : in any case, a good half of Asia. And this same Germany, paralysed in her foreign trade and in her industrial development, is to pay a huge war indemnity to her conquerors ! But how ? She could do so only by manufacturing and selling goods, and those who purpose imposing the war indemnity also purpose to withhold from her as much of the raw material with which to manufacture as they can manage, and to do all in their power to prevent her selling such goods as she may, nevertheless, succeed in manufacturing ! Then, where is she to get the money from wherewith to pay the war indemnity ?

Another thing which seems to be equally lost sight of, although not quite on the same plane of thought, is this : The woes of the world to-day are held, and rightly if we consider visible effects and ignore profound causes, which seems the popular procedure just now, to be in large measure attributable to the existence of huge conscript armies, which means huge armaments ... and the rest. And Germany is regarded, erroneously from the historical standpoint, as the initiatory culprit. Well, were we to succeed, as the result of this war, in forcing Germany to abolish her conscript army without a corresponding measure on the part of the Continental States now opposed to Germany, what would be the upshot ? We should be thereby releasing for commercial and industrial pursuits the whole of the able-bodied population of Germany for the whole period of the year. Having done so, should we impose a veto upon that population carrying on those pursuits ? One might imagine that the ludicrousness of the *impasse* would appeal even to the titled patrons of the Anti-German Union.

Hardly less absurd is the policy of dismembering Germany in order to remove Germany's trade competition. I say, in order to remove Germany's trade competition.

---

[1] Unexpected results sometimes ensue from clumsy attempts to dam up a river. If Germany is forcibly excluded from Africa her obvious policy will be to support Japan in the inevitable conflict which would arise between that Power and Great Britain and the United States should Japan seek special privileges on a large scale in the Chinese markets. Naturally, she would exact her price. But it would be a price which Japan might, under quite conceivable circumstances, be prepared to pay. Of all the follies of which those who direct the policy of this country could be guilty, none could have more enduring and fatal results, than the policy of attempting to stifle the industrial development of Germany in the neutral markets.

because the political disruption of Germany is recommended by the same parties that want to "smash" German trade, although it does not usually figure on their printed programmes. Germany, as we now know her, is to be mutilated by large accessions of territory to France and to Belgium (which does not want them) on the West, to Russia on the East. This, of course, would involve the transference of millions of Germans to the French, Russian, and Belgian States. What would be the consequence from the point of view of human production? It would be that these millions of transferred Germans would continue to produce just the same, tne only. difference being that the merchandise they produced to compete with ours in the world's markets would be made in France, Russia, and Belgium respectively, instead of in Germany. And what difference would that make to the competition? Absolutely none. We should merely have shifted a political frontier, which, incidentally, is becoming a factor of steadily dwindling importance in the life of peoples. We should not, in so doing, have affected trade competition one iota. And in arbitrarily shifting that frontier, thereby violating in flagrant fashion one of the main principles for the upholding of which we are officially stated to be at war, we should, without gaining any compensating advantage, have planted in the breasts of these millions of transferred Germans the determination to strain every nerve to become politically reunited to the bulk of their countrymen. Again, what sort of Europe is this which our hatemongers would create? The sort of Europe that would saddle the British working classes with a permanent war expenditure in peace, from which emigration *en masse* or revolution would be the only means of escape.

Moreover, these short sighted persons have not seemingly grasped the rudiments of what would be involved, in all sorts of ways, by a policy aiming at the penalisation of one of the most numerous and industrious peoples on the face of the globe. They talk and write as though the Teutonic race were confined to Central Europe, or could be confined thereto to-morrow; increasing as it is far more rapidly than the British and, of course, than the French, which was actually decreasing before he war. Have they ever taken into account the millions of Germans scattered throughout our Empire; in the neutral States; in America? What kind of ferment should we be setting

up against us throughout the world by such a policy of
permanent repression? What interminable intrigues we
should be inviting, a constant source of disquietude and
embarrassment; intrigues ready to mature when, later on,
the era of mutual recrimination begins between the Powers
now allied, a process which has invariably succeeded
alliances between Governments for the purpose of waging
war, and which is even more certain and will be even more
than usually rapid in this particular case, owing to the
secret diplomatic manœuvres which involved potential
belligerency without the knowledge of some of the peoples
engaged.

And the mention of America induces me to touch
upon one more aspect of the creed of hate. We
are not, it appears, to ship goods or passengers
in German vessels. We are even to cut off German
ships from British ports—in order to kill German
shipping, which is a branch of German trade competition.
Very well. Now those who at this moment can see
further than the distinguished personages presiding over
the Anti-German Union and its contemporaries must be
fully aware of two factors in this connection. First, that
whatever we may do, or may induce our Allies to do in
the direction of penalising Germany, America is not going
to follow us one step in that direction. This war has
taught America many things, and although consanguinity,
some similar ideals, and detestation of German methods
of warfare have powerfully influenced American opinion
on our side, we have struck a heavy blow at American
trade interests, and we have raised, in a form which hereafter will become acute, that problem of the future of
international commerce as it affects the greatest White
community in the world, which the Germans loosely call
the "freedom of the seas." America will not forget this,
and is, indeed, already taking out insurances for the
future. The other factor is this. Anyone who knows
anything at all about the world's shipping problems knows
that the backbone of German shipping is the North
Atlantic trade, and that this, far and away the most
important section of German shipping, has never received,
because it has never needed, Government assistance.
The traffic between Continental Europe and the United
States has increased enormously during the past twenty
years. The ostracising of German shipping by Britain
would but intensify its activities with American trade, and

one can imagine the tempting offers Germany, if she were excluded from British ports, would make to America, which is ready to move heaven and earth to create a mercantile marine of some consequence, of her own.

This survey, inadequate as it is, shows how essentially antagonistic to the interests of the British people, and especially to the British working classes, any "trade-war" against Germany would be. It has also contributed, I hope, to prove the impracticability and suicidal tendency of such a policy. A great deal might be said as to the causes of Germany's extraordinarily rapid commercial development, and as to our failure to maintain our former lead in certain markets. A profitable field of inquiry also lies open in the direction of demonstrating that communities do not buy from other communities for love, but because they desire the goods those other communities produce. This element in international intercourse must survive the war as it has survived other wars, and must render nugatory any artificial efforts to restrain its influence. Enough has been said to show that in so far as the destruction of German commerce, for the greater benefit of the British people, may be represented to the British nation as an argument in favour of prosecuting the war to the "bitter end"; the destruction of German commerce is, in fact, impossible, and the attempt to ensure its destruction would redound, not to the benefit, but to the disadvantage of the British people.

In the domain of trade interests Britain stands to gain nothing from a prolongation of the war; and a parade of the Allied troops in the Unter den Linden would not lighten by one groat the bill which the prolongation of the war to that point—assuming the feasibility—would create, and which the British people would in the largest measure (they are paying to-day for the maintenance of some three million British troops and some three million Allied troops in the field!) be called upon to foot. The plea for a prolongation of the war on the ground that Germany must be punished by the destruction of her trade, and because, unless she is reduced to "unconditional surrender," and to the acceptance of any terms the Allies choose to impose, British trade would suffer from a renewed period of German trade competition is, therefore, both dishonest and fallacious.

German trade competition is inevitable. There is only one means of removing it : to kill off the German people.

German trade competition is not in itself an evil, because the greater the purchasing powers of the German people, the greater the volume of business our people can transact with them. The mass of the people in both countries are partners in one another's prosperity and in one another's misfortunes. Where German competition hits particular British manufacturers, the remedy is to be sought, not in the elimination of the competitor, but in an increase in efficiency; in maintaining a higher and more universal standard of technical knowledge, in perfecting educationary systems, in revising methods, in cultivating foreign markets with greater assiduity, in creating machinery for the co-ordination and classification of effort, in converting consular functions into intelligence bureaux.

In all these branches of the commercial art we lag far behind because a long undisputed supremacy in every market (which in the nature of things could not, and cannot, be eternalised) has made us careless, and because we suffer from the incompetence of a diplomatic service wholly composed of men of aristocratic connections and wealth, whose upbringing and traditions cause them to look upon the national requirements of trade and commerce as vulgar unessentials, except when some particular commercial or financial combination can be used as a pawn in the diplomatic game of "checking the other fellow."

CHAPTER XXVIII.

Our National and Imperial Problem[1]

WHAT the open door is for trade, the open window is for politics, and a people is wise if it distrusts men who tell them that they can only conduct the public business in the dark. The first requirement of popular control of foreign policy, therefore, is a reasonable publicity. The people must have full opportunity of knowing what is being done and why it is being done, before it has actually been done. Without this provision there is no safety. For a people to grant an unlimited control of their lives and their money to little knots of unrepresentative supermen, who tell them that the arts they practise are too important and too delicate for disclosure, is a monumental act of folly.—*"Towards International Government." By J. A. Hobson (George Allen and Unwin.)*

"At present the control of foreign affairs is centralised in the British Isles. There is in London a group of men who do in fact determine the issues of peace and war for upwards of four hundred and thirty millions of human beings."—X.

IN considering the great task of national and international reconstruction which is laid upon other peoples and upon ourselves, what is the fact which stands out above all the rest?

It is surely this :—

The ignorance in which the population is left as to the policy which its rulers are pursuing, in its name, towards other States.

I propose very briefly to examine our own case, and to give some specific illustrations. Our case is not exceptional. It is typical, although more striking than some others, because we entertain in peculiar degree the illusion that we enjoy a truly democratic constitution. Fifty-seven years ago, speaking in this city of Glasgow, one of the most able, the most honest, and, in the real sense of the word, one of the greatest statesmen Britain has produced—John Bright—said this :—

"When you come to our foreign policy, you are no longer Englishmen, you are no longer free; you are recommended not to inquire. You are told you cannot

---

[1] A speech to the Glasgow Branch of the Union of Democratic Control, at Glasgow, November 23, 1915.

understand; you are snubbed; you are hustled aside. We
are told that the matter is too deep for common understandings like ours."

That was the situation obtaining at the time we fought
our last great war upon the Continent of Europe. That
was the situation obtaining in the years which immediately
preceded the present war. That is the situation obtaining
to-day. Now, as then, when it comes to matters of
foreign policy we are not free men. We are, indeed, less
free, if possible, than we were in 1858, because of late
years—during the past twelve years especially—the strings
of secrecy have been drawn tighter and tighter round the
operations of our foreign policy, with the natural result
that Parliamentary sense of responsibility for foreign
policy has weakened and public interest in foreign policy
has waned.

And yet what are the issues which our foreign policy
decides? They are issues which affect every one of us
more nearly than any national issue can conceivably do.
They are the issues of life and death hanging in the scale
for multitudes.

Those issues, nevertheless, are determined without our
cognisance and without our control. When we inquire
into them, we are snubbed, we are hustled aside.

I enumerate the following facts by way of illustrating
the applicability of John Bright's words to existing conditions, and when I say existing conditions I mean the
conditions which preceded the war and the conditions of
to-day. I make no charges against individuals. I shall
offer no opinion on the merits of the policy itself which the
facts affect. I shall merely give the facts themselves, and
follow them by the briefest of comments.

My first illustration is this. It will be well within your
recollection that in 1905, and again in 1911, this nation
stood on the brink of war in connection with the controversy over Morocco.

Now, for seven years—from 1904 to 1911—the people
of this country were kept in ignorance of the fact that
attached to the published Anglo-French Treaty over
Morocco in 1904 there were secret clauses and a secret
Treaty—the complement of those secret clauses; that these
secret arrangements provided (when the Powers benefiting

under them [1] considered the time was ripe) for the political and economic partition in their favour of Morocco, in which country another European Power[2] had interests formally recognised in one[3], and subsequently in two[4] international conventions, to both of which the British Government was signatory, and the second of which solemnly pledged the signatories to uphold the independence and integrity of Morocco.

Of these secret arrangements it can be said with incontrovertible accuracy, and without raising points of controversy : First, that they weighed upon, and affected in constant fashion, the whole direction of our foreign policy in the ensuing years.   Secondly, that the ignorance in which the nation was kept of their existence affected fundamentally the national judgment in regard to the friction, almost resulting in war, to which the Morocco controversy gave rise.

My second illustration is this : For eight years—from 1906 to 1914—the people of this country were kept in ignorance of the fact that the Cabinet, or a section of it, had authorised periodic consultations and preparations for combined action upon the Continent between the nation's military advisers and the military advisers of the French Republic; and that, arising out of these consultations, this nation was held to have contracted obligations of honour towards that Continental Power.

My third illustration is this :—

For three years—1912 to 1915—the people of this country were kept in ignorance of the fact that, after a protracted effort to find a formula of words which should define with nice exactitude what they conceived their official relations towards one another to be, our Government and the Government of Germany had failed to find that formula—a failure which, in the circumstances of the case, was invested with the utmost gravity for the future of the peoples for whom these Governments were trustees.

Of the two sets of facts which provide my second and third illustrations, it may be said with truth, without entering upon a discussion of events not yet ripe for discussion :—First, that the ignorance in which the nation was kept of them prevented a due appreciation of the

[1] France and Spain.
[2] Germany.
[3] The Madrid Convention, 1880.
[4] The Algeciras Act, 1906.

perils which lay ahead of it; secondly, that these facts
necessitated, and must have occasioned, had the nation
been made aware of them, either a complete and timely
alteration in the accepted conception of national strategy
(which would admittedly have avoided many of the difficulties and dangers with which we are now confronted),
or such a full Parliamentary and national discussion of the
international situation affecting the national policy and
the national interests as might quite conceivably have
averted these threatened perils.

Finally—and this is my last illustration—the nation is
entirely ignorant to-day of the ultimate purposes which
the States with which it is allied—the personnel of whose
Governments has been largely changed since the war broke
out—are pursuing in this war.[1] The nation knows that
there is a quadruple arrangement between its Government
and the Governments of three of its Allies not to conclude
a separate peace. But it has no clear notion of the ideas
entertained by any one of those Governments as to the sort
of settlement it would be prepared to accept, or whether
those views, whatever they may be, are considered by this
Government to be binding upon this nation. Meantime
this nation has already advanced sums to those Governments, sufficient, so we are officially informed, to maintain
three millions of their soldiers in the field, and is pledged,
apparently, to further advances before the end of the
financial year.

I know that I am expressing the conviction of a rapidly
increasing number of thoughtful men, not confined to any
particular school of domestic politics, when I say that to
conduct foreign policy behind the back of the nation in this
way constitutes one of the greatest possible dangers to the
security of the State.

And I know I am expressing the views of a very much
greater number of citizens, who are beginning to realise
that every detail of their lives—the condition of their
homes, the well-being of their families, their employment,
their wages, their food—are intimately connected with the

---

[1] It has been affirmed since this speech was delivered, by such
high authorities on Balkan affairs as Mr. Seton Watson and Sir
Arthur Evans, that a secret understanding has been arrived at
between the Allies whereby the Slav population of Dalmatia is made
over to Italy as part of Italy's price for entering the war. It has
also been affirmed by M. Miluikoff and Dr. Dillon that Great Britain
has agreed to a Russian possession of Constantinople. Neither of
these affirmations have been denied.

conduct and direction of their foreign policy : when I say that the present methods constitute a flagrant injustice to the people at large, and must be abandoned.

The U.D.C. has formulated a series of urgently needed reforms, and there can be no doubt that were these reforms to be loyally and integrally applied they would go a very long way indeed to remove the present anomalies, injustice, and dangers.   They would undoubtedly abolish that secrecy, which is the greatest danger—and which should be the chief object of reform.

But I feel personally convinced that we shall have to accustom ourselves to the idea of contemplating far more drastic changes than any of these, which, in the main, are changes merely of custom and procedure.

When we talk of democracy and democratic control of British foreign policy we have to remember that, while the claim of the democracy of this country to control the issues of national life and death must come first, because they are incomparably greater and because the burden laid upon the democracy of this country is incomparably heavier, there are four other democracies sharing that burden with this democracy, and that the claims of these other democracies cannot be ignored.

It appears to me that it will be quite impossible when the war is over to stave off any longer the demand of our self-governing Dominions, which they have so clearly earned the right to press, for a share, and a full share, in the formation and in the character, control, and discussion of foreign policy.

With the conclusion of peace, and probably before it, we shall find ourselves confronted with this problem.

Even before the war, when the Canadian contribution to the Fleet was carried through the Dominion Parliament, Sir Robert Borden—then, as now, Canadian Premier—was emphatic on the point.   Speaking on December 15, 1912, he said :—

When Great Britain no longer assumes sole responsibility for defence upon the high seas she can no longer undertake to assume responsibility for, and sole control of, foreign policy, which is closely, vitally, and constantly associated with that defence in which the Doninious participate.   It has been declared in the past, and even during recent years, that responsibility for foreign policy would not be shared by Great Britain with the Dominions.   In my humble opinion, adherence to such a position would have but one, and that a most disastrous, result.

Since the war another of Canada's leading men, who enjoys peculiar authority, has used much the same language. Sir Clifford Sifton, at the Canadian Club, Montreal, delivered himself of the following unanswerable proposition last January :—

> Bound by no constitution, bound by no rule or law, equity, or obligation, Canada has decided as a nation to make war. We have levied an army ; we have sent the greatest army to England that has ever crossed the Atlantic to take part in the battles of England. We have placed ourselves in opposition to great world Powers. We are now training and equipping an army greater than the combined forces of Wellington and Napoleon at the Battle of Waterloo, and so I say to you that Canada must now stand as a nation. It will no longer do for Canada to play the part of a minor. The nations will say : "If you can levy armies to make war you can attend to your own business, and we will not be referred to the head of the Empire ; we want you to answer our questions directly."

What holds good for Canada holds good for Australia and New Zealand—whose sons have earned imperishable fame in Gallipoli—and for the Union of South Africa, which is even now engaged, at our Government's request, in raising a large force for operations against the Germans in German East Africa.

We cannot evade the problem. But its solution will necessitate profound and far-reaching changes in our Constitution, changes which, imperfectly understood by the public and badly handled by a Government distrustful of public opinion, might well shake the British Commonwealth to its foundations.

There is only one way by which the ship of State can be steered through the many shoals and rapids with which the chart of our future is marked—for our own people, for the institutions they have built up, for the principles for which we have long stood, for the faiths which we hold—and that way is for the Government of this realm to take the people into its confidence, fully and completely.

Hitherto the nation in all these matters has been treated—the nation has allowed itself to be treated—as an infant in swaddling clothes. Its rulers have committed it, have been allowed to commit it, to unknown courses for ends obscure, even to themselves. They have whittled away the prerogatives of Parliament until that once proud assembly is in danger of sinking to the level of a second-class debating academy as regards these vital issues. They have tried, and they have been permitted to try, to govern without the nation, relying more and more upon cheap and nasty newspaper associations to give the lead they desired the nation to follow, with the not unnatural result that the chosen instruments now call the tune to which Ministers are fain reluctantly to dance.

All this is bad, unwholesome, perilous.

The key to its explanation and the key to its remedy lies here.

Something may be said in favour of a despotic form of government.   A good deal, we think, can be said in favour of a democratic form of government.   But no State can manage its affairs for long upon a mixture of both without inviting consequences fatal to its stability.

And that is what this State is trying to do, and has been trying to do, in all matters which affect the issues of national life and death.

CHAPTER XXIX.

The Alleged "Conflict of Ideals"[1]

I HAVE said that the essential problems which confront
the nations in their international relationship before the
war will not be changed by the war, but will confront the
negotiators at the settlement and the peoples after the
settlement; and that there must be on the part of each
belligerent *people* a conscious and sustained effort of the
will to understand the nature of these problems as their
own destinies and the destinies of their neighbours are
affected by them. This effort is particularly incumbent
upon the people of Great Britain, since, as I have already
remarked, the war to-day is to all intents and purposes
an Anglo-German war, and Anglo-German enmity alone
prevents its collapse. If, therefore, the war is not to be
prolonged to the stage when ordered government itself
becomes impossible, and if the war is not to be followed
by a renewed period of armed peace, with a series of fresh
wars in prospect, a real intellectual effort is needed here
at home to understand what is the paramount necessity
laid upon Germany by the factor of *growth*. And when I
use that word, I mean it as applying to Germany's own
growth in population and in industry, and also to the all-
round growth in the demands of modern industry for the
raw materials of the tropics and subtropics on the one hand
and the all-round growth in the cost of foodstuffs on the
other—both outstanding phenomena of the past two
decades.

Among the tragic failures—of prescience, temper,
common sense—which have led Europe to its present pass,
there is none, after making every allowance for German
mistakes and the arrogance peculiar to the *nouveau riche*
(in individuals as in nations), more tragic, and none which
has been more intimately responsible for this world-war
than the unwillingness or the incapacity—probably, in
major degree, the incapacity—of the British ruling class

[1] The *Labour Leader*, November 25, 1915.

to grasp Germany's economic problem, which during the past quarter of a century has, in increasing measure, governed and determined the character of her international relationships. The blunders of German diplomacy, the crass ignorance of British psychology and British institutions exhibited by the ordinary German official, the apprehensions excited over here by the development of the German Navy, and the unbridled licence of the mischief-making Press in both countries—these have had their full share in obscuring the vital issues beneath a fog of misconception. But the absence in British governing circles of a broad-minded and comprehending grip of Germany's economic situation arising from her automatic growth and the inevitable effect of that situation in creating and justifying her *Weltpolitik;* the absence, in short, of that political insight and discrimination which goes under the name of statesmanship, among those who have directed our foreign policy in recent years, has been (combined with the general secrecy of diplomatic methods everywhere) one of the chief elements in producing that state of tension in Anglo-German relations, thanks to which, *and thanks to which alone,* an Austro-Russian squabble in the Balkans has lit a European conflagration where seven millions of the flower of European manhood have already been consumed.

The attempt to throw the bridge of reason across the torrent of human passion which is hurrying the British and German peoples along the road to bankruptcy is the more difficult to-day, when even those who take the sanest view of our own grave national and Imperial problems endorse the postulate that this war is fundamentally a war between two ideals, the ideal of liberty incarnated in the British Constitution, and the ideal of tyrannous reaction incarnated in the German Confederation. We have advanced so far in that error that the public accepts without a murmur the open threats of violence to Greece indulged in by powerful London newspapers in the event of Greece not doing our bidding; so far, that organs of the Press which used to be "Liberal" complacently envisage, in the name of liberty, a future Europe in which the present Allies, armed to the teeth, shall "permanently hold down" a forcibly disarmed Germany !

What, then, is the nature and significance of Germany's economic problem, arising inexorably from her own growth and the growth of world phenomena affecting her national future? I defined it myself in the last chapter of "Morocco in Diplomacy," published in the spring of 1912, as follows :—

"The guiding motive of German foreign policy to-day is to secure for the German people unfettered access to markets over-seas, as large a share as possible in the development of these markets, and a voice in the acquisition of over-sea territories which may pass, through the course of events, into the International melting pot. It is not land hunger, but trade hunger, which inspires her, and trade hunger responds to the fundamental demand of her national existence."

To every word then written I adhere, and if you want the *statistical* proof of their truth, you will find it in the fact that *more than half of Germany's imports is composed of raw material for manufacture.* German "World-policy," that *Weltpolitik* which the political mind has associated with aggression, because the political mind has regarded it exclusively from a political point of view, and which the Jingo Press has dinned into our ears morning and evening, must be aggressive from its very title (although *Weltpolitik* has been the breath of our own national nostrils since Elisabeth), is the product, not of political design, but of sheer economic necessity, outcome of growth. No doubt it has been expressed, often enough, in a manner calculated to offend susceptibilities, although I hardly think that any German utterance has exceeded the erstwhile performances of Mr. Grover Cleveland. But it is the business of statesmen to discover and appreciate the motive forces lying beneath the surface of diplomatic or royal demonstrations.

Let us consider this economic problem of Germany, whence it springs, and how it has revolutionised the conditions of her national existence—for the problem is not a thing of yesterday, but of to-day and to-morrow. It governs the future as well as the present. In the last forty-five years the population of Germany has more than half doubled itself. It has risen from 40,000,000 to 65,000,000, and before the war it was increasing from three-quarters of a million to a million *per annum*. To find food and work for an immense natural growth of this kind must ever be the primary obligation laid upon the Government of a community so prolific. As Mr. Dawson pointed out with irrefutable truth some years ago :—

"The position of Germany is that of a prolific nation which is growing beyond the physical conditions of its surroundings."

And Germany *alone among the nations of Europe* has been faced with the tremendous perplexities incidental to a problem of this kind. Her Government had either to sustain this population at home, or encourage its emigration to foreign countries. Now, so long as the spirit of national entity exists, no Government and no national organism will be satisfied that foreign countries should benefit exclusively from the surplusage of its population. Germany possessed no over-sea territories affording the necessary climatic requirements for the expansion of a White people. The policy of her statesmen was, therefore, bound to be centripetal and not centrifugal. In other words, they had to meet their problem by centralisation and not by decentralisation. They had to concentrate and not disseminate their human material.

Two points have to be noted, first, the necessity; secondly, the decision. The centrifugal policy, the policy of radiation from the centre, was impracticable, because the means were not available : no temperate zones were in the market. The centripetal policy, the policy of concentration of national effort within the boundaries of the State, was, therefore, deliberately adopted, and has been deliberately and scientifically pursued and systematised. Both food and work were found for the population at home. Emigration dwindled, virtually to vanishing point. An immense industrial system was built up. While other Powers—the lambs of the international picture as painted to-day—were waging war here, there, and everywhere, in Manchuria, South Africa, Tripoli, Abyssinia, Morocco, the Sudan; Germany, while fully prepared for war, did not wage it, but devoted the national energy to consolidating, perfecting, and training her population in industrial pursuits, calling upon all the inventive genius and laborious, painstaking, hardworking qualities of the race; improving her hygienic and municipal undertakings to a degree which caused other nations to seek her counsels; penetrating every foreign market accessible, rivalling and outpacing old-established competitors by sheer application of intellect and system to commercial and industrial development. Two years before the war broke out Germany's foreign trade stood at £982,615,000; in 1888 her foreign trade only amounted to £323,585,000.   In 24 years it had trebled itself, showing an annual average rate of increase of 8.5 per cent., compared with Great Britain's 4.1 per cent.

And it is precisely when we contemplate these facts that the fallacy of so much that is now being written about the divergence between British "Imperial" ideals and German "Imperial" ideals becomes so apparent. German professors and publicists may rave to-day about "destroying" the British Empire, just as British professors and publicists rave about "destroying" Germany and "grinding her to powder." But the policy *actually followed* by Germany's rulers—imposed upon Germany's rulers by accomplished facts—during the past quarter of a century, has been a policy moving in a direction absolutely contrary to the forcible wresting of temperate zones over-seas from the peoples which inhabit those zones in order to create therein German-speaking communities. The belief which attributes to the rulers of Germany a deep-laid plot, hatched for years past, to acquire Canada, Australia, New Zealand, South Africa ("destroy the British Empire," in other words), is a belief founded in ignorance of the whole trend of German policy and of the economic necessities dictating it, and also upon a radically faulty concept of the relationship existing between Great Britain and her self-governing Dominions. The British self-governing Dominions are inhabited by a white population of 14 millions invested with complete control over their own affairs, except (and it is a big exception which cannot be perpetuated without wrecking the Empire), in so far as their own affairs are affected by the foreign policy of Downing Street. The Germans would not "possess" these countries even if they could conquer them, any more than we possess them; and, in practice, Germany, having conquered these countries, would be no more able to coerce and control them than we are, without coming to grief, even as we came to grief when we tried that procedure in the case of the American Colonies.

And when we are gravely told, as we are to-day, that this war is a struggle between irreconcilable British and German "Imperial" ideals, between two "opposing systems," and so forth, meaning thereby the fundamental divergence between the British and German notions of the relationship which should exist between the Central Authority and over-sea communities of the same stock on the one hand, and between the Central Authority and communities of alien stock, but incorporated within the boundaries of the Central State, on the other hand; when we are told these things, what is our reply? Our reply is this. The similitude implied, in order to point a moral from the divergence, is non-existent. There is no material for comparison, for the simple reason that Germany has never had to face an Imperial problem involving the creation of any kind of relationship between the Mother Country and over-sea communities of German stock; and, secondly, because we have never had to face the German Imperial problem of determining the character of the relationship which should prevail between the Central Authority and alien communities within the territorial boundaries of the State subject to that Central Authority. Our nearest approach to the German Imperial problem is the case of Ireland, and our record in Ireland should make us chary of using the sort of arguments current to-day, because the very faults committed by Germany in Poland and Alsace-Lorraine, covering a few decades in the matter of time, have been committed by us in Ireland for centuries, and an influential Party in the State is still bitterly opposed to our correcting them.

All this talk about a conflict of ideals being the rock bottom of the war, a conflict so deep-seated and racial that it can only be settled by the "complete overthrow" of either Britain or Germany, is, therefore, as applied to the domain of actual facts, an extraordinary hallucination, typical of that looseness of thought which catch-phrases engender. There is no such conflict, because Germany has never had the opportunity of demonstrating whether she possesses or does not possess the political sagacity to treat great white communities of her own stock over-seas as we have learned by bitter experience is the right way to treat them. There is no such conflict, because we have not been called upon to handle the problem of the government of vast agglomerations of alien peoples within our territorial boundaries, the case of the Irish— separated from us by sea, but at our doors—approximating most nearly to the German problem, and our dealings with the Irish not having been of a character such as to entitle us to declare that our regard for alien communities subjected to our immediate control places us upon a moral pedestal compared with the Germans. There is no such conflict, because the part Britain and Germany have had to play in the world has been utterly different; permitting of no possible political analogy.

If the war is indefinitely prolonged, a direct or subsidised attack upon any portion of the British Empire, territorially accessible to Germany or her Allies, is probable enough. But that will be part of the strategy of war, and not of any supposed conflict of political ideals responsible for the war itself.

CHAPTER XXX.

Germany's Human and Economic Problem[1]

A PEOPLE which increases fifty per cent. in a generation must be a colonising people, must have a great over-seas commerce, must, therefore, have a great navy.—*J. Holland Rose, in "Germany in the Nineteenth Century."*

Germany has a population to-day of over 65,000,000 of people, who are confronted with problems at home as well as abroad. They are the best clients of the United Kingdom ; they also do a very large trade with France (buying more from her than they sell), and an enormous trade—an average of £90,000,000 annually—with Russia. Therefore, if the Governments of the Powers who form the Triple Understanding are business men, they will desire that Germany may solve not only her foreign difficulties, but her anomalies in home administration, as well as the social and fiscal questions in dispute, so that her toiling millions may increase in numbers and in wealth, and require larger and larger supplies of foreign products for their manufactures and their bodily consumption.—*Sir Harry Johnston, in "Views and Reviews." (Williams and Norgate. 1912.)*

IF I return to Germany's economic problem, resulting from the growth in her population, it is because there can be no "New Europe" if that problem, and its effect upon international relations, is not understood; and, above all, by the people of this country. It is one of the capital issues underlying the condition of Europe to-day, and it is one of the capital issues inseparably bound up with the sort of future which is reserved for Europe after the war. The problem will subsist substantially unimpaired in its essentials by the war. If the settlement does not take it into account, the settlement cannot in the nature of things be a permanent one. A few years, at the most a decade or two, and the problem re-asserts itself automatically. Its solution can be sought, however, by action which would not only relieve the arterial pressure in Germany, but at one and the same time confer lasting benefit upon humanity at large. That action would consist in the establishment, by common consent, of freedom of commerce and the "open door" for all commercial transactions (*i.e.*, unrestricted by differential tariffs and exclusive privi-

[1] The *Labour Leader*, December 2, 1915.

leges) by the nationals of every European State in the dependencies which have been, or may be, acquired by those States outside Europe. It would mean ridding Africa and Asia of the curse of the monopolist, the protectionist, and the concessionaire, whose selfish interests provide the Chancelleries of Europe with most of their recriminating matter and with the raw material of their intrigues. It would make for peace in Europe, in Asia,[1] and in Africa. It would make for commercial and political honesty and international decency. It would not benefit Germany at the expense of other nations. It would ensure a fair field and no favour for all nations, and prove an inestimable boon to the "coloured" subjects of colonising States.

So far as Germany is concerned, let us glance at her problem once more. We have seen that her rulers were compelled, in the absence of colonisable areas suitable for white settlement, to concentrate the tremendous elemental force with which Nature was endowing their country, within the boundaries of the State, which necessitated providing that force with sustenance and with labour. Now, despite artificial fiscal efforts the agricultural resources of the State were insufficient to supply foodstuffs in adequate quantity for the increased population. Germany's position has been steadily approximating to our own. She has become more and more dependent upon imported food. But to buy food from abroad you must pay for it, and, in the ultimate resort, you can only pay for it in goods. Put otherwise, a population unable to sustain itself with the necessaries of life from its own territory must be in a position to purchase its requirements by producing articles to sell to foreign food-producers in exchange. Similarly, a population increasing prodigiously, but concentrated at home by force of circumstances, must be kept employed. To furnish these articles and to provide this employment the raw material from which goods can be manufactured must be available in abundance. To sell these articles to the best advantage in the face of a universal competition entails not only access to existing markets in Europe, where in most cases discriminating tariffs have to be reckoned with; it entails unhampered access to new markets overseas of vast potentiality in raw material,

---

[1] I am assuming that the "open-door" in China is not closed by Japan as the outcome of an attempt on the latter's part to exercise complete control over China's internal and external policy.

both for trade and for the employment of capital designed to intensify the flow of that raw material towards the centres of home manufacture.   In the measure in which tariffs, set up by those who control these new markets access to these new markets is hampered by discriminating and by other restrictive measures, the problem confronting a Power in Germany's unique position must be rendered more complex and more difficult to solve.   Free and expanding markets have become for Germany an idispensable necessity of her people's livelihood.   As Mr. Dawson, writing at a time when men's judgments were not obscured by the passions of war, has put it : "To the nation collectively extended markets are a condition of life."

Dr. Paul Rohrbach, the well-known German economist, quoted by the same writer, states the case with admirable lucidity :—

"The number of those who must live on foreign corn increase, and the increases will soon be a million a year. Whoever cannot get rid of this million is bound to answer the question how otherwise he will feed them than by the produce of our industry—in the manufacture of raw material brought from abroad and the sale of our products to foreign nations, or the produce of the capital created here and invested abroad.   If that is so, then for Germany all questions of foreign politics must be viewed from the standpoint of the creation and maintenance of markets abroad, and especially in trans-oceanic countries.   For good or ill, we must accustom ourselves in our political thinking to the application of the same principles as the English.   In England the determination of foreign policy according to the requirements of trade, and, therefore, of industry, is an axiom of the national consciousness which no one any longer disputes.   If the possibility of disposing of its industrial products abroad were one day to cease or to be limited for England, the immediate result would be, not merely the economic ruin of millions of industrial existences on both sides of the ocean, but the political collapse of Britain as a Great Power.   Yet the position is not materially different for ourselves."

Now, if we can lay hold of this pivotal fact and get it firmly fixed in our minds, we shall be able not only to understand how utterly impossible it is to expect that a durable peace in Europe can be secured by any of the

nostrums for penalising Germany which are being dangled
before the national vision, but how impossible it is to
suppose that a permanent cure for Europe's ills is to be
found if enormous regions in Africa and Asia continue to
be treated by the States which administer them as privileged preserves for their own nationals, especially when
the States which so administer them are free from the
internal problems which press upon Germany; and, too,
if an area of the world's surface one quarter larger than
Europe, inhabited by a population only 33 millions less
than that of Europe, is liable to become a privileged area
for British nationals by the accident of a British General
Election.

The three great Imperial colonising Powers (excluding
Germany), are Britain, France, and Russia. Excluding
the self-governing Dominions of the Empire, which are,
of course, in all fiscal matters independent States, the
British Government can determine the fiscal policy of an
area covering one-tenth of the world's surface and
inhabited by a little more than one-fourth of the world's
total inhabitants.[1] Britain has hitherto discriminated
against none of her commercial rivals throughout this
gigantic area, and that is one of the reasons why, as
Britons, we are justified in asserting that the British
administration of those vast tracts is unselfishly exercised
so far as other European nations are concerned. Were a
strong Protectionist Party, however, to come into power
at the end of this war and carry out its long threatened
programme, the whole world, and especially the nation
which comes next to our own in productive capacity, would
suffer, and international relations would again become
poisoned in consequence. For us, the result would be
that we should have to build against the whole world, and
maintain a permanent army on a large scale to prepare for
the Continental coalition which would infallibly come about
sooner or later.

The case of France and Russia is different. France
now owns very nearly half Africa and over 300,000 miles
in Asia. In Asia the Russian Empire extends over just
under one-third of that continent; and both France and
Russia discriminate to the uttermost practicable extent
against foreign merchandise and foreign enterprise, except
where restricted from doing so—and the restrictions are

[1] The area of the British *dependencies* is 5,091,000 square miles,
and the population is 369,000,000.

confined to a few areas in French West Africa, and these
only for a term of years which has nearly expired—by international agreement.[1]

The case of France and Germany respectively may be
taken by way of illustration of the impossible situation
which is created in the world so long as great colonial
Powers use their privileges to create for themselves and
their nationals exclusive advantages, to the detriment of
other Powers, for whom the need of free markets over-
seas is a national necessity.   This can best be shown in
a table :—

Population :—

France	39,601,509
Germany	64,925,993

Excess of deaths over births :—

France	34,869

Excess of births over deaths :—

Germany	740,431

Foreign trade (1912) :—

France	£583,488,000
Germany	£982,615,000

That was the situation before the war.[2]   It is, it would
seem, to be further aggravated after the war.   France and
England are to drive Germany from the African Continent
altogether.   They are to seize and retain her dependencies
therein, and they are to combine for the purpose of
"smashing" her over-seas trade.   Yet Germany is driven
by the immutable laws which govern the existence of
States either to secure free markets over-seas or to secure
over-sea territory which she can develop free from the
unfair competition of hostile tariffs, or perish !   Of course,
if you can really "destroy" Germany the problem is solved.
Personally, I do not regard that operation as within the
range of possibility.

The Government of every nation engaged in this war
has repeatedly declared that it is waging war in order to
secure a durable peace at the end of it.   A durable peace
cannot be secured from the military results of the war.   It
can only be secured by a joint effort to recognise the

[1] I assume, of course, that the Franco-German Convention in
Morocco has gone by the board.

[2] In the decade preceding the last census, which in France was
taken in 1911, and in Germany in 1912, the population of Germany
increased by 8½ millions, and the population of France by 639,564.

peculiar needs of each nation, and by- the admission, expressed in political acts, that natural growth must find an outlet and cannot be artificially stifled. The following table illustrates a further aspect of the problem we have been here considering, and, like the preceding one, crystallises a series of facts which can only be disregarded by the expedient the ostrich is said to adopt when pursued. The States of Europe are being pursued to-day by the nemesis of their own past follies, and they cannot find salvation by imitating the ostrich.

Population :—
 United Kingdom 45,369,090
 Germany 64,925,993

Increase in last decade :—
 United Kingdom 3,392,263
 Germany 8,558,815

Foreign trade :—
 United Kingdom £1,344,168,421
 Germany £943,050,000

Growth of foreign trade in last 25 years :—
 United Kingdom .... 100.7 per cent.
 Germany .... 204 per cent.

Actual increase in aggregate value of foreign trade in last 25 years :—
 United Kingdom £562,025,000
 Germany £659,030,000

I shall now show that the enormous importance which attaches to the future colonial policy of European States in determining what the future of Europe is to be, is fully apprehended by representative men belonging to neutral and even to belligerent States.

CHAPTER XXXI.

The Eternal International Irritant[1]

IF you think that, *not being able to sell freely, we should mend ourselves by giving up the power to buy freely,* I must leave you to that opinion, only expressing my wonder at it. But you will perhaps say that we can force other nations to reduce their tariffs if we impose a tariff against them. You forget, probably, that we have tried that in past times, and that it has wholly failed.—*John Bright.*

THE war of to-morrow will be a war, not between nations, but between influences and forces within nations divided into two opposing camps, those upholding the conception that force must be the ultimate Court of Appeal for conflicts between nations, and those determined that other means must be found. If we are to equip ourselves efficiently for this struggle we must look out upon the world as it is and frame our action in conformity therewith. We must not act and argue as though the world were what we wished it to be, and what, no doubt, it ought to be. Nor shall we achieve our ends by supposing that it is within our power to start right away fashioning a new world. The new world will grow out of the reformed world. But first the existing world has to be reformed. The struggle for the internal reform of nations, *i.e.*, fairer adjustment of nationally earned wealth, equality of opportunity, the obligation upon the State to find work for all and to exact work from all, and so forth, can proceed side by side with the struggle for the reform of international relationships. But so long as the latter problem is not solved, the former proceeds under a perpetual menace. For what measure, not merely of finality, but even of assured and cumulative progress, can be achieved within a State when the whole internal economy of that State is open to violent dislocation at any moment by war—by war which diverts the national resources from the amelioration of internal conditions to the destruction of the nation's clients in neighbouring States, thus in a double sense hampering the nation's advance? The utmost precariousness and

[1] The *Labour Leader,* December 23, 1915.

perennial delay must of necessity characterise the internal improvement of States until the wider problem is solved.

And when we look out upon the world as it is, what is the irritant we observe everywhere at work poisoning the relationship between nations? The tariff. And it is a poison which increases in virulence with the growth of population. The closer the intercommunication between peoples, the greater the facilities for the exchange of commodities, the nearer the peoples are drawn to one another by mutual needs. How singular is it to reflect that while the operation of natural forces tends more and more to the abolition of frontiers as obstacles to human intercourse and to a fusing and commingling of human interests, a restricted section of every community is permitted by the Governments to interpose artificial barriers thereto, and how grimly ironic that the very influences which ought to make for increasingly harmonious relations become charged, owing to these artificial barriers, with matter making for bitterness, jealousy, and discord. Tariffs produced the tension which in the middle of last century almost determined war between France and England. Within the present generation France and Italy have nearly come to blows over tariffs. In the last twenty-five years tariffs have over and again embittered the relations of Britain and France, and France and Germany. The Tariff Reform campaign here gathered copious harvests of international ill-will from the home tariffs of Germany, and the threat of constructing a tariff wall round the British Empire provoked German anger and alarm. The decision of the Russian Government in March of last year to impose heavy tariffs upon German rye and flour helped to precipitate the events of August. And to-day our tariff worshippers are busy laying plans to sow the seeds of future hatreds when this war is over.

The opening up of new vast markets over-seas, primarily due to the rapid development of European industries and consequent demand for increased quantities of raw material, has intensified the friction and quadrupled the dangers arising out of it. For to tariffs pure and simple have been added special forms of monopolies and privileges of an exclusive character. True, neither Britain nor Germany has been guilty in this respect. Germany has not imported her home tariffs into her colonial possessions. She has preserved therein the open door. Britain has maintained her home traditions in all her dependencies, although she has accepted preferential treatment from the *Dominions*.   But while British fiscal policy has remained sound, British foreign policy has for the past twelve years been identified with the political interests of *Colonial Protectionist Powers,* and against the interest of the only other *Colonial Free Trade* Power[1] except Britain.   This association has led on the one hand to the present topsy turvydom—Free-Trade Britain helping Protectionist France and Russia in their extra-European interests against Free-Trade Germany—and, on the other, has undoubtedly strengthened the tariff elements in Britain in their agitation for Imperial Protection, an agitation promoted by the immense increase in German trade, and assisted, in its popular appeal, by the Protectionism of Germany at home. The part this fatal economic policy has played in shaping the events which led to the war is beyond question, and here lies, perhaps, the most vital of all the reforms which clamour for broad and far-seeing international statesman-ship, if the "New Europe" of the future is to emerge from the region of hope to the region of fact.   Cobden's vision not only went to the root of the actual, it pierced the future. We read his utterances with reverence, for if they embodied the truth in his time, they apply with tenfold significance to the world of to-day.   Unhampered commercial inter-course, the right of all peoples to exchange their produce and their merchandise on a basis of mutual equality—this still remains the greatest of all reforms to be accom-plished in the relationship of States.   The evil needs attacking all along the line, both in its actual manifesta-tions and in its potential threats.   It can be attacked more effectively where its establishment is recent and where, for a multiplicity of reasons, it is more easily approached— *i.e.,* in the Colonial field.

This is realised by the able and distinguished men who have drawn up the "Minimum Programme for a Durable Peace," and who before many months—perhaps weeks— will assemble at Berne to discuss it.   Twenty-six countries are represented upon the Council of the coming conference, including the United States, the Argentine, Austria-Hungary, Belgium, Britain, Brazil, Canada, Denmark, France, Greece, Holland, Switzerland, Norway, Sweden, Italy, Spain, and Roumania.   One of the resolutions reads as follows :—

---

[1] *I.e.,* among the Great Powers.   Holland pursues a Free Trade Colonial policy.

"The Powers shall agree to introduce freedom of trade, or, at least, equality of treatment for all nations, into their colonies, protectorates, and spheres of influence."

Here are some notable passages from the statement issued in support of the resolution :—

"The opinion is universally entertained that economic rivalry has contributed more than has any other motive to the present war; it is evident in any case that the commercial competition between Germany and Great Britain profoundly troubled the relations of the two countries; thus a conflict was created which became one of the principal causes of the world war."

Were the friends of peace of the last century mistaken, then, the document asks, when in urging freedom of trade, which implies the most widespread competition, they argued that the unrestricted exchange of goods between peoples was symbolic of human solidarity? Obviously not. For it is not international competition in the purchase and sale of merchandise which leads to armed conflict between States. What does so is the action of Governments in seeking to create, in specific cases, privileged conditions for their nationals at the expense of other nations.

"German trade" and "British trade" are often spoken of as though these two Empires were joint-stock companies, one and indivisible in their interests and pursuing commercial enterprises under the direction of their Governments. Everyone knows that nothing of the kind exists, and that, in point of fact, commercial competition in regular trade and in the exchange of ordinary goods is much more intense between two British merchants or between two German merchants than between English and German merchants; and, on the other hand, that the majority of the citizens of both countries have common and identical interests."

After pointing out that the Protectionism adopted by many States at home will only perish by degrees as a democracy, growing in enlightenment and in power, is able more and more to impose its will upon selfish interests, the document contends that collective international action in regard to Colonial Dependencies is perfectly feasible and urgently necessary, and is the only policy compatible with the duties of civilised nations towards races in a more backward state. The document lays stress upon the fact that :—

"Exclusivism in the Colonial field has become more and more a fertile source of conflicts between States. It is in the Colonial field that commercial competition tends to assume a political complexion, and, consequently, to be provocative of war."

Britain, Germany, and Holland have adopted the policy of the "open-door" in their Colonial Dependencies. Why should not other countries? The remedy is simple, and would consist "in an undertaking between all colonising States to put an end to a system of Colonial privilege, preference, and favouritism." The compilers of the Minimum Programme rightly insist that "freedom of commerce" must mean more than mere "freedom of exchange." Freedom of navigation, of employment of capital, of the location of commercial undertakings, of mineral enterprises—these must be free for all nations in all Colonial Dependencies, i.e., the enterprise of all nations must be on a footing of equality. If Customs dues are imposed for revenue purposes, they must not be differential dues, but applied to all goods, whatever their origin.

The document stigmatises as an illusion the idea that national interests are really concerned in the international friction to which the policy of the "shut door" in Colonial Dependencies gives rise. It is individual interests which are at stake, and these, by the influence they are able to bring to bear upon Governments and in the Press, create among the masses the illusion that national interests are at stake.

It is cheering to read so lucid and truthful a statement drawn up by well-known men from so many different countries, and to find distinguished Belgians like M. Henri Lambert and M. Paul Otlet devoting themselves, the former especially,[1] to the spread of the truth. It encourages the hope that the immense movement which will everywhere arise after the war against war as a medium for the solution of international disputes, will

[1] I would earnestly commend to those who may not have read it, Lambert's "The Ethics of International Trade," published by Humphrey Milford, Oxford University Press (London, Edinburgh, and Glasgow), and printed at the price of 2d. by Frederick Hall, Oxford.

concentrate upon the removal of positive factors in international relations which, so long as they exist, render a durable peace utterly impossible.

It must come as a shock to those evil or ignorant advisers of the British nation, who go on dinning into our ears that the inherent wickedness and vile ambitions of Germany were alone responsible for this war, and that a durable peace can only come as the result of her destruction as a first-class Power; it must come as a shock to them to find, after fifteen months of declamation, that they can impose less and less upon international intelligence, and to find that men of eminence, belonging to neutral, and even Allied nations, are preparing for a rational solution.

But let us face the truth quite frankly. The stumbling block to a Colonial understanding between the three great Colonial Powers which are articulate—Britain, France, and Germany—is the Colonial policy hitherto pursued by France. Let us see whether, by the exercise of statesmanship in all three countries, that stumbling block cannot be removed, and whether its removal, if practicable, might not be the first step to the breaking down of the tariff barriers which play such havoc with the interests of European peoples.

CHAPTER XXXII.

The Way Out[1]

A N arrangement for the internationalisation of commercial activity in the extra-European Dependencies[2] of the Colonial Powers and for the neutralisation of the Dependencies themselves would remove three-fifths, possibly four-fifths, of the cause of potential conflicts between States. It would be a self-denying ordinance on the part of the Governments, but the peoples would be the material gainers thereby, apart altogether from the immense gain derivable by them from the elimination of the chief irritant in international relations. And if the European Governments could be induced to go thus far, it would be comparatively easy to extend the principle to China, Persia, and other parts of Asia and Africa ruled over by indigenous Governments free from direct European tutelage, but necessarily accessible to and swayed by European influence. In other words, if agreement were possible in regard to the Dependencies, there could be agreement to refrain from pursuing exclusive commercial or political advantages (which are usually the cloak to cover the former) in independent Asiatic and African territories. There is nothing Utopian or visionary in these suggestions. They are eminently practicable. Their execution would involve no diminution of commercial activity and business enterprise on the part of the nationals of any European State.

[1] Written on December 24, 1915, *i.e.,* before Mr. Runciman's pronouncement in the House of Commons (January 10, 1916) : published in the *Labour Leader,* January 20, 1916.

[2] In using the term "Dependencies," instead of "Colonies," I desire to avoid that confusion in ideas which leads to so much muddled thinking on this subject. The term "Colony" is not applicable to the vast tropical and sub-tropical areas which have been drawn into the vortex of European political ambitions owing to Europe's economic need for the raw material these areas produce. They are not *colonisable* by white peoples. At the present time these non-colonisable areas and the self-governing Dominions of the British Empire are all lumped together as "Colonies."

261

But all would compete on equal terms. Acumen, applicability to local conditions, up-to-date methods, hard work—these would be the criterions of success.

I mean by the expression "internationalisation of commercial activities" in the Dependencies of the Powers, tnat the nationals of all European States shall compete on an equal footing in the Colonial Dependencies of each, whether in commerce, industry, banking, mining, shipping, or any other form of legitimate enterprise. I mean that a Frenchman, an Italian, a Russian, a Dutchman, a German, a Belgian, an Englishman shall carry on his business on equal terms in a French, British, German, Italian, Russian, Dutch, or Belgian Dependency as the case may be. I mean that representatives of all nationalities that care to do so shall have equal rights of tendering for the construction of public works, and a share, if they desire it, in enterprises necessitating large capital outlay, in the Dependencies of the various Powers. I do not mean that the local administration of a Dependency should not impose taxes on European enterprises in order to raise revenue, but that such taxes, whatever form they take, should be imposed without differentiation. Neither do I suggest that the administration itself should be internationalised, although the creation of international Boards for the discussion and adjustment of local difficulties, upon which commercial representatives of the nations interested would sit, might suggest itself as a feasible development in course of time.

The subject has another side to it, superficially irrelevant, but to those who look beneath the surface indissolubly connected, viz., the treatment of the native races. If economic rivalry between the colonising Powers in the undeveloped or partly developed areas of the world's surface could be done away with, the rights and the wrongs of the native races would receive closer and more sympathetic consideration by the Governments. At present the native races are callously sacrificed to rivalries between the Governments—perfectly futile rivalries for the most part; and the Governments have not yet realised that the perpetration of, or the acquiescence in, moral wrongs inflicted upon the natives, affect in the most detrimental fashion those very economic interests for which these Governments intrigue and agitate. So long as the European Governments look upon these vast African and Asiatic territories as areas for the pursuit of privileges and monopolies, carried on behind closed doors, in favour of a microscopic fraction of their respective nationals, so long will these territories continue to be one of the prime causes of European unrest and European armaments, and so long will their inhabitants be sacrificed—and sacrificed not only immorally but stupidly, without the slightest advantage to the European peoples, and for the sake of purely ephemeral and exclusively selfish interests.

By the "neutralisation" of the Dependencies themselves, the writer means the removal of these oversea areas from the operations of European war. This was intended by the Berlin and Brussels Acts to apply to a considerable part of the African Continent. But that provision, like everything else, has gone by the board. What chance, then, the sceptic will exclaim, of extending that principle on a vaster and, indeed, universal scale after the war, or by the terms of settlement? Every chance, if public opinion will but apply itself to the problem in the meantime; and, intrinsically, a very good chance, for a multiplicity of reasons. The Berlin and Brussels Acts laying down the neutralisation of the Congo Basin had been so frequently violated both in the letter and spirit before the war, that it may have been said to have been a dead letter from the start. The war itself has produced many weighty arguments in favour of the neutralisation of African and Asiatic Dependencies. When passions have cooled down and a sense of perspective reasserts itself, I do not suppose the British or French Governments will feel particularly proud, or particularly easy in their minds as to the ultimate effects of their action—at having imported Asiatics[1] and Africans to fight their battles upon the plains of Europe. Experience will suggest to them the doubtful wisdom of consecrating that policy.

It would be idle to deny that the neutralisation of the European Dependencies over-seas would entail a sacrifice on Britain's part; while, on the other hand, the internationalisation of commercial activities within them would be to her advantage, because of her commercial experience. For it is evident, of course, that in time of war the Dependencies of every European State are at the mercy,

---

[1] The tribute to the general character of our Indian administration involved in the generous support Indian potentates have given us is gratifying and deserved. It is the wisdom of having profited by it that is doubtful.

virtually speaking, of the Power which commands the seas. Their neutralisation would, therefore, involve on the part of Britain the loss of an advantage which her sea power gives to her. Let us face the fact frankly. But let us also ask ourselves, with an equal desire to deal honestly with ourselves, whether the voluntary surrender of that advantage would really injure the vital interests of the British people; and, too, whether, in the long run, the Powers of Europe can be expected to acquiesce in a situation which makes all their over-seas enterprise subject to British sufferance in time of war. To-day, no doubt, this is a German grievance. But yesterday it was a French grievance. To-morrow it may be a grievance collectively urged. The way to envisage the problem is not in terms of the grievance of this or that particular State at a particular moment; but in terms of the future of Europe, humanity, and of Britain herself. Continental Powers can never be expected to disarm on land, even approximately, still less to abandon the idea of challenging us on the seas, so long as their policy over-seas is carried out subject to our good will and pleasure. The safety of an island-Empire whose nerve-centres depend upon sustenance from abroad can never be jeopardised without a radical elimination of the causes which might place that safety in jeopardy. But neither can an island-Empire in a future world of man's increasing mastery over air arrogate with safety to itself the right to maintain a perpetual mortgage over the extra-European activities—the Imperial policy— of Europe. But that has been, and is, the attitude of British statesmanship. We say, in effect, to the Powers of Europe : "You can have an over-seas policy if you wish. You can acquire Dependencies, spend money on them, build up a big trade with them. But if you are so foolish as to fall foul of us, understand that we shall promptly seize them." Most Englishmen believe to-day that this war was caused by the German Government's desire to dictate to Europe, in Europe. Assuredly some Germans have put forward views which, logically interpreted, mean nothing else. But in our own case we quite deliberately, and as the most natural thing in the world, claim to dictate, by virtue of our overwhelming sea power, the policy of European Powers outside Europe. To me it appears utterly impossible, either that a better Europe can arise from the ashes of the old while that claim remains the bed-rock of our foreign policy, or that we can continue indefinitely to exercise it with safety to our own country or Empire. The neutralisation of the over-seas Dependencies of all Powers offers a just and feasible way of escape from the accumulation of fresh hatreds and of fresh rivalries; and from a position which, ultimately, must in the very nature of things become impracticable to sustain.

Britain is in a position to take the lead in the matter of the neutralisation of the Dependencies; quite obviously this great reform could not be consummated without her consent. In the matter of the internationalisation of commercial activities in the Dependencies, on the lines here laid down, the word rests primarily with France, which, after Britain, possesses the largest over-seas Empire and treats it as a protectionist reserve. But Germany, too, would have to consent to make sacrifices, for there must be a German *quid pro quo.* The internationalisation of "colonial" trade would be the first step towards undermining the tariff in Europe itself. Both in her over-seas policy and in her home policy Europe must gravitate towards freedom of trade, or continue to nurse within her bosom the asp of international strife. At present her ruling classes, pushed forward by vested interests and at their wits' ends to conciliate the most superficially powerful elements in their public opinion for the horrors and losses of the war, would seem to be busily preparing for renewed economic conflicts, rendered the more bitter by pumping into them the passions of the time; and hence preparing for fresh political conflicts and increased armaments. For let this incontestable truth sink into the minds of all the peoples. If, when the cannon cease to boom, the blight of the tariff war ensues, the hopes of humanity, which centre in this frightful catastrophe being the last of its kind, are blasted. Were European frontiers remodelled, as the result of this war, upon the most approved lines of national boundaries and political consciousness, and the tariff and the colonial monopoly not only remained in being but were aggravated by a further strengthening of the artificial barriers between peoples, the most fundamental of all causes of international friction would subsist. When one reads about this plotting and counter-plotting on the part of the British, German, French, Austrian, Russian, and Italian Governments to hamper Britons, Germans, Frenchmen, Austrians, Russians, and Italians in the exchange of commodities, one is tempted to ask whether statesmanship has not become utterly bankrupt in ideas. While its spokesmen declare that a durable peace is their one end and aim, they are deliberately engineering war under the spur of a spurious patriotism. They are arranging to plunge Europe back into the morass.

Imagine a draught of pure, wholesome air sweeping through the musty atmosphere of the Chancelleries, and you might picture to yourself these men, appalled at the consequences of their own past incompetence, concocting no more poisonous brews, but some healing balsam to cure the wounds they have inflicted. You might perceive a germ of common-sense expanding into some such constructive set of proposals as these. For a period of, say, twenty-five years—no agreement should be unlimited in time—the British Government would pledge itself to the continued maintenance of the open-door throughout the British Dependencies. It would surrender for that period the preference granted by the Dominions. The French Government would initiate the policy of the open-door throughout the French Dependencies, and would undertake to maintain it for that period. The German Government would pledge itself to maintain the policy of the open-door throughout the Dependencies remaining to Germany as the outcome of the general settlement; and would further take the first stride towards European free trade by lowering its home tariff towards all countries alike—a measure which would benefit the Allies primarily, since it is the Allies which do the greatest volume of business with her. Substantially the British Government would say to the German :—

"We guarantee to you a continuance of that equality of commercial treatment in the United Kingdom and in the British Dependencies which you have always enjoyed. For a quarter of a century you would thus be freed from the fear of a tariff wall round the British Empire. As a proof of the sincerity of our intentions, we are even willing to forego the preference accorded to us by our self-governing Dominions. In return we ask for reciprocity both in your Dependencies and in your home market. So far as your home market is concerned, we recognise that you cannot immediately abolish your tariff, but it should be substantially lowered. In stipulating this we are demanding from you considerably less than we have ourselves always accorded you, and what we are prepared, under these conditions, to go on according you. But we realise the economic problem you have to face, and we feel that the British people and the British Empire are sufficiently great and powerful to give this earnest of their desire to eliminate future international friction." In so acting the British Government would be laying the foundations of international concord, saving its own people from the disabilities and restrictions inherent in Protection receiving in return a substantial concession from Germany. Instead of maturing further impediments to human intercourse, elaborating further schemes for the manufacture of human bitterness—the prospect of consolidating an existent freedom of human intercourse where such freedom prevails, of undermining the ramparts of existing Protection where such prevails, of making the first serious effort to ensure the ultimate economic freedom of the nations. Which alternative offers most to humanity? Which is the wisest?

What of France? What advantages would she derive from the establishment of commercial freedom in her African and Asiatic Empire? What disadvantage would she suffer? "France" would suffer no disadvantage. "France" would gain priceless advantages. A few specific French interests would be affected. A certain pestilent type of politician, journalist, and financier who has been the curse of the Third Republic, and who thrives on colonial jobberies, would find his occupation gone, to the lasting benefit of political purity at home and administrative decency in the French Dependencies. On the other hand, it is a fact that nearly all the great exporting French firms are in favour of "colonial" free trade, and many of the most experienced French colonial administrators also. Notably is this the case in French West Africa, where the most considerable colonial effort of France has been exercised, and where the greatest volume of French colonial trade has been attained. The French West African merchants are dead against Protection, and always resist an increase in differential taxation. The French Dependencies themselves would grow richer and more prosperous with the disappearance of the differential tariff. Their trade would increase by leaps and bounds, and as the natural result there would be more revenue to spend on public works, sanitation, agricultural development, and native affairs. The whole

character of French over-seas activity would be affected
for the good.

What of Germany? As already stated, Germany, like
ourselves and Holland, has kept the open door in her
Dependencies. But what of the *quid pro quo* in the shape
of a lowering of the home tariff? Observe, first of all, the
justice of the standpoint. A British open-door policy
throughout the Empire is of enormous value to Germany.
Granted that we have not kept the open door all these
years from altruistic motives. The fact remains that our
action in so doing has benefited Germany in the measure
of her commercial ability, and as her commercial
ability is very considerable, the advantage has been
very considerable Why should she not begin to
reciprocate in her own market ? She is surrounded
by Protectionist Powers. True. But a very little
actual experience would show her rulers that the
German people as a whole would benefit if the German
tariff were lowered to all comers. And if Germany once
took this step, reciprocity would undoubtedly eventuate.
The mass of the German people would be unquestionably
favourable to such a course of action, and were Britain to
put forward a policy such as this, instead of indulging in
tall talk about crushing, dismembering, overthrowing, and
so forth, the peace and anti-militarist party in Germany
would be enormously strengthened. The vested interests,
the agrarians, the "Junkers" would be up in arms. But
it would be a square fight between them and the German
masses. Who can doubt the ultimate result? Here is a
true democratic policy for Britain to follow, a policy which
would automatically and inevitably cut away the props
which sustain Continental militarism.

Will the British people think it out for themselves?
Will the leaders of British Labour look ahead, or continue
dully to acquiesce in being swept away by a torrent of
loose thought, faulty economics, and sterile passions? Is
it possible that at least the North of England and Scotland
does not even now contain sufficient elements impregnated
with Cobden's teaching to evolve a counter-programme to
that tariff war which the Government in power, the Northcliffe Press, which is its insolent master, and the selfish
interests represented by Leagues and combines, are
undoubtedly hatching? If so, these various forces in our
national life must rouse themselves to action before it is
too late.   .   .   .   .

Since the above article appeared a great many statements have been made in the Press, not only by Jingo editors and contributors of no particular importance to Jingo newspapers, but by personages who certainly ought to know better, concerning the future division of the African and Asiatic tropics between Britain and France to the exclusion of Germany. Nobody has argued this case more fiercely than Sir Harry Johnston, whose notable contributions to our geographical and ethnological knowledge of Africa it would savour almost of impertinence for me to praise. And it is with genuine regret that I find myself in diametrical opposition on this matter with one who rendered valuable help at critical moments to the movement for the reform of the Congo, and to whom I am personally indebted for much generous appreciation and support of my African work.

Having said so much, I am bound to state that Sir Harry Johnston's proposal to exclude Germany from any share in African territorial sovereignty appears to me bad and impracticable. From the point of view of the interests of the native population it would be justifiable if German rule in Africa had shown itself very much worse than that of other Powers who have exercised, or who exercise, African territorial rights. But it has not. There has been nothing comparable in German administration with the hideous tragedies of the Congo Free State and French Congo—the latter in such marked contrast to French administrative rule north of the Bights. The guerilla warfare against the Hottentots in South-West Africa was characterised by many atrocious incidents, but so have other African campaigns waged by other Powers, as Sir Harry Johnston would be the first to admit. A European administration in Africa is not to be fairly judged by what occurs in a state of war; else whose records would be clean? German rule in Africa has had certain patent defects. But it was steadily improving. The last two German Colonial Secretaries were sincere reformers. The last one had personally visited the British West African Dependencies (which is more than any British Colonial Secretary has ever done), and had openly expressed his admiration for our policy in Nigeria. He was engaged in orienting German policy in the same direction when the war broke out. A powerful school of thought had arisen in Germany under the leadership of Westermann and Vohsen in favour of a native policy similar to that which we have pursued with success in Nigeria and the Gold Coast. The administration of native races was quite a new problem to Germany. She was learning and profiting by her mistakes. One decided point to her credit as against the other European Powers, Britain excepted, was her maintenance of the open door for international trade, and this has an important indirect bearing upon native interests. From the point of view of the natives a policy aimed at excluding Germany from Africa would not, therefore, be justified.

From the wider point of view it would be very short-sighted. Assuming, for the sake of argument, that the Allies are eventually in a position to "dictate" peace-terms to Germany and to impose, as part of those peace-terms, Germany's exclusion from the Colonial field; they would, if they so acted, be sowing the seeds, not of a lasting peace, but of a renewed conflict. It is a moral, physical and strategic impossibility to bottle up an elemental force such as that which the German people incarnate. It simply cannot be done. I suppose no Englishman living has written more, or more eulogistically, than I have done of many aspects of France's rule in her vast African Empire (except where her true policy became deflected for a time through Leopoldianism). But it is only necessary to consider the problem of, for instance, the future of French and German territorial sovereignty in Africa in the hard, cold light of figures to realise how futile is the idea that any permanent peace among the nations can be looked for under a settlement which, while changing nothing in the fiscal policy of France in Africa, would extend still further French sovereign rights and exclude Germany from Africa entirely.

When the war broke out France's Dependencies in Africa covered an area of 4,421,934 square miles, including the African Islands, but minus Morocco (if you throw Morocco in, the total is increased by 219,000 square miles). In other words, France's African possessions were nearly 1,000,000 square miles larger than the area of the United States. Throughout this area, except where restricted by Treaties, France differentiated heavily against foreign merchandise. Before the war France's foreign trade amounted to £583,488,000; her population (1911) was 39,601,509; her surplusage of deaths over births being (1911) 34,869. Germany's Dependencies in Africa covered 931,460 square miles; her foreign trade amounted to

£982,615,000, having increased by 204 per cent. in 22 years (double the ratio of increase of even Britain's foreign trade). Her population was (1910) 64,925,993, and her surplusage of births over deaths (1910) 740,431. Now these figures do not suggest that a nation with a large and expanding population and a phenomenally developing foreign trade, a nation more and more dependent, therefore, upon imported raw materials for the employment of its industrial population, should dispossess another nation with a much smaller and a stationary population and far less dependent upon imported raw material, of the latter's footing in the tropical world acquired by the blood and treasure of its sons. But they do suggest the folly of expecting that any rational scheme of international reconstruction in Europe can evolve from a policy which purposely intends to exclude the more numerous, industrially powerful and expanding unit from a footing in that same tropical world. If the Allies succeed in reducing Germany to an unconditional surrender, it is clear they will be in a position to impose such terms as they choose. But they cannot destroy the German people or that people's industrial capacities. Hence I fear that the sort of "punishment" which Sir Harry Johnston would like to see inflicted upon Germany would be a punishment inflicted, not only upon the German people, but upon the British and French people as well.

The essential condition of Germany's industrial requirements is, and has been for the past two decades, free markets over-seas. If she cannot obtain free markets over-seas under foreign flags, she must acquire over-sea territories for herself. Short of destroying the German nation, which is impossible, and undesirable if it were possible, I fail to see how the problem can be disposed of. It certainly cannot be by ignoring it. No doubt it would in the long run be to the advantage of the German people if they could obtain over-sea free markets without territorial responsibility. But, putting that consideration aside, on what logical grounds could "France" be made to say to "Germany" : "I, with my forty millions of people, claim the right to possess four and a-half million square miles of territory in Africa, where I differentiate against your goods, and I claim the right to increase my possessions still further. But I deny you, with your sixty-five millions of people and expanding birth rate and foreign trade, the right to hold a single inch of African soil'' ? Or on what grounds of reason could ''Britain'' be made to say to ''Germany'' : ''My flag flies over one-fifth of the world's surface, but although your population is greater than mine and increasing more rapidly, as is your trade, than mine, I deny to you, not only the right to possess an inch of African territory, but I also claim the right, whenever it may suit me, to encircle the whole of my enormous domain with a tariff wall against you''? That way lies, not peace, but endless strife; not statesmanship, but madness; not relief for the peoples of France, Britain, and Germany, but added burdens.

CHAPTER XXXIII.

The Betrayal of the Nation, 1906-1911

THE honour of a country depends much more on removing its faults than on boasting of its qualities.—*Mazzini.*

The great danger of England is the Foreign Office—and much more the Foreign Office than the Foreign Minister.—The *Candid Quarterly Review. November, 1915. (Conducted by Mr. Thomas Gibson Bowles.)*

When war was decided upon, it was not decided upon by the House of Commons or by the electorate, but by the concurrence of Ministers and ex-Ministers.—*Lord Hugh Cecil in "The Times," April 29, 1916.*

In practice the Foreign Office and the Chief Ministers of the Crown direct our foreign policy. There is, it is true, a modern and fashionable doctrine that Parliament has usurped this control; but no sensible man believes it. Sir Edward Grey made a show of consulting Parliament when the country had already been committed to the Entente policy and, indeed, to the war.—*"Morning Post," May 24, 1916.*

Allied armies have usually had difficulties in the field, for different national modes of thought are not harmonised in a moment. But in the case of France and Britain the union of arms began under fortunate auspices. For some years the two General Staffs had been in the habit of considering certain problems together, and British officers had been regular guests at the French manœuvres.—*Mr. John Buchan, in "Nelson's History of the War." (Thomas Nelson and Sons.)*

I AM profoundly convinced, and I believe the great mass of Englishmen will be convinced within a very few years, that if our foreign policy in the last decade had been controlled by the nation, the situation which has involved all the great European Powers, ourselves included, in a general war, would never have arisen.

I am convinced that if the nation had been treated honestly and fairly by the Liberal Government, the national future would have been infinitely more secure today than it is; and that hundreds of thousands of the flower of British manhood, now dead or crippled, would have been alive and well.

I am convinced that if British foreign policy had been an open, unshackled policy, the influence of Great Britain in the councils of the nations would have saved

Western Europe assuredly, and quite possibly, all Europe, from the catastrophe which mutual fears and jealousies were preparing.

I am convinced that at no period in our history had such an opportunity been given to Liberal statesmen to lead the world along the road of international sanity as was provided in the decade preceding the war; that the opportunity was not taken because they allowed themselves to become implicated almost immediately after they assumed the reins of power in the Continental maze of groupings and alliances, and that their implication therein would never have occurred had the nation enjoyed real democratic control. What was required was high and honest statesmanship, not bad and furtive diplomacy.

I hold that the supreme national issue which this war compels us to confront, is the secrecy with which our foreign policy has been conducted since 1904, the consequences which have arisen from it, and the appalling dangers inherent in such a system.

To slur over that issue, lest in facing it with candour and in our own most obvious interest, we be forced to shed the mantle of impeccability in all that touches the origins of this war, and our part therein, which our rulers have cast about their shoulders, would be unworthy of our greatness as a people, and would be to inflict a grave injustice upon our sons.

.   .   .   .

It is a misfortune that criticism of our foreign policy should be interpreted by its apologists merely, or chiefly, as evidence of a desire on the part of the critic to attack the particular Minister nominally responsible for its direction. Inevitably the Minister is comprised in the criticism. But the trouble from which this country suffers, the trouble which is its greatest danger, and will, if unremedied, bring it to ruin, lies much deeper than the mistakes of a Minister who, like all human beings, is liable to err, and to err with the best of motives. The trouble is, that the system this nation tolerates as regards its foreign policy is a system which suffers from a fundamental contradiction. It is a system which *in reality* allows to that Minister, and to such of his colleagues as he may choose to consult, a power, virtually uncontrolled, to compromise the national destinies; while *professedly* allowing him no such power. The result of this conflict between practice and theory is to create, in the management of our foreign affairs, an autocracy more complete than that wielded by Tsar or Kaiser, but unlike the latter, ineffective, because unaccompanied by executive functions. Thus its Foreign Minister can—without putting his signature to any particular document, which would require Cabinet and ultimately Parliamentary sanction—commit this country to a line of action involving war under certain contingencies, without informing the Cabinet or Parliament. But he cannot, without informing the Cabinet and Parliament, carry out the measures necessary to give practical effect, should occasion require it, to the policy he is pursuing. If he informs the Cabinet, he may split it. If he succeeds in carrying the Cabinet, the difficulty is not overcome. There is Parliament and the country to be dealt with. He is, therefore, at once responsible and irresponsible. A system of this kind is a sword of Damocles continuously suspended over the head of the nation. It has all the disadvantages of an autocracy without any of its advantages. It makes "democratic" government quite impossible, and is hideously unjust to the democracy. The would this system has inflicted upon the country is deep. If it is not to prove mortal, the nation *must* bring itself to realise how the system has operated and how the wound has been inflicted. "My country, right or wrong," is an expression replete with good intentions. The road to Hell, it has been said, is paved with good intentions. It was, I think, one of Lincoln's advisers who supplied the complementary corrective : "My country, right or wrong ! If right, to be kept right. If wrong, to be set right."

When the Unionist Administration left office in December, 1905, it had succeeded in the task of rehabilitating the credit of this country, which had found itself during the Boer War without a single well-wisher in Europe. It had settled a series of long outstanding disputes with France, and it had slightly improved our relations with Russia. On the other hand, Anglo-German relations had become marked by mutual suspicion and ill-feeling. The Kaiser's telegram to President Kruger; Germany's determination to build a powerful navy, and her manner of announcing it; Mr. Chamberlain's Tariff Reform campaign, in which the growth of German trade figured so prominently; the personal friction between King Edward and his nephew, the Kaiser; Germany's ostensible exclusion from the international agreements over China;[1] Britain's opposition to the Bagdad railway scheme—these things were probably the chief contributory causes for the change, with one exception. That exception was Morocco. I shall not discuss Morocco again here, beyond remarking that the year 1906, which opened with the advent of a Liberal Government in England, ushered in a second International Conference (at Algeciras) over Moroccan affairs, a Conference demanded by Germany, invited by the Sultan, and resisted until the last moment by the British and French Foreign Offices. It is at this stage, the specific starting point leading to Britain's eventual participation in the world-war, that the system under which the British nation permits its foreign affairs to be conducted becomes capable of illustration. The illustration can, I think, be given more fittingly in the form of a brief chronological *précis*.

FIRST STAGE, 1906 (First Morocco Crisis).

Sir E. Grey expresses to the French and German Ambassadors his personal belief that in the event of a war between France and Germany over Morocco, British public opinion would rally to the "material support" of France.[2]

The French Ambassador urges that the potential military and naval co-operation of Britain and France shall be facilitated, and for this purpose that the military and naval staffs of the two countries shall be authorised to meet in periodic consultation.[3]

Sir E. Grey consults Sir Henry Campbell Bannerman,[4] Lord Haldane, and Mr. Asquith, and consents to the

[1] "These three agreements practically closed the ring round China for the exclusive benefit of what has been described as the China Pooling Syndicate. This consisted of Great Britain, Japan, Russia, and France, and excluded Germany and the United States."—(Editorial note to Baron Hayashi's "Memoirs.")

[2] Revealed by Sir E. Grey to the House of Commons on August 3, 1914.

[3] Ditto.

[4] It seems incredible that the information can have been conveyed to Sir Henry Campbell Bannerman in a way which enabled him to grasp its full significance.

French Ambassador's proposal,[1] which, however, is to leave the hands of the Government free.

The Cabinet is not informed of this step until "much later on."[2] There is presumptive evidence that the Cabinet was not informed until the advent of the second Morocco crisis in the summer of 1911—five years and a-half later.

Parliament is not, of course, informed at all.

There is presumptive evidence that the official leaders of the Opposition were given at least a hint of what had been done; whether in 1911 or earlier must be a matter at present of conjecture. There is presumptive evidence that the consultation of the military and naval staffs became thenceforth a permanent feature of our secret relations with France.

SECOND STAGE, 1911 (Second Morocco Crisis).

Sir E. Grey takes "precisely the same line" as he had taken in 1906.[3]

Mr. Lloyd George makes, obviously by agreement with the Foreign Office, a threatening speech against Germany at the Mansion House; punctuated as such by *The Times* the next morning.[4]

Towards the end of the year, when the crisis is over, it becomes a matter of common knowledge in political, military and naval circles in Britain, France, and Germany, that in the event of a Franco-German rupture, British aid would have been given to France.

THIRD STAGE, 1912.

Spring.—Anglo-German negotiations on the subject of Britain's neutrality in the event of a European war break down.[5]

November 22.—As the result of Cabinet discussions, Sir E. Grey writes an "unofficial" letter to the French Ambassador, to the effect that consultations between the

[1] Revealed by Sir E. Grey to the House of Commons on August 3, 1914.
[2] Ditto.
[3] Ditto.
[4] "Ten Years of Secret Diplomacy" (p. 144).
[5] Partially revealed for the first time by Mr. Asquith in October, 1914. Negotiations of a similar character, apparently at Germany's suggestion, had taken place in 1909, and again in 1910—without result.

British and French military and naval staffs "does not restrict the freedom of either Government to decide at any future time whether or not to assist the other by armed force."[1]

FOURTH STAGE, 1913.

March 10.—Lord Hugh Cecil asks the Prime Minister whether there is foundation for the general belief that the Prime Minister and the Foreign Secretary, "have entered into an arrangement, or, to speak more accurately, have given assurances which, in the contingency of a great European war, would involve heavy military obligations on this country?"; and states that, "there is a very general belief that this country is under an obligation, not a treaty obligation, *but an obligation arising owing to an assurance* given by the Ministry in the course of diplomatic negotiations, to send a very large armed force out of this country to operate in Europe. This is the general belief."

Mr. Asquith replies: "I ought to say it is not true." Similar denials by the Prime Minister follow questions of a similar tendency asked in Parliament on March 24, 1913, and April 28 and June 11, 1914.

.   .   .   .

Let us explore this record.

In the spring of 1906 the Minister in charge of our foreign relations, with the concurrence of three of his colleagues, takes a step involving the nation in the issues of life and death. He authorises the military and naval advisers of this country to work out a plan of campaign in the event of war arising in Europe, with the military and naval advisers of a Power which forms part of one of the two great rival Groups into which Europe is divided. In so doing he stipulates that he is not pledging the Government, of which he is, next to the Prime Minister, the most important member, to take part in such a war on the side of the Power with whose military and naval advisers the military and naval advisers of this country are henceforth collaborating, and which is itself formally pledged in a military alliance with another Great Power. This is *literally true*, inasmuch as there is no written bond. But the mere setting out of the fact in other than diplomatic language shows that the reserve then made (and confirmed in writing six years later) is in the very nature

[1] Revealed by Sir E. Grey to the House of Commons on August 3, 1914.

of the case precarious, and must become more and more
so the longer the collaboration exists.   This becomes at
once apparent when the circumstances are examined.

The fact of such an authorisation being given
constitutes an unwritten bond of a moral, and also of a
material and positive kind, which involves the personality
of the Minister who sanctions it and of the colleagues
whom he consults.   Henceforth the whole war mechanism
of the two Powers is linked together : a community of
professional interest and professional thought is created
among the influential national elements connected with the
profession of arms on both sides of the Channel.   Those
elements are themselves and of necessity closely related
with the organisations concerned in the manufacture of
engines of war.   Between the latter and the world of
politics and Press and finance there are a hundred
filaments.   Time alone must tend to strengthen the link
thus originally created.   Time will give additional potency
to the unwritten bond in influencing political events. Time
will commit the Ministers responsible more and more
deeply to the logical sequence of their initial action, should
the events which their action contemplated actually occur.
Moreover, contemporary happenings themselves are bound
to be affected by the existence of this secret and unwritten
bond.   Its existence will, and must, mould those happenings consciously, or unconsciously, and give them a
particular tendency and a particular direction. To question
all this is surely puerile?   We *know* that the existence of
this unwritten bond had these effects, and we know it from
the Minister chiefly responsible.

Eight years later (August 3, 1914) Sir E. Grey was to
make the operative force of the unwritten bond, both in its
moral and material aspects, quite clear to the nation.   He
told the House in effect that, in his opinion, its existence,
although unknown to the House until that moment, had
placed us under a moral obligation to assist the French.
And he also told the House that *on the strength of that
unwritten bond, as part of her share in the authorised plan
of campaign,* France had concentrated her fleet in the
Mediterranean, and had left her western and northern
coast-line undefended, and at the complete mercy of the
German fleet.[1]

_____

[1] It is astonishing that the suspicions of the House of Commons
were not aroused earlier in the year, when Mr. Churchill brought in

Let us carry our exploration a step further.

The years that follow the crisis of 1906 are troubled years. The ill-feeling between Britain and Germany remains an increasingly menacing portent upon the horizon. Two efforts to define their respective relations fail to mature. A naval panic, engineered by interested parties in this country upon, as it eventually transpires, inaccurate information, intensifies the prevailing bitterness. The reactionary Press on both sides plays its sinister *rôle*. Graver than aught else, from the point of view of the liabilities contracted in the unwritten bond, of which three men in England are now the sole legatees—Sir Henry Campbell Bannerman having passed away—the Morocco clouds gather steadily in volume. In France, Cabinet succeeds Cabinet, and each fresh Ministry sees its capacity to control the militarists and colonial Chauvinists, who are bent upon the conquest of Morocco over the ashes of the Algeciras Act, becoming weaker and weaker. In vain the Chamber ignorant, as our Parliament is ignorant, of the secret clauses to the Anglo-Franco-Spanish Treaties, repeatedly asserts its intention of safeguarding the independence and integrity of Morocco. While the Chamber talks, the militarists act. Germany watches with an impatience which grows as negotiations begun with one French Cabinet are upset by another.

And all the while, unknown to the Cabinet, unknown to Parliament, unknown to the nation, British and French military and naval experts are carrying out their instructions, and with devoted zeal are discussing and arranging all the larger problems of strategy, and all the

his Navy Estimates, and made his statement about the Mediterranean. The estimates were contested by the Unionists on the ground of reduction, and a resolution was moved on the subject of the political and strategic position in the Mediterranean. In a speech he made on that occasion Sir Edward Grey said he would "pass very lightly over the question of naval strength in the Mediterranean." He further said that the policy contested could not "fairly be called abandoning the Mediterranean." No one, except Lord Charles Beresford, seems to have realised that such a re-arrangement must have been the result of some strategic *quid pro quo* with France. He indeed remarked :—

"They (the French) are to look after our enormous interests in the Mediterranean, because we cannot have a fleet there. What are we going to do for France? It may be very disagreeable, but we are liable with these Ententes and Alliances."

But apparently the House paid no attention.

details of organisation incidental to a great campaign waged in common against a common potential foe.

And now the storm bursts.   The Algeciras Act has become in the eyes of all men merely a "scrap of paper." The secret Treaties have come to fruition, although their existence is still undisclosed.   Germany bangs her fist upon the diplomatic table.   At the request of the Foreign Office, the Minister in the Cabinet who enjoys the greatest popular following speaks to Germany in diplomatic language of open menace.

A long smouldering hostility has come to a head. Britain and Germany are on the brink of open rupture. But this time the storm passes, and with its passing, something akin to consternation at the imminence of the peril infects political circles in this country.   Once again negotiations to reach a *modus vivendi* are attempted. Once again they fail.

.   .   .   .

Let us now consider the situation reached at this period, *i.e.,* the summer of 1912, after the failure of the Anglo-German negotiations following the Franco-German settlement over Morocco.[1]

Let us consider it from the point of view of the terrible injustice and perils inflicted upon the people of this country by the system under which the nation's foreign relations are carried on.   Three members of the Cabinet have authorised military and naval consultations based upon the assumption that the armed forces of the Crown will, in the event of a general European war, co-operate on land and sea with one of the Continental Groups, whose rivalry keeps Europe permanently under arms.   I say, with   one   of   the   two   *Groups*   advisedly,   because co-operation with France must mean co-operation with her partner Russia, and involves us, therefore, in contingent   liabilities   to   Russia.   Obviously   these consultations have led to the adoption by the responsible experts on either side of strategic measures designed to give practical effect thereto; otherwise the consultations would   be   farcical.   Here, then, is a positive factor in actual being which must needs exercise a dominating influence over our whole international relationships.   It constitutes, on our side, a definite preparation for war. In the summer of 1911 its significance is increased tenfold,

[1] The   failure   was   not   admitted   *then;* on   the   contrary—*vide* Chapter XXXIV.

owing to the fact that our diplomacy has openly taken the side of the Power with which we have been carrying on these professional consultations—even to the point of a veiled threat of war upon that Power's rival if the quarrel should end in armed collision. But until that event, until, *i.e.*, the summer of 1911, knowledge of this portentous step has not only been concealed by the three responsible Ministers from Parliament, but from their colleagues in the Cabinet. What has been the consequence of this?

The consequence has been that other members of the Cabinet have delivered speeches in the country during the period covered by these consultations, of a kind calculated to make the nation believe that its relations with Germany are not really dangerous; *whereas, in point of fact and in the event of a European war, the nation's relations with Germany have become compromised in advance, virtually beyond redemption, and, short of a miracle, the nation's participation in such a war has become a foregone conclusion.* Not only have the other members of the Cabinet been permitted to speak in this optimistic strain by their three colleagues, but the latter *have themselves made exactly the same kind of speeches.*

In 1908 we find Mr. Asquith stating in the House of Commons that Britain and Germany "are every year advancing nearer and nearer to a complete understanding";[1] Mr. Churchill asserting that "there is no real cause of difference" between them, that they "have nothing to fight about, have no prize to fight for, and have no place to fight in";[2] Mr. Harcourt declaring, "with knowledge and a sense of deep responsibility," that their relations, "commercial, colonial, political, and dynastic," have at no period in the last ten or fifteen years been on a firmer and more friendly footing than they are to-day," denouncing those who seek to set them at variance as "footpads of politics and enemies of the human race," as "pariah curs who foul the kennel in which they live."[3] More interesting still, we discover Mr. Lloyd George emphasising Germany's precarious strategic position in Europe, explaining the anxieties incidental thereto, and the necessity for her to increase and perfect her army; proclaiming, in other words, as natural, right and proper, for Germany to do that which, for having done, she is

[1] March 2, 1908.
[2] August 15, 1908, to a demonstration of Miners at Swansea.
[3] October 2, 1908, in a speech to his constituents.

denounced six years later by the same speaker. In 1909 Sir Rufus Isaacs, Mr. Churchill, Mr. Robertson, Colonel Seely, Mr. Birrell, and Lord (then Mr.) Haldane, all speak in language identical in tendency. Lord Haldane asseverates that he has many friends in Germany, and that the Germans are much misunderstood.[1]   Mr. Churchill is most emphatic as to there being between the two countries, no "racial, territorial, dynastic, or religious causes of quarrels which have in the past set the world on edge," while the "foundations of European peace are laid more broadly every year,"[2] and, again, declaiming that it is a "monstrous error" to speak of a "profound antagonism of interests between the British and German nations which can only be resolved by a supreme trial of strength, towards which the tides of destiny are irresistibly bearing us. . . . If a serious antagonism is gradually created between the two peoples, it will not be because of the workings of any natural or impersonal forces, but through the vicious activity of a comparatively small number of individuals in both countries and the culpable credulity of larger classes." In 1910, Mr. Asquith, Mr. Lloyd George, and Mr. McKenna, figure on the public boards; "unhesitatingly" does Mr. Asquith assert that there is no single Power, "basing its calculations upon the assumption that war between Great Britain and Germany is inevitable or even possible," in no quarter of the political horizon is there "any cause of quarrel, direct or indirect, between us and that great and friendly nation."[3] Mr. Lloyd George scorns the very idea of an "inevitable" war with Germany.[4] Mr. McKenna ridicules the scaremongers.[5]

The nation has not only been led to believe that an Anglo-German collision is unthinkable, the while its military and naval experts are silently preparing for that very contingency with their French colleagues. The nation has been warned off any further military expenditure both by members of the Cabinet who are not "in the know," and this is natural enough; but incredible as it

---

[1] December 14, 1909, speaking in the Town Hall, Tranent, East Lothian.

[2] April 14, 1909, letter to the Chairman of the Liberal Association at Dundee.

[3] January 6, 1910, speech at Bath.

[4] January 6, 1910, speech at Peckham.

[5] October 20, 1910, speech in Wales.

may seem, by the Ministers who have authorised the secret military and naval consultations.

At the very moment these consultations are initiated, Lord Haldane,[1] then in charge of the War Office, we see, is adopting measures to reduce expenditure on the Army. "My Government"—King Edward states on July 28, 1906, in addressing the 3rd Battalion of the Scots Guards—"has considered it necessary to reduce the expenses of the Army, in consequence of which there is to be a reduction both of our artillery and infantry, and in this reduction your battalion is included." Mr. Harcourt, in October, has expressed great satisfaction at "notable retrenchments" in the Army.[2] On a later occasion he has prayed God we shall never "be organised as a great military nation with a people in arms."[3] Mr. Runciman has congratulated the country upon a steadily dwindling expenditure on the Army, and has looked forward to further reductions.[4] In 1910, Lord Haldane has gone so far as to declare : "*In naval and military defence we are absolutely and completely equipped to meet all emergencies and situations. The person who says we are not is in a blue funk.*"[5] These words are uttered by one of the Ministers who is cognisant of the fact that a decisive step has been taken on the road to commit this country, with an expeditionary force of under 200,000 men, to participation in a land war against a State *then* perfectly well known to be the most formidably equipped and organised for war of any on the Continent, capable of placing several millions of men in the field.

.   .   .   .

Thus for the five years 1906-1911 was the nation permitted to live in a fool's paradise, not as Ministers have since induced the nation to believe, because they, and, therefore, the nation, were innocent victims of Machiavellian cunning on the part of Germany; but because Ministers were steering a secret course which reduced all these fine utterances of theirs and of their

---

[1] I pass no opinion upon the value or otherwise of Lord Haldane's Army reforms. I know nothing about it. I am here merely recording facts in the light of the unwritten bond with France.
[2] October 17, 1906, speech to Rossendale Liberal Council.
[3] October 2, 1908, speech to his constituents.
[4] October 8 and November 18, 1907.
[5] December 28, 1910, speech at Grimsby.

colleagues to so much gibberish, a secret course which demanded, not reductions in Army expenditure, but a complete revolution in the whole character of the military strategy of the Empire, including the adoption of national service.

CHAPTER XXXIV
The Betrayal of the Nation, 1912-1914

THE story in brief is one of action—hidden from all and especially from the Cabinet, secretly taken by the Three from 1906 to 1911, and bringing England to unavoidable war in 1914. The Three had all the time been preparing for the war, which they believed was so probable that it needed a detailed plan of operations beforehand, yet all the time concealing all from their confidential colleagues in the Cabinet. The point and the appalling significance of the story lie in the proof it affords that we live under a political system which leaves the greatest of all issues in the absolutely uncontrolled hands of one, or two, or three, acting secretly and without the knowledge of what they are doing being shared by any of those on whom the real burden must fall, or even by their own most confidential and trusting colleagues. For the Wisdom of the many we have substituted the Conspiracy of the few.—*"The Candid Quarterly." May, 1915.*

We were all caught unprepared.—*Mr. Lloyd George: interview with the Editor of "Il Secolo." (Sunderland "Daily Echo," January 29, 1916.)*

SO far the terrible story, for terrible posterity will deem it. But there is much yet left to explore, and I shall attempt it in this chapter.

. . . .

The year 1912 was marked by two notable events. Public opinion here (and also in Germany) had given unmistakable proof of its desire to heal the breach. Among the political supporters of the Ministry the feeling was strong and emphatically expressed. Nor were there lacking voices on the other side of British politics. Sundry unofficial bodies sprang, just about this time, into existence on both sides of the North Sea having reconciliation and understanding as their aim. The Government sent Lord Haldane over to Berlin. It was an unfortunate selection, although at the time public opinion—knowing nothing of the unwritten bond—regarded the Government's choice as a particularly happy one. For Lord Haldane was well known to the Kaiser and to Germany's leading statesmen. But Lord Haldane was also one of the triumvirate responsible for the unwritten bond, and he was, moreover, the head of the Department which was supervising the execution of the bond. In other words, he was head of the Department which was working out a combined plan of action with the analogous Department in France, a combined plan of action in the event of a European war, *i.e.,* a combined plan of action against Germany, the country with which he proposed to negotiate. And the analogous Department in France was working at the same plan with the analogous Department in Russia— Russia's hypothetical intentions being at that moment the object of German fears and suspicions. No Minister placed in such a false position could possibly have succeeded in bridging the gulf of Anglo-German misunderstanding. But the public knew nothing of all this. And, when Lord Haldane returned, the public was once again deceived. It was led to believe that Lord Haldane had smoothed matters over and brought about a permanent improvement, whereas the smoothing process could only be superficial and evanescent, by reason of the unwritten bond. Nevertheless, everything that could be done to convey the belief that Lord Haldane's mission had been highly successful was done. Lord Haldane's own florid references thereto may be set aside, in view of the Prime Minister's clear and emphatic pronouncement.

Speaking in the House of Commons on July 25 (1912) Mr. Asquith said :—

"Our relations with the great German Empire are, I am glad to say, at this moment, *and, I feel sure, are likely to remain,* relations of amity and goodwill. Lord Haldane paid a visit to Berlin early in the year; he entered upon conversations and an interchange of views, which have been continued since *in a spirit of perfect frankness* and friendship, both on one side and the other."

Thus Mr. Asquith on the Haldane negotiations in 1912. Now listen to Mr. Asquith on those same Haldane negotiations two years later. (October 3, 1914.)

"They (the German Government) wanted us to *pledge ourselves absolutely to neutrality* in the event of Germany being engaged in war, and this, mind you, at a time when Germany was enormously increasing both her aggressive and defensive resources, and especially upon the sea. *They asked us—to put it quite plainly—they asked us for a free hand so far as we were concerned, if, and when, they selected the opportunity to overbear, to dominate, the European world.''*

Thus, in 1912, the Prime Minister of Great Britain despatches one of his most intimate colleagues on a delicate mission to the Sovereign and Government of one of the most powerful States in Christendom, a State united to our own by ties of Royal blood and by centuries of co-operation, but over whose relations with our own a sinister shadow of distrust and suspicion has recently been cast. This mission is of enormous importance to the people of both States. For, bearing in view the events of the year preceding it, and the general condition of Europe, that mission constitutes the touchstone of the future. If it succeeds, both nations can breathe freely once more. If it fails, this nation is confronted with one of the most momentous crises in its history. Even to the "man in the street" this is dimly apparent. To the Prime Minister of Britain, who knows how deeply the nation is committed in ties of honourable obligation towards the potential foes of that State to which this confidential emissary has proceeded, realisation of all that hangs upon the mission must be acute. The emissary returns, and the negotiations begun by him are continued after his return. The public mind is full of contradictory rumours. Finally, the Prime Minister deems the time has come to enlighten the nation. He solemnly informs Parliament that the negotiations have been marked throughout by "a spirit of perfect frankness and friendship" on both sides, and that our relations with our powerful neighbour are not merely excellent at the moment, but, he feels sure, are likely to remain so. . . . Two years pass. For the first time in a thousand years the British and Germanic peoples are at war. And how does the Prime Minister of Great Britain then refer to the proceedings which he had precedently characterised in the manner stated? He now indignantly asseverates that they disclosed an attempt on the part of the German Government to bind Great Britain to a shameful neutrality. The "perfect frankness and friendship" have become transmuted into a species of bullying blackmail. This State, with which, he assured the nation, we were likely to retain "relations of amity and goodwill," had, nevertheless, made clear to us with a cynicism as indiscreet as it was brutal, that it proposed, when the time had come, to "dominate the European world."

Comment would be superfluous.

. . . .

Whether Mr. Asquith's second version of the Haldane negotiations—substantially endorsed by Sir E. Grey in May, 1916—is a fair and accurate account of the German attitude on that occasion, is a matter upon which students of the published British and German versions must form their own judgment. Mr. Lowes Dickinson has put the matter with great judiciousness and penetration[1] :—

"The Triple Alliance was confronting the Triple Entente. On both sides were fear and suspicion. Each believed in the possibility of the others springing a war upon them. Each suspected the others of wanting to lull them into a false security, and then take them unprepared. In that atmosphere what hope was there of successful negotiations? The essential condition—mutual confidence—was lacking. What, accordingly, do we find? The Germans offer to reduce their naval programme, first, if England will promise an unconditional neutrality; secondly, when that was rejected, if England will promise neutrality in a war which should be 'forced upon' Germany. Thereupon the British Foreign Office scents a snare. Germany will get Austria to provoke a war, while making it appear that the war was provoked by Russia, and she will then come in under the terms of her alliance with Austria, smash France, and claim that England must look on passively under the neutrality agreement! 'No, thank you!' Sir Edward Grey accordingly makes a counter proposal. England will neither make nor participate in an 'unprovoked' attack upon Germany. This time it is the Chancellor's turn to hang back. 'Unprovoked! H'm! What does that mean? Russia, let us suppose, makes war upon Austria, while making it appear that Austria is the aggressor. France comes in on the side of Russia. And England? Will she admit that the war was 'unprovoked,' and remain neutral? Hardly, we think!' The Chancellor, therefore, proposes this addition: 'England, of course, will remain neutral if war is forced upon Germany? That follows, I presume?' 'No!'

[1] "The European Anarchy"; *op. cit.*

from the British Foreign Office.   Reason as before.   And
the negotiations fall through.   How should they not under
the conditions?   There could be no understanding,
because there was no confidence.   There could be no
confidence because there was mutual fear.   There was
mutual fear because the Triple Alliance stood in arms
against the Triple Entente.   What was wrong?   Germany?
England?   No.   The European tradition and system.''

It is an admirable passage, and a tribute to the equable-
ness of judgment and the sanity of mind which one of our
very few distinguished intellectuals has succeeded in
retaining amid the general declension.

But I cannot altogether subscribe to it.   It would, I
think, have been more accurate to say : The Teutonic
combination and the Franco-Russian combination confronted one another—for the Triple Alliance by that time
was a myth : Italy stood apart, and was rapidly gravitating
towards the Franco-Russian combination.   These two
combinations, then, confronted one another.   But where
did England come in?   Her statesmen denied that she was
bound to the Franco-Russian combination.   Yet, only the
previous year, she had clearly intimated that she would
support France, even to the lengths of going to war with
the Teutonic combination, in a quarrel over Morocco where
Germany's case rested upon international law and the case
of France upon the violation of international law on behalf
of French interests.   What was the *real* situation?   Would
England lay her cards on the table?   Was England's
support of France on that occasion due to the particular
circumstances of the case, or was her support permanent
and unconditional?   Would England say what she would do
if Russia dragged in France over a Near-Eastern struggle
on the strength of her alliance with that country?

.   .   .   .

The negotiations of 1912 failed, and were bound to
fail, not because either side desired war.   They failed
because, while the commitments on one side were avowed,
the commitments on the other side were concealed.   The
primary cause of their failure was not the lack of desire,
but the impossibility in which the British Ministers, in
whose hands the negotiations rested, found themselves
to devise any formula of neutrality which could be made
to square with the obligations they had contracted.   The

plain fact was that British neutrality, in the event of war involving the Teutonic combination and the Franco-Russian combination, had been morally bartered away. British neutrality in such an event, *which was the only event at issue,* was a non-existent quantity at the time these negotiations took place. It had, morally speaking, vanished, with the initiation, early in 1906, of the secret Anglo-French military and naval consultations. It had disappeared *in esse* when, on the basis of those consultations, continued from 1906 onwards, and the accumulating moral obligations they set up, the British Government had, in the summer of 1911, announced its intention, through Mr. Lloyd George and *The Times,* of giving material aid to France in trampling upon the Algeciras Act. It was with the latter fact overshadowing their deliberations that the negotiators met. Under such circumstances the negotiations were foredoomed to sterility. This country was ignorantly and rapidly drifting into a potential land war, for which Ministers could make no adequate preparation without informing the country what they had done and without disclosing the position into which the country had been manœuvred. This Ministers did not dare to do, for it would have split the Liberal Party from top to bottom, and probably have sent them individually into the wilderness. No doubt they honestly believed that such a double event would be bad for the country. But in every denunciation of the "preparedness" of the German Government before the war, which they have uttered since the war, they pass condemnation upon themselves and upon the system of which they form part.

For they knew of that preparedness. They knew its efficiency, its scale, its thoroughness. They proclaimed their knowledge.

.   .   .   .

Did not Lord Haldane, for instance, speak on one occasion of the "great advantage" he had experienced from frequent visits to Berlin, "and there studying the German War Office and the German Army system"? Did he not express his gratitude for the opportunities freely given him for studying "the wonderful system, dating from the days of Moltke and Bismarck, with its lessons of clear thinking and its instruction of how to produce definiteness in organisation"?

Moreover, Ministers testified to the inevitableness of, and the justification for, that preparedness down to the very eve of the war.

Did not Mr. Lloyd George, for instance, thus unburden himself to a London newspaper on January 1, 1914 :—

"The German Army is vital, not merely to the existence of the German Empire, but to the very life and independence of the nation itself, surrounded, as Germany is, by other nations, each of which possesses armies almost as powerful as her own."

Did he not point out, as he had already pointed out in 1908, that Germany was compelled by her geographical and strategic position, to be the strong man armed? Did he not insist that while we demanded for our own national security a 60 per cent. superiority in ships, Germany had nothing like that military superiority over France alone? And did he not remind the nation that Germany had, "of course, in addition, to reckon with Russia on her Eastern frontier"? Did he not acknowledge, and defend as natural and inevitable, in view of "recent events" (the increasing tension between Austria and Russia in the Balkans) Germany's immense army increases?

. . . .

Similarly, Ministers condemn themselves when, to cover up their own conduct towards the nation, they spread the legend of a Germany desirous of "subjugating Europe," and of having laboured to that end for forty years—a statement which at any time but the present would be held to qualify the maker of it for a lunatic asylum. If this was the Germany which displayed its hand to Lord Haldane, why was Mr. Asquith so confident, in 1912, of remaining on terms of amity and goodwill with so detestable a neighbour?

This sort of garment, in which to clothe their failures and inconsistencies, has been worn threadbare on previous occasions by other Ministers, with more justification, perhaps. Was not the Crimean War attributed to Russia's aims at "universal dominion," to her "arrogant attitude," to the existence in Russia of a "threatening military autocracy"?[1] Was not Russia then described as

---

[1] "The Life of Lord Granville." Lord E. Fitzmaurice.

"a Power which has violated the faith of Treaties and défies the opinion of the civilised world"?[1] But the people swallowed it all in 1854 as they swallow it all to-day. For war psychology, it would seem, never changes.

There were Russians then (and there are Russians now) who thus insensately boasted, re-echoing in their fashion the testamentary effusions of Peter the Great. There have been Germans (and there are Germans to-day) who have raved to the same purpose. It is always easy · select matter of that kind from the Chauvinistic literature of every nation, in order to hypnotise the masses with a fixed idea. But never has the practice been systematised as it has been in the present war with the sanction of those for whom the rooting of that legend in the public mind was essential to their political salvation. Never before has officialdom stooped to such grotesque falsification of history in order to clean its own historical records. Never before have a few books, written by a handful of Jingoes, and scarcely read in the enemy country, been poured upon the station bookstalls in cheap editions, in order to prove that a people whose blood has fertilised our own institutions, which has given us our reigning line, and many of those most eminently concerned in building up our own Empire—is putrid to the core. Never before has the inculcation of hate, the advertisement given to the brutal acts of a maddened soldiery, the appeal to the passions of revenge and unreason been pursued, in this country, at all events, as a fine art, with Governmental support. Never before have our leading men given their patronage to such vulgar declamation against a foe who has committed many brutalities, but to whom our soldiers, at least, do not deny the gift of bravery or the perpetration of many acts of kindliness and chivalry. Never before have our newspapers stooped—again with encouragement from above—to such odious vituperation of a monarch whose faults, doubtless, are conspicuous but who, as the ruling classes of every country in Europe, not least our own, know full well has stood out during the greater part of his reign as a bulwark of European peace; a monarch who could have unchained war, and successful war from the militarist point of view, half a dozen times over in the past twenty years if he had so willed. We used to pride ourselves upon being above this sort of thing.

---

[1] Royal declaration. March 28, 1854.

(21)

And those who protest against these aberrations, which have done us incalculable harm among all neutral peoples, are denounced as "unpatriotic." Unpatriotic, forsooth ! It is "patriotic" to pitchfork your country into a general European war with a military equipment adequate for dealing with a few thousand South African Dutchmen. But it is unpatriotic, after nearly two years' slaughter and waste, to recommend that your country should be extracted with honour from the shambles.

.   .   .   .

It is, then, beyond dispute that the Haldane negotiations in the spring of 1912, while they improved the general atmospheric conditions, left untouched the crux of the difficulty between Britain and Germany—*i.e.*, the true character of the relations between the British Government and the Franco-Russian Alliance. They paved the way for minor accommodations, for the re-opening under more favourable conditions of certain African and Asiatic problems which had already formed the subject of mutual discussion, such as the future of the Portuguese possessions, the Bagdad railway, the oil deposits of Mesopotamia, and so on. They must also have influenced very considerably the collaboration which prevailed in the critical situation arising out of the Balkan War of 1912, and its sequel the following year.

But, fundamentally, the situation remained exactly what it was, what it had been since the unwritten bond in 1906. The perils of that situation had increased enormously. The Pan-Slavists, whose High-Priest in the Balkans was M. de Hartwig,[1] and whose inspirer in the background was M. Isvolski,[2] were in full cry against Russian official diplomacy for its alleged lack of vigour, and were rapidly acquiring ascendency in the councils of the Empire. The Pan-Slavists had with them all the forces of reactionary officialdom. Their prototypes in Austria-Hungary were stirring up the same sort of trouble. The growth of the latter's influence was assisted by the incessant anti-Austrian propaganda in Bosnia directed from Belgrade and fostered by de Hartwig, and by the continuous intriguing in Galicia through the instrumentality

[1] Russian Minister at Belgrade.
[2] The predecessor of M. Sazonoff.

of unofficial Russian agents.   All this was common knowledge.   An explosion had been averted in 1912 owing to
French and British pressure upon Russia on the one hand,
and to German pressure upon Austria on the other.   But
Austro-Russian relations had become stretched to cracking
point.   They were at the mercy of any untoward incident.
And if they snapped, the divisions of Europe at once came
into play—with Austria stood Germany, with Russia
France : *and between France and Britain was the unwritten
bond,* constituting, as Lord Lansdowne afterwards
described it in the House of Lords, "obligations not less
sacred, because they are not embodied in a signed and
sealed document."[1]

Britain's equivocal position was thus infinitely more
dangerous to herself in 1912 than in 1906, or even in
1911.   The British people went gaily about their business,
believing that their Government was free and untrammelled.

. . . .

It was in these circumstances that the most distinguished
of living British soldiers came into the open.   He knew
the facts.   He knew that his country had become so far
involved by its governing statesmen, but without its knowledge, on the side of one of the two great combinations of
potential belligerents that it stood morally committed, with
ludicrously inadequate material, to participation in the
most terrific land war ever waged.   He flung himself
personally, at an advanced age, into a public campaign on
behalf of universal military training, which he had
advocated for several years previously.   The campaign
failed, just as the Anglo-German negotiations of 1912
failed, and substantially for the same reason.   It failed
because the truth could not be disclosed.   British traditions
of public life precluded Lord Roberts from saying what he
knew.   All that he could do was to try and avert the danger
by the only means open to him.   That he should have been
supported by the militarist and jingo elements in the nation
was natural enough.   That he should have been opposed
by those whose conception of the international duties and
national interests of Britain differed from theirs, was also
natural.   But that he should have been opposed, and not
only opposed, but attacked, by the very men who had
secretly placed the British people in a position where their
national and Imperial future was imperilled without their
cognisance, and, therefore, without adequate preparation

[1] August 6, 1914.

—that, surely, will be regarded by future historians as one of the most amazing incidents in our national annals.

Is it necessary to recall how Lord Haldane in particular strenuously opposed Lord Roberts' campaign all over the country, both on the ground of policy—*i.e.,* absence of necessity—and on the ground of economy? The thing would be incredible were it not recorded in black and white.

. . . .

All through 1913 and in the spring of 1914 "the drums of Armageddon—as Mr. Walton Newbold expresses it in that remarkable book of his, which may be particularly recommended to those who place the blame for Europe's follies upon the shoulders of Germany alone[1]—were rolling more insistently for a struggle now not long to be deferred." The Teutonic combination and the Franco-Russian combination were arming to the teeth, each accusing the other of being the cause of their doing so. The international armament ring, in which British capital and many personalities of influence in British official and professional life were interested, was making enormous profits. Our armament firms were turning out with frantic haste and with sublime impartiality every kind of killing machine for potential friend and potential foe alike. The incendiary Press in Germany, France, Russia, Austria, and Britain was inflaming and exacerbating public opinion —none playing a more sinister and influential part than the Northcliffe papers.

Yet all through this period, during which the storm clouds were gathering, the British people were allowed to remain in the same fools' paradise in which they had dwelt since 1906. By this time, as it has been well said[2] "we were tied to France inextricably, tied by countless invisible threads such as fastened down Gulliver while he slumbered in the land of little men." The analogy is a doubly perfect one. And as we were tied to France, so France was tied to Russia. But in her case the threads were all too visible ! But the Ministers who had so tied us, and such of their colleagues and prominent personalities among the Opposition leaders, who must by then have become acquainted with the facts, persisted in their immoral course of keeping the truth from the country.

[1] "How Europe Armed for War." (Blackfriars Press Ltd.)
[2] *The Candid Review.* May, 1915.

Ministers denied point blank in Parliament that the country was in any sense committed.

They denied it on the public platform.

They insisted that our relations with Germany were satisfactory and improving.

They insisted that our Army was fully sufficient to meet the requirements of our foreign policy and of our national strategy founded thereon.

They urged a reduction of our naval expenditure up to within a fortnight of the outbreak of war.

. . . .

Then the blow fell. The bullet which put an end to the life of the Archduke Ferdinand penetrated the magazine which both the European Groups had been so long and so diligently filling with explosives. Into that magazine a dozen middle-aged and elderly gentlemen, half in blind panic, half in criminal disarray of mind, let fall the torch which, in falling, lit the funeral pyre of Europe's youth.

But at least the peoples *they* governed were fore-armed.

Our people were not.

The Nemesis of their own secret acts gripped our Ministers by the throat. It paralysed their sincere and desperate efforts to maintain peace. It cast dissension among them. They could steer no clear or consistent course. They were unable to take up a definite attitude towards either party in the quarrel. They could afford to be honest neither to the British people nor to the world. They could not hold in check the elements making for war in Germany by a timely declaration of solidarity with France and Russia, although morally committed to France, and, therefore, to Russia; lest by a premature acknowledgment to Parliament of their long course of secret negotiations they should plunge the country into utter confusion and bring disaster upon themselves. They could not hold in check the elements making for war in Russia and France because their military and naval staffs had long since made all arrangements, with their authority, for common action with those of France, and, therefore, contingently, with those of Russia. In vain the Russians and French implored them to make a pronouncement of British policy while there was yet time. The Cabinet, as a Cabinet, could make no such pronouncement, for the Cabinet, as a Cabinet, declined to admit that it and the country were committed to the Franco-Russian combination. To the Cabinet as a whole the character and significance which the eight years' secret military and naval collaboration had gradually assumed in the eyes of those members of the Cabinet who had originally sanctioned it, came as a staggering and appalling prospect.

The critical days rushed by. The struggle between contending factions in the Cabinet became acute. Finally the section which contended that war, having now become inevitable, we must enter it, being bound in honour to France and Russia, carried the day. It was materially assisted by the leaders of the Official Opposition, who, on August 2, expressed in a letter to the Premier—*which contains no allusion, however distant, to Belgium*—their opinion that "it would be fatal to the honour and security of the United Kingdom to hesitate in supporting France and Russia at the present juncture."

Whereupon a number of members of the Cabinet resigned.

All but Mr. Burns and Lord Morley reconsidered their decision when Germany invaded Belgium.

. . . .

Mr. Lloyd George has since asserted[1] that if Belgium had not been invaded he would not have been a party to a declaration of war upon Germany. And he added this very positive statement :—

"If Germany had been wise she would not have set foot on Belgian soil. *The Liberal Government, then, would not have intervened.*"

It will not do. Mr. Ramsay Macdonald has been overwhelmed with abuse because he has from the first resisted the dishonest plea that the Liberal Cabinet determined upon war because of Belgium. Mr. Lloyd George's statement is a legend. That the invasion of Belgium was the chief factor which inspired the bulk of our people to the greatest voluntary effort in arms which any people has ever made in the history of the world (by way of reward, it has been conscripted !) is unquestionable. That it was the invasion of Belgium which gave the war its popular backing—that, too, is unquestionable. That it was the invasion of Belgium which fired the self-governing Dominions is equally true. But that the invasion of Belgium determined our official entry into the war is simply untrue. And its untruth is conclusively demonstrable. Thus :—

July 31, 1914. Sir E. Grey informs the German Ambassador that if France and Germany become involved

[1] *Pearsor's Magazine.* March, 1915.

in war, Britain will be drawn in. (White Book No. 119: Yellow Book No. 110.)

August 1, 1914. Sir E. Grey refuses to say that Britain will remain neutral if Germany undertakes not to violate Belgian neutrality, and refuses, when further pressed by the German Ambassador, to name any terms upon which Britain will remain neutral. (White Book No. 123.)

August 2, 1914. Sir E. Grey definitely pledges British naval aid to France if Germany attacks the French coasts or shipping.

August 3, 1914. (Afternoon.) Sir E. Grey informs the House of Commons that this definite commitment has been made to France; that our national honour, in his opinion, is involved in supporting France; he reveals the military and naval consultations which have been going on since 1906, and states that France has, by agreement with us, concentrated her fleet in the Mediterranean and left her other coasts undefended.

August 3, 1914. (Evening.) Sir E. Grey informs the House of Commons of Germany's threat to invade Belgium (dated 7 p.m., August 2), and adds that he did not possess that information when he made his statement to the House in the afternoon.

The final and irrevocable act had, therefore, taken place before Germany had invaded Belgium; before she had threatened to invade Belgium; and before the Cabinet was in possession of the information that she had issued that threat.

And the final and irrevocable act was the fatal and necessary consequence of the unwritten bond.

. . . .

A few days later, without any notification to Parliament, the small British Expeditionary Force was being despatched to the Continent, there to be extricated only by consummate generalship and consummate valour from absolute annihilation.

Where is the original Expeditionary Force to-day?

. . . .

Such is the story of how the British people were committed, in blissful ignorance of the fact, step by step, to support one of the two great rival Groups of the Continent of Europe, and to a land war on an unprecedented scale, with an available Expeditionary Force (sufficient, they had precedently been informed, for all their needs) of under 200,000 men; of how, being gradually, imperceptibly, and furtively so committed, the British people were, nevertheless, lulled into a sense of false security by those who had so committed them; of how those who so committed them repeatedly assured them that their relations with Germany were excellent; of how those who so committed them concealed from the British people that the negotiations of 1912 with Germany had failed to establish an accord between the two Governments, but led the British people, on the contrary, to believe that they had been successful; of how those who had so committed the British people opposed every attempt to increase the military forces of the Crown, and took credit for reducing the expenditure upon those forces; of how those who so committed the British people constantly held out hopes of a reduction on naval expenditure, and even urged publicly that such reduction should be effected; of how those who so committed the British people, having also borne witness on numerous occasions to the efficiency, preparedness, and magnitude of German military resources, and having explained and justified the same in view of Germany's geographical and strategic situation, proceeded, when war broke out, to describe this efficiency, preparedness and magnitude of the German military resources, as conveying proof that the rulers of Germany had plotted in secret for a treacherous assault upon uninformed and unsuspecting neighbours, for the purpose of dominating Europe.

. . . .

The moral is clear; the lesson plain. No Democracy which tolerates a system capable of producing such results can live.

CHAPTER XXXV

The Two Roads

LET us listen only to the experience that urges us on. It is always higher than that which keeps us back. Let us reject all the counsels of the past that do not turn toward the future.—*Maeterlinck.*

THE ruling classes in every belligerent State advise their peoples not to be content with an "inconclusive peace." And there are not wanting professional men of God who echo that advice in the name of the merciful Christ. By an "inconclusive peace" the ruling classes in each belligerent State mean, although they take care not to avow it, a settlement of the war which shall deprive them of the sweet triumph of standing on the necks of the ruling classes opposed to them.

For this world-war was made possible by personal friction between a very few individuals among the ruling castes in the respective countries engaged in it. These people now feel their personal prestige to be at stake. They feel it so much that the horrors of the war take a secondary place in their minds. They keep away from the actual battlefields. They live well, feed well; their ears are deaf to the wailing of the women. If this were not so the war would have ended long ago. If this were not so every individual who had had a share in promoting this war would either have committed suicide or lost his reason. The war could end to-morrow if these people would think less about themselves and more about the dead.

It is a staggering thought, is it not, that this war might end to-morrow but for the stiff-necked pride of a few—a very, very few—middle-aged and elderly gentlemen, whose incompatibility of temper, unlimited capacity for intrigue, and traditional notions of dignity brought the war about? But it is God's truth. A turn of the wrist; the touching of a lever in the obedient journalistic machine, and the soldiers would rest in their trenches, the cannon would cease to growl, and the diplomatists would be packing their traps to assemble at the appointed meeting place . . . to talk together instead of *at* each other. Yes, it is God's truth, for these middle-aged and elderly gentlemen are the principals in this gigantic duel. The people are their seconds. But the parts are reversed, for it is the seconds that fight while the principals look on and extol the peoples' virtues aloud, while musing in silence upon their gullibility.

. . . .

When a man has given you advice which you followed, and which has turned out to be wholly bad, you are a very foolish person if you grant him your blind confidence again. The ruling classes in every belligerent State have been telling the democracy for years that while they themselves were extremely anxious to keep the peace, the fellows next door were a quarrelsome lot, and that the only way to keep them quiet was to arm to the teeth. "If you want peace—they said—you must spend and go on spending your substance on battleships and guns, on explosives and air-craft; then you will maintain peace, but not otherwise." Now that advice was hopelessly wrong. But, undeterred, the very same people who gave it, now come along with equal assurance and amazing effrontery with another piece of advice. "If you want peace—they say—you must go on fighting until the fellows next door own themselves in the wrong." Now, this is arrant nonsense. Moreover, this arrant nonsense is preached to every belligerent people, and, do not forget, every belligerent people is persuaded, more than ever persuaded after a two years' war, that the fellows next door were the cause of all the trouble. So, a complete *impasse* is reached.

Well, we must reject that advice, and every people must reject it.. . . . . .

The only compensation possible for the miseries which this war has inflicted upon the present generation and for the burdens it has laid upon the next, is that it shall be militarily inconclusive, and that it shall be brought to a speedy end by general consent.

A conclusive war, i.e., a war which enables one side to impose its unfettered will upon the other, means an inconclusive peace.

A war closing amid universal exhaustion, followed by a sullen peace, holding out no prospect of international reconstruction on a different basis of motive and outlook, means an inconclusive peace.

A militarily inconclusive war, so recognised by general consent, offers the only prospect of a conclusive peace.

. . . .

Only if the war be militarily inconclusive will the nations concerned perceive that the philosophy of war has become unsound.

Only if the war be militarily inconclusive will the nations be led collectively to repudiate the doctrines regulating the intercourse of peoples which their respective Governments inherited, and which they have maintained in an age when these doctrines present no permanent advantage to be reaped nor true glory to be gained.

Only if the war be militarily inconclusive will each belligerent nation be induced to examine both the origins and the lessons of the war with the determination to seek, and to find, a road which all nations can tread henceforth with safety and without dishonour.

A militarily inconclusive termination of the war is the defeat of "Prussian militarism." It is the defeat of the French school of *La Revanche.* It is the defeat of Pan-Slavism. It opens the door to a Balkan Confederation, the one constructive policy for that tumultuous area. It compels a more equitable distribution of political power in that political mosaic, the Dual-Monarchy. It opens the eyes of the British people to the injustices, the dangers, and the ineffectiveness of their political system.

At present the articulate elements in each belligerent State are busily engaged in distracting attention from national perplexities, by emphasising the perplexities of the enemy.

But the national attention everywhere would be better employed in focusing its own problems, which are numerous.

. . . .

In what light does our own national and Imperial future appear, assuming what I have termed a "sullen" peace, the result of universal exhaustion; a peace laying foundations for no real change in the mechanism and procedure of international intercourse, effecting no settlement of those international problems of economics and of race distribution which, in the blundering grasp of so-called statesmen, have produced this war : a peace, therefore, which will be nominal and ephemeral, little more than an armistice, which the belligerents will employ in recuperation and in preparation for another attempt to solve these problems by another war?

That is what concerns our people primarily.

There is much which must give food for grave reflection in the actual and potential changes which this war has created in the strategic conditions of our country, when we consider those changes in connection with the great racial movements now in process, and our relation thereto.

.   .   .   .

Let us glance, first of all, at a capital factor in the life of States, the factor of population, and the light which it throws upon our national and Imperial future.   The great commercial, industrial, and expanding peoples of the world are the American, the British, the German, and the Russian.   Of the four the British people are now numerically by far the weakest.   This can be seen at a glance. The totals given are in round figures :—

United States (white population, 1910 census) 82 millions.
United Kingdom (1911 census) .... 45 millions.
Germany (1910 census) .... 65 millions.
European Russia (1911 census) ....121 millions.

Moreover, of the four the people of the United Kingdom are increasing at a much less rapid rate, largely owing to the mishandling of the Irish problem, the population of Ireland to-day being less by more than a million than it was in the opening years of the nineteenth century. The reliability of the Russian census of 1897 is open to doubt.   If it be accepted, then the population of European Russia has increased 27 millions in fourteen years.   In any case, the rate of increase is admittedly very large. The figures for the other countries are as follows :—

The white population of the United States in the 40 years preceding the last census increased by 47 millions.

The population of Germany in the 39 years preceding the last census increased by 23 millions.

The population of the United Kingdom in the 40 years preceding the last census increased by 14 millions.

These comparative rates of increase are even more striking if we take the respective increases in the decade preceding the last census (the figures for Russia are not available).   We then find that :—

In ten years (1900-10) the white population of the United States increased 14,832,552.

In ten years (1900-10) the population of Germany increased 8,558,825.

In ten years (1901-11) the population of the United Kingdom increased 3,392,263.

If that ratio of increase is maintained during the 50 years following the last census, the result will be as follows, in round numbers :—

In 1965 the white population of the United States will be 156 millions.

In 1965 the population of Germany will be 108 millions.

In 1965 the population of the United Kingdom will be 68 millions.

. . . .

The above figures, and the lessons they convey, must be continually in mind when we discuss the problem of Britain's future in the event of a "settlement" of the war which leaves its deep seated origins unconfronted, and, therefore, without prospect of remedy; a "settlement" which leaves legitimate ambitions unsatisfied, economic needs disregarded, open sores still festering; a settlement under which Europe, with a forced temporary respite due to financial drain, will begin once more to arm.

The first consequence for the United Kingdom (henceforth dragged into the Continental system) of such a "settlement" must be a double burden upon the back of the people of these Islands. For to the burden of maintaining a supreme Navy would need to be added the burden of a conscript Army. That Army might in the early stages be moderate in size, but it would increase as the recuperative forces of the Continental States reasserted themselves. Is this double burden one which the people of the United Kingdom can bear?

Before the war the single burden was proving heavy enough. It was absorbing large sums urgently required for domestic purposes, lacking which millions of our people were suffering severely from preventible poverty, from preventible disease, and from preventible educational and other kindred handicaps. It may be said : "You are reckoning without the Empire. The Empire will henceforth share that burden " Yes, the self-governing Dominions will share it, and gladly share it, provided you allow them to share in the direction and control of your foreign policy. But whatever their contribution may amount to, it cannot cover the difference between the single and the double burden. The white population of the Dominions, it may be noted, is not more than fourteen millions.　On the other hand, the burden of existing taxation upon India cannot be wisely or justly increased.

. . . .

In considering the future military requirements of the United Kingdom under the foreshadowed conditions, the position of France cannot be disregarded.　France will emerge from the war more exhausted than at the close of the Napoleonic wars.　She has already lost—lost definitely in dead—more than a million of her most virile elements, and, perhaps, as many more permanently disabled.　What this loss means for France can only be understood when it is borne in mind that her population was only 39½ millions at the last census (1911); that its increase in the preceding 30 years had been under two millions, and that before the war she, unlike Germany, had enrolled every unit into military service, and that the utmost limit of her military man-power had, therefore, been reached.　France will be in no position to take any but a secondary part in another great European war.　And her willingness to do even that may well be doubted. The course the rulers of France have pursued during the past decade they have pursued with their eyes open. *They* at least cannot shift the blame upon others.　But it remains true, nevertheless, that a malign fate has caused the French people to be ground between the upper and nether millstones of Russian exigencies and Anglo-German rivalry.　This they will clearly perceive at the end of the war, and a great reaction is sure.　Only the bitterest enemy of France would wish to see her involved in another European war.　Her only chance of surviving this one is generations of peace, and this she cannot have unless she establishes a *modus vivendi* with her Eastern neighbour.　That she will do so may be taken as one of the certainties of the future.　Her most enlightened sons had been working along those lines for the past twenty years, and if France had been free from external commitments they would have succeeded.

. . . .

But would this assumption by the people of the United Kingdom of a double burden be sufficient, under the foreshadowed conditions, to meet the potential modifications this war has occasioned in offensive strategy?　Assuredly not.

We have had a long start in sea supremacy, and we have maintained it.　For a thousand years the sea has saved us from the invader. We have been immune from the desolation which has ravaged the Continent, and in which our own legions have often participated. But the future holds for us none of the security which the past has held. That security was threatened when we went to war. At the present moment it is still our rampart. But the days that it will be so are numbered. And this for two reasons. In the first place, we cannot build against the world, and after this war the world will never consent that one Power—even though that Power may justly claim not to have abused its strength in time of peace—shall hold undisputed sway over the natural highways of the globe in time of war, and so arrogate to itself the right of regulating, according to its strategic interests, the sea-borne traffic of all nations. Had our situation been other than it is we should have done our utmost to dispute such a claim. After the experiences of the war the world cannot be expected to tolerate it. In itself the claim is far more comprehensive than would be a claim on the part of a Continental Power to exercise a military dictatorship in Europe. And for either claim the future can hold no place.

We might for some years, by a desperate effort which would wear us to the bone, succeed in building against a Continental coalition. But we cannot build against a Continental coalition and against America as well. And America appears firmly resolved that if she cannot obtain by diplomatic action at the settlement, freedom for the exercise of her sea-borne trade in time of war, and the abolition of the British claim to capture private property at sea other than contraband, and to convert into contraband, at British pleasure, any article whatsoever; she will do so by other means. And as she has long contended for the abolition of the right of capture, she will be consistent. What other means can she adopt? She can construct a battle fleet of such dimensions that even the most powerful maritime State must respect her wishes. This she will do if we do not abate our claim, and in this her position is identical with that of Germany. The community of interest is there; patent, irrefutable. No consideration of sentiment or of historical connection; no passing indignation at the ruthlessness of German methods of warfare; not even a rupture of relations can permanently remove it. And sooner or later—sooner rather than later—it must prove a decisive factor in inter national relationships if the old system of international intercourse is to continue.

This acknowledgment of an unpalatable truth permeates Mr. Balfour's recent pronouncement to the American journalist, Mr. Edward Marshall (May 18, 1916). For if that statement be carefully read, it will be observed to be, in substance, a bid for joint Anglo-American control of the high seas. "Give up—says Mr. Balfour in effect—the demand for the immunity from capture of private property which you have persistently urged at the Hague, and which Britain has as persistently opposed, and we will take you into partnership as controllers of the high seas." The scheme contains the flaw common to all proposals which have as their object the concentration in the hands of a limited number of States, of a power to dictate the destinies of all nations. On these lines there can be no permanent solution of the naval problem or of the military problem. It has no moral sanction behind it. The true solution, which must, however, be bracketed with an analogous solution for Continental militarism, has been well and tersely put by Sir Charles Bruce :—

"The only way seems to be for the Powers to recognise that the interests of one are the interests of all; that the world's commerce can only be protected by a world's navy, and that, accordingly, the policy of the open-door must be supplemented by the policy of an open path, under the protection of an International Naval Police Force, to be composed of ships of all nations in proportion to the interests of individual States. Such a force would dispel the anxieties of those States which possess fleets inferior in power, but which are becoming increasingly dependent upon over-sea commerce for their means of existence. It would put an end to the perpetual unrest arising out of the apprehension of a sudden attack by one sea-Power on another, without a declaration of war, and insure for international commerce the security now enjoyed by national trade."[1]

That is one of the reasons why the future holds for us none of the security that the past has held. More and more does commerce claim, and rightly claim, to be immune from the effects of the madness and selfishness of contending rulers and castes. More and more does

[1] "The English Navy and the Peace of the World." By Sir Charles Bruce, in *The Statist.* July 13, 1912.

the sea belong to all men, and not only to some men.[1]
But there is another reason. Even were we able by
our own unaided efforts, or in conjunction with America,
to retain a monopoly of sea power—and this would
assume a corresponding ability to cope with any possible
development of submarine power—sufficiently comprehensive for our war needs, we should not have solved our
difficulties. For another and rival element has allowed
itself to be partly subjugated by the genius of man, and
his complete triumph over it is only a matter of time.
Sea power alone can no longer assure our security, even
though we maintain directly, or in part by proxy, our
mastery upon it. Air power has circumvented it. And
in air power we do not even compete on equal terms with
some at least of the great States of the Continent.
Germany notably has the start of us, and although Fleet
Street affects to laugh at the Zeppelins, you will not find
naval, or military men, or air men doing so. A decade,
maybe two decades, may pass before air power is sufficiently developed to permit of anything like a serious
military invasion. But we must reckon upon air power
attaining within a comparatively short time such a degree
of perfection that our vulnerable centres will be open to
accurately directed attack, and upon chemistry devising
some further devilish ingredients in the destructive pro-
perties of projectiles.

Moreover, the events of the past two years have shown
that modern warfare will henceforth be waged with
increasing implacability, not against the armies and
navies of the contending Powers alone, but against the
civilian population, which by its monetary contributions,
by its manufacture of the fuel of slaughter, by its agricultural and industrial labours, and by its sanction, maintain
those armies and navies in being. It will become less and
less possible for belligerent States, and more and more
futile for international lawyers, to draw any distinction
between combatants and non-combatants. It is flying in
the face of logic to maintain that the man (or woman)
who fashions the projectiles or the explosive which another
man discharges with deadly effect, is a non-combatant.

---

[1] This Chapter was written before Mr. Wilson's speech at
Washington, on May 27, in which he outlined the kind of Settlement
which would meet with America's support, postulating *inter alia*.

    A universal association of nations to maintain inviolate the
security of the highway of the seas for the common, unhindered
use of all the nations of the world.

Germany has deliberately adopted the practice of treating civilian life as of no account when civilian life interferes with military exigencies—or merely gets in the way. But is our own procedure different, except in the character of its manifestation? What does a "war of attrition" involve? What do our efforts to stop food supplies from reaching our enemies involve? We know full well what they involve. By those measures we seek, with equal deliberation, to inflict such hardships upon the civilian population of Germany as will result in sufficient pressure being placed upon the German Government by that civilian population as will, in turn, compel the German Government to sue for peace and to accept the terms we and our Allies see fit to impose. When the Germans say that we are making war upon their women and children, they are but giving rhetorical expression to what is true in substance and in fact.[1]

In their respective ways, therefore, both Germany and England have, by their actual practices in this war, admitted that, in order to be fully effective, modern warfare must be waged against the civilian population.

The effect of this admission upon air power and its perfectibility and upon our national position in relation thereto, is obvious. In any future war the population of our cities and towns will be at least equally exposed to wholesale slaughter as the population of the cities and towns of the Continent—unless we all take to living underground.

Our strategical situation has, therefore, undergone a complete revolution. Formerly the Continent could not get at us. Our officials, well-to-do City men, and Fleet Street heroes could afford to be intensely patriotic at the expense of the soldiers and sailors whom they sent to fight and whom (incidentally) they paid (and pay) very meanly, and to whom they denied (and deny) full political rights. The Continent can now get at us sufficiently to make us feel uncomfortable at nights. But to-morrow it will be

---

[1] Hardly a day passes that our Press does not express jubilation at the thought of a starving civilian population in Germany. One wonders whether the anonymous persons who are responsible for these effusions ever bear in mind that Germany claims nearly two million Allied prisoners, and whether they ever ask themselves what the fate of these prisoners is likely to be if the time really comes when the German Government is unable to feed its civilian population? The levity, to say nothing of other aspects, with which the matter is treated in the British Press is as staggering as it is revolting.

air fleets, not nocturnal visitors in twos or threes, that we must contemplate.

In a word, we have ceased, strategically speaking, to be an Island.
.   .   .   .

And this revolution in our strategic situation, occasioned by the new aspect of the exercise of sea power which this war has projected upon the international screen; by the double burden resulting from our entry into the Continental system, and by the development of air power, must needs modify very profoundly our ability to sustain what has been for several centuries the chief purpose of our traditional foreign policy. We need not here discuss whether, in endeavouring throughout the centuries to prevent any one Power or combination of Powers from acquiring a leading position on the Continent [however fitted to exercise such it or they might be, through the possession of the same kind of qualities which we think justify us in controlling one-fifth of the habitable globe], our policy has been dictated by a desire to preserve the liberties of Europe; or whether that policy has been due to a perfectly intelligible ambition to minister to our own security and to increase the boundaries of our overseas Empire. It is enough to point out that whatever the guiding inspiration may have been, the conditions which ensured the successful prosecution of the policy have passed away. This war will bring many revelations as well as many revolutions. It will reveal to the peoples of Europe that their divisions are not fundamental, but superficial. This process of revelation was, indeed, making rapid headway when the war came. As its natural complement is the growth of democratic tendencies within States, which makes for a corresponding weakening of autocracy, monopoly, and militarism—the triple demons which curse humanity—it is more than probable that resistance to the process by the latter played its part in precipitating the conflict. Be that as it may, the Europe of Pitt and Palmerston is a thing of the past, and can never be revived. Alike through the growth of population, the centralisation of authority, the ramifications of commerce and finance, and the realisation of a basic solidarity among the peoples—which in the fullness of time will rise, phœnix-like, from these ashes—British traditional foreign policy is no longer practicable. We cannot now prevent the Power or Powers most qualified, from acquiring a leading position on the Continent of Europe. We can, however, materially influence that Power, or those Powers, towards liberalism or towards reaction, by the course our statesmen steer during the next few years, which will be crucial ones in casting the mould of the new Europe. For example, the future of the European peoples—of the whole world, indeed—depends for many generations to come upon whether reaction in Russia and Germany joins hands against Democracy in Germany and Russia—or the other way about. We can turn the hopes of the German people towards the more liberal West or towards the reactionary East in the measure in which we attempt—or do not attempt—to make this war an excuse for interference in their constitutional and domestic affairs; and in the measure in which we either ignore their economic needs, and endeavour to stifle their legitimate expansion, or recognise that there is room in the world for them and for us, and that "if you press down the lid upon an industrial and commercial country that lid will infallibly be blown off."[1] Far-reaching consequences will ensue from the choice we make.

But, having made that choice, we shall no longer be able to control the issue. We can always influence, for good or ill: we can no longer control the destinies of Europe. The sooner we recognise it the better for ourselves, and the better for Europe.

. . . .

Having these various factors in consideration, I am led to conclude that events have brought—more speedily than might a few years ago have been anticipated—the British Empire to a point whence two roads diverge. One leads straight to eventual decay and disruption. The other leads to the only safe and tolerable future, alike for the British people and their kith and kin across the seas, for the people of the Continent, and for the races whom Europe, in her arrogance, calls "coloured." The fundamental interests of all these people are common. Injustice to either is injustice to all.

If we wish to direct our footsteps along the former road, all that we have to do is to adopt the policy so vociferously commended by the Jingo and ultra-Imperialist

[1] "Peace with Honour." By Vernon Lee. (The Union of Democratic Control: Price 3d.)

section of the official and political classes, and their following in all classes. It looks the easiest road to tread. Probably it is, for it requires little or no mental effort and allows of plenty of cheerful shouting in the approved "patriotic" style. *Facilis descensus averni.* If we select it, we shall make up our minds to prolong the war as long as our Allies can do so. We shall even urge them to prolong it, in the hope of "bringing Germany to her knees." We might conceivably succeed in doing that, and, assuredly, quarrel with our present Allies as the outcome. But, whether or no, we shall, in any case, resolve to make it as difficult as possible for the Central Powers to make peace. We shall do our utmost permanently to cripple the States of Central Europe, whose divisions and accessibility to invasion were the bane of Europe for five centuries. We shall welcome a large increase of Russian territory in Europe at the expense of Austria-Hungary. We shall decline to countenance any solution of the Polish problem which does not put back the greater part of the Poles under the Tsar. In defiance of our claim to be fighting for the liberties of the smaller peoples and for the rights of nationality, we shall agree to an Italian protectorate over a considerable proportion of the Southern Slavs, and we shall restore Macedonia to Serbia. We shall insist either upon retaining for ourselves, and the Dominions, all the overseas possessions we have taken from Germany, or make a present of them to France, and we shall obstruct any combination by which Germany can obtain compensation for their loss in other directions. We shall encourage the French to maintain their monopolistic and differential fiscal systems in the French dependencies. We shall exclude Germany from any share in the economic development of Asia-Minor.

Having gone thus far, we shall proceed to erect a tariff barrier against the trade of the Central Powers, both in our home market and in our dependencies, as a first step towards that Protectionist and self-contained Empire which is the dream of Mr. Hughes. Having thus invited the world to ask itself how long 59 million white people are to be permitted to monopolise the natural resources and the labour of one-fifth of the habitable globe, we shall continue to direct our foreign policy on the cherished principle of the "Balance of Power." Having thus definitely consecrated the British Empire to an aggressive

policy, we shall jealously observe any signs of recuperation in Germany.   We shall watch with equal suspicion
the enormous accretion of Russia's power which our
policy will have given her.   And, whenever the "Balance"
seems to us endangered we shall be as ready to shift our
friendships and to promote fresh combinations as we have
been in the past, recalling with complacency that we have
fought now against, now in alliance with, almost every
State in Europe, and have come out top every time.   We
shall refuse to modify the advantage which our para-
mountcy at sea gives to us to superimpose our will in time
of peace upon the over-sea expansion of Continental
Powers; and, in time of war, to sweep enemy merchant-
men from the seas, confiscate our enemy's trade, and seize
our enemy colonies—if he has any.   If America objects
we will be hectoring at first, but as a *pis aller* we will
grumblingly endeavour to buy her off and probably quarrel
with her irremediably.

In our domestic concerns we shall continue to mis-
manage the affairs of the nation and Empire within the
portals of a single Legislature.   We shall continue to
make the health and education of the proletariat a matter
of Party controversy, wasting the time of our legislators
in fantastic discussions while the nation perishes.   And,
of course, we shall preserve in all its essential features
a land system as ridiculous as it is iniquitous.

Our ruling classes will have finally elected to present
the spectacle of a class perishing through sheer lack of
intellectuality and, through its own invincible repugnance
to learn, leading the nation to suicide.

.   .   .   .

Or we can follow the other road.

The goal at the end of it is an Internationalism, which,
while asking no people to part with the institutions and the
body of tradition which have made them one; while asking
no people to surrender one iota of their pride in the land
of their birth, in the social customs, the ideals and associations clinging about it : *will* demand of every people, in
the interests of all peoples, some sacrifice of accepted
sentiment, some surrender of national vanity, some abandonment of a philosophy largely rooted in arrogance and
largely founded upon phrases meaning very little in themselves, but which long familiarity has invested with an

artificial significance. That Internationalism will be directed to ensuring the interests of all States, not merely the most powerful in size, in the number of their inhabitants, and in their financial resources.

It will be directed to the preservation of the welfare of the peoples, not the white peoples alone, but the non-white peoples whose evolution has not yet reached the point where they can stand alone and confront, single-handed, the powerful economic and financial forces of modern civilisation.

It will be creative of the spirit by which alone the motive inspiring the relationship of nations shall respond to the real needs and aspirations of humanity, and through whose operating force the monstrous doctrine of defensive and offensive armaments shall be extirpated finally and for all time.

That Internationalism must embrace *all* States : none must be excluded from its beneficent operations. It must be directed by a Council to whose judgment in inter-State disputes all States must give allegiance, and whose deliberations and decisions shall be public.

Behind its sanction every State must feel secure. Every State must feel that there is advantage to itself in entering it. And for the false conception of the word "State," which rulers and small privileged castes, politicians, and militarists have imposed upon the world to its undoing, must be substituted the true conception which shall enable the people at last to come into their own and to be the conscious, controlling guides of their destiny.

. . . .

The indispensable preliminary to an advance upon that road must be a speedy settlement of this war, marked by mutual concessions.

If that be attained, progress along it will be rapid or slow, according to the sincerity of the statesmen and the capacity of the democracies to select the right men and to keep them to their mandate.

For British statesmanship the opportunity is unique and will not recur.

Is British statesmanship capable of rising to it?

Is British democracy sufficiently determined to *will* that the opportunity shall be taken?

EPILOGUE

To the Belligerent Governments

Wider and wider the spread of your devastations.

Higher and higher the mountains of the dead—the dead because of you.

Ever more extensive the boundaries of the cemetery you fashion.

All the wars and all the plagues were as nought to the madness of your doings.

Like unto the breath of a pestilence this madness sweeps through the plains and valleys of Europe, destroying in multitudes the children of men.

The weeping of women is unceasing; their tears mingle with the blood which flows continuously at your bidding.

. . . .

What have the people done to you that you should treat them so?

Have they not sweated for you?

Have they not grovelled to you and licked the hand that smote them?

Have they not stocked your Treasuries?

Have they not lacked that you might be filled?

Have not great masses of them submissively endured poverty, squalor and want while you prated to them of Liberty and Equality, of Patriotism and Empire?

. . . .

And, in return, what have you done for the peoples?

*You have abandoned them in their need, neglected their
    interests, mishandled the substance their labours
    brought you, abused the powers their loyalty and
    trustfulness gave you.*

You have cheated them and laughed at their bewilderment.

*You have kept them asunder and traded on the prejudices
    you fostered in them.*

*You have humiliated and pauperised them and waxed
    strong on their weaknesses.*

*You have left them ignorant, the better to hold them sub-
    servient to your purposes.*

*You have taught them a false ideal of national honour and
    national greatness.*

*You have pumped fear into their hearts in order to uphold
    that militarism you use to crush and drain them.*

*You have encircled them with chains which, with grim
    irony, you have lured them to fashion and fasten upon
    themselves.*

*Continuously, cynically, deliberately you have sacrificed
    them to your secret manœuvres and your sordid
    quarrels.*

.   .   .   .

*Your armies, dead-locked in foul embrace, sway backwards
    and forwards advancing here a little, there a little—but
    at immense cost.*

*Long and weary months they have grappled thus, the
    while your coffers run dry and the peoples murmur.*

*At this spectacle apprehension and rage possess you. For
    you have staked all on "Victory," and if "Victory" is
    for none of you, therein your common doom is writ;
    the doom of your systems, your caste-privileges, your
    monopoly of the sources of production, your unfettered
    command of the labour of millions of men—aye and of
    women and children too.*

*Baffled, you order the death and mutilation of multitudes,
    you rain death upon sleeping cities, you decree the
    slow starvation of whole communities, you strew the
    floor of the sea with the bodies of the helpless.*

*And the scribes and pharisees you pay with this intent,
    dupe and mystify the peoples.*

Your hireling Priests call upon the Deity to sanctify your deeds, and nail once more the Christ upon the Cross.

. . . .

Constantly you seek to invoke more peoples in the general ruin of which you are the architects.

From the uttermost ends of the earth you conduct fresh contingents to the slaughter, men with brown skins and yellow; black men of whom you boasted awhile ago that you had rescued them from barbarism.

For your lust is insatiable and your hypocrisy measureless.

. . . .

You sow the world with lies, with malice and with uncharitableness.

You ingeminate the cancer of unreason.

You invent and trick, distort and vilify.

Under your moulding Humanity becomes misshapen, ghoulish, revolting.

You murder the body and you putrefy the mind.

An' you were able, you would kill the soul.

. . . .

You hope to mitigate your crimes against the day of reckoning by repudiating an initial responsibility which is collective.

For you are all guilty—every one.

One and all you prepared for this saturnalia of massacre.

One and all you squandered the communally earned wealth of your peoples in engines of destruction, and gave high awards for the most potent.

One and all you lied and plotted and spied, span webs of intrigue, dug pits, laid traps, contrived ambushes for your neighbours.

One and all you betrayed your peoples.

. . . .

"Victory!"

What means this "Victory" you proclaim to be your goal?

The victory you seek is a victory which shall perpetuate your empire over mankind; keep Humanity bound in fetters to your cruel and senseless systems; maintain your castes and your monopolies; strengthen your embargo upon the peoples' liberties; leave your heel firmly planted on the peoples' necks.

Profiting by the passions you have loosed, you hope to blind men for ever to your designs.

They will be richer, you say, if more territory be added to your demesnes which, you falsely tell them, are their demesnes.

They will be more secure, you say, if you can crush, humiliate and dictate terms to your rivals who, you falsely state, are their rivals.

They will prosper, you say, from the ruin of their neighbours, with whom they must henceforth neither buy nor sell.

All this is false, and you know that it is false.

It is false, because if you rob, the robbed will not rest until they have won back what you stole from them, and your people must once more bear the burden of your predatory instincts.

It is false, because dictation, humiliation and crushing bring no security to those who inflict them, but only breed hatred and revenge against which the perpetrators must be ever on their guard.

It is false, because the more impoverished your neighbours, the less they have to spend, and your people who supply their wants and whose wants are supplied by them, will suffer from their lessened ability to perform these human functions.

Thus your notion of "Victory" means for the peoples increased poverty and a renewal of fears and hatreds upon which you have thriven, by which you retain them in subjection to your will and through which they perish.

For the peoples, your "Victory" means Death.

There is but one victory which can bring salvation to the peoples and heal the wounds which your disorderly ambitions and monumental selfishness have inflicted upon them; and which can create a fairer world for their descendants.

That victory is the victory which shall prove, finally and for all time, that warfare between great nations can yield no decisive results, can achieve nothing but disaster and misery for all concerned.

It is a victory which shall secure the practical demonstration of the futility as well as the vileness of your practices, expel your philosophy from the councils of mankind, shatter your systems and sweep them, and you along with them, into oblivion.

It is the victory which shall precipitate a great awakening in the hearts and minds of men, causing the scales to fall from their eyes, and the jungle of error in which they have so long wandered to be clearly revealed.

It is the victory which shall turn the nations in loathing from you and from the idols of power and greed, and jealousy you have bidden them worship to their undoing and to your profit; which shall open out to them the road to Peace and good-will towards all men, domination over none, co-operation and partnership with all in the common tasks of social service which know no frontiers; and in the concentration of human effort upon honourable rivalry in arts and crafts, and all branches of constructive knowledge.

It is the victory which out of this chaos of desolation will lead to Understanding.

For none but YOU does that victory spell defeat.

And without your defeat, utter and complete, Understanding is hidden from the peoples.

·　·　·　·　·　·　·　·　·　·　·

So, in praying that the kind of victory you one and all desire shall not be yours, we pray for the victory of justice over injustice, of truth over falsehood, of liberty over thraldom, of understanding over ignorance—that ignorance wherein lie the seeds of every sin against the light.

May, 1916.

INDEX

INDEX

323